SQUID'S WONDERFUL BIG, GIANT BOOK 🙂 OF 🙂 UNSPEAKABLE HORRORS

THIS BOOK REPRINTS MATERIAL PREVIOUSLY SEEN IN SQUEE! #1
-4, AND JOHNNY THE HOMICIDAL MANIAC #1-7, SO YOUR REASONS
FOR BUYING THIS BOOK ARE BEYOND ME. PERHAPS IT IS THE
MIGHTY NEAT-O NEW COVER AND BACK COVER THAT HAS
LURED YOU INTO MY EVIL SCHEME TO MAKE YOU GET THE
SAME STUFF AGAIN. PERHAPS YOU JUST DO NOT FEEL COMPLETE
WITHOUT THIS COLLECTION. I CANNOT TRULY UNDERSTAND YOUR
MOTIVES. THIS FONT IS HARD TO READ, HUH?

CREATED BY JHONEN VASQUEZ

PUBLISHED BY
SLAVE LABOR GRAPHICS

DAN VADO — PRESIDENT AND GIANT PIG TAMER.

JENNIFER DE GUZMAN — DIABOLICAL EDITING
MUTANT

SLUNCHY — A STINKING HOMELESS CHILD WHO
LIVES IN MY HEAD

My sincere...hee! hee!...thanks to anyone who helped inspire the thoughts
and ghastly images portrayed in this book. You inspre me by being there
when I need to spout off about ideas, or by giving me dirty looks when I
walk in to a restaurant.

SQUEE'S Wonderful Big Giant Book of Unspeakable Horrors August 1998 • published by the amorphous
cloud of sentience that is Slave Labor Graphics, who, when you poke their collective belly, giggle and
then obliterate you with deathbeams. Their secret base of operations is 848, The Alameda, San
Jose CA, 95126. No part of this fine publication may be reproduced without the written comsent of
Jhonen "Jiggy" Vasquez, and that scary, cloudy Slave Labor thing, unless you wish to incur the wrath
of SLUNCHY!! As is the way, this book is printed in Canada, where, from what I have been able to
gather, food comes from. Rashes are never funny. Sixtheenth printing, February 2005.

SLEEP DEPRIVED
INTRODUCTION . . .

MMM....THIS IS INTERESTING. I REMEMBER STARTING OFF THE SQUEE! SERIES WITH
MENTION OF HOW I USED TO HIDE UNDER THE COVERS LIKE A LITTLE BURRITO WHEN
CAME TIME FOR ME TO GO TO BED AS A WEE JHONEN. AND HERE I AM, TYPING
IS ALL OUT WHILE LYING IN BED, THE BLANKETS OVER MY HEAD AND LIT BY THE SCREEN
THIS LITTLE COMPUTER. IT NEVER CEASES FREAK ME OUT, JUST HOW THINGS HAVE
VELOPED SINCE THOSE TIMES - THE VERY THINGS THAT HORRIFIED ME AS THAT LITTLE
RRITO VERSION OF MYSELF ARE THE SAME THINGS THAT I NOW DERIVE COMFORT FROM.
E UNCERTAINTY OF WHAT MIGHT BE AROUND THE CORNER, OR AT THE FOOT OF THE
, OR EVEN IN PEOPLE'S PANTS, IS WHAT MAKES THE TEDIUM OF REAL LIFE TOLERABLE.
VE SEEN PEOPLE GROW UP AND INTO SUCH UNINTERESTING, UNIMAGINATIVE SHELLS,
ERLY DEVOID OF WHAT MADE THEM FUN TO BE AROUND WHEN WE WOULD MAKE UP STORIES,
ETEND TO BE GIANT ROBOTS, AND SAW OFF PEOPLE'S WOODEN LEGS. WHAT THE HELL
I TALKING ABOUT? WHAT THE HELL IS THE POINT I WAS TRYING TO MAKE? OH,
LL, IT'S FUN ENOUGH JUST LETTING THIS NONSENSE SPILL OUT OF MY HEAD - SORT
TIES INTO WHAT I WAS SAYING ABOUT THE LITTLE BURETTE KID, ACTUALLY. SEE
E BURETTE KID IS MAGICAL, AND CAN FLY WITHOUT LEGS. . .WAIT . . . NO, I
AN IT TIES INTO THE IDEA OF NO DEFINED BARRIERS OF THOUGHT OR CONCEPTUALIZING
UST FREE-FORM AWARENESS. OF COURSE, THIS ALL LED TO SOME NIGHTMARISH
CIONS AS A CHILD, AND THIS PRETTY MUCH FED THE IDEA BEHIND THE LITTLE BOY
AT IS NOW SQUEE!, OR TODD, AS HE WAS KNOWN BEFORE HIS PARENTS REALIZED THEY
D TO TAKE HIM HOME FROM THE HOSPITAL. I WANTED TO DO THE SQUEE! SERIES
OUND THE TIME I HAD REACHED THE FOURTH ISSUE OF JTHM, AS I WANTED TO TAKE
A SERIES THAT WAS NOT SO MUCH A SLAVE TO CONTINUOUS STORYLINES (NOT THAT
HM DID MUCH OF THAT). SQUEE! GAVE ME THE OPPORTUNITY TO DO A BOOK THAT
TS NONSENSE OVER CONTENT, IF YOU KNOW WHAT I MEAN. I MEAN, THERE ARE IDEAS
PRESSED IN THE BOOKS THAT MEAN QUITE A BIT TO ME, BUT THEY TAKE SECOND SEAT
SIMPLE, HORRID GOOFINESS. IT WAS THE MOST FUN I HAD DOING COMICS! JTHM
IS MY FIRST ATTEMPT AT A COMIC BOOK THING, SO I LOOK BACK ON IT WITH A MIXTURE
AFFECTION, AND SEETHING DISGUST. SO SQUEE! WAS MORE THAN JUST AN ESCAPE
OM THE STORY-TELLING STYLE OF JTHM, BUT ALSO A CHANCE TO START SOMETHING
= WITH A BIT MORE SKILL, AND I THINK IT SHOWS. CAN YOU POSSIBLY DENY THE
UE ARTISTIC MIGHT THAT IS EXPLOSIVE POOH STORIES, AND ZOMBIE SCHOOLMATES?
N YOU?!! REALLY, THE SQUEE! RUN WAS ALL ABOUT CHANNELING STRAIGHT BACK IN
ME AND DIRECTLY INTO THE FEVERISHLY PARANOID MIND OF THAT GIBBERING, SENTIENT,
G-EYED BURETTE. MAN, I'M REALLY OBSESSED WITH THIS BURETTE THING. IT'S
GINNING TO BOTHER ME, AS I'M NOT EVEN BIG ON BURRITOS, AND IT'S NOT REALLY

    WHY AM I BOTHERING TO START ANOTHER PARAGRAPH HERE, AT THIS SPECIFIC POINT
THIS INTRODUCTION GONE HORRIBLY WRONG? I MEAN, THAT FIRST PARAGRAPH WAS ONE
THE MOST GODAWFUL THINGS I HAVE EVER WRITTEN (AND I'M THE GUY WHO WRITES
E BAD ART COLLECTION, AND WHO STILL, FOR SOME REASON, PUTS OUT HAPPY NOODLE
Y.) I WAS HOPING TO MAKE SOME CHARMING POINT ABOUT CRUCIAL IT HAS BEEN TO
TO NEVER LOSE SIGHT OF THAT PERSPECTIVE THAT HAS YOU STANDING ON YOUR TIPPY
ES JUST TO SEE OVER THE SINK WHEN YOU'RE BRUSHING YOUR TEETH. WHAT? SOMEBODY
T STOP ME FROM WRITING THIS! I'VE MANGLED THE ENGLISH LANGUAGE AND HAVE
PLAYED MY LAZINESS BY NOT GOING BACK AND CORRECTING THIS MESS. I'VE BEEN
AKE FOR MAYBE THREE MONTHS NOW, GETTING MY ONLY REST IN THE FORM OF EXTENDED
NKING, SO IS IT ANY REAL SURPRISE THAT I AM DUMPING, MERCILESSLY, THE PRODUCT
THIS PSYCHOSIS THAT RESULTS FROM . . . BURRITO. UGH. . . THERE'S STILL
ME TO MAYBE ADD SOMETHING COHERENT TO THIS INTRO. AH, YESSS, I CAN SAY,
UTHFULLY, THAT OF ALL THE CHARACTERS IN MY HEAD, SQUEE WOULD HAVE TO BE ONE
THE CLOSEST TO ME, AS I KNOW WHAT IT IS TO BE AFRAID, AND TO NOT GET TWISTED
O THOSE VERY THINGS THAT FRIGHTEN ME. WHILE JOHNNY DISPLAYS HIS EVERY DEFECT
HIS EVERY ACTION, SQUEE'S SAD, PASSIVE STANCE SEEMS THE MORE INTELLIGENT,
D MAKES ME LOVE HIM MORE.

                                    JHONEN VASQUEZ

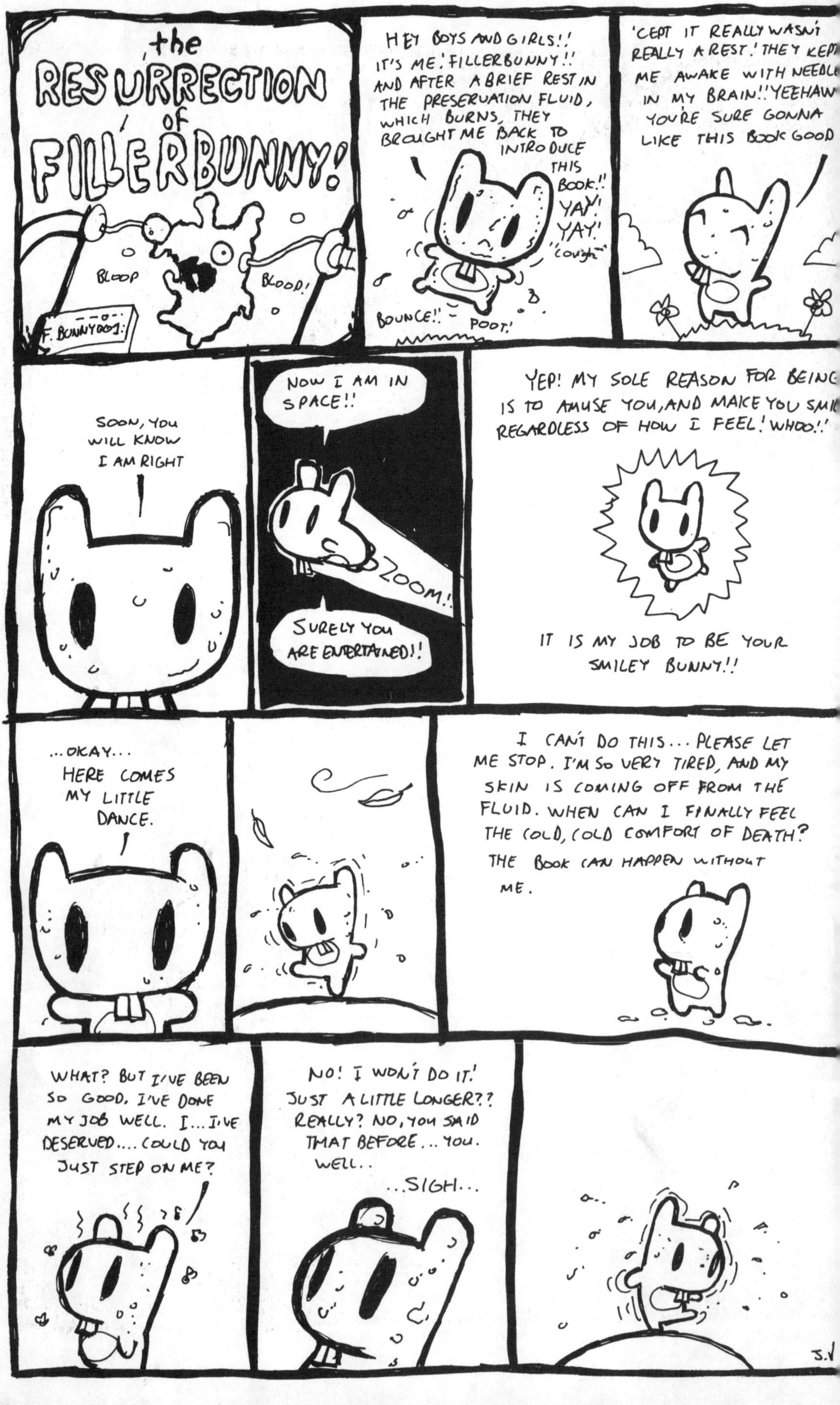
the RESURRECTION of FILLERBUNNY!
BLOOP
BLOOD!
F. BUNNY001
HEY BOYS AND GIRLS!! IT'S ME! FILLERBUNNY!! AND AFTER A BRIEF REST IN THE PRESERVATION FLUID, WHICH BURNS, THEY BROUGHT ME BACK TO INTRODUCE THIS BOOK!! YAY! YAY! *cough*
BOUNCE!! POOT!
'CEPT IT REALLY WASN'T REALLY A REST! THEY KEPT ME AWAKE WITH NEEDLE IN MY BRAIN!! YEEHAW YOU'RE SURE GONNA LIKE THIS BOOK GOOD
SOON, YOU WILL KNOW I AM RIGHT
NOW I AM IN SPACE!!
ZOOM!!
SURELY YOU ARE ENTERTAINED!!
YEP! MY SOLE REASON FOR BEING IS TO AMUSE YOU, AND MAKE YOU SMIL REGARDLESS OF HOW I FEEL! WHOO!!
IT IS MY JOB TO BE YOUR SMILEY BUNNY!!
...OKAY... HERE COMES MY LITTLE DANCE.
I CAN'T DO THIS... PLEASE LET ME STOP. I'M SO VERY TIRED, AND MY SKIN IS COMING OFF FROM THE FLUID. WHEN CAN I FINALLY FEEL THE COLD, COLD COMFORT OF DEATH? THE BOOK CAN HAPPEN WITHOUT ME.
WHAT? BUT I'VE BEEN SO GOOD. I'VE DONE MY JOB WELL. I... I'VE DESERVED.... COULD YOU JUST STEP ON ME?
NO! I WON'T DO IT! JUST A LITTLE LONGER?? REALLY? NO, YOU SAID THAT BEFORE... YOU. WELL..
...SIGH...
J.V

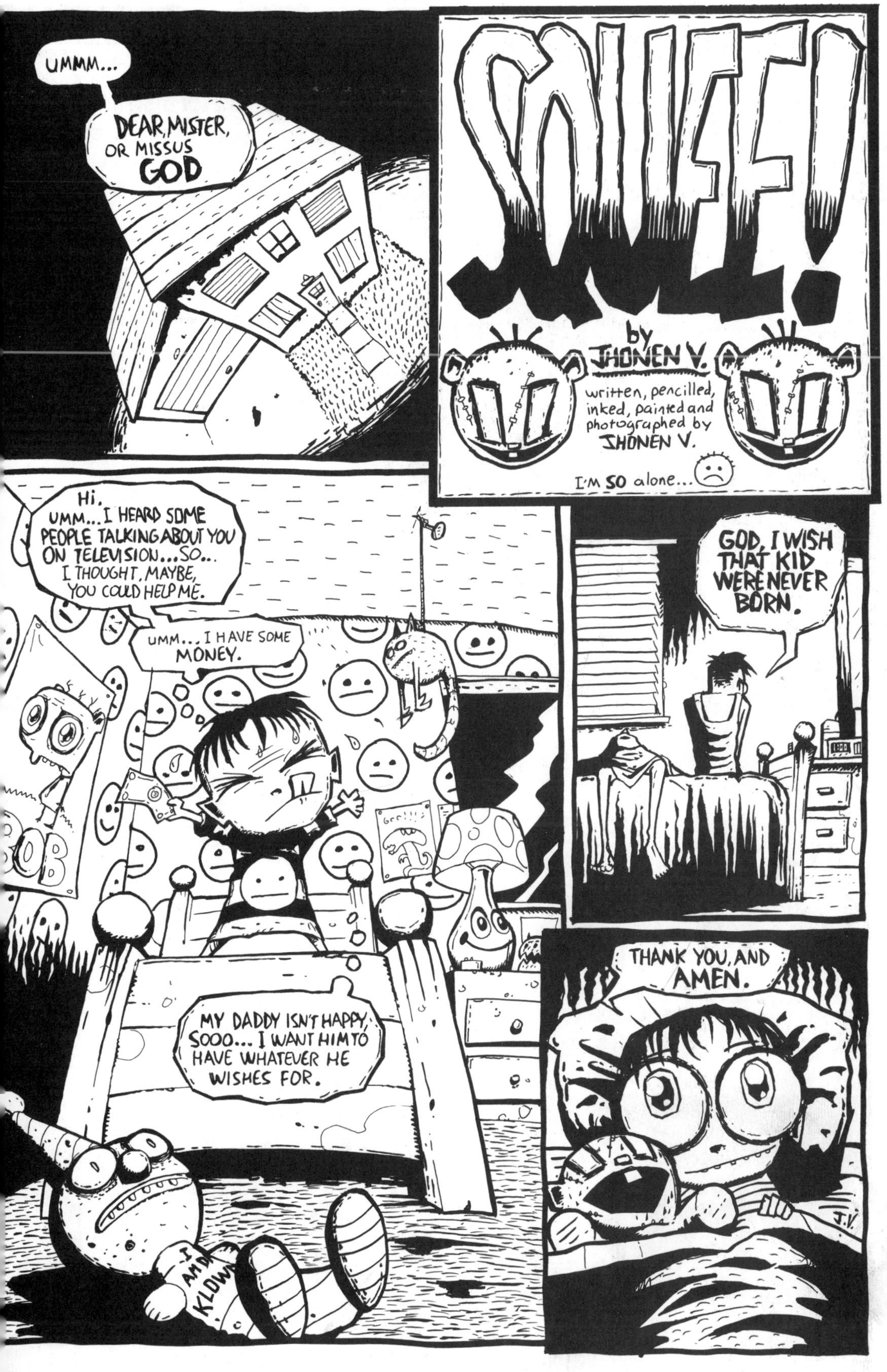
UMMM...
DEAR, MISTER, OR MISSUS GOD
SQUEE!
by JHONEN V.
written, pencilled, inked, painted and photographed by JHONEN V.
I'M SO alone...
Hi. UMM... I HEARD SOME PEOPLE TALKING ABOUT YOU ON TELEVISION... SO... I THOUGHT, MAYBE, YOU COULD HELP ME.
UMM... I HAVE SOME MONEY.
MY DADDY ISN'T HAPPY, SOOO... I WANT HIM TO HAVE WHATEVER HE WISHES FOR.
I AM A KLOWN
GOD, I WISH THAT KID WERE NEVER BORN.
THANK YOU, AND AMEN.
J.V.

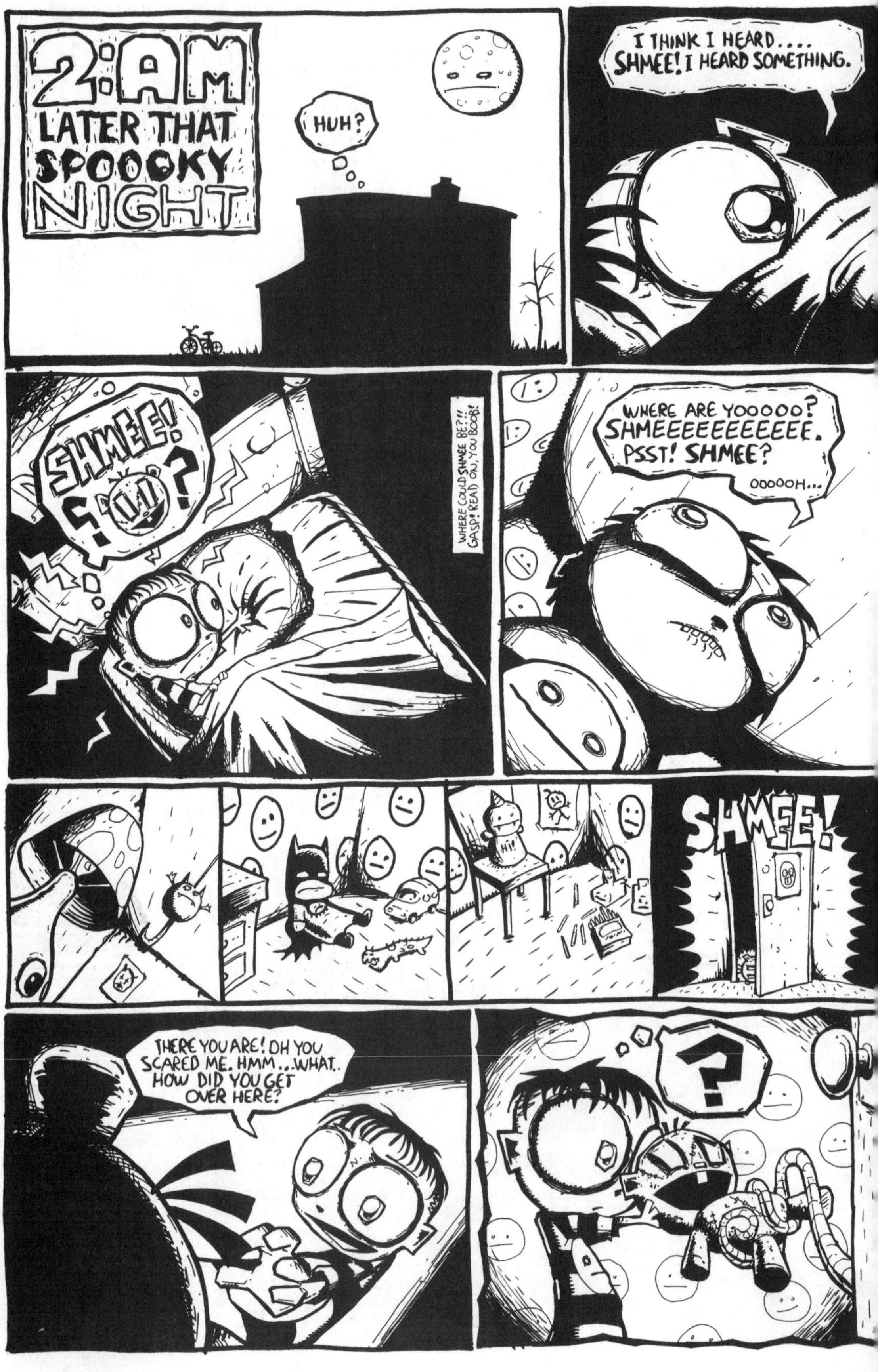
2:AM LATER THAT SPOOOKY NIGHT
HUH?
I THINK I HEARD.... SHMEE! I HEARD SOMETHING.
SHMEE? ?
WHERE COULD SHMEE BE?!! GASP! READ ON, YOU BOOB!
WHERE ARE YOOOOO? SHMEEEEEEEEEEE. PSST! SHMEE?
OOOOOH...
HI!
SHMEE!
THERE YOU ARE! OH YOU SCARED ME. HMM...WHAT. HOW DID YOU GET OVER HERE?
?

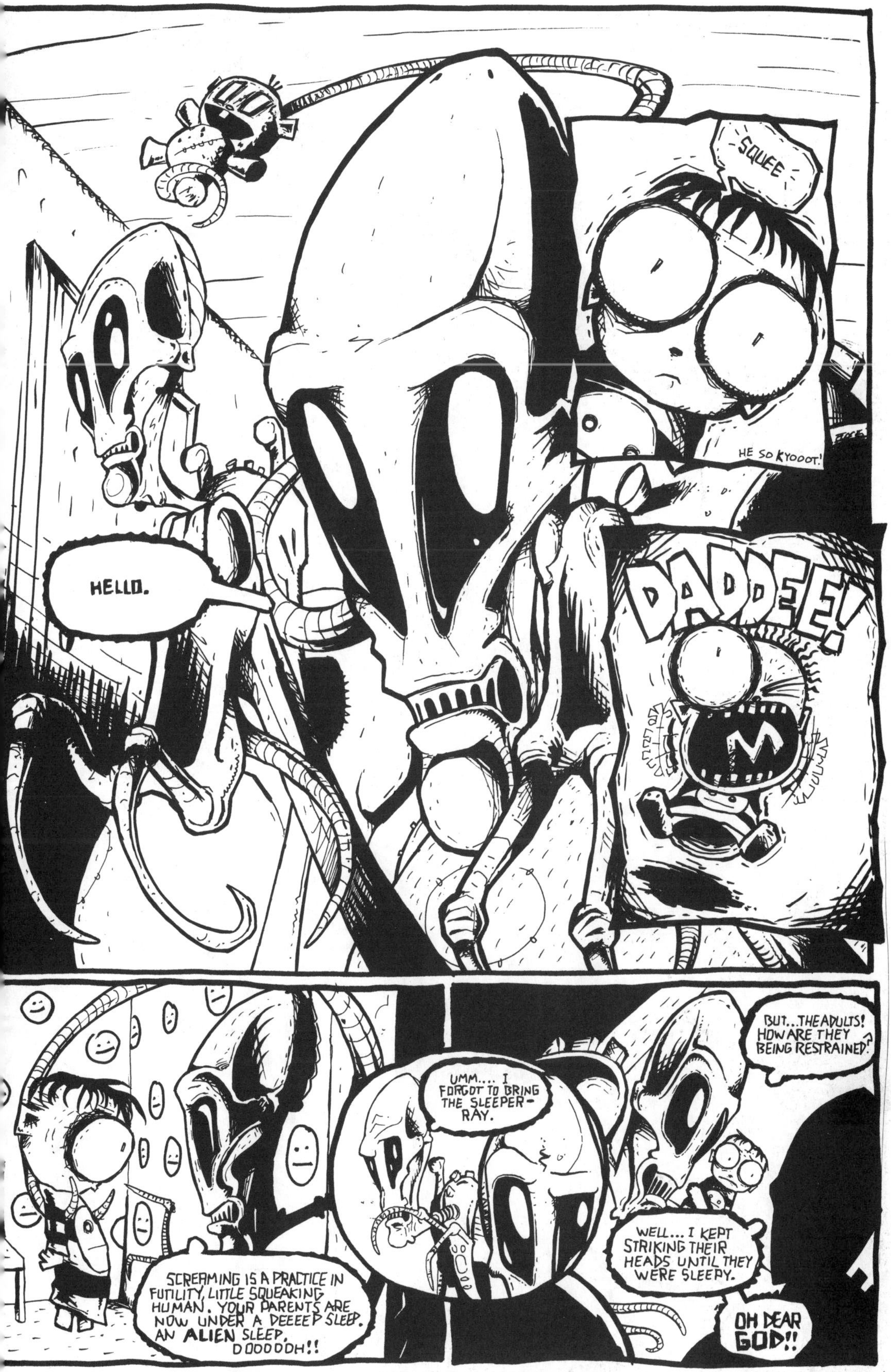

SQUEE
HE SO KYOOOT!
HELLO.
DADDEE!
SCREAMING IS A PRACTICE IN FUTILITY, LITTLE SQUEAKING HUMAN. YOUR PARENTS ARE NOW UNDER A DEEEEP SLEEP. AN ALIEN SLEEP, DOOOOOH!!
UMM.... I FORGOT TO BRING THE SLEEPER-RAY.
BUT...THE ADULTS! HOW ARE THEY BEING RESTRAINED?
WELL... I KEPT STRIKING THEIR HEADS UNTIL THEY WERE SLEEPY.
OH DEAR GOD!!

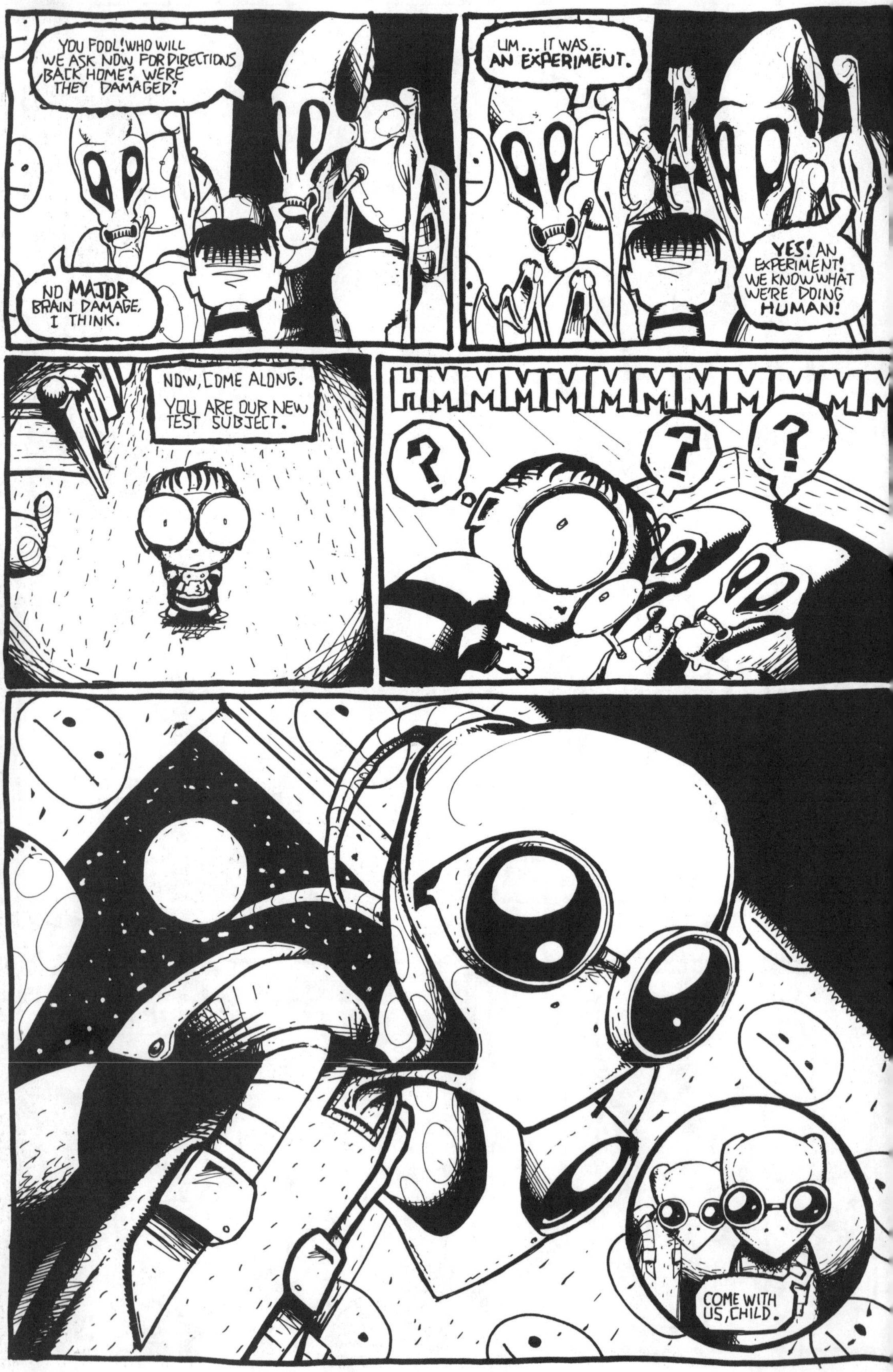
YOU FOOL! WHO WILL WE ASK NOW FOR DIRECTIONS BACK HOME? WERE THEY DAMAGED?
NO MAJOR BRAIN DAMAGE, I THINK.
UM... IT WAS... AN EXPERIMENT.
YES! AN EXPERIMENT! WE KNOW WHAT WE'RE DOING HUMAN!
NOW, COME ALONG.
YOU ARE OUR NEW TEST SUBJECT.
HMMMMMMMMMMMMM
?
?
?
COME WITH US, CHILD.

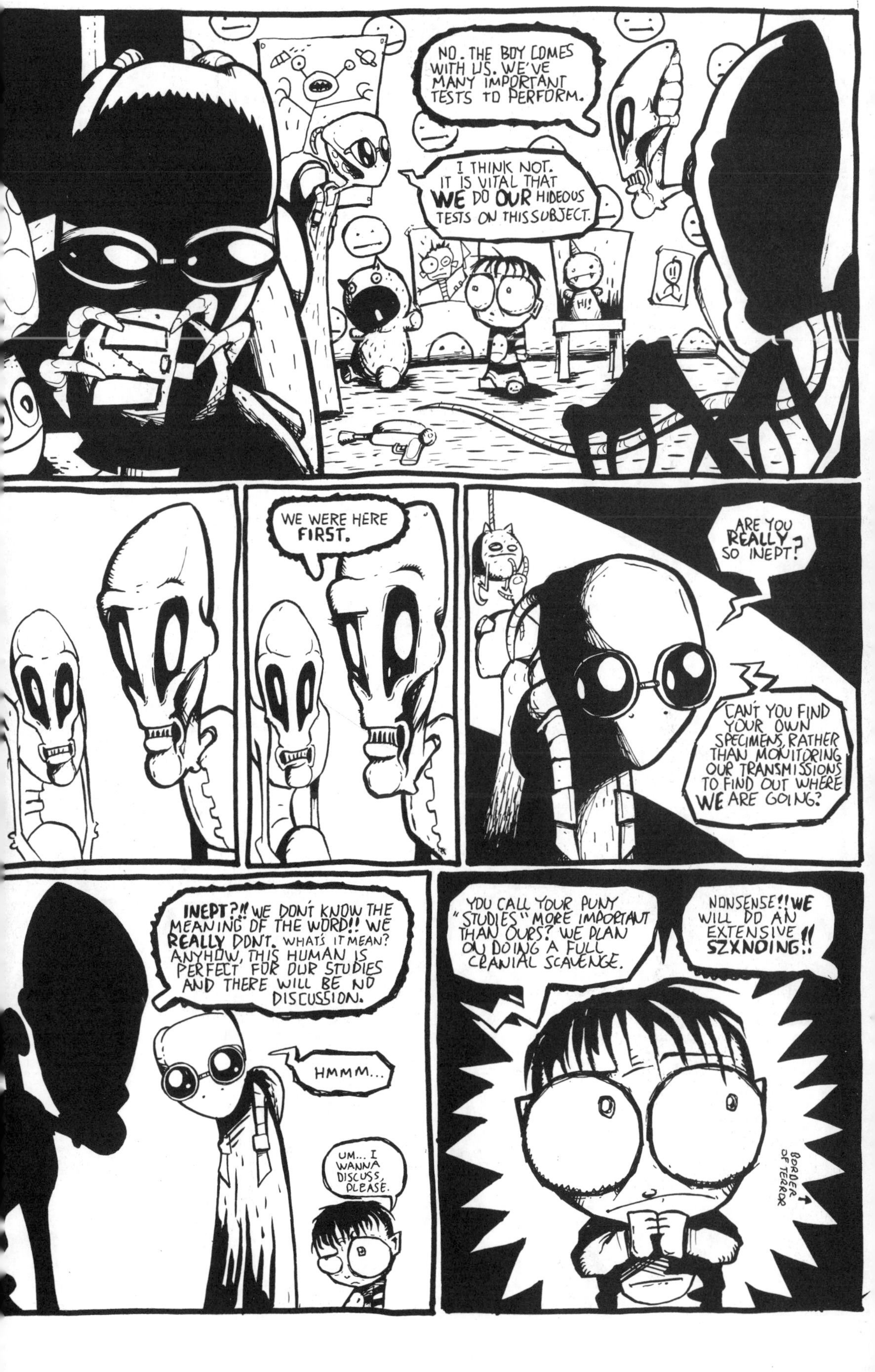
NO. THE BOY COMES WITH US. WE'VE MANY IMPORTANT TESTS TO PERFORM.
I THINK NOT. IT IS VITAL THAT WE DO OUR HIDEOUS TESTS ON THIS SUBJECT.
HI!
WE WERE HERE FIRST.
ARE YOU REALLY SO INEPT?
CAN'T YOU FIND YOUR OWN SPECIMENS, RATHER THAN MONITORING OUR TRANSMISSIONS TO FIND OUT WHERE WE ARE GOING?
INEPT?!! WE DON'T KNOW THE MEANING OF THE WORD!! WE REALLY DON'T. WHAT'S IT MEAN? ANYHOW, THIS HUMAN IS PERFECT FOR OUR STUDIES AND THERE WILL BE NO DISCUSSION.
HMMM...
UM... I WANNA DISCUSS, PLEASE.
YOU CALL YOUR PUNY "STUDIES" MORE IMPORTANT THAN OURS? WE PLAN ON DOING A FULL CRANIAL SCAVENGE.
NONSENSE!! WE WILL DO AN EXTENSIVE SZXNOING!!
BORDER OF TERROR

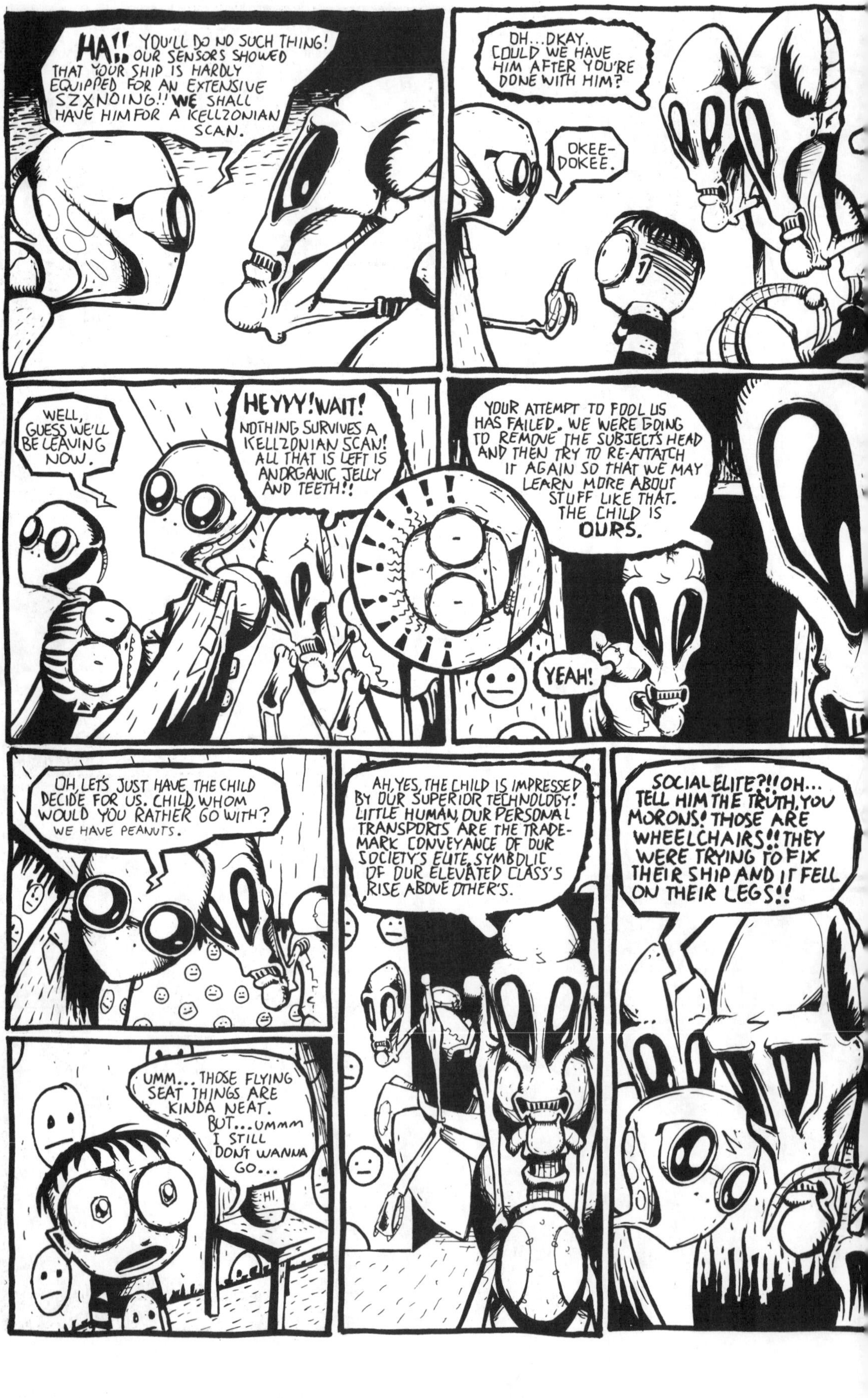
HA!! YOU'LL DO NO SUCH THING! OUR SENSORS SHOWED THAT YOUR SHIP IS HARDLY EQUIPPED FOR AN EXTENSIVE SZXNOING!! WE SHALL HAVE HIM FOR A KELLZONIAN SCAN.
OH...OKAY. COULD WE HAVE HIM AFTER YOU'RE DONE WITH HIM?
OKEE-DOKEE.
WELL, GUESS WE'LL BE LEAVING NOW.
HEYYY! WAIT! NOTHING SURVIVES A KELLZONIAN SCAN! ALL THAT IS LEFT IS ANORGANIC JELLY AND TEETH!!
!!!
YOUR ATTEMPT TO FOOL US HAS FAILED. WE WERE GOING TO REMOVE THE SUBJECT'S HEAD AND THEN TRY TO RE-ATTATCH IT AGAIN SO THAT WE MAY LEARN MORE ABOUT STUFF LIKE THAT. THE CHILD IS OURS.
YEAH!
OH, LET'S JUST HAVE THE CHILD DECIDE FOR US. CHILD, WHOM WOULD YOU RATHER GO WITH? WE HAVE PEANUTS.
UMM... THOSE FLYING SEAT THINGS ARE KINDA NEAT. BUT...UMMM I STILL DON'T WANNA GO...
HI.
AH, YES, THE CHILD IS IMPRESSED BY OUR SUPERIOR TECHNOLOGY! LITTLE HUMAN, OUR PERSONAL TRANSPORTS ARE THE TRADE-MARK CONVEYANCE OF OUR SOCIETY'S ELITE, SYMBOLIC OF OUR ELEVATED CLASS'S RISE ABOVE OTHER'S.
SOCIAL ELITE?!! OH... TELL HIM THE TRUTH, YOU MORONS! THOSE ARE WHEELCHAIRS!! THEY WERE TRYING TO FIX THEIR SHIP AND IT FELL ON THEIR LEGS!!

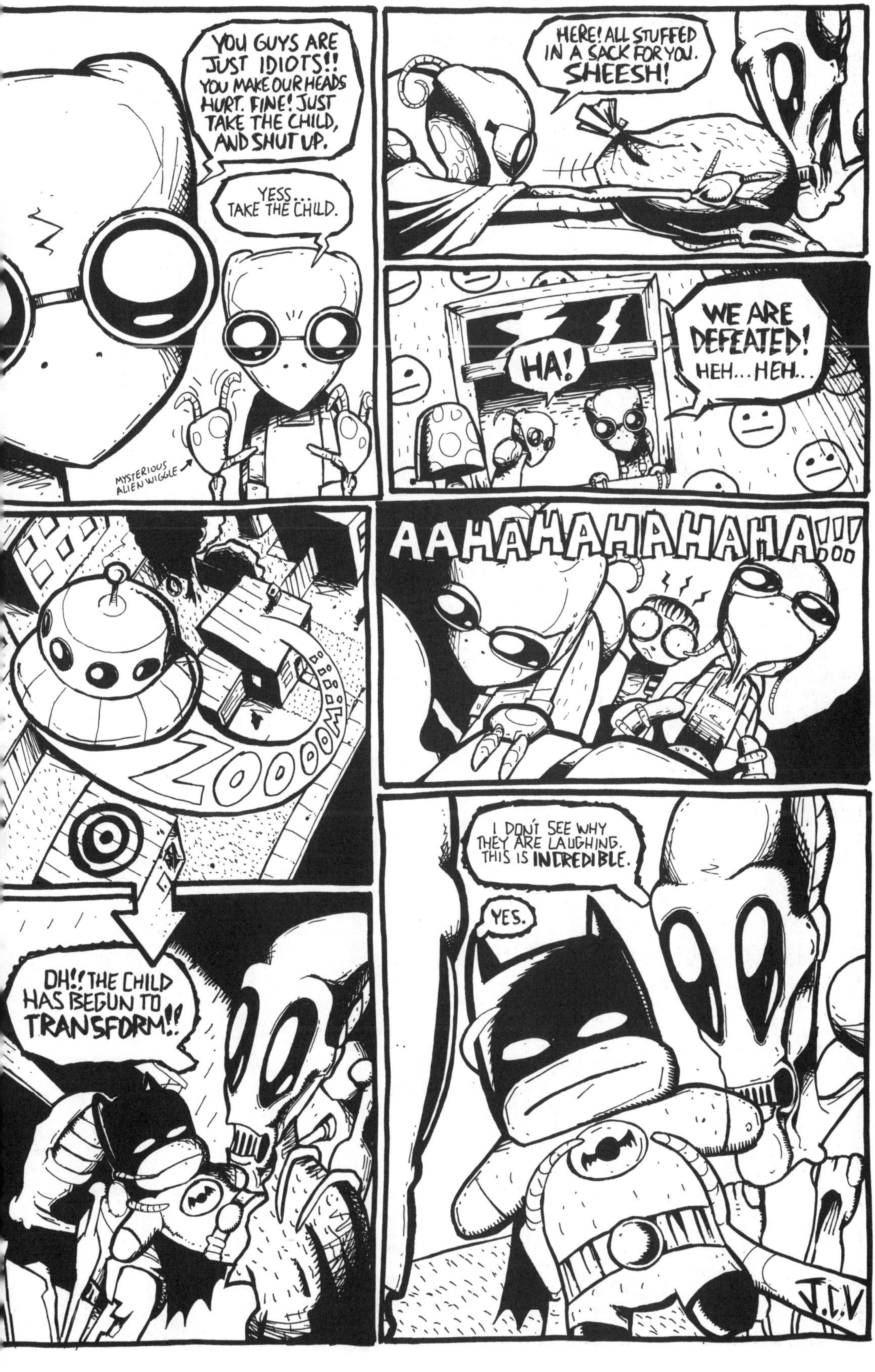
YOU GUYS ARE JUST IDIOTS!! YOU MAKE OUR HEADS HURT. FINE! JUST TAKE THE CHILD, AND SHUT UP.
YESS... TAKE THE CHILD.
MYSTERIOUS ALIEN WIGGLE
HERE! ALL STUFFED IN A SACK FOR YOU. SHEESH!
HA!
WE ARE DEFEATED! HEH... HEH...
ZOOOOOOOM
AAHAHAHAHAHAHA!!!
OH!! THE CHILD HAS BEGUN TO TRANSFORM!!
I DON'T SEE WHY THEY ARE LAUGHING. THIS IS INCREDIBLE.
YES.
J.C.V

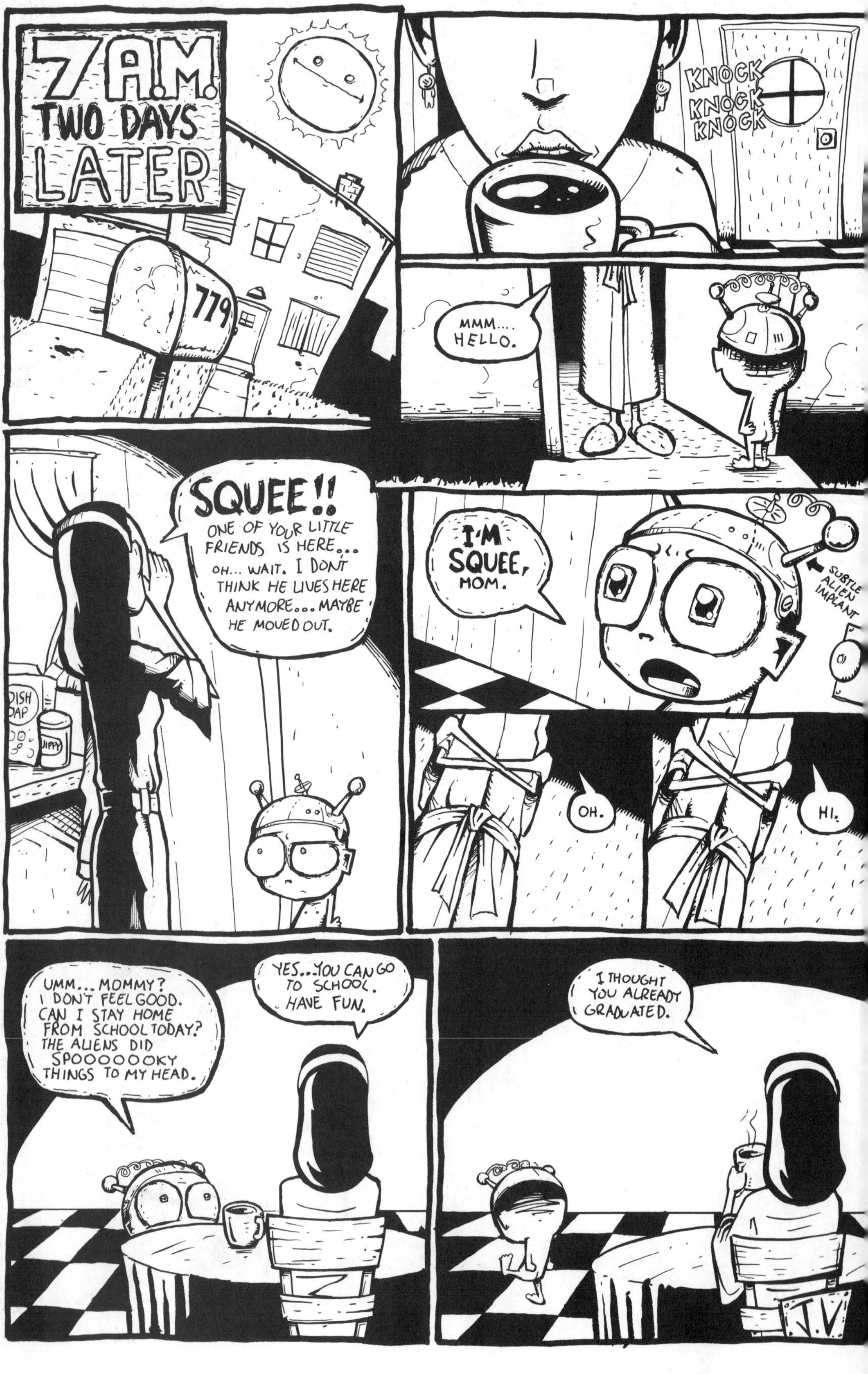
7 A.M. TWO DAYS LATER
779
KNOCK KNOCK KNOCK
MMM.... HELLO.
SQUEE!! ONE OF YOUR LITTLE FRIENDS IS HERE... OH... WAIT. I DON'T THINK HE LIVES HERE ANYMORE... MAYBE HE MOVED OUT.
DISH OAP
JIPPY
I'M SQUEE, MOM.
SUBTLE ALIEN IMPLANT
OH.
HI.
UMM... MOMMY? I DON'T FEEL GOOD. CAN I STAY HOME FROM SCHOOL TODAY? THE ALIENS DID SPOOOOOOOKY THINGS TO MY HEAD.
YES... YOU CAN GO TO SCHOOL. HAVE FUN.
I THOUGHT YOU ALREADY GRADUATED.
J.V

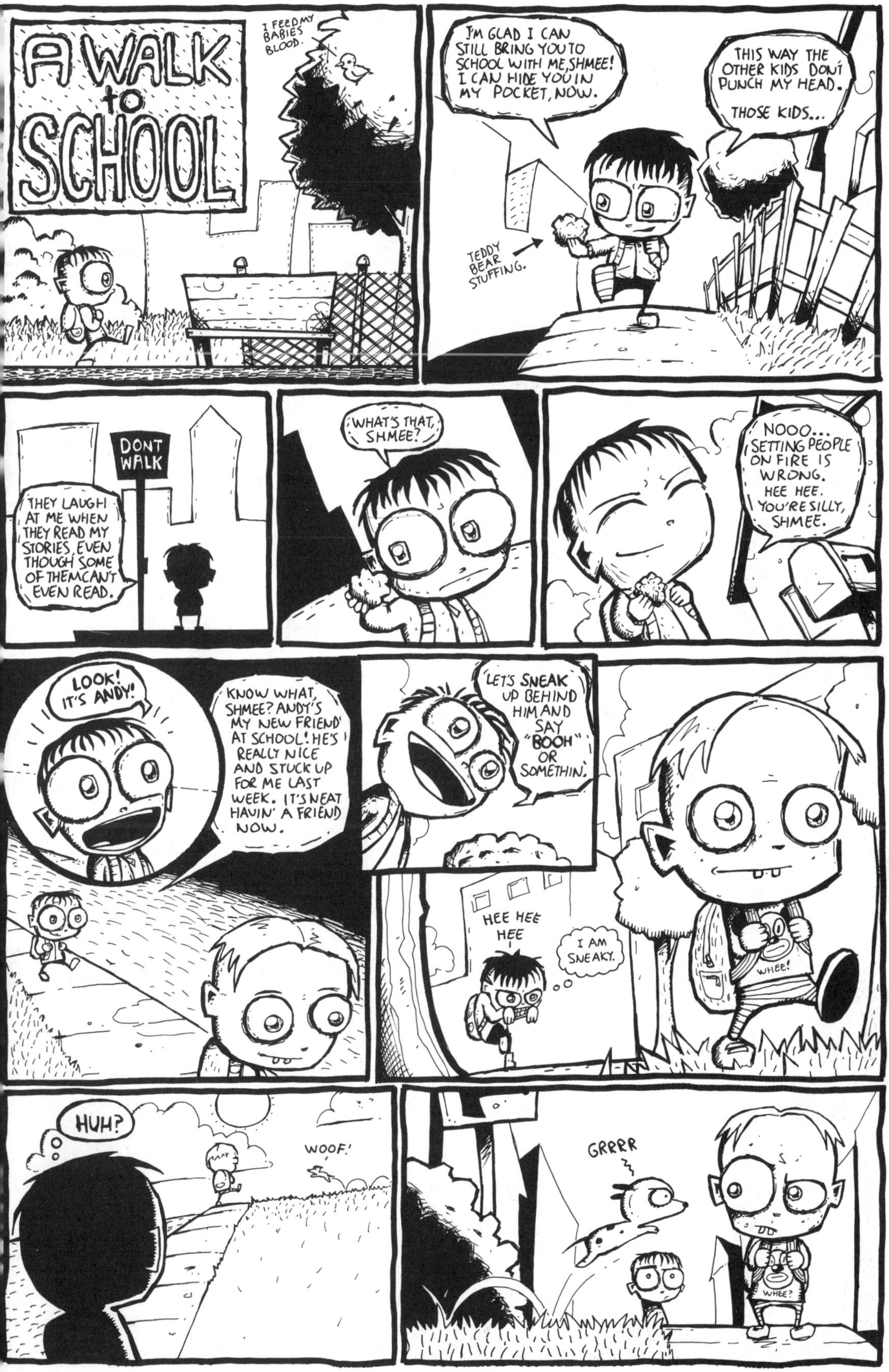
A WALK to SCHOOL
I FEED MY BABIES BLOOD.
I'M GLAD I CAN STILL BRING YOU TO SCHOOL WITH ME, SHMEE! I CAN HIDE YOU IN MY POCKET, NOW.
THIS WAY THE OTHER KIDS DON'T PUNCH MY HEAD.
THOSE KIDS...
TEDDY BEAR STUFFING.
DONT WALK
THEY LAUGH AT ME WHEN THEY READ MY STORIES, EVEN THOUGH SOME OF THEM CAN'T EVEN READ.
WHAT'S THAT, SHMEE?
NOOO... SETTING PEOPLE ON FIRE IS WRONG. HEE HEE. YOU'RE SILLY, SHMEE.
LOOK! IT'S ANDY!
KNOW WHAT, SHMEE? ANDY'S MY NEW FRIEND AT SCHOOL! HE'S REALLY NICE AND STUCK UP FOR ME LAST WEEK. IT'S NEAT HAVIN' A FRIEND NOW.
LET'S SNEAK UP BEHIND HIM AND SAY "BOOH" OR SOMETHIN'.
HEE HEE HEE
I AM SNEAKY.
WHEE!
HUH?
WOOF!
GRRRR
WHEE?

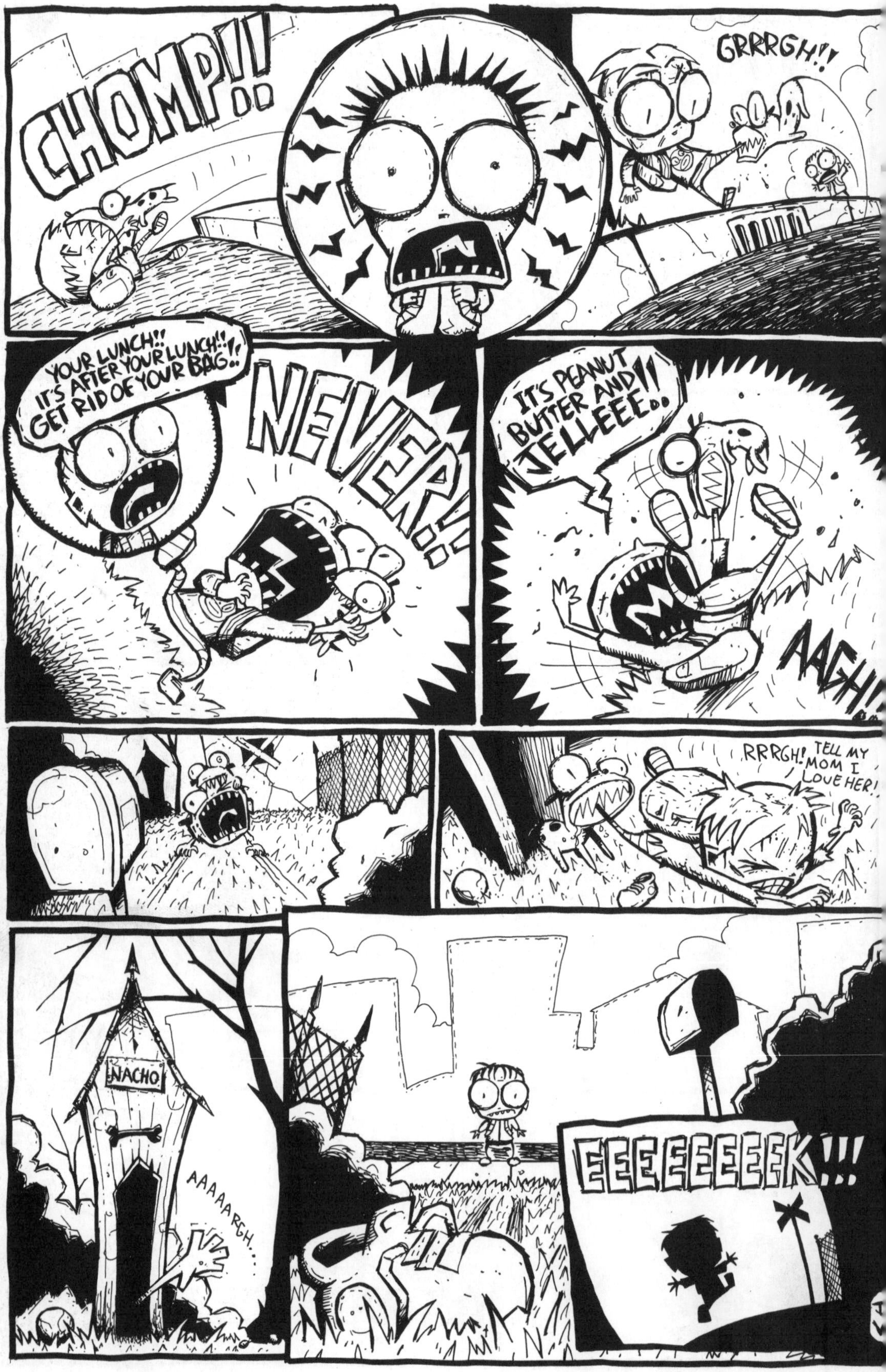
CHOMP!!
GRRRGH!!
YOUR LUNCH!! IT'S AFTER YOUR LUNCH!! GET RID OF YOUR BAG!!
NEVER!!
IT'S PEANUT BUTTER AND JELLEEE!!
AAGH!!
RRRGH!
TELL MY MOM I LOVE HER!
NACHO
AAAAARGH...
EEEEEEEEK!!!

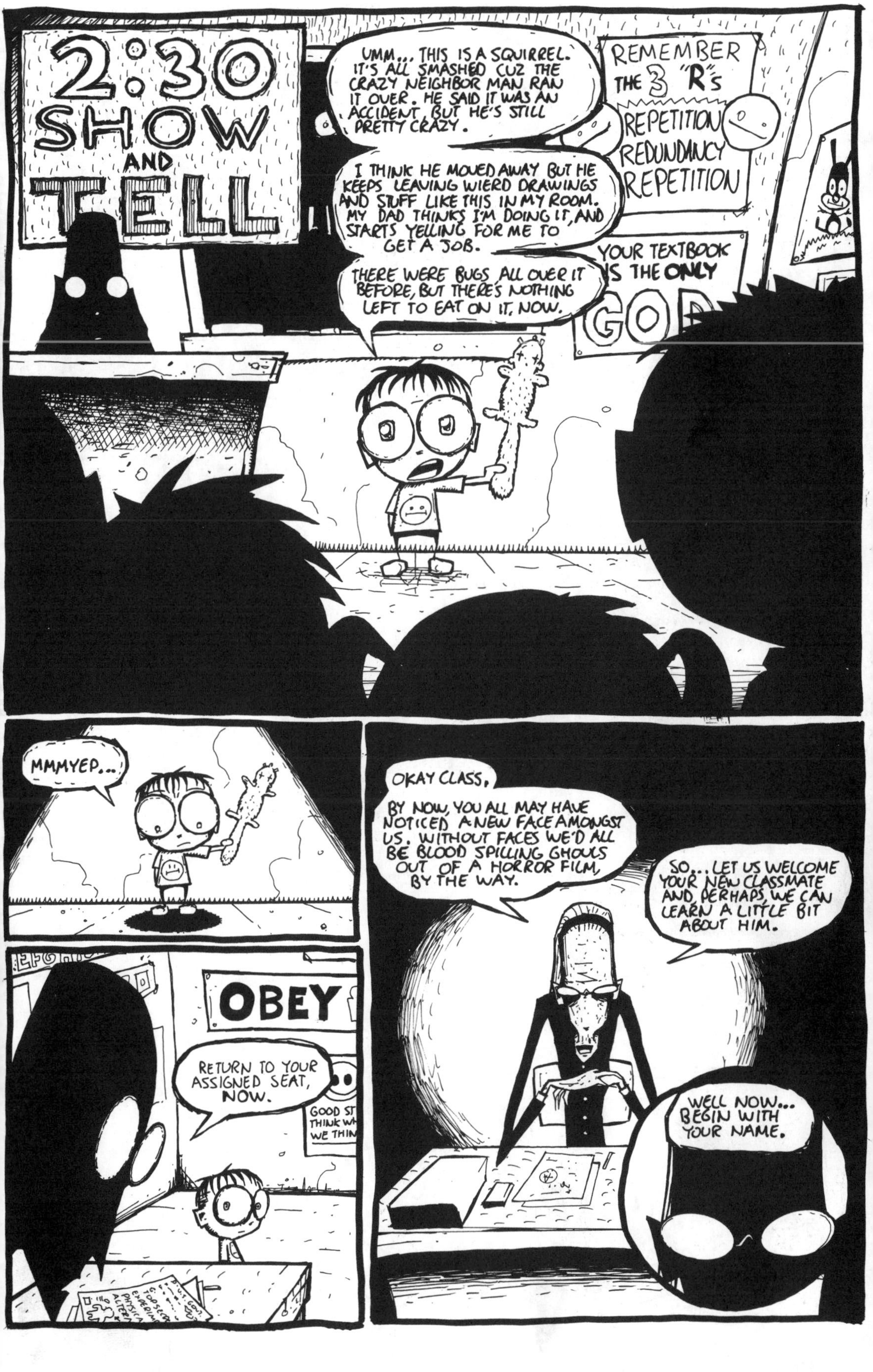
2:30 SHOW AND TELL
UMM... THIS IS A SQUIRREL. IT'S ALL SMASHED CUZ THE CRAZY NEIGHBOR MAN RAN IT OVER. HE SAID IT WAS AN ACCIDENT, BUT HE'S STILL PRETTY CRAZY.
REMEMBER THE 3 "R"s
REPETITION
REDUNDANCY
REPETITION
I THINK HE MOVED AWAY BUT HE KEEPS LEAVING WIERD DRAWINGS AND STUFF LIKE THIS IN MY ROOM. MY DAD THINKS I'M DOING IT, AND STARTS YELLING FOR ME TO GET A JOB.
YOUR TEXTBOOK IS THE ONLY GOD
THERE WERE BUGS ALL OVER IT BEFORE, BUT THERE'S NOTHING LEFT TO EAT ON IT, NOW.
MMMYEP...
OKAY CLASS,
BY NOW, YOU ALL MAY HAVE NOTICED A NEW FACE AMONGST US. WITHOUT FACES WE'D ALL BE BLOOD SPILLING GHOULS OUT OF A HORROR FILM, BY THE WAY.
SO... LET US WELCOME YOUR NEW CLASSMATE AND, PERHAPS, WE CAN LEARN A LITTLE BIT ABOUT HIM.
OBEY
RETURN TO YOUR ASSIGNED SEAT, NOW.
WELL NOW... BEGIN WITH YOUR NAME.

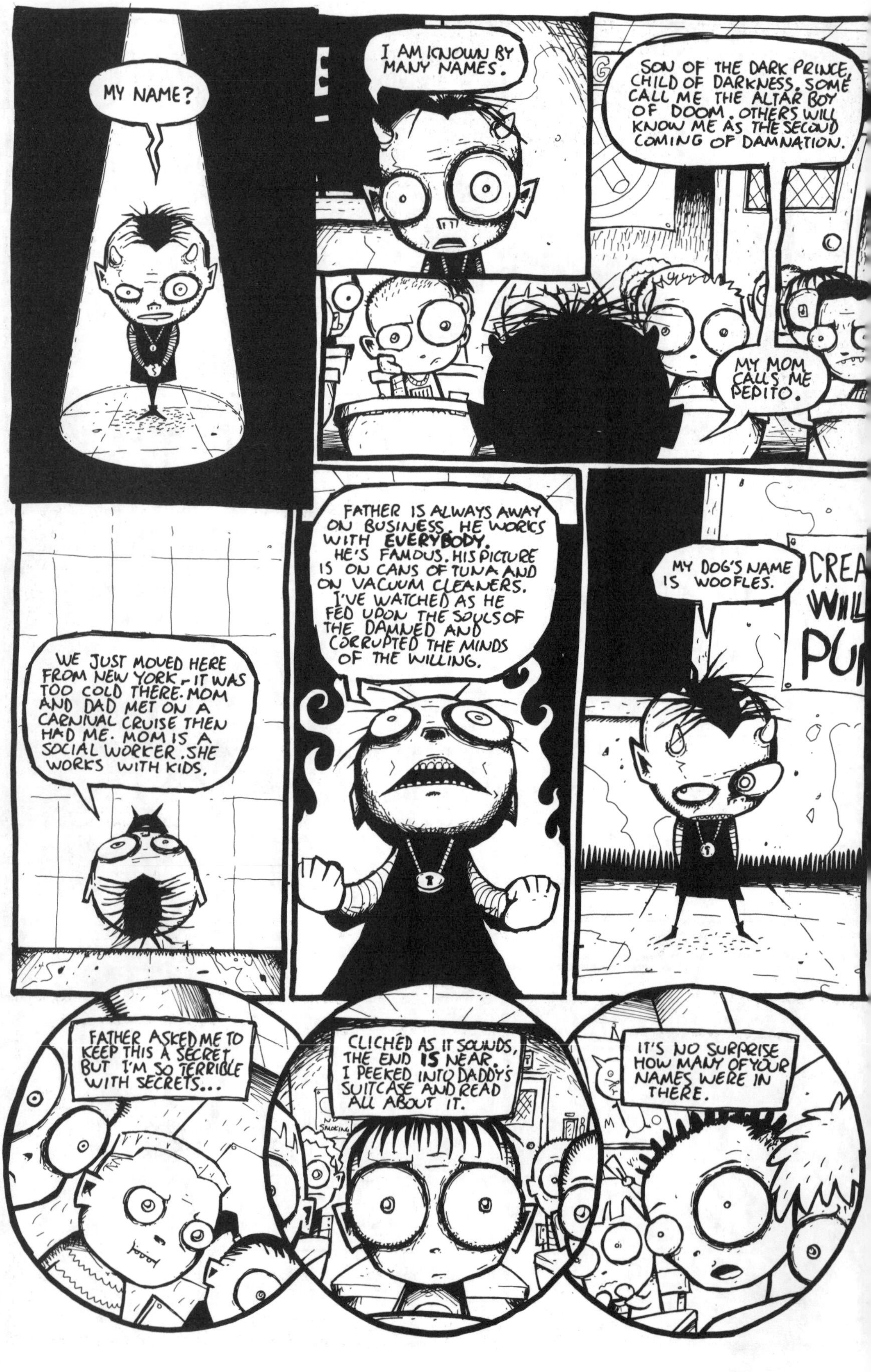
MY NAME?
I AM KNOWN BY MANY NAMES.
SON OF THE DARK PRINCE, CHILD OF DARKNESS. SOME CALL ME THE ALTAR BOY OF DOOM. OTHERS WILL KNOW ME AS THE SECOND COMING OF DAMNATION.
MY MOM CALLS ME PEPITO.
WE JUST MOVED HERE FROM NEW YORK - IT WAS TOO COLD THERE. MOM AND DAD MET ON A CARNIVAL CRUISE THEN HAD ME. MOM IS A SOCIAL WORKER. SHE WORKS WITH KIDS.
FATHER IS ALWAYS AWAY ON BUSINESS. HE WORKS WITH EVERYBODY. HE'S FAMOUS. HIS PICTURE IS ON CANS OF TUNA AND ON VACUUM CLEANERS. I'VE WATCHED AS HE FED UPON THE SOULS OF THE DAMNED AND CORRUPTED THE MINDS OF THE WILLING.
MY DOG'S NAME IS WOOFLES.
FATHER ASKED ME TO KEEP THIS A SECRET BUT I'M SO TERRIBLE WITH SECRETS...
CLICHÉD AS IT SOUNDS, THE END IS NEAR. I PEEKED INTO DADDY'S SUITCASE AND READ ALL ABOUT IT.
IT'S NO SURPRISE HOW MANY OF YOUR NAMES WERE IN THERE.

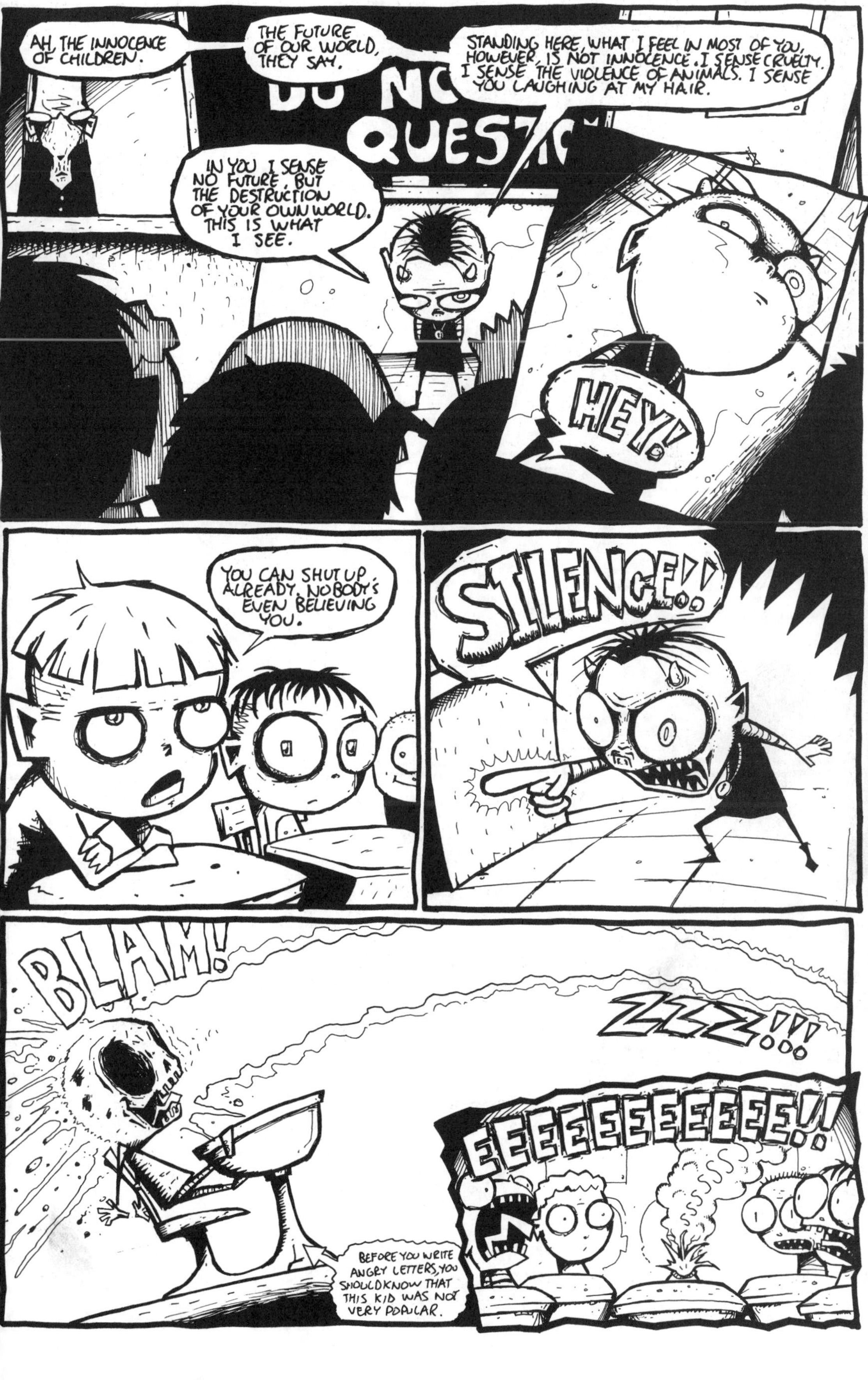
AH, THE INNOCENCE OF CHILDREN.
THE FUTURE OF OUR WORLD, THEY SAY.
STANDING HERE, WHAT I FEEL IN MOST OF YOU, HOWEVER, IS NOT INNOCENCE. I SENSE CRUELTY. I SENSE THE VIOLENCE OF ANIMALS. I SENSE YOU LAUGHING AT MY HAIR.
DO NO
QUESTIO
IN YOU I SENSE NO FUTURE, BUT THE DESTRUCTION OF YOUR OWN WORLD. THIS IS WHAT I SEE.
HEY!
YOU CAN SHUT UP ALREADY. NOBODY'S EVEN BELIEVING YOU.
SILENCE!!
BLAM!
ZZZ!!!
EEEEEEEEEEEE!!
BEFORE YOU WRITE ANGRY LETTERS, YOU SHOULD KNOW THAT THIS KID WAS NOT VERY POPULAR.

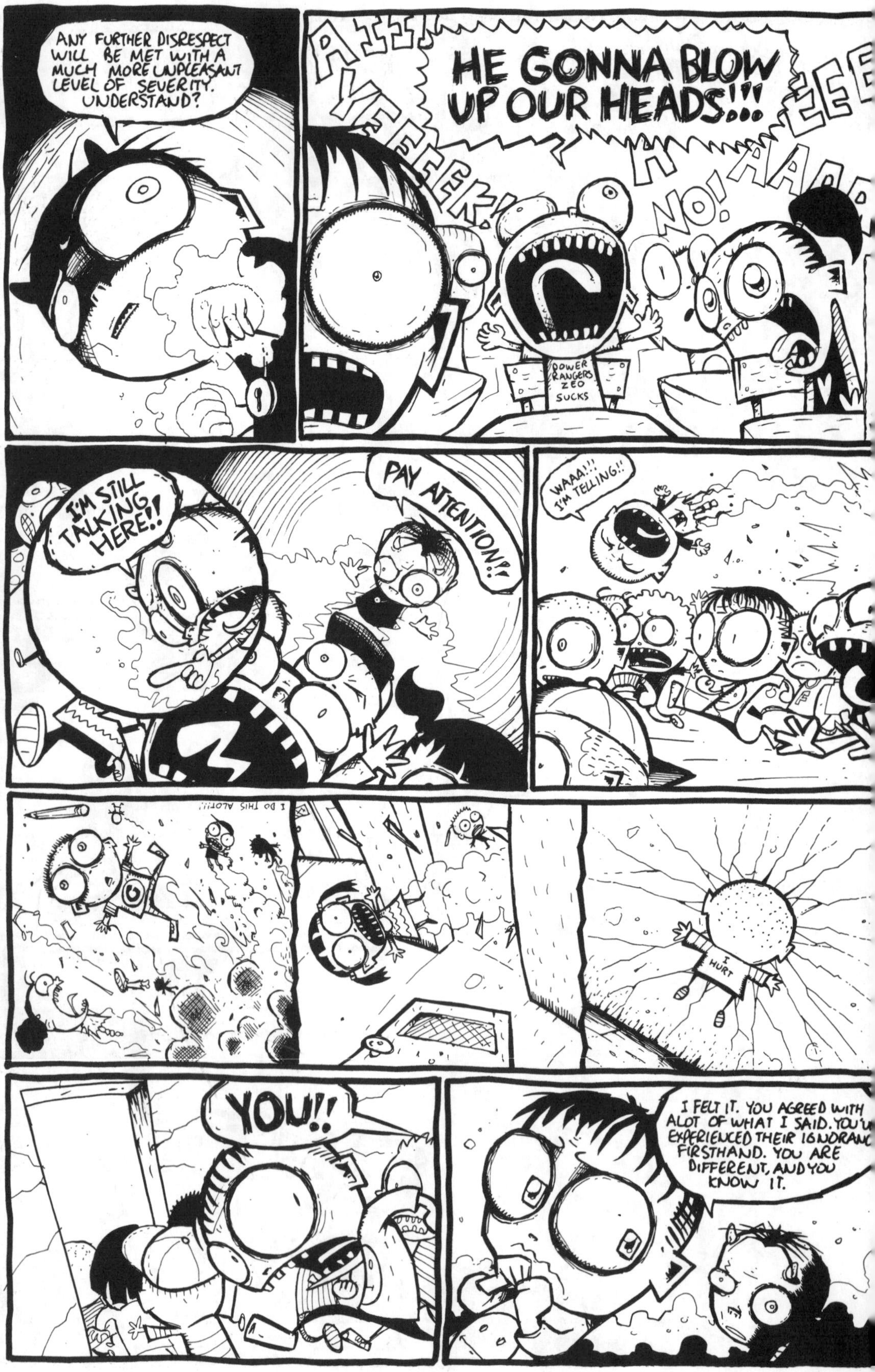
ANY FURTHER DISRESPECT WILL BE MET WITH A MUCH MORE UNPLEASANT LEVEL OF SEVERITY. UNDERSTAND?
AIII!
YEEEEEK!
HE GONNA BLOW UP OUR HEADS!!!...
EEE
NO!
POWER RANGERS ZEO SUCKS
I'M STILL TALKING HERE!!
PAY ATTENTION!!
WAAA!!! I'M TELLING!!
I DO THIS ALOT!!!
I HURT
YOU!!
I FELT IT. YOU AGREED WITH ALOT OF WHAT I SAID. YOU'
EXPERIENCED THEIR IGNORANC
FIRSTHAND. YOU ARE DIFFERENT, AND YOU KNOW IT.

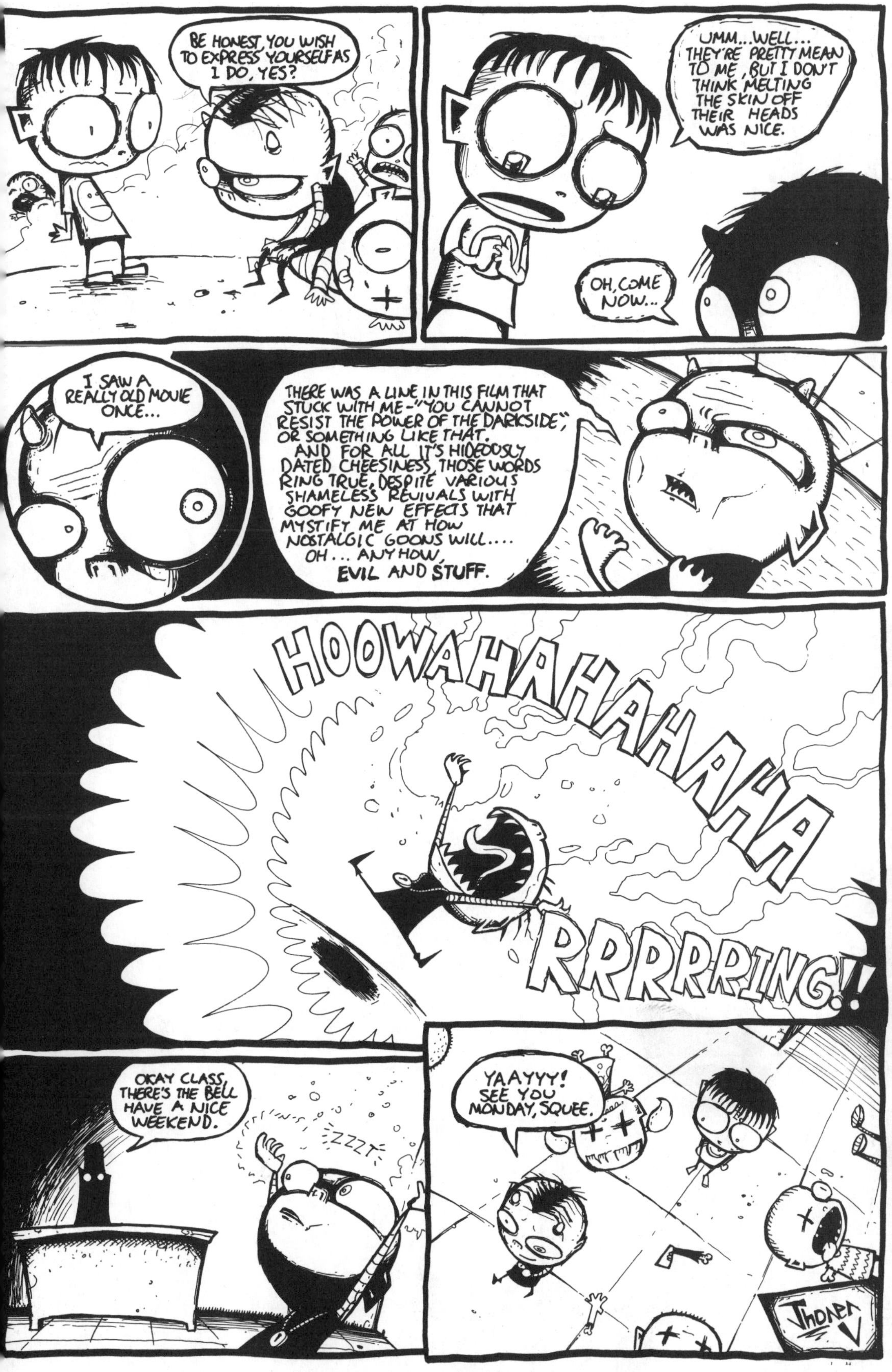
BE HONEST, YOU WISH TO EXPRESS YOURSELF AS I DO, YES?
UMM... WELL... THEY'RE PRETTY MEAN TO ME, BUT I DON'T THINK MELTING THE SKIN OFF THEIR HEADS WAS NICE.
OH, COME NOW...
I SAW A REALLY OLD MOVIE ONCE...
THERE WAS A LINE IN THIS FILM THAT STUCK WITH ME- "YOU CANNOT RESIST THE POWER OF THE DARKSIDE", OR SOMETHING LIKE THAT.
AND FOR ALL IT'S HIDEOUSLY DATED CHEESINESS, THOSE WORDS RING TRUE, DESPITE VARIOUS SHAMELESS REVIVALS WITH GOOFY NEW EFFECTS THAT MYSTIFY ME AT HOW NOSTALGIC GOONS WILL....
OH... ANYHOW, EVIL AND STUFF.
HOOWAHAHAHAHAHA
RRRRRING!!
OKAY CLASS, THERE'S THE BELL HAVE A NICE WEEKEND.
ZZZT
YAAYYY! SEE YOU MONDAY, SQUEE.
JHONEN V

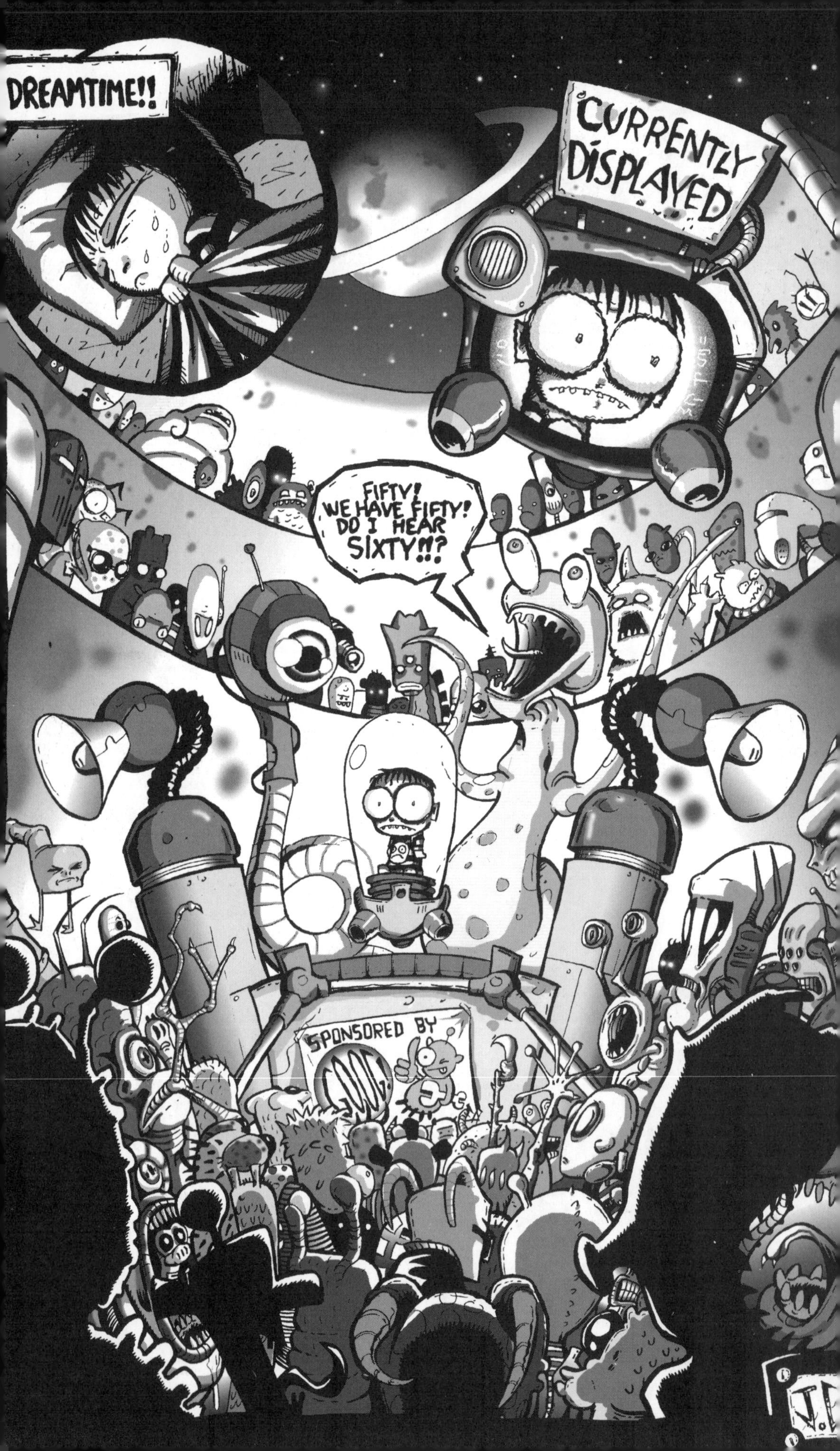
DREAMTIME!!
CURRENTLY DISPLAYED
FIFTY! WE HAVE FIFTY! DO I HEAR SIXTY!!?
SPONSORED BY

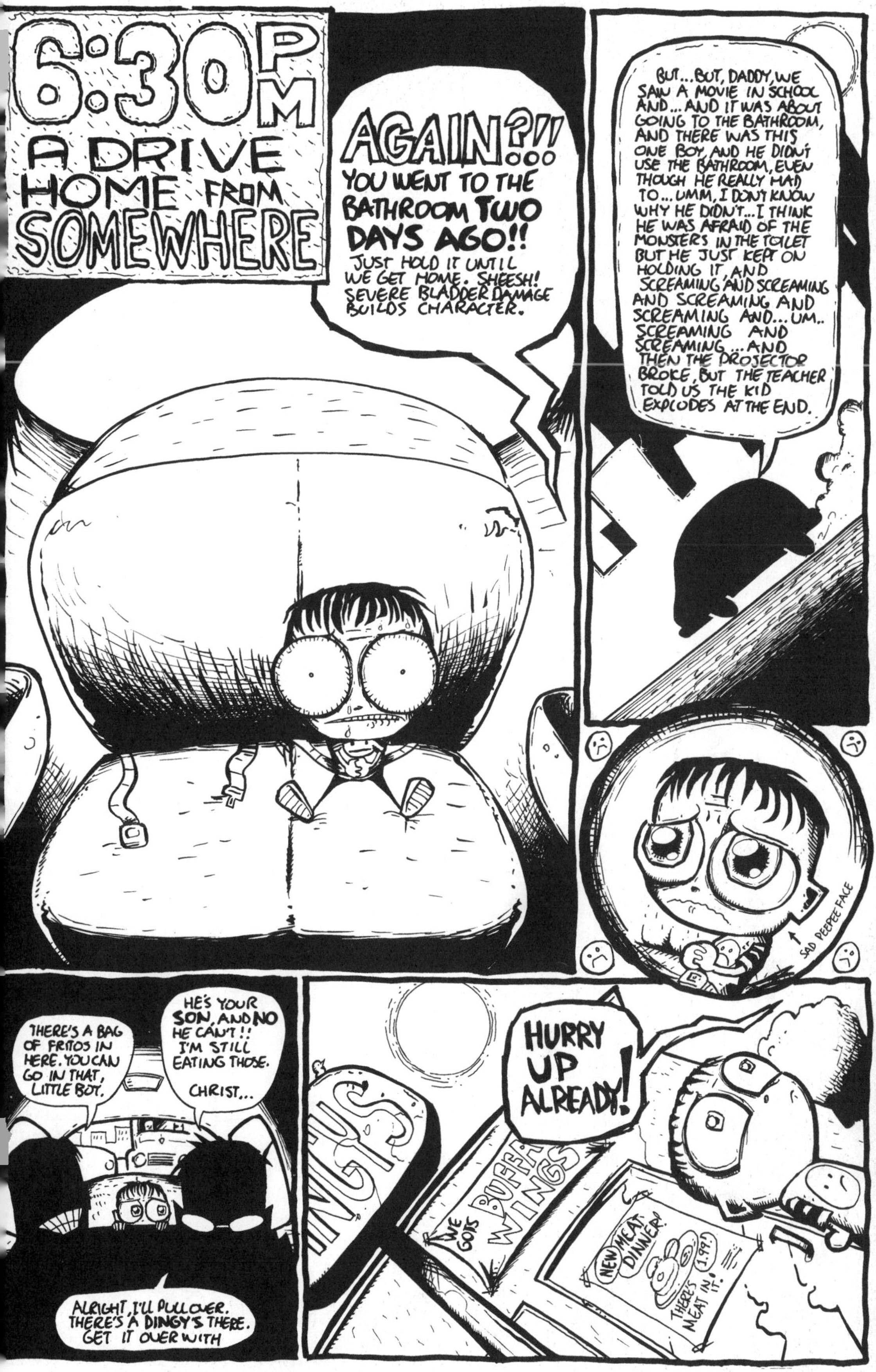
6:30 PM
A DRIVE HOME FROM SOMEWHERE
AGAIN?!! YOU WENT TO THE BATHROOM TWO DAYS AGO!! JUST HOLD IT UNTIL WE GET HOME. SHEESH! SEVERE BLADDER DAMAGE BUILDS CHARACTER.
BUT... BUT, DADDY, WE SAW A MOVIE IN SCHOOL AND... AND IT WAS ABOUT GOING TO THE BATHROOM, AND THERE WAS THIS ONE BOY, AND HE DIDN'T USE THE BATHROOM, EVEN THOUGH HE REALLY HAD TO... UMM, I DON'T KNOW WHY HE DIDN'T... I THINK HE WAS AFRAID OF THE MONSTERS IN THE TOILET BUT HE JUST KEPT ON HOLDING IT, AND SCREAMING AND SCREAMING AND SCREAMING AND SCREAMING AND... UM.. SCREAMING AND SCREAMING... AND THEN THE PROJECTOR BROKE, BUT THE TEACHER TOLD US THE KID EXPLODES AT THE END.
SAD PEEPEE FACE
THERE'S A BAG OF FRITOS IN HERE. YOU CAN GO IN THAT, LITTLE BOY.
HE'S YOUR SON, AND NO HE CAN'T!! I'M STILL EATING THOSE.
CHRIST...
ALRIGHT, I'LL PULL OVER. THERE'S A DINGY'S THERE. GET IT OVER WITH
HURRY UP ALREADY!
WE GOTS BUFFA WINGS
NEW MEAT DINNER! 1.99!
THERE'S MEAT IN IT!

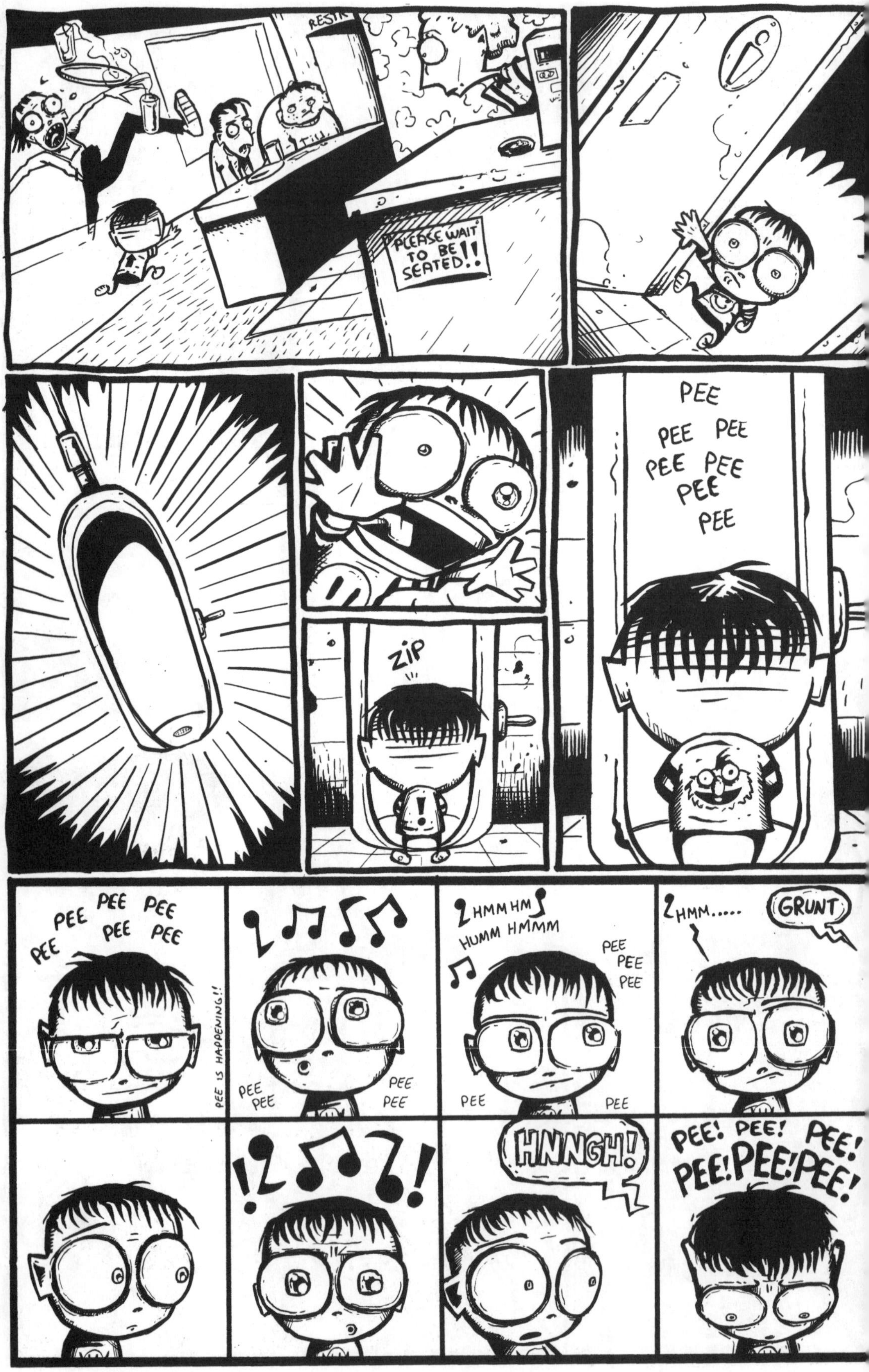
RESTR
PLEASE WAIT TO BE SEATED!!
PEE
PEE PEE
PEE PEE
PEE
PEE
ZIP
PEE PEE PEE PEE PEE PEE
PEE IS HAPPENING!!
PEE PEE
PEE PEE
HMM HM
HUMM HMMM
PEE PEE PEE
PEE
PEE
HMM.....
GRUNT
HNNGH!
PEE! PEE! PEE!
PEE! PEE! PEE!

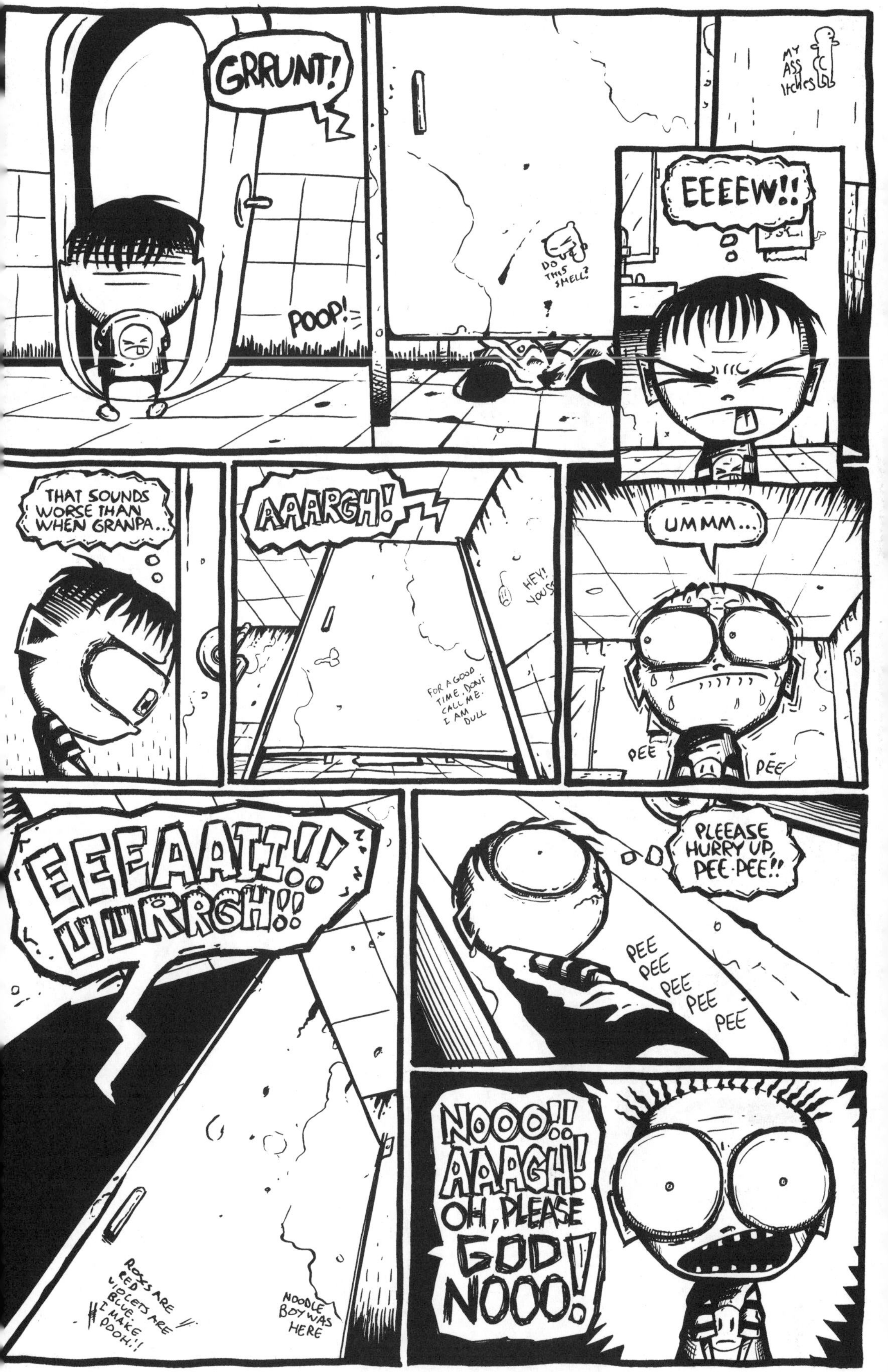
GRRUNT!
POOP!
DO U C THIS SMELL?
MY ASS ITCHES
EEEEW!!
THAT SOUNDS WORSE THAN WHEN GRANPA...
AAARGH!
HEY! YOU'S
FOR A GOOD TIME, DON'T CALL ME. I AM DULL
UMMM...
PEE
PEE
EEEAAII!! UURRGH!!
ROSES ARE RED VIOLETS ARE BLUE. I MAKE POOH!!
NOODLE BOY WAS HERE
PLEEASE HURRY UP, PEE-PEE!!
PEE PEE PEE PEE PEE
NOOO!! AAAGH! OH, PLEASE GOD NOOO!

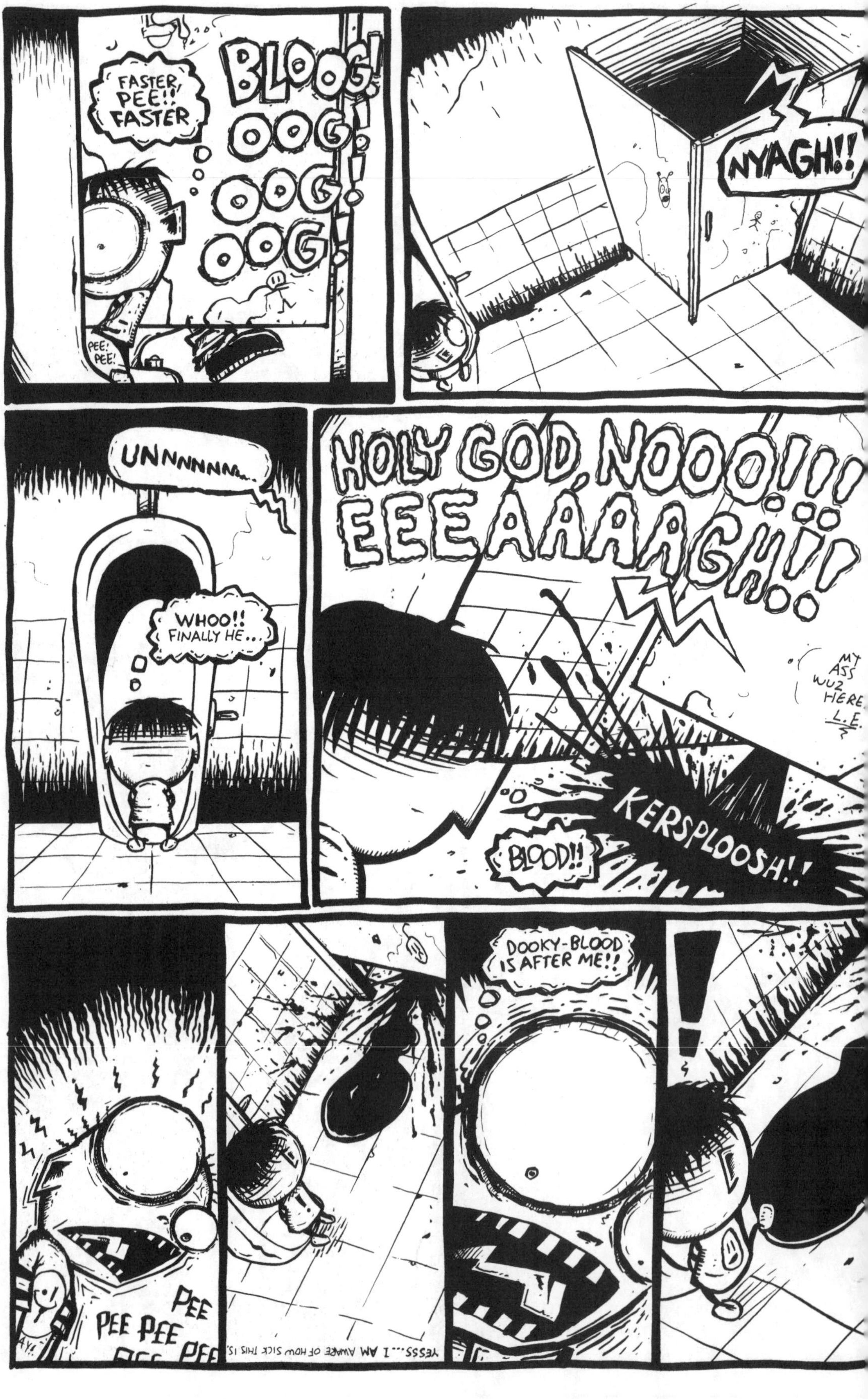
FASTER PEE!! FASTER
BLOOG! OOG! OOG! OOG!
PEE! PEE!
NYAGH!!
UNNNNNN...
WHOO!! FINALLY HE...
HOLY GOD, NOOO!!! EEEAAAAGH!!
MY ASS WUZ HERE. L.E.
KERSPLOOSH!!
BLOOD!!
PEE PEE PEE PEE
YESSS.... I AM AWARE OF HOW SICK THIS IS.
DOOKY-BLOOD IS AFTER ME!!
!

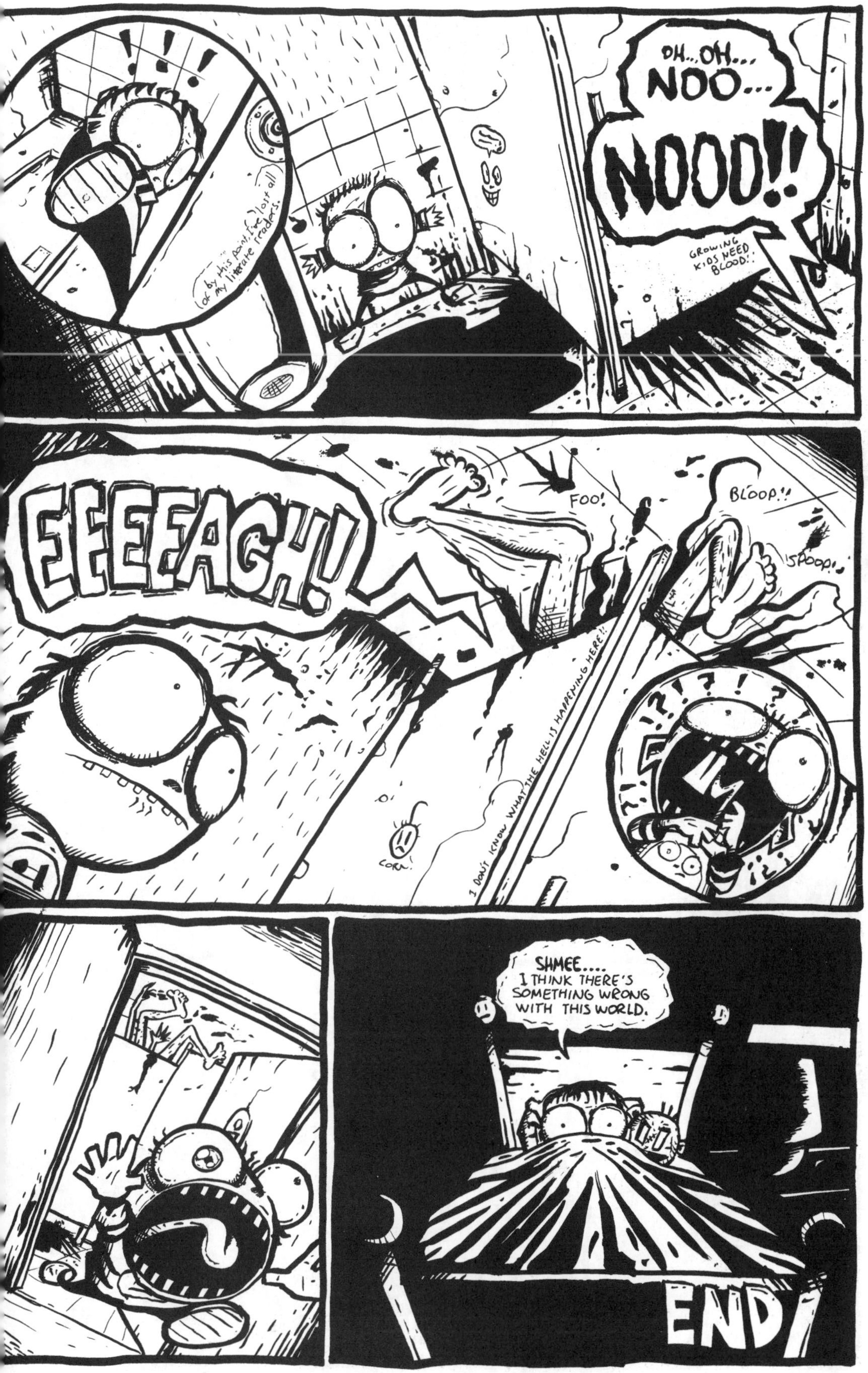

!!!
(by this point, I've lost all of my literate readers.
OH...OH... NOO...
NOOO!!
GROWING KIDS NEED BLOOD!
EEEEAGH!!
FOO!
BLOOP!!
SPOOP!
CORN!
I DON'T KNOW WHAT THE HELL IS HAPPENING HERE!!
!?!?!?
SHMEE.... I THINK THERE'S SOMETHING WRONG WITH THIS WORLD.
END

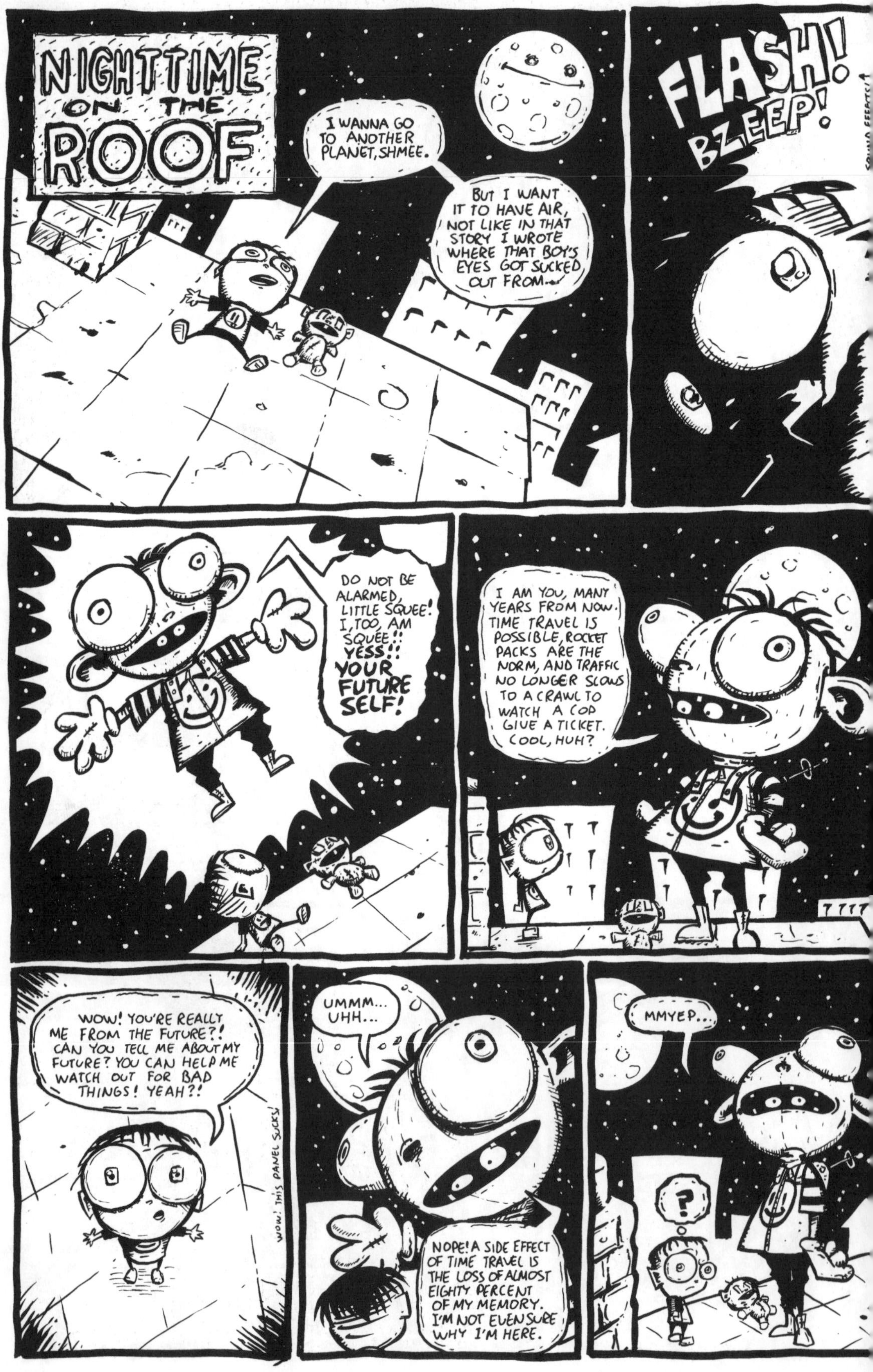
NIGHTTIME ON THE ROOF
I WANNA GO TO ANOTHER PLANET, SHMEE.
BUT I WANT IT TO HAVE AIR, NOT LIKE IN THAT STORY I WROTE WHERE THAT BOY'S EYES GOT SUCKED OUT FROM...
FLASH! BZEEP!
DO NOT BE ALARMED, LITTLE SQUEE! I, TOO, AM SQUEE!! YESS!! YOUR FUTURE SELF!
I AM YOU, MANY YEARS FROM NOW. TIME TRAVEL IS POSSIBLE, ROCKET PACKS ARE THE NORM, AND TRAFFIC NO LONGER SLOWS TO A CRAWL TO WATCH A COP GIVE A TICKET. COOL, HUH?
WOW! YOU'RE REALLY ME FROM THE FUTURE?! CAN YOU TELL ME ABOUT MY FUTURE? YOU CAN HELP ME WATCH OUT FOR BAD THINGS! YEAH?!
WOW! THIS PANEL SUCKS!
UMMM... UHH...
NOPE! A SIDE EFFECT OF TIME TRAVEL IS THE LOSS OF ALMOST EIGHTY PERCENT OF MY MEMORY. I'M NOT EVEN SURE WHY I'M HERE.
MMYEP...
?

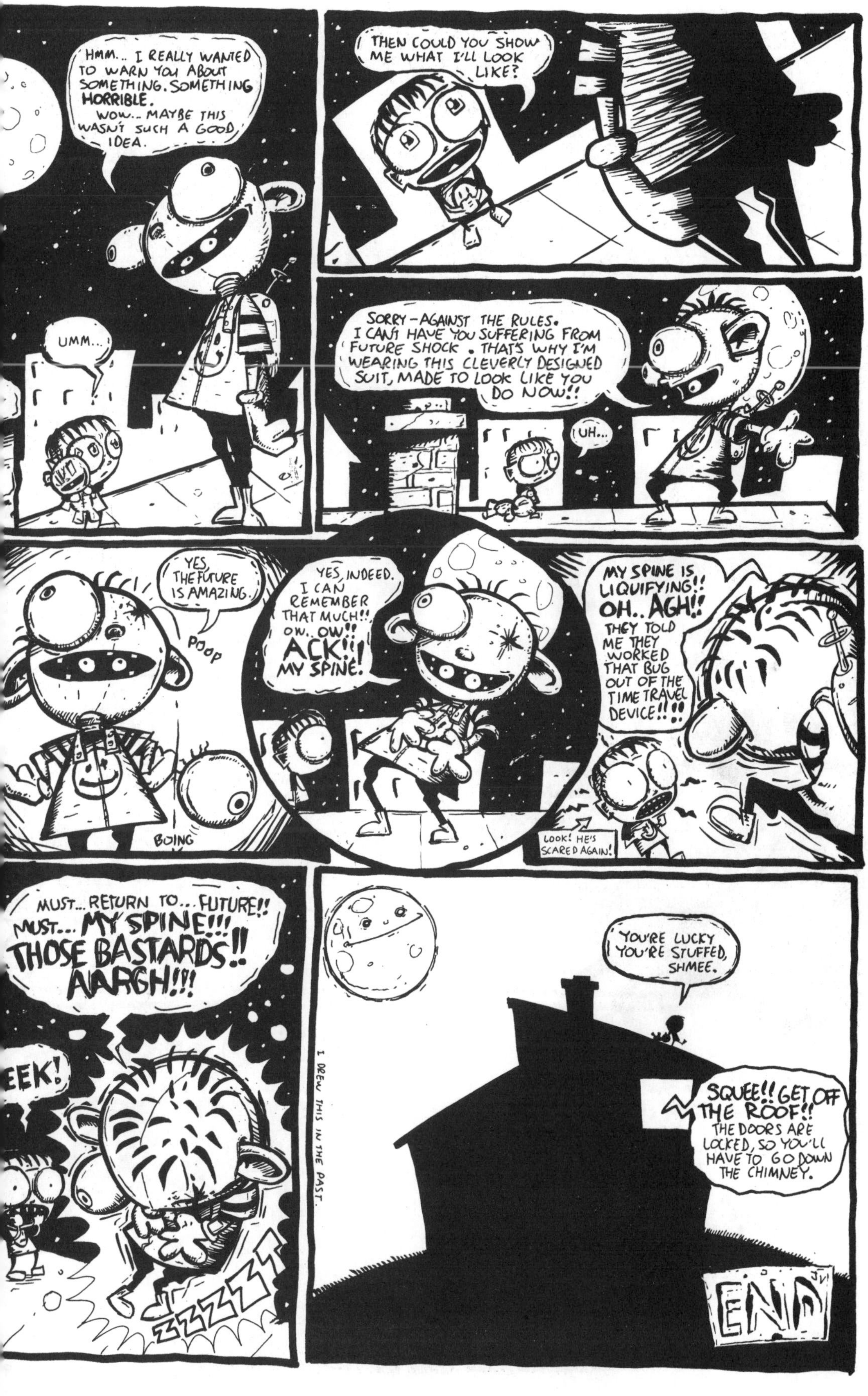
HMM... I REALLY WANTED TO WARN YOU ABOUT SOMETHING. SOMETHING HORRIBLE. WOW... MAYBE THIS WASN'T SUCH A GOOD IDEA.
UMM...
THEN COULD YOU SHOW ME WHAT I'LL LOOK LIKE?
SORRY - AGAINST THE RULES. I CAN'T HAVE YOU SUFFERING FROM FUTURE SHOCK. THAT'S WHY I'M WEARING THIS CLEVERLY DESIGNED SUIT, MADE TO LOOK LIKE YOU DO NOW!!
UH...
YES, THE FUTURE IS AMAZING.
POOP
BOING
YES, INDEED. I CAN REMEMBER THAT MUCH!! OW.. OW!! ACK!!! MY SPINE!
MY SPINE IS LIQUIFYING!! OH.. AGH!! THEY TOLD ME THEY WORKED THAT BUG OUT OF THE TIME TRAVEL DEVICE!!!!
LOOK! HE'S SCARED AGAIN!
MUST... RETURN TO... FUTURE!! MUST... MY SPINE!!! THOSE BASTARDS!! AARGH!!!
EEK!
ZZZZZT
I DREW THIS IN THE PAST.
YOU'RE LUCKY YOU'RE STUFFED, SHMEE.
SQUEE!! GET OFF THE ROOF!! THE DOORS ARE LOCKED, SO YOU'LL HAVE TO GO DOWN THE CHIMNEY.
END

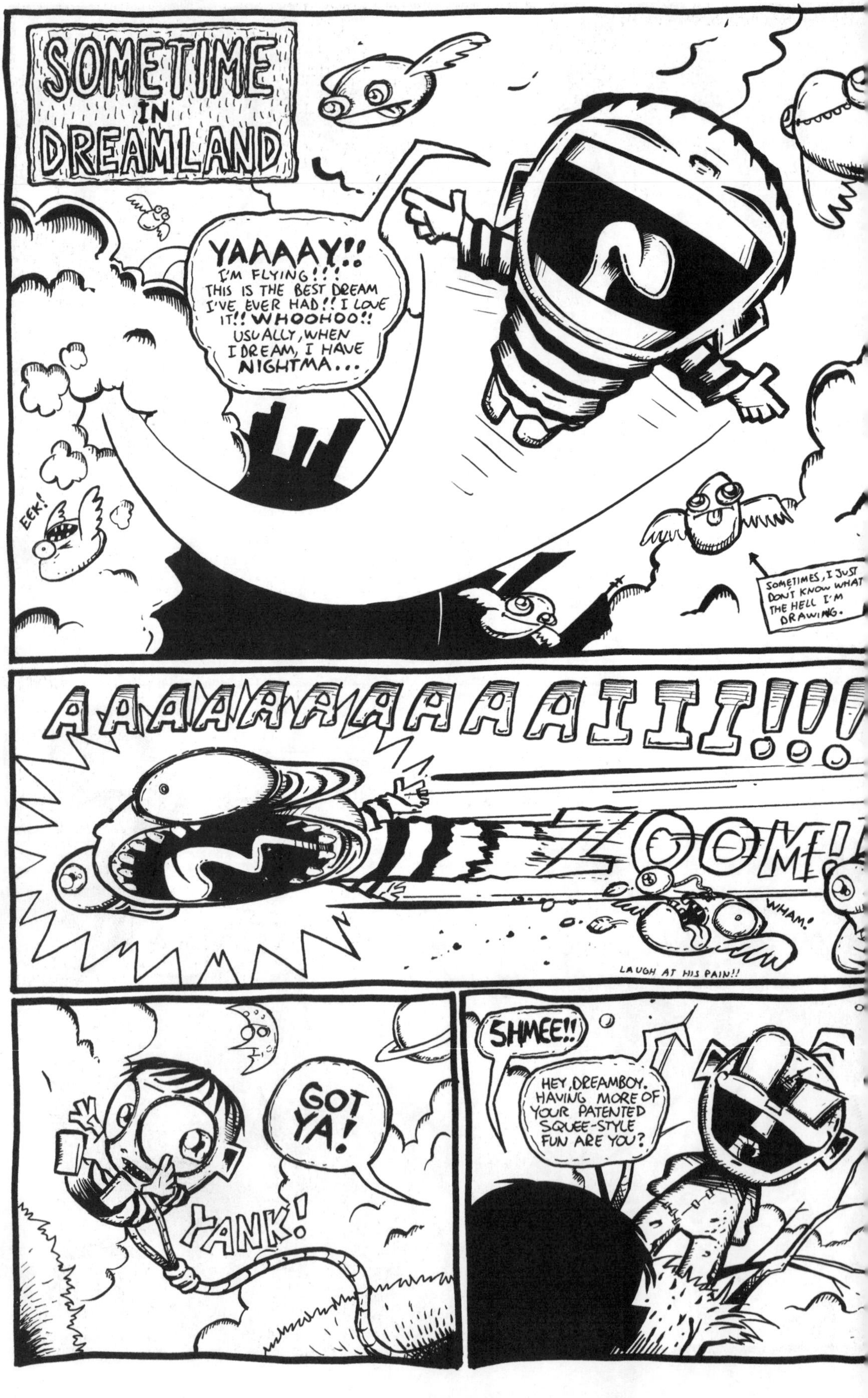
SOMETIME IN DREAMLAND
YAAAAY!! I'M FLYING!!! THIS IS THE BEST DREAM I'VE EVER HAD!! I LOVE IT!! WHOOHOO!! USUALLY, WHEN I DREAM, I HAVE NIGHTMA...
EEK!
SOMETIMES, I JUST DON'T KNOW WHAT THE HELL I'M DRAWING.
AAAAAAAAAAAIIII!!!
ZOOM!!
WHAM!
LAUGH AT HIS PAIN!!
GOT YA!
YANK!
SHMEE!!
HEY, DREAMBOY. HAVING MORE OF YOUR PATENTED SQUEE-STYLE FUN ARE YOU?

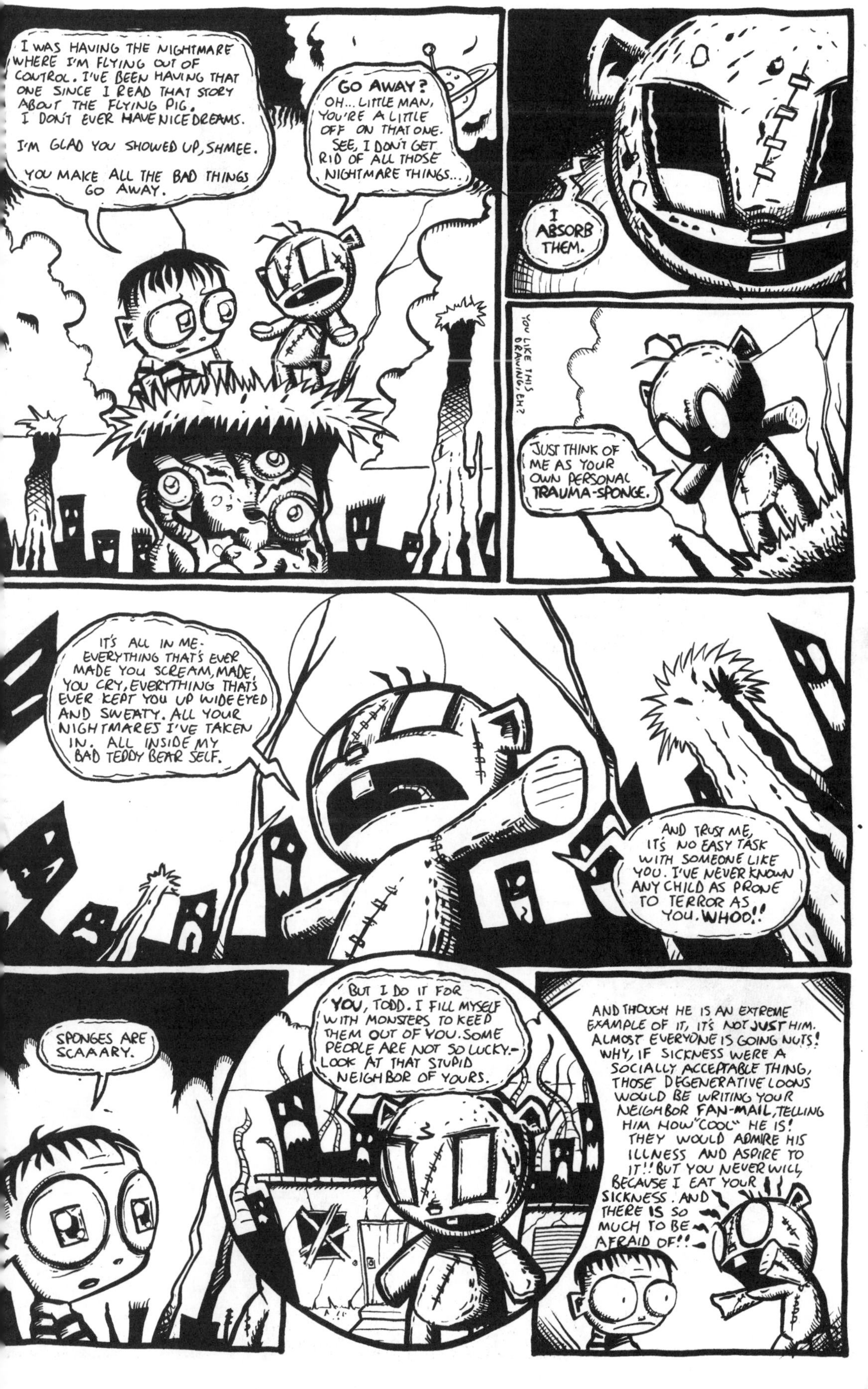
I WAS HAVING THE NIGHTMARE WHERE I'M FLYING OUT OF CONTROL. I'VE BEEN HAVING THAT ONE SINCE I READ THAT STORY ABOUT THE FLYING PIG. I DON'T EVER HAVE NICE DREAMS.
I'M GLAD YOU SHOWED UP, SHMEE.
YOU MAKE ALL THE BAD THINGS GO AWAY.
GO AWAY? OH... LITTLE MAN, YOU'RE A LITTLE OFF ON THAT ONE. SEE, I DON'T GET RID OF ALL THOSE NIGHTMARE THINGS...
I ABSORB THEM.
YOU LIKE THIS DRAWING, EH?
JUST THINK OF ME AS YOUR OWN PERSONAL TRAUMA-SPONGE.
IT'S ALL IN ME- EVERYTHING THAT'S EVER MADE YOU SCREAM, MADE YOU CRY, EVERYTHING THAT'S EVER KEPT YOU UP WIDE EYED AND SWEATY. ALL YOUR NIGHTMARES I'VE TAKEN IN. ALL INSIDE MY BAD TEDDY BEAR SELF.
AND TRUST ME, IT'S NO EASY TASK WITH SOMEONE LIKE YOU. I'VE NEVER KNOWN ANY CHILD AS PRONE TO TERROR AS YOU. WHOO!!
SPONGES ARE SCAAARY.
BUT I DO IT FOR YOU, TODD. I FILL MYSELF WITH MONSTERS TO KEEP THEM OUT OF YOU. SOME PEOPLE ARE NOT SO LUCKY.- LOOK AT THAT STUPID NEIGHBOR OF YOURS.
AND THOUGH HE IS AN EXTREME EXAMPLE OF IT, IT'S NOT JUST HIM. ALMOST EVERYONE IS GOING NUTS! WHY, IF SICKNESS WERE A SOCIALLY ACCEPTABLE THING, THOSE DEGENERATIVE LOONS WOULD BE WRITING YOUR NEIGHBOR FAN-MAIL, TELLING HIM HOW "COOL" HE IS! THEY WOULD ADMIRE HIS ILLNESS AND ASPIRE TO IT!! BUT YOU NEVER WILL, BECAUSE I EAT YOUR SICKNESS. AND THERE IS SO MUCH TO BE AFRAID OF!!

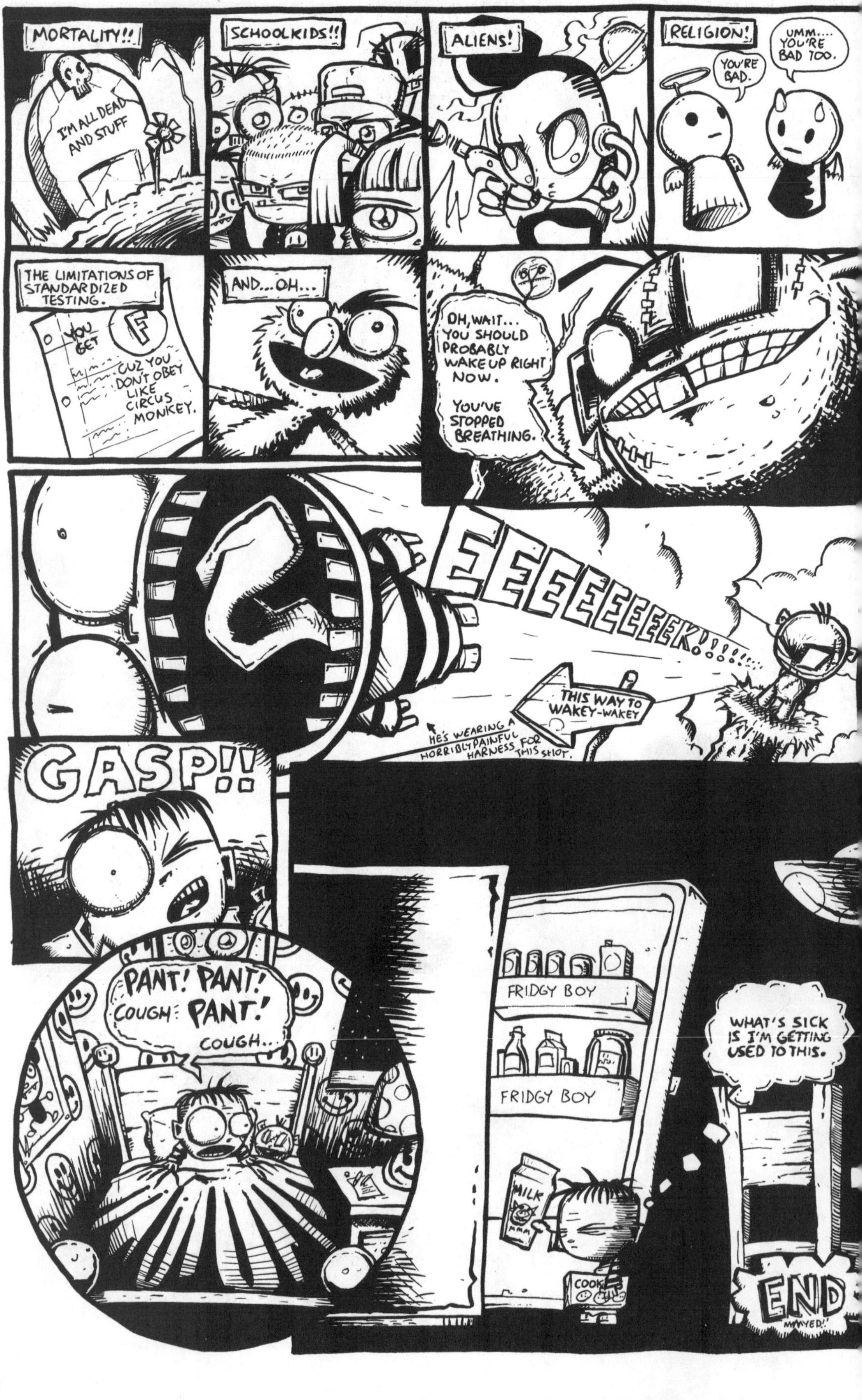
MORTALITY!!
I'M ALL DEAD AND STUFF
SCHOOLKIDS!!
ALIENS!
RELIGION!
YOU'RE BAD.
UMM.... YOU'RE BAD TOO.
THE LIMITATIONS OF STANDARDIZED TESTING.
YOU GET F
CUZ YOU DON'T OBEY LIKE CIRCUS MONKEY.
AND...OH...
OH, WAIT... YOU SHOULD PROBABLY WAKE UP RIGHT NOW.
YOU'VE STOPPED BREATHING.
EEEEEEEEEK!!!!!
THIS WAY TO WAKEY-WAKEY
HE'S WEARING A HORRIBLY PAINFUL HARNESS FOR THIS SHOT.
GASP!!
PANT! PANT! COUGH PANT! COUGH...
FRIDGY BOY
FRIDGY BOY
MILK
COOK
WHAT'S SICK IS I'M GETTING USED TO THIS.
END

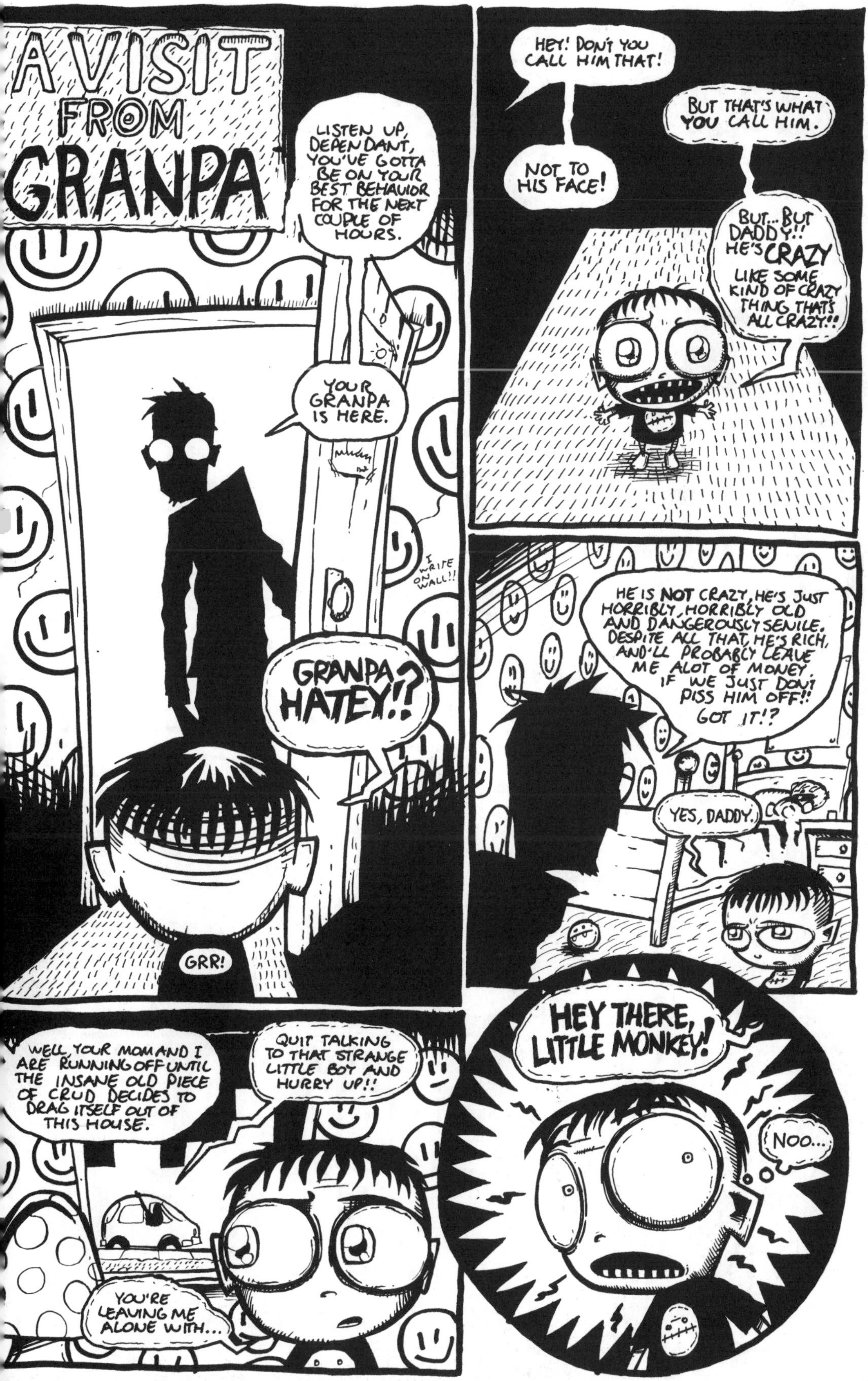
A VISIT FROM GRANPA
LISTEN UP, DEPENDANT, YOU'VE GOTTA BE ON YOUR BEST BEHAVIOR FOR THE NEXT COUPLE OF HOURS.
YOUR GRANPA IS HERE.
I WRITE ON WALL!!
GRANPA HATEY!!?
GRR!
HEY! DON'T YOU CALL HIM THAT!
BUT THAT'S WHAT YOU CALL HIM.
NOT TO HIS FACE!
BUT... BUT DADDY!! HE'S CRAZY LIKE SOME KIND OF CRAZY THING THAT'S ALL CRAZY!!
HE IS NOT CRAZY, HE'S JUST HORRIBLY, HORRIBLY OLD AND DANGEROUSLY SENILE. DESPITE ALL THAT, HE'S RICH, AND'LL PROBABLY LEAVE ME ALOT OF MONEY, IF WE JUST DON'T PISS HIM OFF!! GOT IT!?
YES, DADDY.
WELL, YOUR MOM AND I ARE RUNNING OFF UNTIL THE INSANE OLD PIECE OF CRUD DECIDES TO DRAG ITSELF OUT OF THIS HOUSE.
QUIT TALKING TO THAT STRANGE LITTLE BOY AND HURRY UP!!
YOU'RE LEAVING ME ALONE WITH...
HEY THERE, LITTLE MONKEY!
NOO...

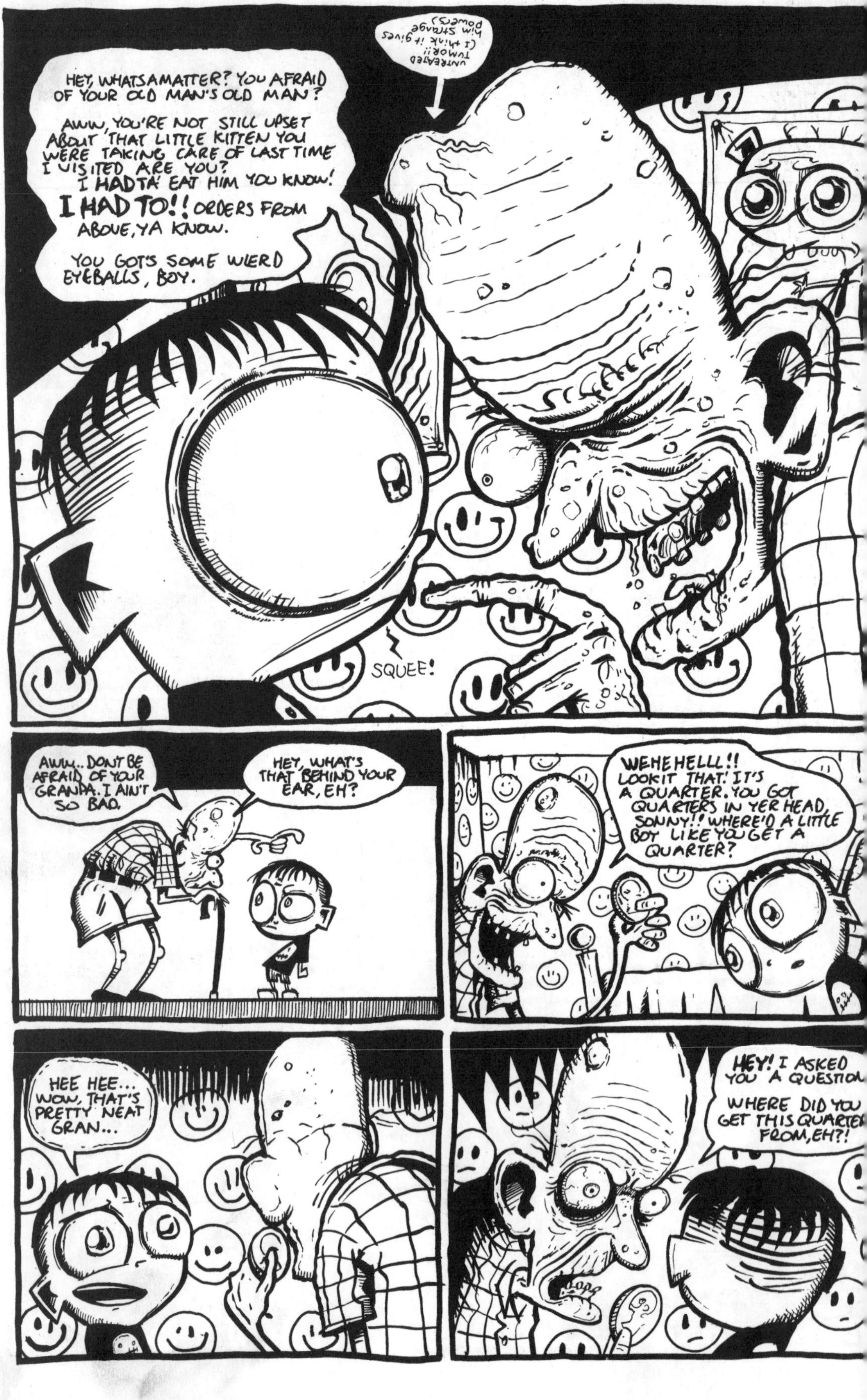

UNTREATED TUMOR!! (I think it gives him strange powers)
HEY, WHATSAMATTER? YOU AFRAID OF YOUR OLD MAN'S OLD MAN?
AWW, YOU'RE NOT STILL UPSET ABOUT THAT LITTLE KITTEN YOU WERE TAKING CARE OF LAST TIME I VISITED ARE YOU?
I HADTA' EAT HIM YOU KNOW!
I HAD TO!! ORDERS FROM ABOVE, YA KNOW.
YOU GOT'S SOME WIERD EYEBALLS, BOY.
SQUEE!
AWW... DONT BE AFRAID OF YOUR GRANPA. I AIN'T SO BAD.
HEY, WHAT'S THAT BEHIND YOUR EAR, EH?
WEHEHELLL!! LOOKIT THAT! IT'S A QUARTER. YOU GOT QUARTERS IN YER HEAD, SONNY!! WHERE'D A LITTLE BOY LIKE YOU GET A QUARTER?
HEE HEE... WOW, THAT'S PRETTY NEAT GRAN...
HEY! I ASKED YOU A QUESTION
WHERE DID YOU GET THIS QUARTER FROM, EH?!

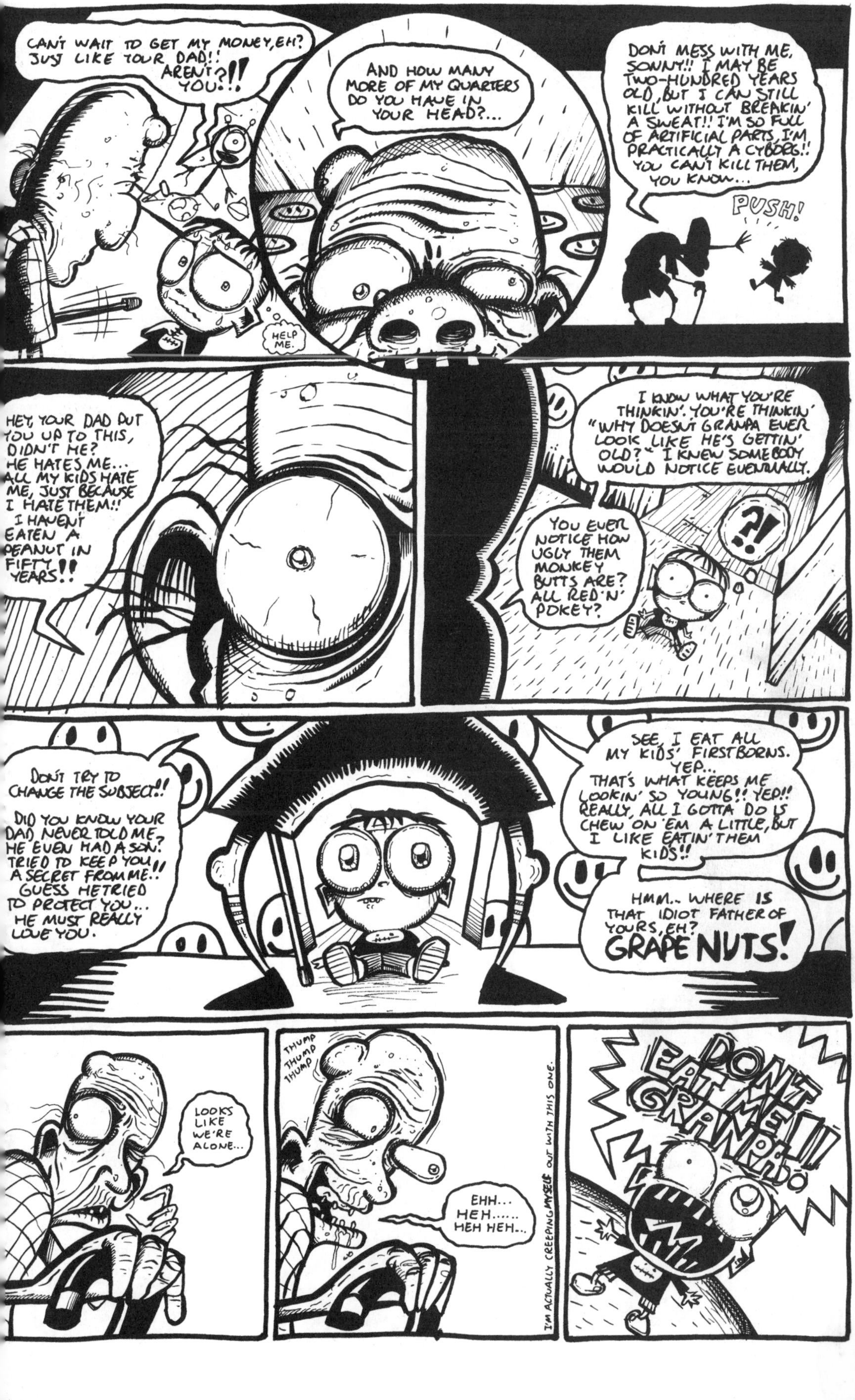
CAN'T WAIT TO GET MY MONEY, EH? JUST LIKE YOUR DAD!! AREN'T?!! YOU?!!
HELP ME.
AND HOW MANY MORE OF MY QUARTERS DO YOU HAVE IN YOUR HEAD?...
DON'T MESS WITH ME, SONNY!! I MAY BE TWO-HUNDRED YEARS OLD, BUT I CAN STILL KILL WITHOUT BREAKIN' A SWEAT!! I'M SO FULL OF ARTIFICIAL PARTS, I'M PRACTICALLY A CYBORG!! YOU CAN'T KILL THEM, YOU KNOW...
PUSH!
HEY, YOUR DAD PUT YOU UP TO THIS, DIDN'T HE? HE HATES ME... ALL MY KIDS HATE ME, JUST BECAUSE I HATE THEM!! I HAVEN'T EATEN A PEANUT IN FIFTY YEARS!!
I KNOW WHAT YOU'RE THINKIN'. YOU'RE THINKIN' "WHY DOESN'T GRANPA EVER LOOK LIKE HE'S GETTIN' OLD?" I KNEW SOMEBODY WOULD NOTICE EVENTUALLY.
YOU EVER NOTICE HOW UGLY THEM MONKEY BUTTS ARE? ALL RED 'N' POKEY?
?!
DON'T TRY TO CHANGE THE SUBJECT!! DID YOU KNOW YOUR DAD NEVER TOLD ME HE EVEN HAD A SON? TRIED TO KEEP YOU A SECRET FROM ME!! GUESS HE TRIED TO PROTECT YOU... HE MUST REALLY LOVE YOU.
SEE, I EAT ALL MY KIDS' FIRSTBORNS. YEP... THAT'S WHAT KEEPS ME LOOKIN' SO YOUNG!! YEP!! REALLY, ALL I GOTTA DO IS CHEW ON 'EM A LITTLE, BUT I LIKE EATIN' THEM KIDS!!
HMM.. WHERE IS THAT IDIOT FATHER OF YOURS, EH? GRAPE NUTS!
LOOKS LIKE WE'RE ALONE...
THUMP THUMP THUMP
EHH... HEH...... HEH HEH...
I'M ACTUALLY CREEPING MYSELF OUT WITH THIS ONE.
DON'T EAT ME GRANPA!!!

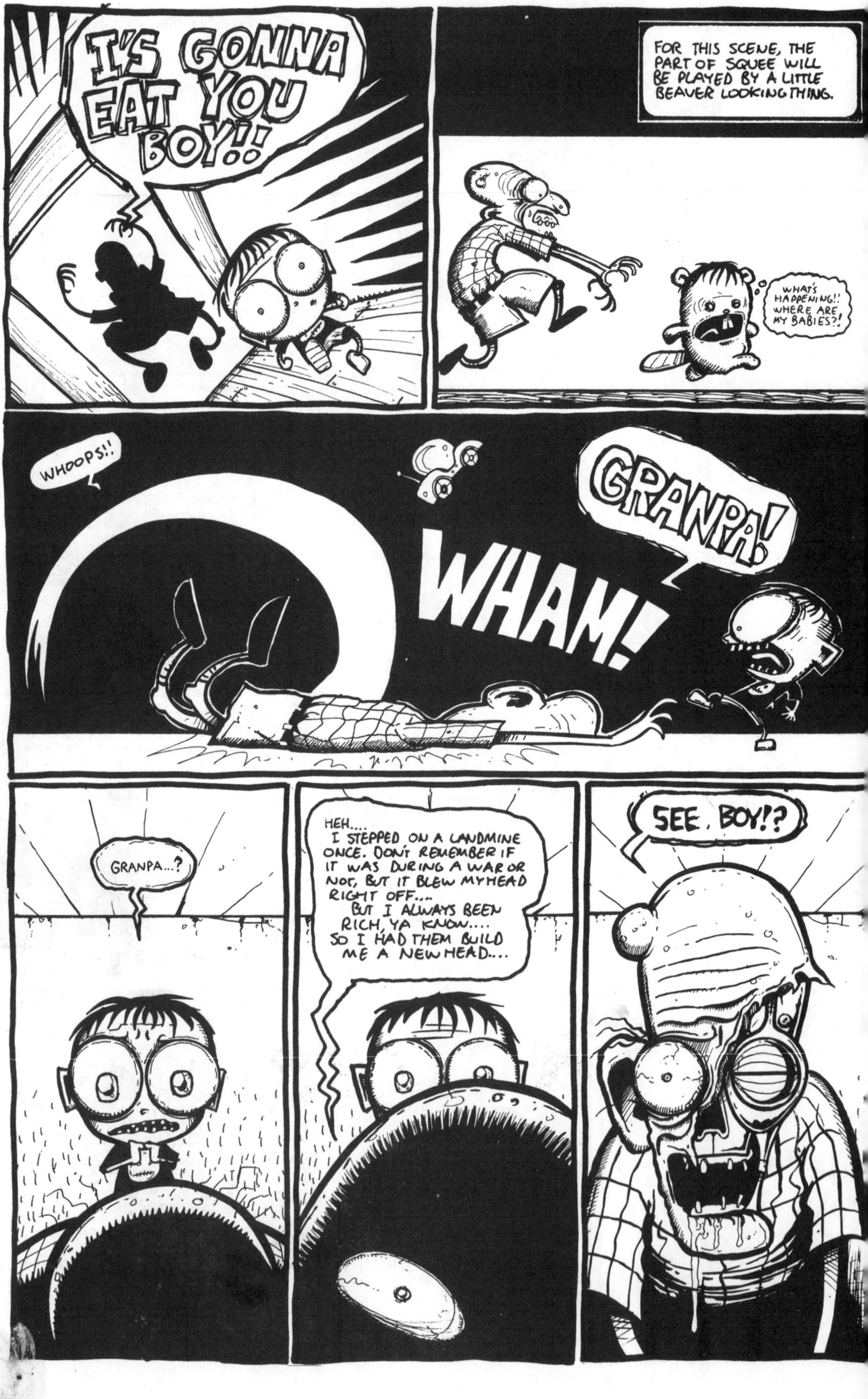
I'S GONNA EAT YOU BOY!!
FOR THIS SCENE, THE PART OF SQUEE WILL BE PLAYED BY A LITTLE BEAVER LOOKING THING.
WHAT'S HAPPENING!! WHERE ARE MY BABIES?!
WHOOPS!!
WHAM!
GRANPA!
GRANPA...?
HEH.... I STEPPED ON A LANDMINE ONCE. DON'T REMEMBER IF IT WAS DURING A WAR OR NOT, BUT IT BLEW MY HEAD RIGHT OFF.... BUT I ALWAYS BEEN RICH, YA KNOW.... SO I HAD THEM BUILD ME A NEW HEAD....
SEE, BOY!?

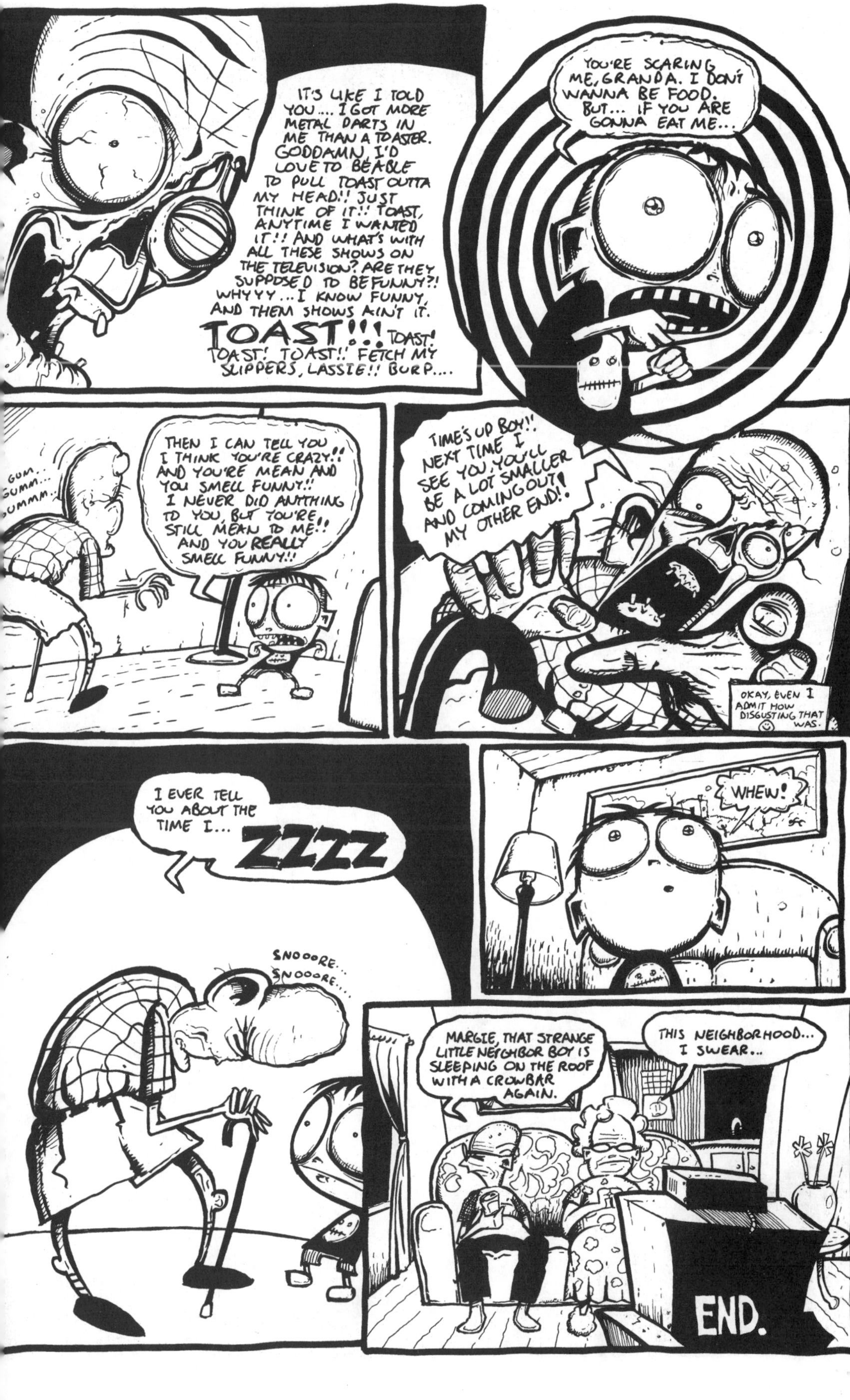
IT'S LIKE I TOLD YOU.... I GOT MORE METAL DARTS IN ME THAN A TOASTER. GODDAMN, I'D LOVE TO BE ABLE TO PULL TOAST OUTTA MY HEAD!! JUST THINK OF IT!! TOAST, ANYTIME I WANTED IT!! AND WHAT'S WITH ALL THESE SHOWS ON THE TELEVISION? ARE THEY SUPPOSED TO BE FUNNY?! WHYYY... I KNOW FUNNY, AND THEM SHOWS AIN'T IT. TOAST!!! TOAST! TOAST! TOAST!! FETCH MY SLIPPERS, LASSIE!! BURP....
YOU'RE SCARING ME, GRANDA. I DON'T WANNA BE FOOD. BUT... IF YOU ARE GONNA EAT ME...
GUM.. GUMM... GUMMM...
THEN I CAN TELL YOU I THINK YOU'RE CRAZY!! AND YOU'RE MEAN AND YOU SMELL FUNNY!! I NEVER DID ANYTHING TO YOU, BUT YOU'RE STILL MEAN TO ME!! AND YOU REALLY SMELL FUNNY!!
TIME'S UP BOY!! NEXT TIME I SEE YOU, YOU'LL BE A LOT SMALLER AND COMING OUT MY OTHER END!!
OKAY, EVEN I ADMIT HOW DISGUSTING THAT WAS.
I EVER TELL YOU ABOUT THE TIME I... ZZZZ
SNOOORE... SNOOORE...
WHEW!
MARGIE, THAT STRANGE LITTLE NEIGHBOR BOY IS SLEEPING ON THE ROOF WITH A CROWBAR AGAIN.
THIS NEIGHBORHOOD... I SWEAR...
END.

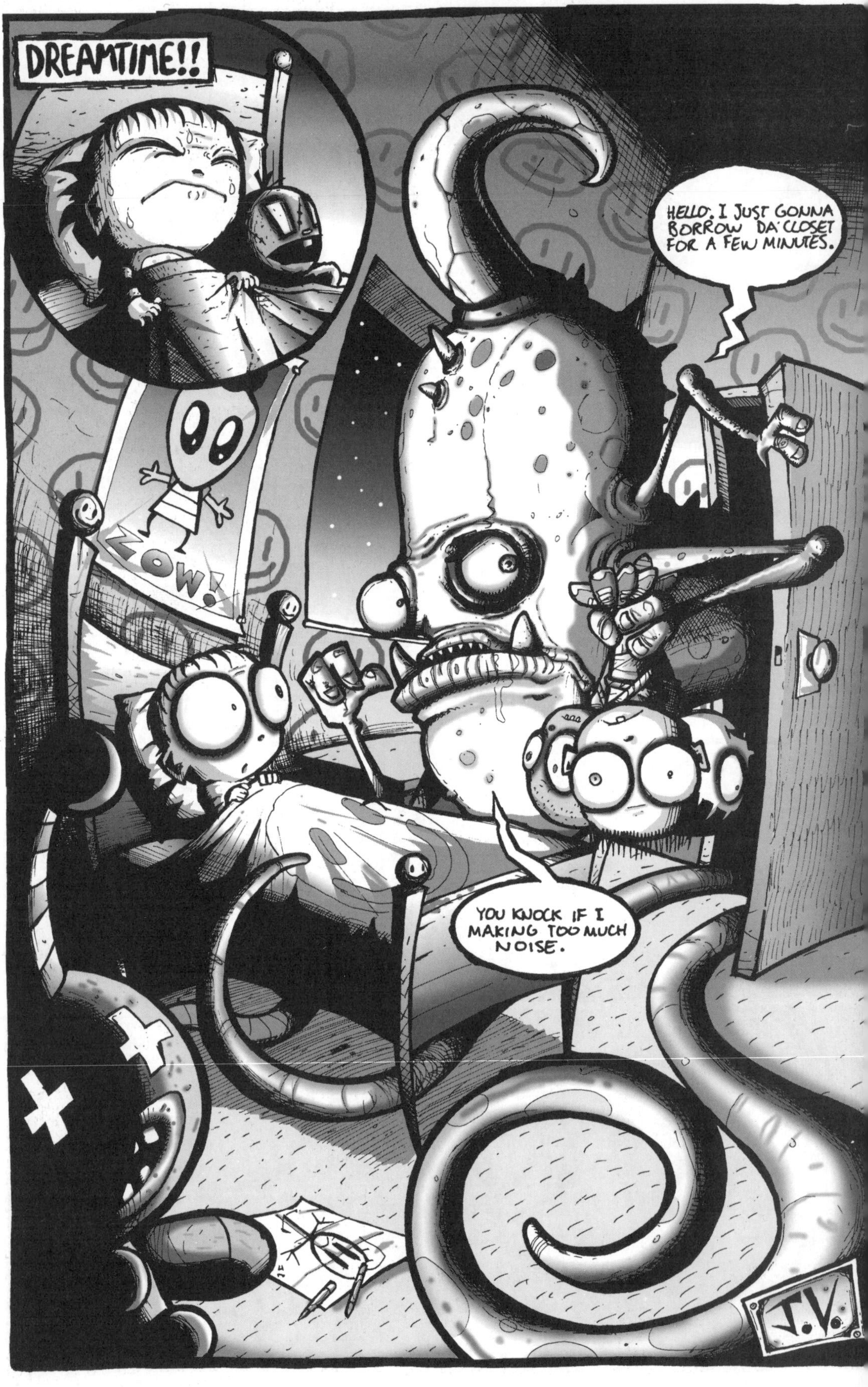
DREAMTIME!!
ZOW!
HELLO. I JUST GONNA BORROW DA CLOSET FOR A FEW MINUTES.
YOU KNOCK IF I MAKING TOO MUCH NOISE.
J.V.

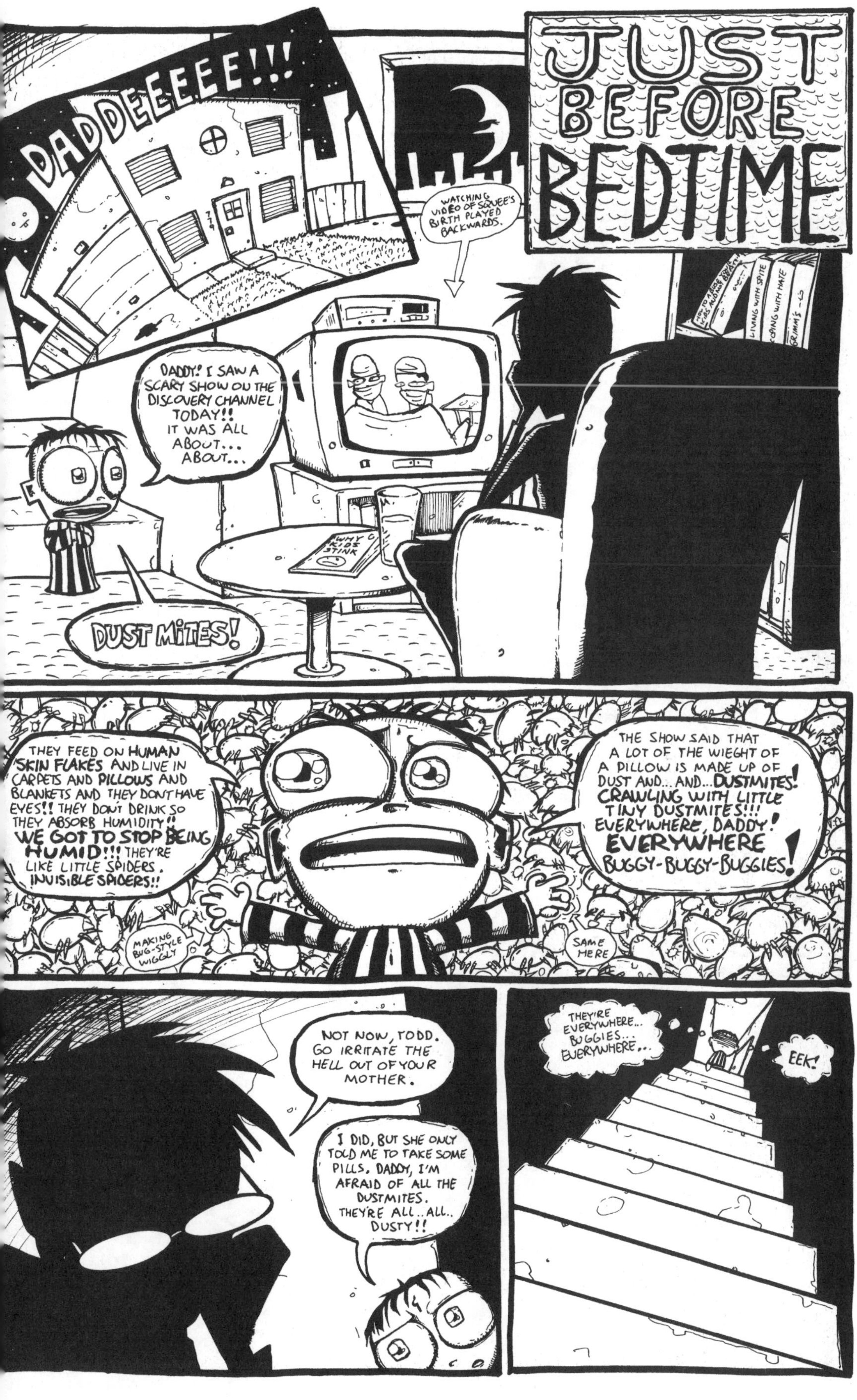
DADDEEEEEE!!!
JUST BEFORE BEDTIME
WATCHING VIDEO OF SQUEE'S BIRTH PLAYED BACKWARDS.
LIVING WITH SPITE
COPING WITH HATE
GRIMM'S
DADDY! I SAW A SCARY SHOW ON THE DISCOVERY CHANNEL TODAY!! IT WAS ALL ABOUT... ABOUT...
WHY KIDS STINK
DUST MITES!
THEY FEED ON HUMAN SKIN FLAKES AND LIVE IN CARPETS AND PILLOWS AND BLANKETS AND THEY DON'T HAVE EYES!! THEY DON'T DRINK SO THEY ABSORB HUMIDITY!! WE GOT TO STOP BEING HUMID!!! THEY'RE LIKE LITTLE SPIDERS. INVISIBLE SPIDERS!!
THE SHOW SAID THAT A LOT OF THE WIEGHT OF A PILLOW IS MADE UP OF DUST AND... AND... DUSTMITES! CRAWLING WITH LITTLE TINY DUSTMITES!!! EVERYWHERE, DADDY! EVERYWHERE BUGGY-BUGGY-BUGGIES!
MAKING BUG-STYLE WIGGLY
SAME HERE
NOT NOW, TODD. GO IRRITATE THE HELL OUT OF YOUR MOTHER.
I DID, BUT SHE ONLY TOLD ME TO TAKE SOME PILLS. DADDY, I'M AFRAID OF ALL THE DUSTMITES. THEY'RE ALL.. ALL.. DUSTY!!
THEY'RE EVERYWHERE.. BUGGIES... EVERYWHERE...
EEK!

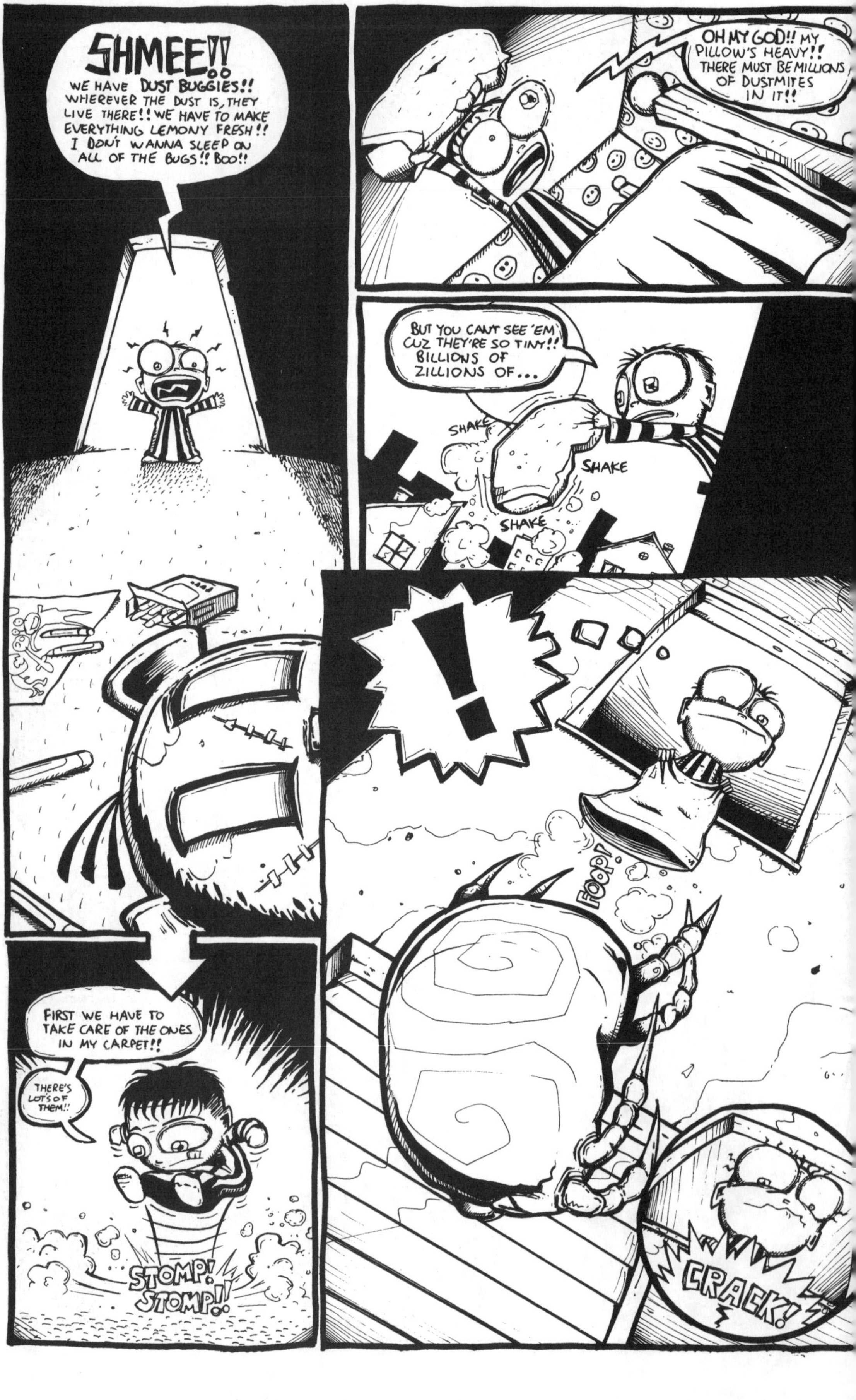
SHMEE!!
WE HAVE DUST BUGGIES!! WHEREVER THE DUST IS, THEY LIVE THERE!! WE HAVE TO MAKE EVERYTHING LEMONY FRESH!! I DON'T WANNA SLEEP ON ALL OF THE BUGS!! BOO!!
OH MY GOD!! MY PILLOW'S HEAVY!! THERE MUST BE MILLIONS OF DUSTMITES IN IT!!
BUT YOU CAN'T SEE 'EM CUZ THEY'RE SO TINY!! BILLIONS OF ZILLIONS OF...
SHAKE
SHAKE
SHAKE
FIRST WE HAVE TO TAKE CARE OF THE ONES IN MY CARPET!!
THERE'S LOTS OF THEM!!
STOMP! STOMP!!
!
FOOP!
CRACK!

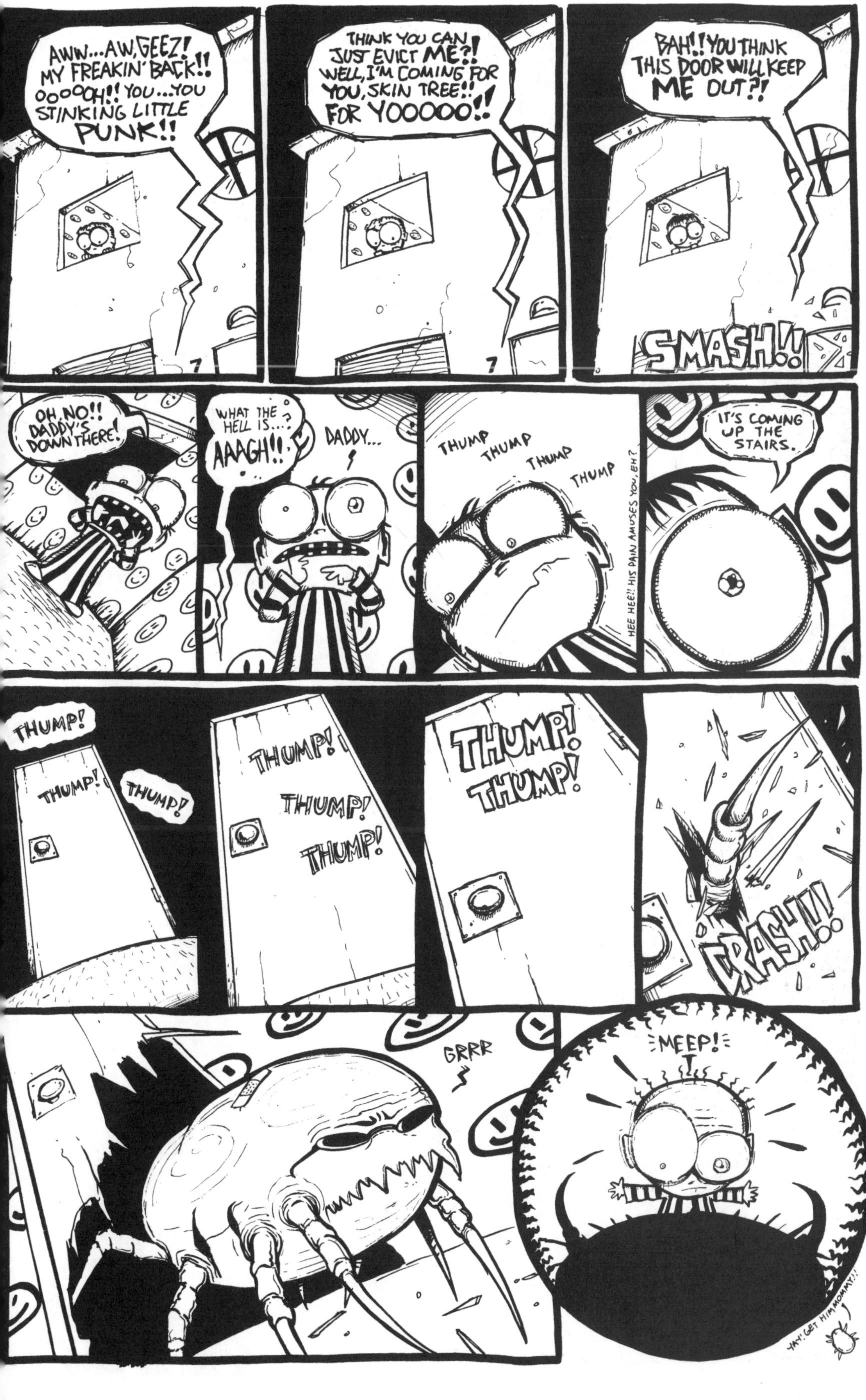
AWW...AW, GEEZ! MY FREAKIN' BACK!! OOOOOH!! YOU...YOU STINKING LITTLE PUNK!!
THINK YOU CAN JUST EVICT ME?! WELL, I'M COMING FOR YOU, SKIN TREE!! FOR YOOOOO!!
BAH!! YOU THINK THIS DOOR WILL KEEP ME OUT?!
SMASH!!
OH, NO!! DADDY'S DOWN THERE!
WHAT THE HELL IS...?
AAAGH!!
DADDY...
THUMP THUMP THUMP THUMP
HEE HEE!! HIS PAIN AMUSES YOU, EH?
IT'S COMING UP THE STAIRS.
THUMP! THUMP! THUMP!
THUMP! THUMP! THUMP!
THUMP! THUMP!
CRASH!!
GRRR
MEEP!
YAY! GET HIM MOMMY!!

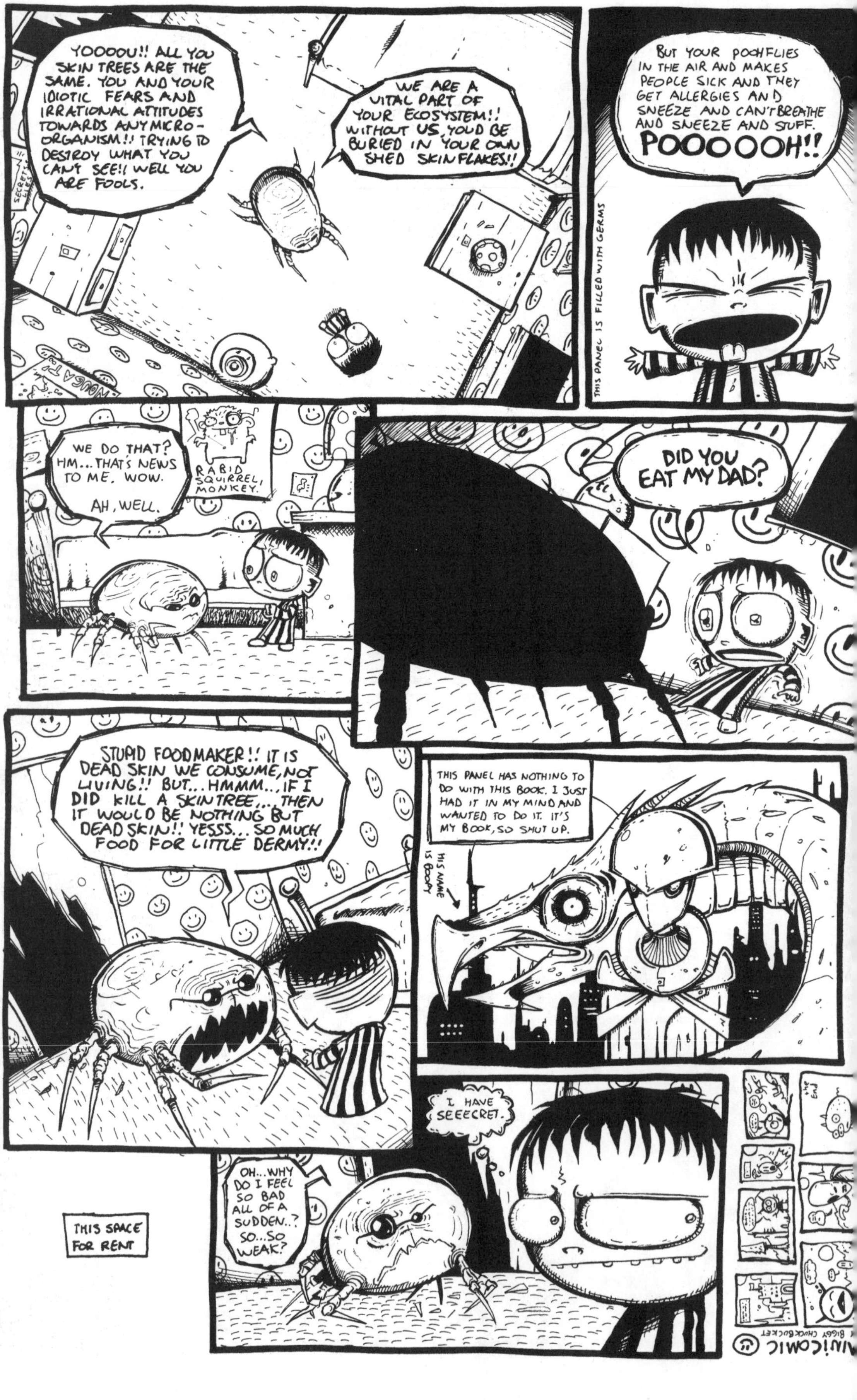
YOOOOU!! ALL YOU SKIN TREES ARE THE SAME. YOU AND YOUR IDIOTIC FEARS AND IRRATIONAL ATTITUDES TOWARDS ANY MICRO-ORGANISM!! TRYING TO DESTROY WHAT YOU CAN'T SEE!! WELL YOU ARE FOOLS.
WE ARE A VITAL PART OF YOUR ECOSYSTEM!! WITHOUT US, YOU'D BE BURIED IN YOUR OWN SHED SKINFLAKES!!
NOUGAT
BUT YOUR POOH FLIES IN THE AIR AND MAKES PEOPLE SICK AND THEY GET ALLERGIES AND SNEEZE AND CAN'T BREATHE AND SNEEZE AND STUFF.
POOOOOH!!
THIS PANEL IS FILLED WITH GERMS
WE DO THAT? HM... THAT'S NEWS TO ME. WOW.
AH, WELL.
RABID SQUIRREL, MONKEY.
DID YOU EAT MY DAD?
STUPID FOODMAKER!! IT IS DEAD SKIN WE CONSUME, NOT LIVING!! BUT... HMMM..., IF I DID KILL A SKINTREE..., THEN IT WOULD BE NOTHING BUT DEAD SKIN!! YESSS... SO MUCH FOOD FOR LITTLE DERMY!!
THIS PANEL HAS NOTHING TO DO WITH THIS BOOK. I JUST HAD IT IN MY MIND AND WANTED TO DO IT. IT'S MY BOOK, SO SHUT UP.
HIS NAME IS POOPY
I HAVE SEEECRET.
OH... WHY DO I FEEL SO BAD ALL OF A SUDDEN..? SO... SO WEAK?
THIS SPACE FOR RENT

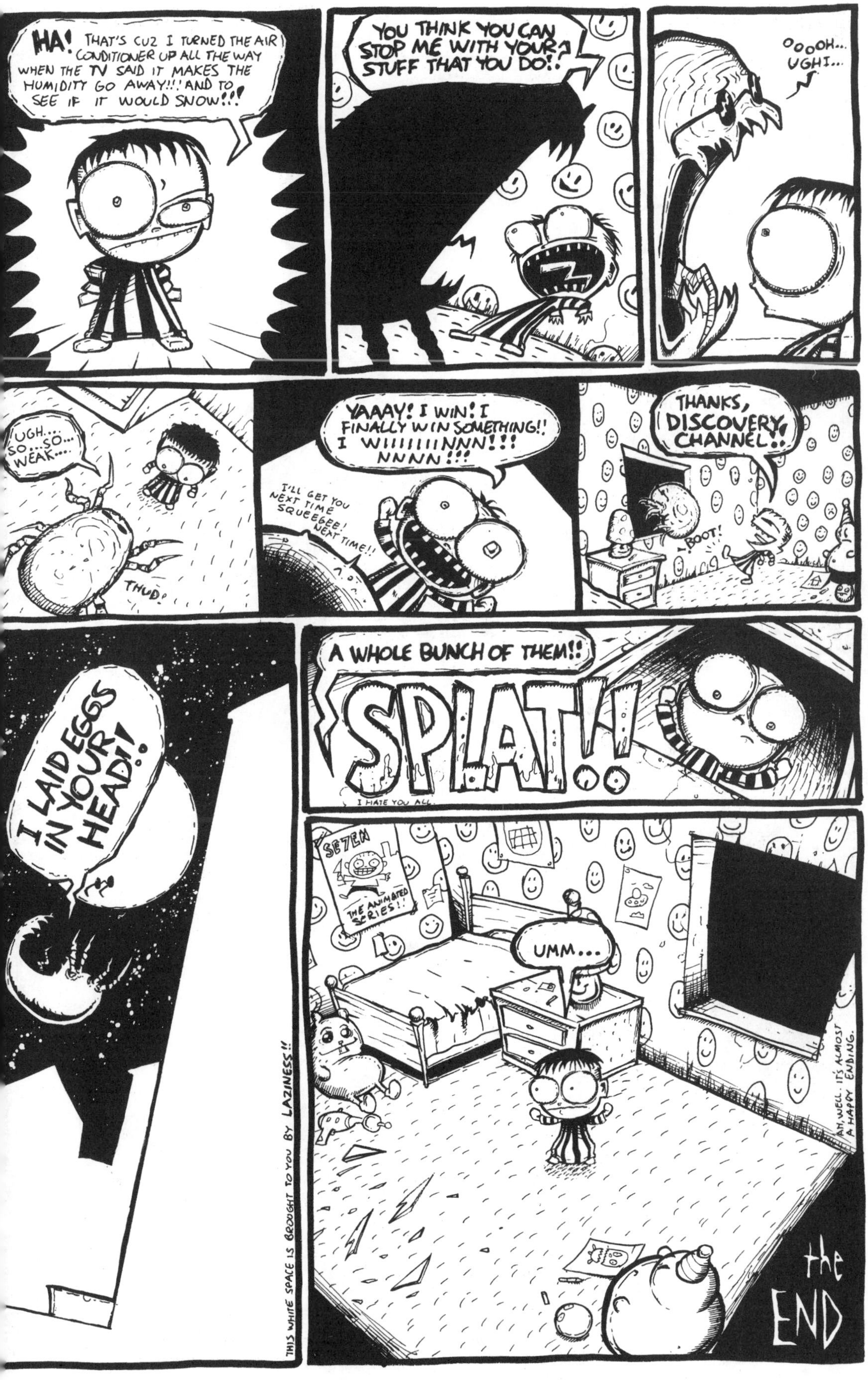
HA! THAT'S CUZ I TURNED THE AIR CONDITIONER UP ALL THE WAY WHEN THE TV SAID IT MAKES THE HUMIDITY GO AWAY!!! AND TO SEE IF IT WOULD SNOW!!!
YOU THINK YOU CAN STOP ME WITH YOUR STUFF THAT YOU DO!?
OOOOH... UGH!...
UGH.... SO...SO... WEAK....
THUD.
YAAAY! I WIN! I FINALLY WIN SOMETHING!! I WIIIIIIIINNN!!! NNNN!!!
I'LL GET YOU NEXT TIME SQUEEGEE! NEXT TIME!!
THANKS, DISCOVERY CHANNEL!!
BOOT!
I LAID EGGS IN YOUR HEAD!!
A WHOLE BUNCH OF THEM!!
SPLAT!!
I HATE YOU ALL.
SE7EN
THE ANIMATED SERIES!!
UMM...
AH, WELL. IT'S ALMOST A HAPPY ENDING.
THIS WHITE SPACE IS BROUGHT TO YOU BY LAZINESS!!
the END

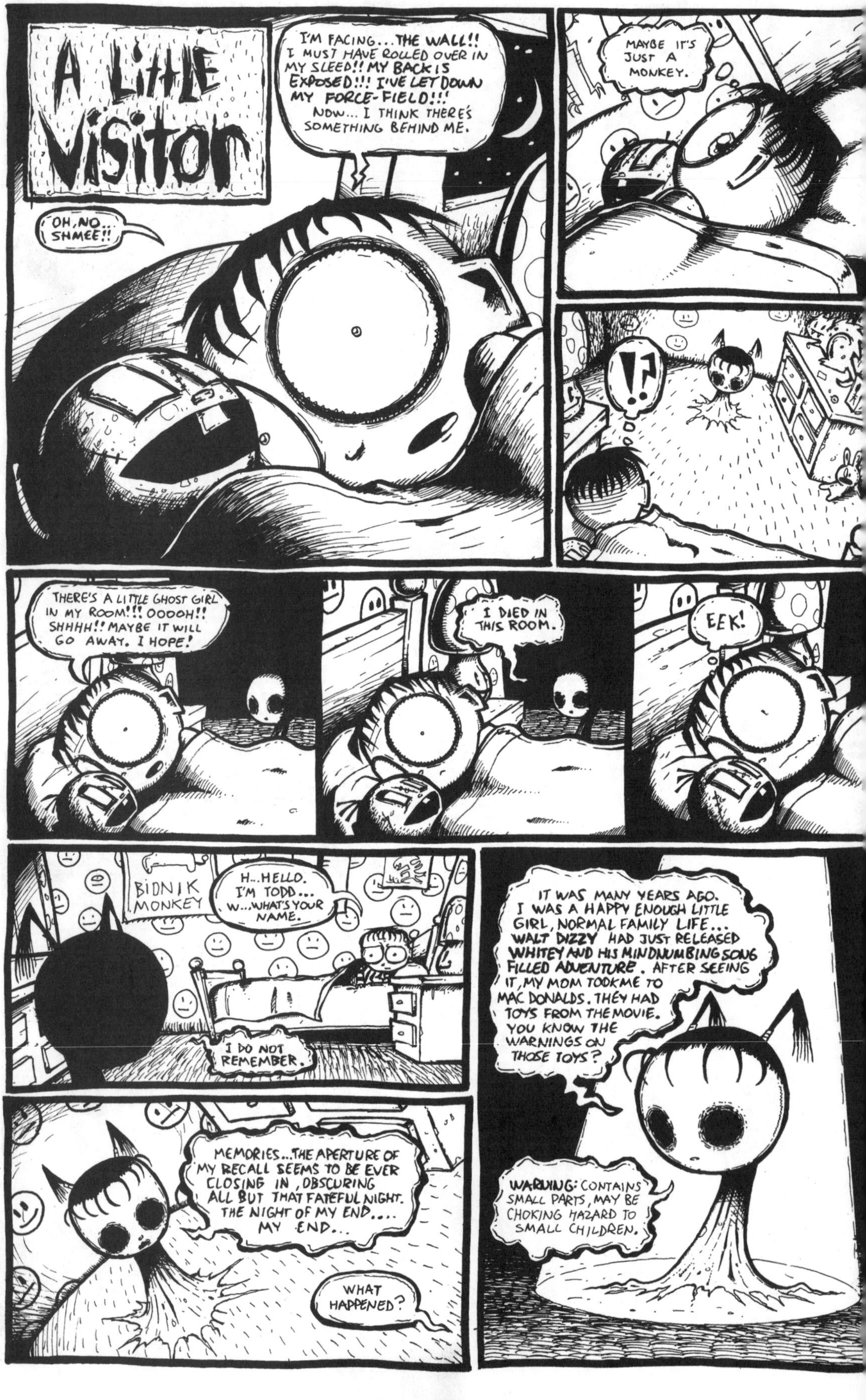
A Little Visitor
I'M FACING... THE WALL!! I MUST HAVE ROLLED OVER IN MY SLEEP!! MY BACK IS EXPOSED!!! I'VE LET DOWN MY FORCE-FIELD!!! NOW... I THINK THERE'S SOMETHING BEHIND ME.
OH, NO... SHMEE!!
MAYBE IT'S JUST A MONKEY.
!?
THERE'S A LITTLE GHOST GIRL IN MY ROOM!!! OOOOH!! SHHHH!! MAYBE IT WILL GO AWAY. I HOPE!
I DIED IN THIS ROOM.
EEK!
BIDNIK MONKEY
H...HELLO. I'M TODD... W...WHAT'S YOUR NAME.
I DO NOT REMEMBER.
MEMORIES...THE APERTURE OF MY RECALL SEEMS TO BE EVER CLOSING IN, OBSCURING ALL BUT THAT FATEFUL NIGHT. THE NIGHT OF MY END.... MY END...
WHAT HAPPENED?
IT WAS MANY YEARS AGO. I WAS A HAPPY ENOUGH LITTLE GIRL, NORMAL FAMILY LIFE... WALT DIZZY HAD JUST RELEASED WHITEY AND HIS MINDNUMBING SONG FILLED ADVENTURE. AFTER SEEING IT, MY MOM TOOK ME TO MAC DONALDS. THEY HAD TOYS FROM THE MOVIE. YOU KNOW THE WARNINGS ON THOSE TOYS?
WARNING: CONTAINS SMALL PARTS, MAY BE CHOKING HAZARD TO SMALL CHILDREN.

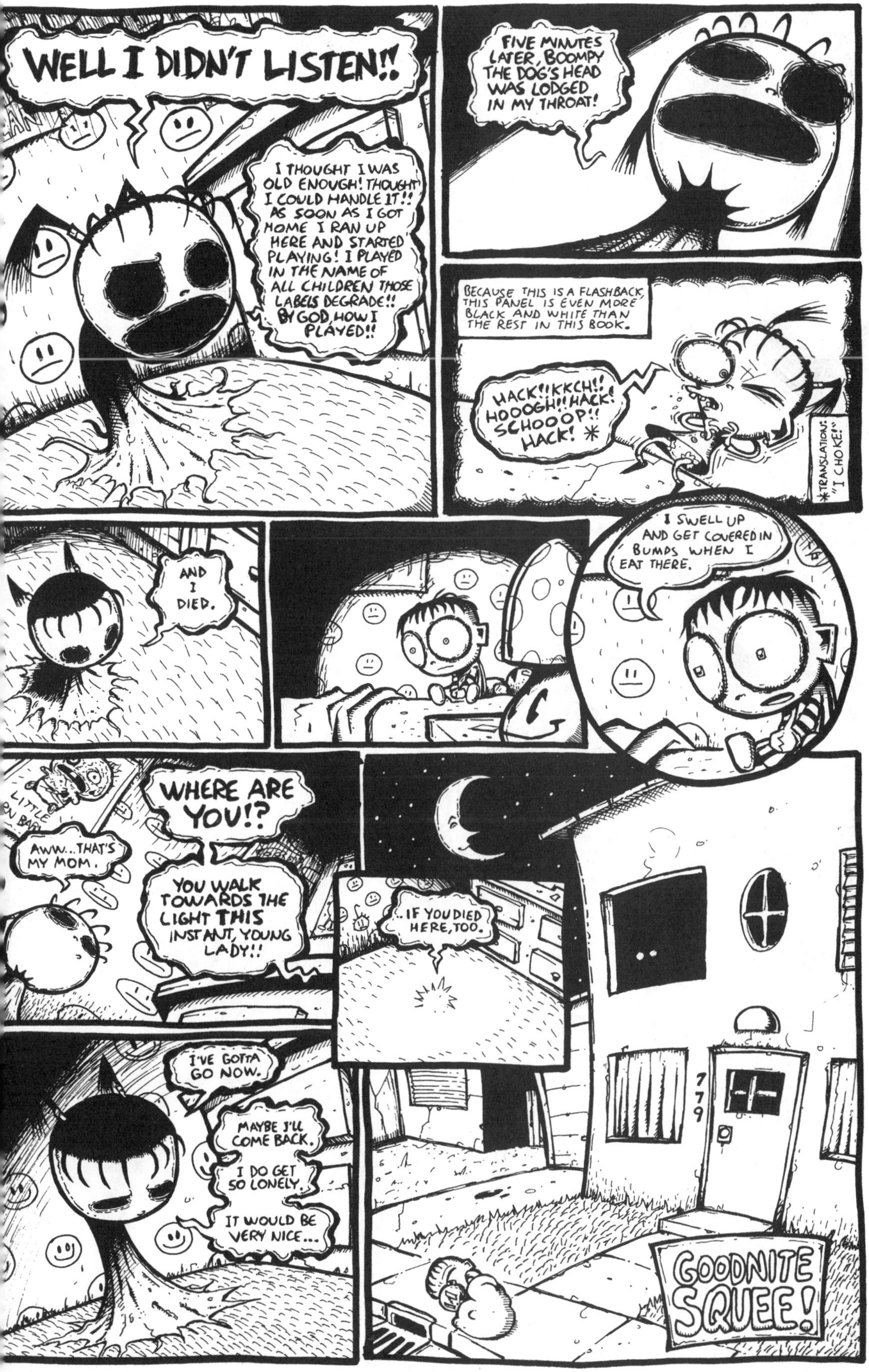
WELL I DIDN'T LISTEN!!
I THOUGHT I WAS OLD ENOUGH! THOUGHT I COULD HANDLE IT!! AS SOON AS I GOT HOME I RAN UP HERE AND STARTED PLAYING! I PLAYED IN THE NAME OF ALL CHILDREN THOSE LABELS DEGRADE!! BY GOD, HOW I PLAYED!!
FIVE MINUTES LATER, BOOMPY THE DOG'S HEAD WAS LODGED IN MY THROAT!
BECAUSE THIS IS A FLASHBACK, THIS PANEL IS EVEN MORE BLACK AND WHITE THAN THE REST IN THIS BOOK.
HACK!!KKCH!! HOOOGH!! HACK! SCHOOOP!! HACK! *
*TRANSLATION: "I CHOKE!"
AND I DIED.
I SWELL UP AND GET COVERED IN BUMPS WHEN I EAT THERE.
WHERE ARE YOU!?
AWW...THAT'S MY MOM.
YOU WALK TOWARDS THE LIGHT THIS INSTANT, YOUNG LADY!!
..IF YOU DIED HERE, TOO.
I'VE GOTTA GO NOW.
MAYBE I'LL COME BACK.
I DO GET SO LONELY.
IT WOULD BE VERY NICE...
779
GOODNITE SQUEE!

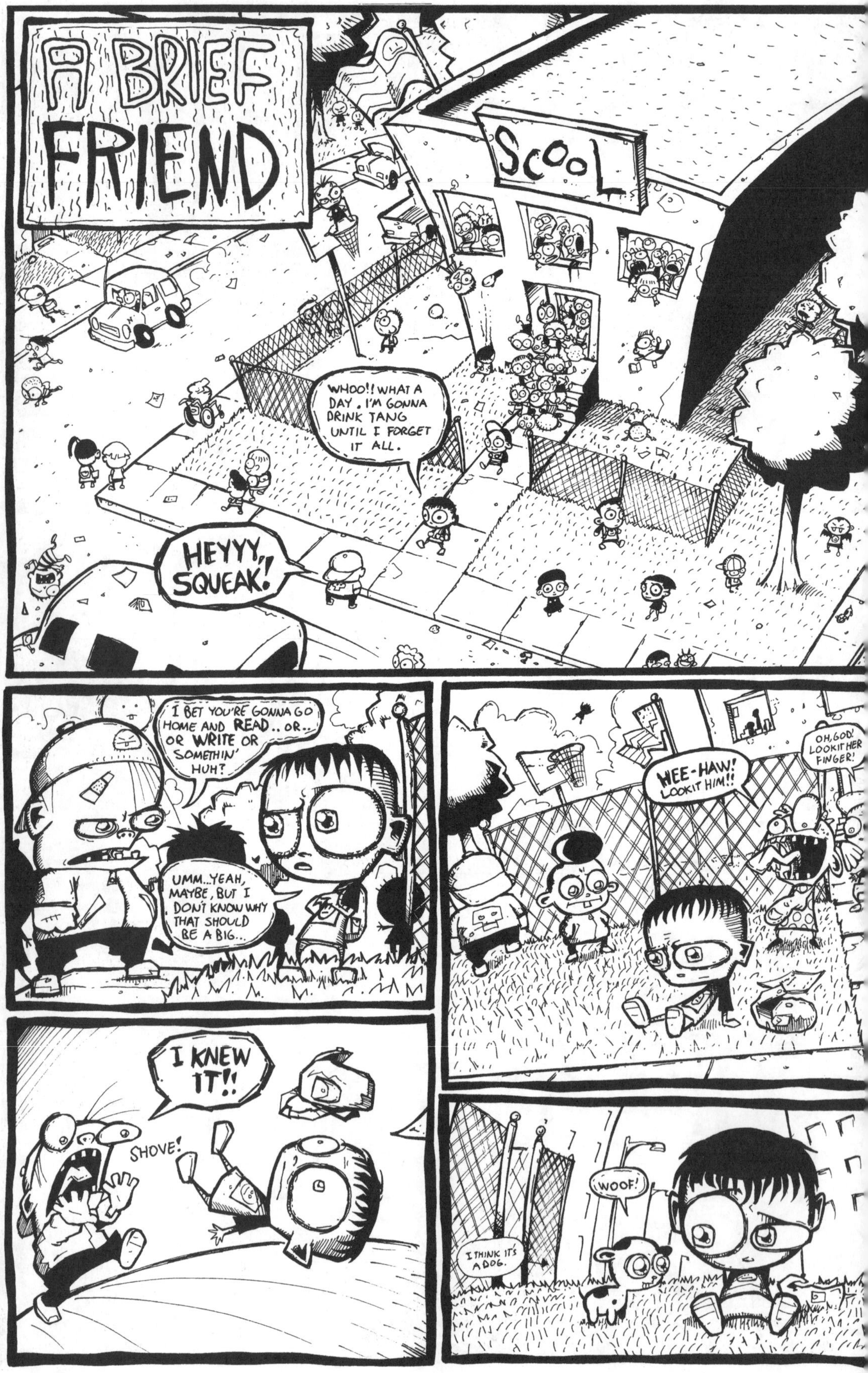
A BRIEF FRIEND
SCOOL
WHOO!! WHAT A DAY. I'M GONNA DRINK TANG UNTIL I FORGET IT ALL.
HEYYY, SQUEAK!
I BET YOU'RE GONNA GO HOME AND READ.. OR.. OR WRITE OR SOMETHIN' HUH?
UMM...YEAH, MAYBE, BUT I DON'T KNOW WHY THAT SHOULD BE A BIG...
WEE-HAW! LOOKIT HIM!!
OH, GOD! LOOKIT HER FINGER!
I KNEW IT!!
SHOVE!
WOOF!
I THINK IT'S A DOG.

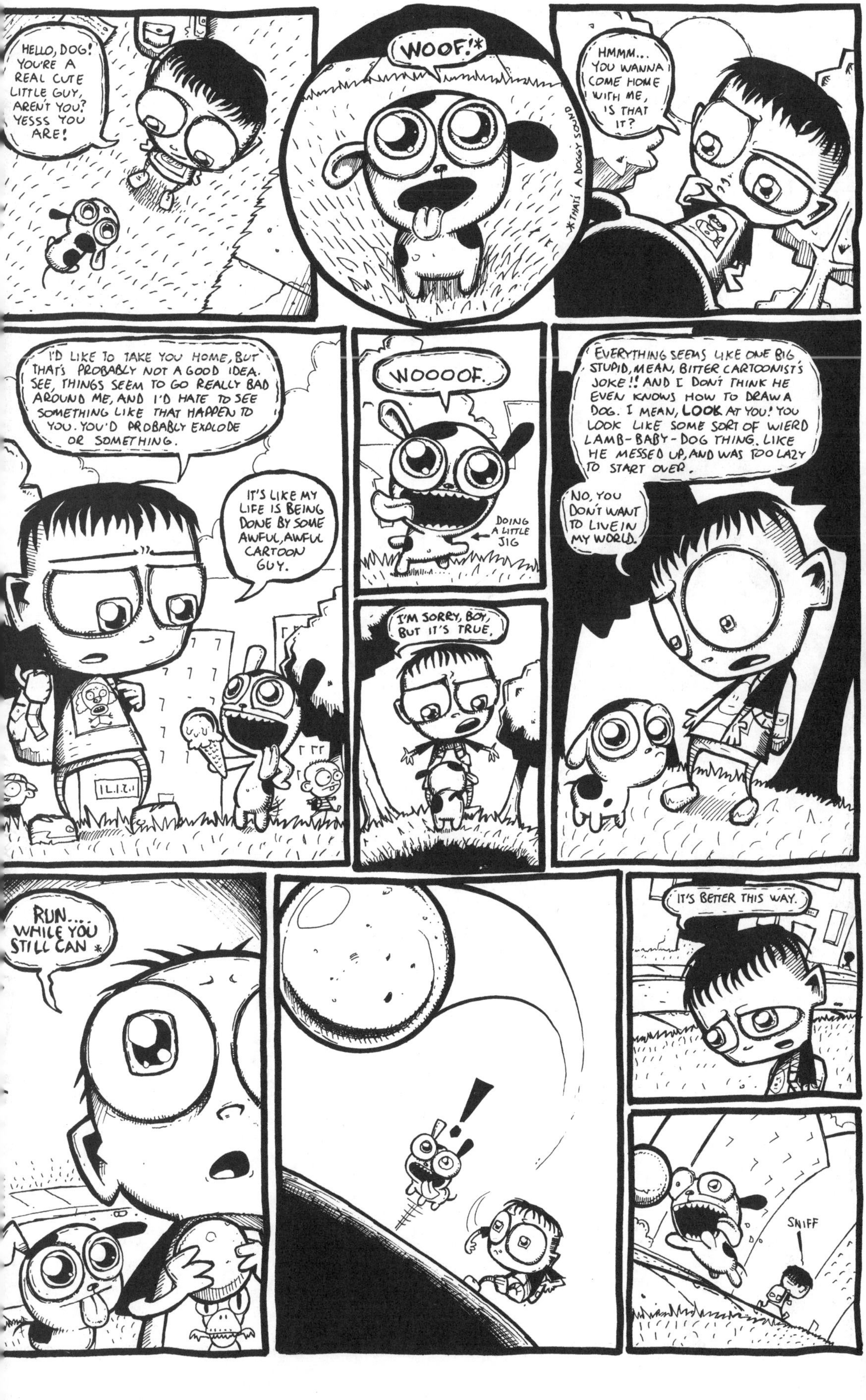
HELLO, DOG! YOU'RE A REAL CUTE LITTLE GUY, AREN'T YOU? YESSS YOU ARE!
WOOF!*
*THAT'S A DOGGY SOUND
HMMM... YOU WANNA COME HOME WITH ME, IS THAT IT?
I'D LIKE TO TAKE YOU HOME, BUT THAT'S PROBABLY NOT A GOOD IDEA. SEE, THINGS SEEM TO GO REALLY BAD AROUND ME, AND I'D HATE TO SEE SOMETHING LIKE THAT HAPPEN TO YOU. YOU'D PROBABLY EXPLODE OR SOMETHING.
IT'S LIKE MY LIFE IS BEING DONE BY SOME AWFUL, AWFUL CARTOON GUY.
WOOOOF.
DOING A LITTLE JIG
I'M SORRY, BOY, BUT IT'S TRUE.
EVERYTHING SEEMS LIKE ONE BIG STUPID, MEAN, BITTER CARTOONIST'S JOKE!! AND I DON'T THINK HE EVEN KNOWS HOW TO DRAW A DOG. I MEAN, LOOK AT YOU! YOU LOOK LIKE SOME SORT OF WIERD LAMB-BABY-DOG THING. LIKE HE MESSED UP, AND WAS TOO LAZY TO START OVER.
NO, YOU DON'T WANT TO LIVE IN MY WORLD.
RUN.... WHILE YOU STILL CAN *
!
IT'S BETTER THIS WAY.
SNIFF

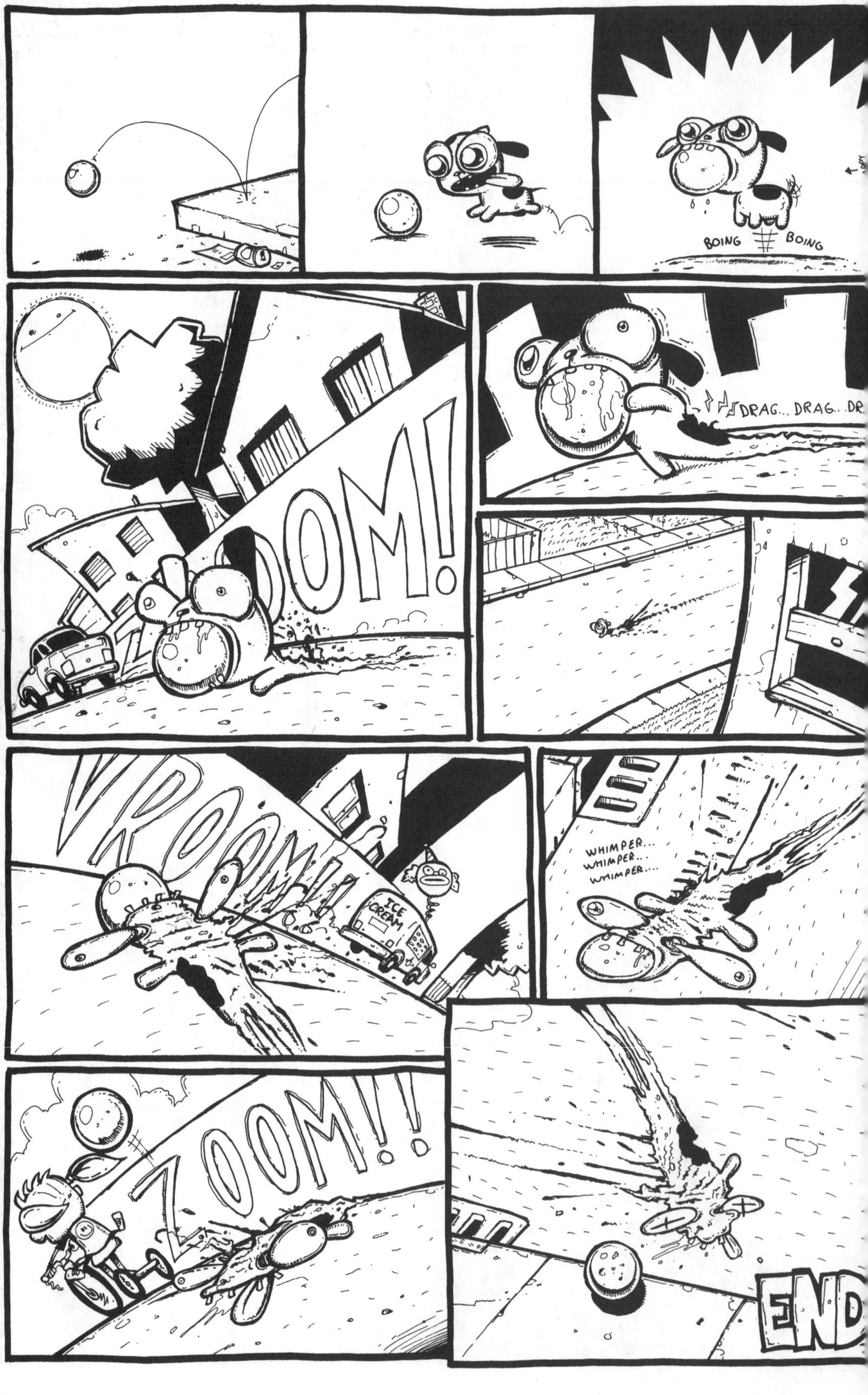
BOING
BOING
OOM!
DRAG... DRAG... DR
VROOOM!!
ICE CREAM
WHIMPER...
WHIMPER...
WHIMPER....
ZOOM!!
END

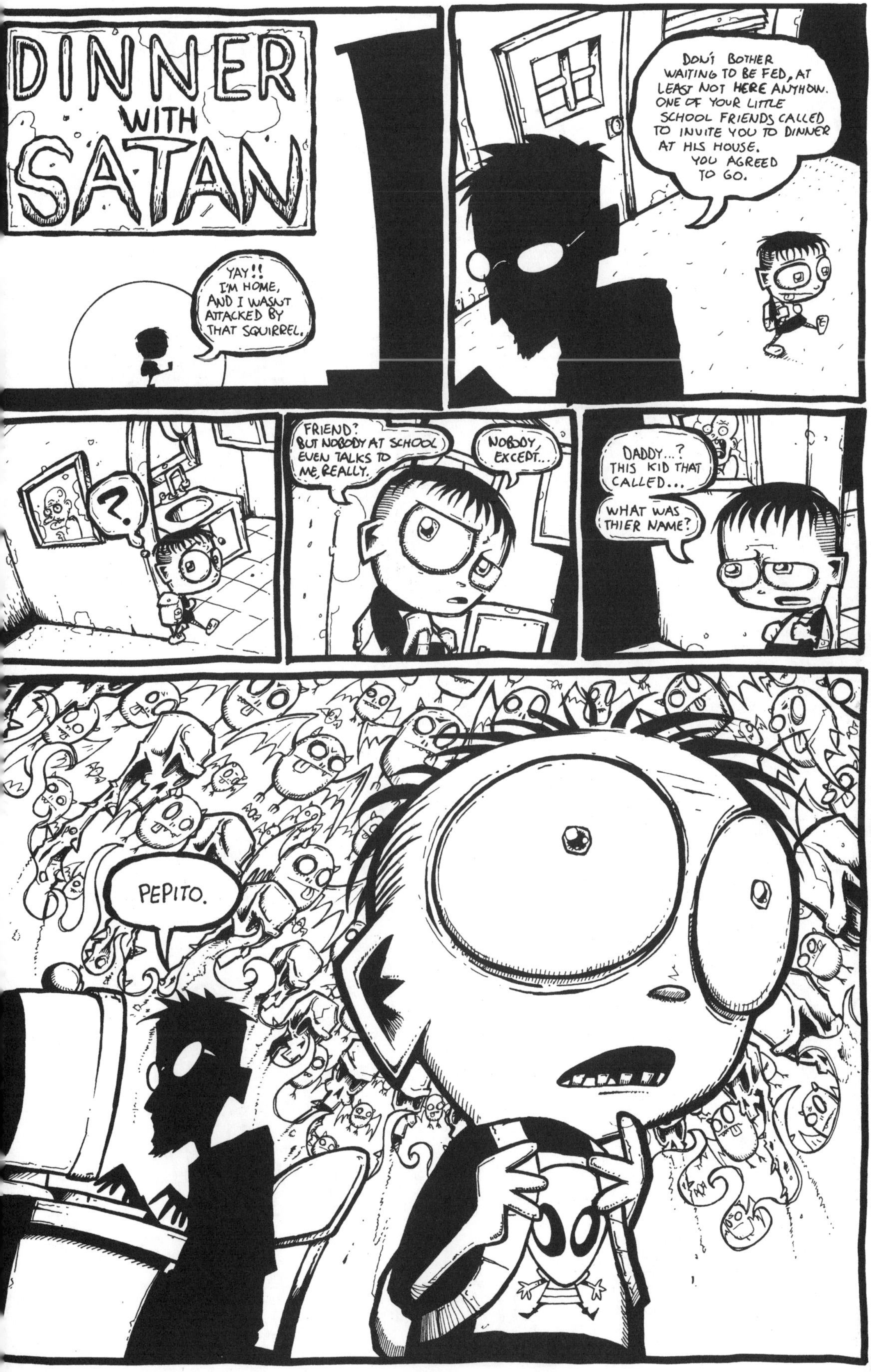
DINNER WITH SATAN
YAY!! I'M HOME, AND I WASN'T ATTACKED BY THAT SQUIRREL.
DON'T BOTHER WAITING TO BE FED, AT LEAST NOT HERE ANYHOW. ONE OF YOUR LITTLE SCHOOL FRIENDS CALLED TO INVITE YOU TO DINNER AT HIS HOUSE. YOU AGREED TO GO.
?
FRIEND? BUT NOBODY AT SCHOOL EVEN TALKS TO ME, REALLY.
NOBODY, EXCEPT...
DADDY...? THIS KID THAT CALLED...
WHAT WAS THIER NAME?
PEPITO.

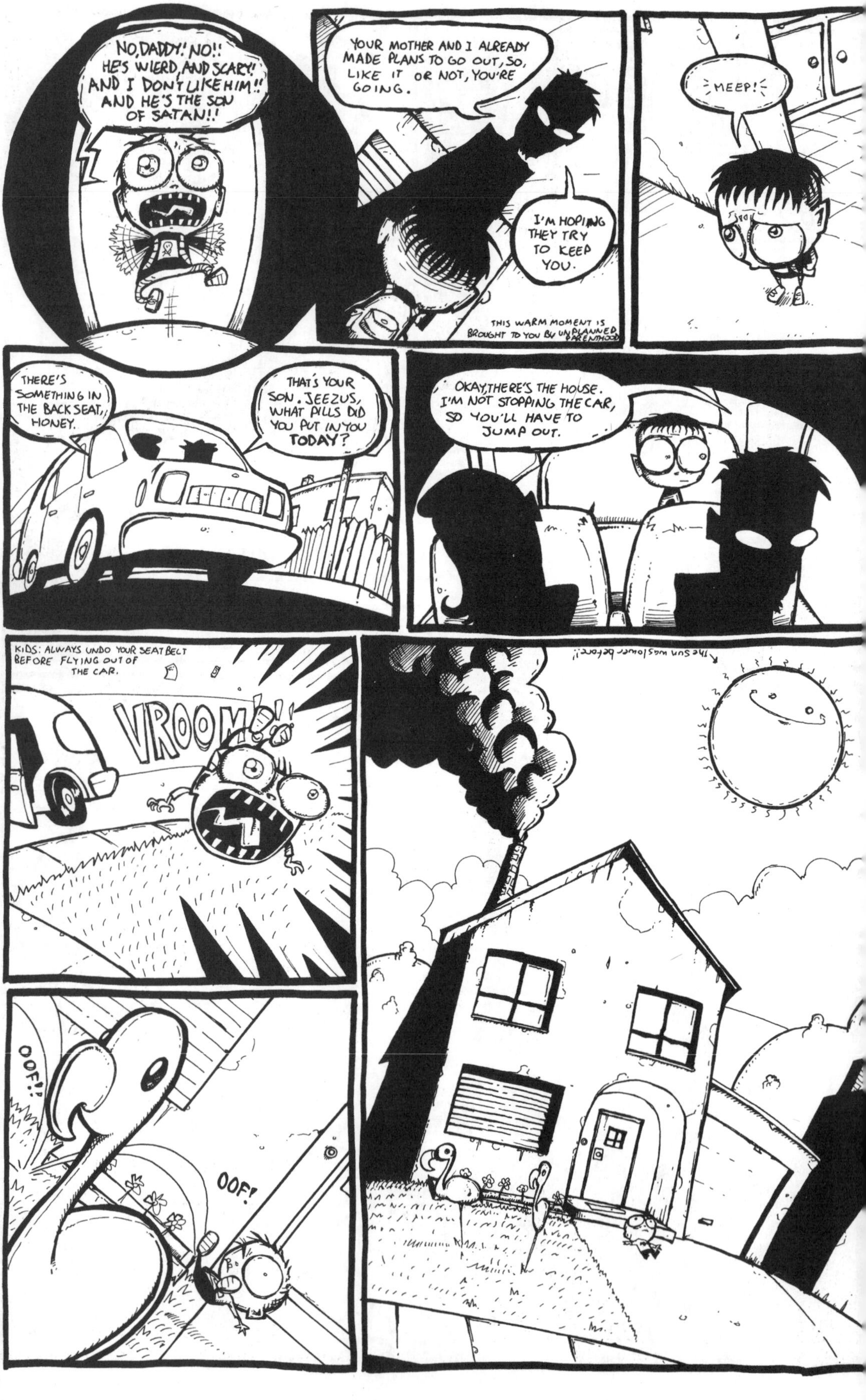
NO, DADDY! NO!! HE'S WIERD, AND SCARY! AND I DON'T LIKE HIM!! AND HE'S THE SON OF SATAN!!
YOUR MOTHER AND I ALREADY MADE PLANS TO GO OUT, SO, LIKE IT OR NOT, YOU'RE GOING.
I'M HOPING THEY TRY TO KEEP YOU.
THIS WARM MOMENT IS BROUGHT TO YOU BY UNPLANNED PARENTHOOD
MEEP!
THERE'S SOMETHING IN THE BACK SEAT, HONEY.
THAT'S YOUR SON. JEEZUS, WHAT PILLS DID YOU PUT IN YOU TODAY?
OKAY, THERE'S THE HOUSE. I'M NOT STOPPING THE CAR, SO YOU'LL HAVE TO JUMP OUT.
KIDS: ALWAYS UNDO YOUR SEATBELT BEFORE FLYING OUT OF THE CAR.
VROOM!
OOF!?
OOF!
the sun was lower before!!

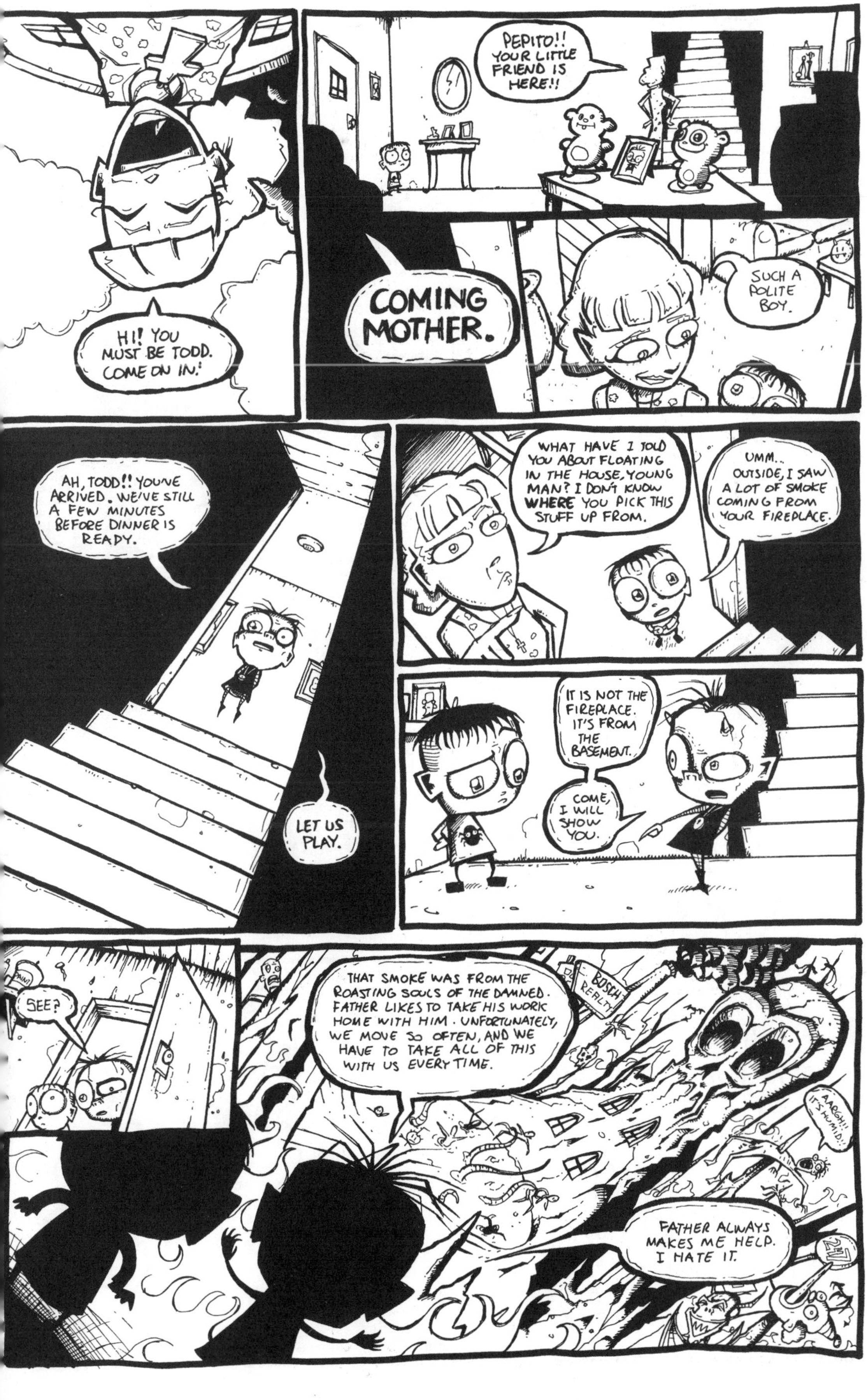
HI! YOU MUST BE TODD. COME ON IN!
PEPITO!! YOUR LITTLE FRIEND IS HERE!!
COMING MOTHER.
SUCH A POLITE BOY.
AH, TODD!! YOU'VE ARRIVED. WE'VE STILL A FEW MINUTES BEFORE DINNER IS READY.
LET US PLAY.
WHAT HAVE I TOLD YOU ABOUT FLOATING IN THE HOUSE, YOUNG MAN? I DON'T KNOW WHERE YOU PICK THIS STUFF UP FROM.
UMM.. OUTSIDE, I SAW A LOT OF SMOKE COMING FROM YOUR FIREPLACE.
IT IS NOT THE FIREPLACE. IT'S FROM THE BASEMENT.
COME, I WILL SHOW YOU.
SEE?
THAT SMOKE WAS FROM THE ROASTING SOULS OF THE DAMNED. FATHER LIKES TO TAKE HIS WORK HOME WITH HIM. UNFORTUNATELY, WE MOVE SO OFTEN, AND WE HAVE TO TAKE ALL OF THIS WITH US EVERY TIME.
BOSCH REALTY
AARGH!! IT'S HUMID!!
FATHER ALWAYS MAKES ME HELP. I HATE IT.
247

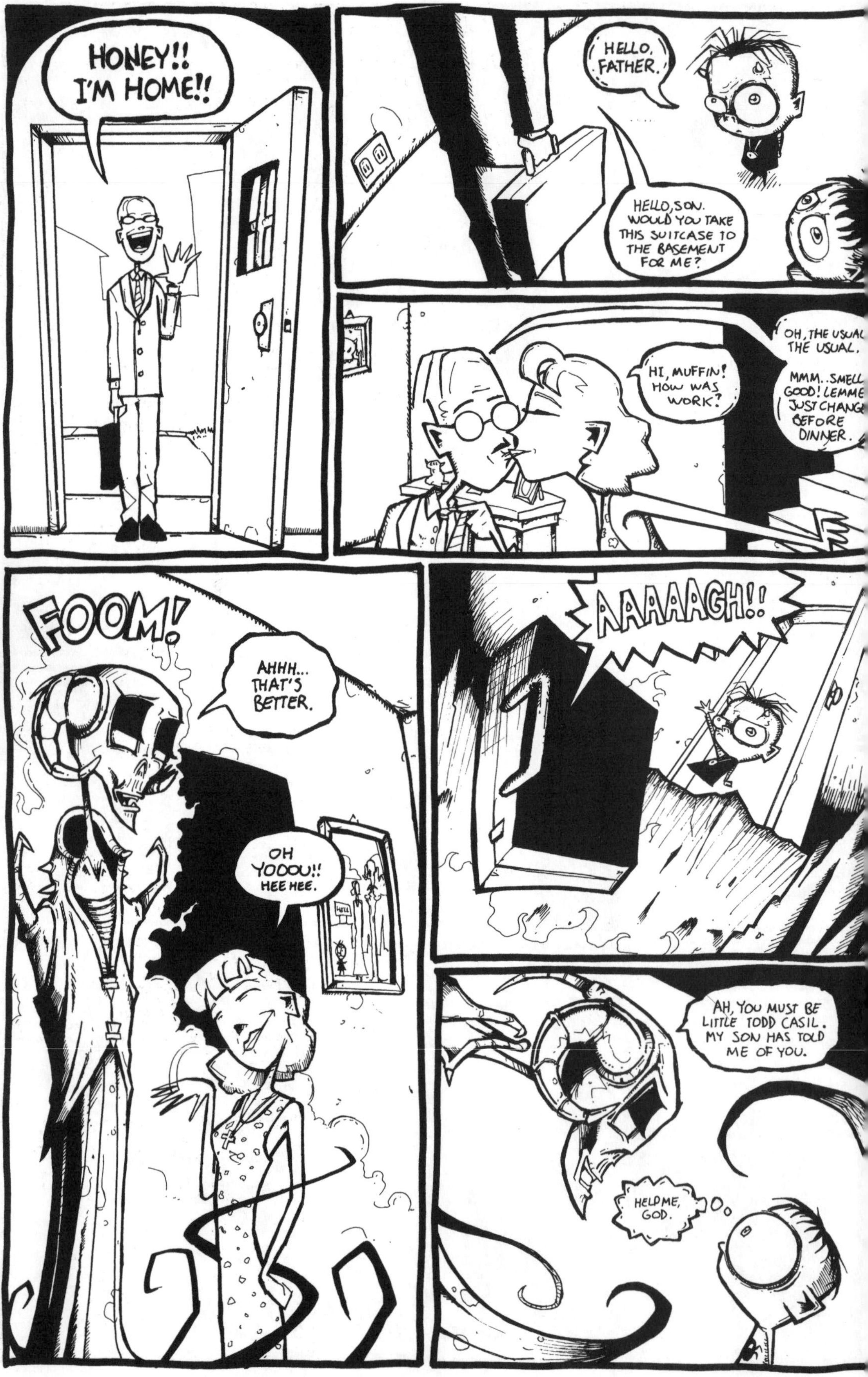
HONEY!! I'M HOME!!
HELLO, FATHER.
HELLO, SON. WOULD YOU TAKE THIS SUITCASE TO THE BASEMENT FOR ME?
HI, MUFFIN! HOW WAS WORK?
OH, THE USUAL THE USUAL.
MMM.. SMELL GOOD! LEMME JUST CHANGE BEFORE DINNER.
FOOM!
AHHH... THAT'S BETTER.
OH YOOOU!! HEE HEE.
HELL
AAAAAGH!!
AH, YOU MUST BE LITTLE TODD CASIL. MY SON HAS TOLD ME OF YOU.
HELP ME, GOD.

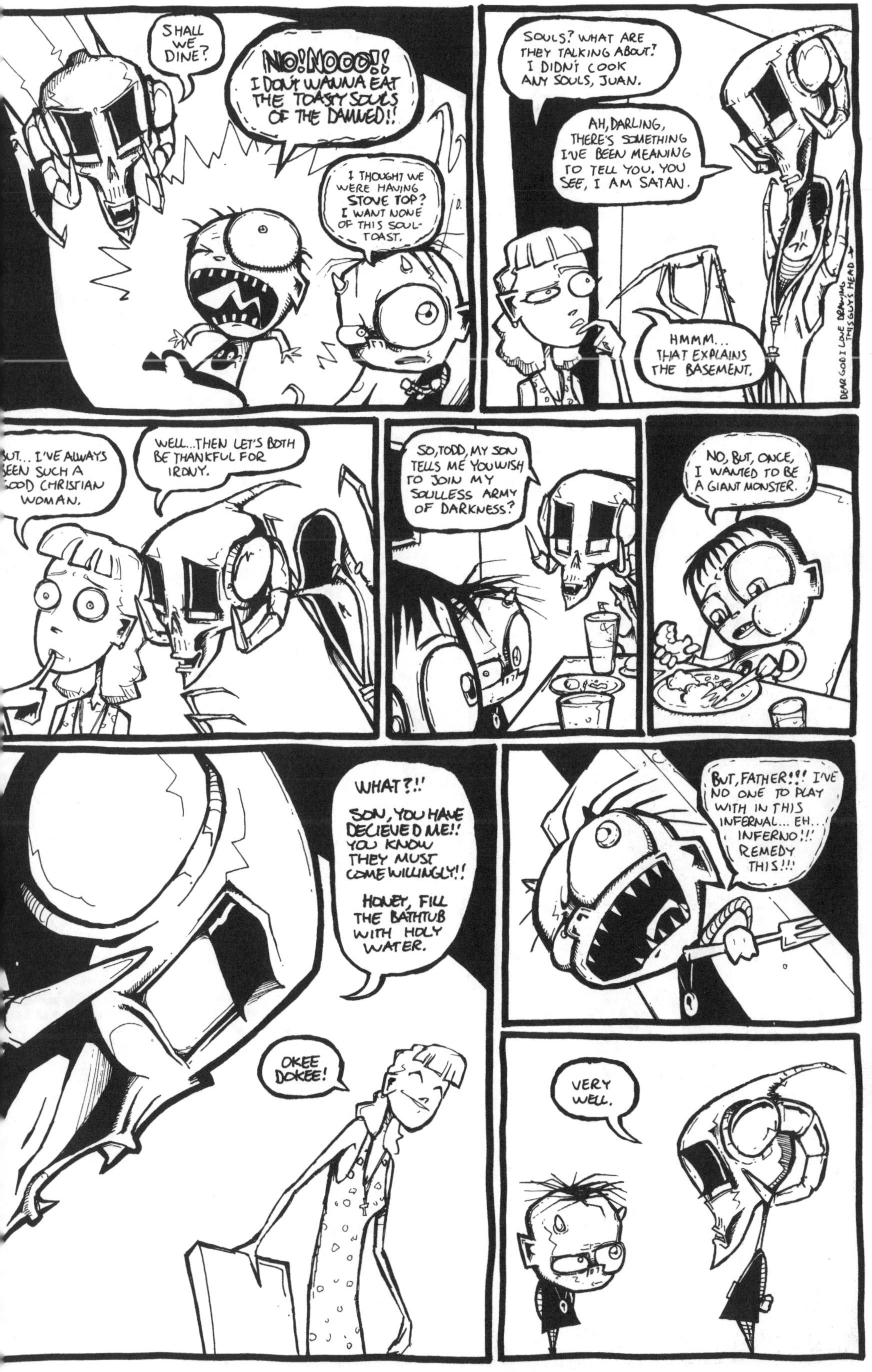
SHALL WE DINE?
NO! NOOO!! I DON'T WANNA EAT THE TOASTY SOULS OF THE DAMNED!!
I THOUGHT WE WERE HAVING STOVE TOP? I WANT NONE OF THIS SOUL-TOAST.
SOULS? WHAT ARE THEY TALKING ABOUT? I DIDN'T COOK ANY SOULS, JUAN.
AH, DARLING, THERE'S SOMETHING I'VE BEEN MEANING TO TELL YOU. YOU SEE, I AM SATAN.
HMMM... THAT EXPLAINS THE BASEMENT.
DEAR GOD I LOVE DRAWING THIS GUY'S HEAD
BUT... I'VE ALWAYS BEEN SUCH A GOOD CHRISTIAN WOMAN.
WELL...THEN LET'S BOTH BE THANKFUL FOR IRONY.
SO, TODD, MY SON TELLS ME YOU WISH TO JOIN MY SOULLESS ARMY OF DARKNESS?
NO, BUT, ONCE, I WANTED TO BE A GIANT MONSTER.
WHAT?!!
SON, YOU HAVE DECIEVED ME!! YOU KNOW THEY MUST COME WILLINGLY!!
HONEY, FILL THE BATHTUB WITH HOLY WATER.
OKEE DOKEE!
BUT, FATHER!!! I'VE NO ONE TO PLAY WITH IN THIS INFERNAL... EH... INFERNO!!! REMEDY THIS!!!
VERY WELL.

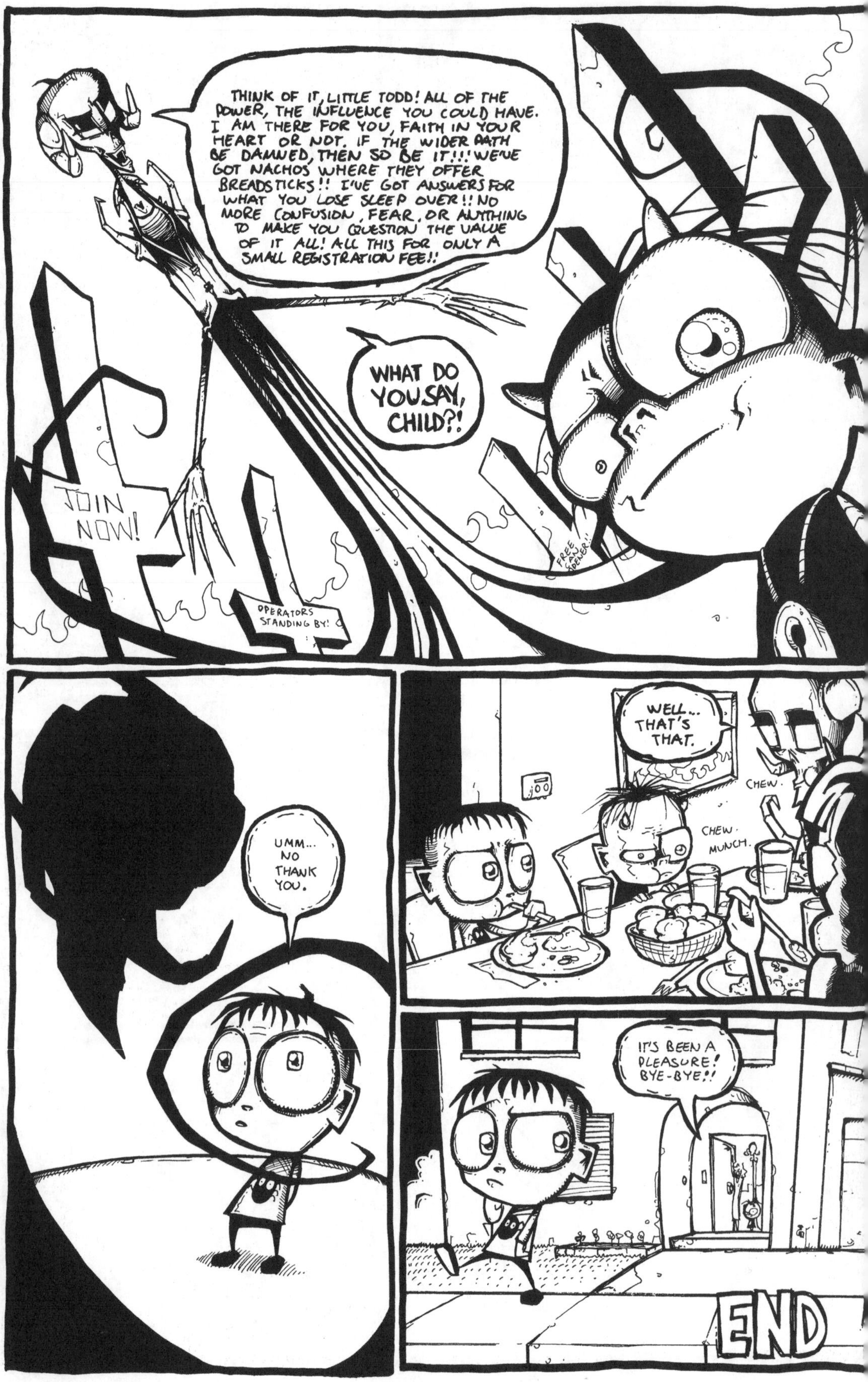
THINK OF IT, LITTLE TODD! ALL OF THE POWER, THE INFLUENCE YOU COULD HAVE. I AM THERE FOR YOU, FAITH IN YOUR HEART OR NOT. IF THE WIDER PATH BE DAMNED, THEN SO BE IT!!! WE'VE GOT NACHOS WHERE THEY OFFER BREADSTICKS!! I'VE GOT ANSWERS FOR WHAT YOU LOSE SLEEP OVER!! NO MORE CONFUSION, FEAR, OR ANYTHING TO MAKE YOU QUESTION THE VALUE OF IT ALL! ALL THIS FOR ONLY A SMALL REGISTRATION FEE!!
WHAT DO YOU SAY, CHILD?!
JOIN NOW!
FREE CAN OPENER!!
OPERATORS STANDING BY!
UMM... NO THANK YOU.
WELL... THAT'S THAT.
CHEW.
CHEW.
MUNCH.
IT'S BEEN A PLEASURE! BYE-BYE!!
END

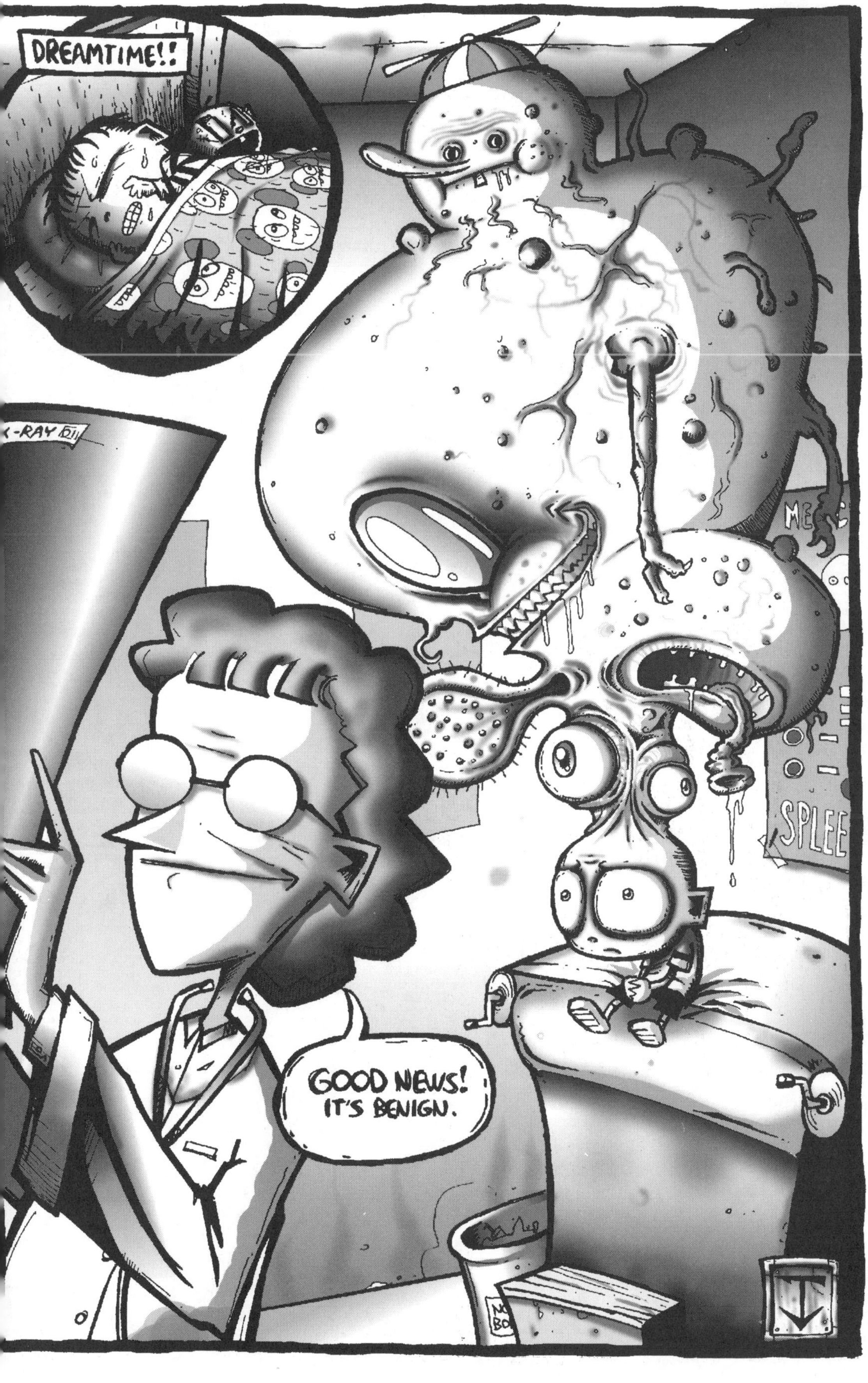
DREAMTIME!!
-RAY
ME
SPLEE
GOOD NEWS!
IT'S BENIGN.

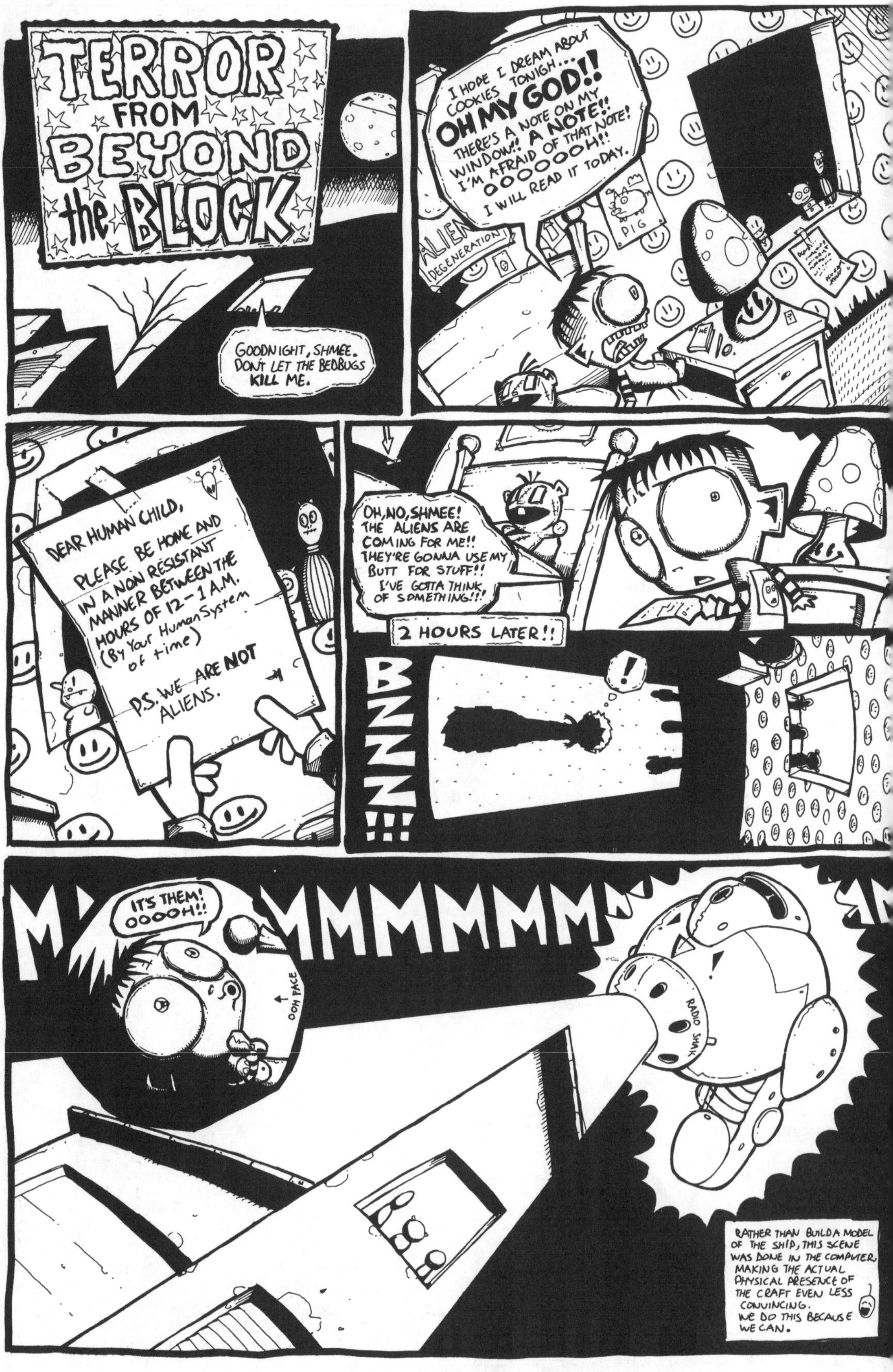
TERROR FROM BEYOND the BLOCK
GOODNIGHT, SHMEE. DON'T LET THE BEDBUGS KILL ME.
I HOPE I DREAM ABOUT COOKIES TONIGH... OH MY GOD!! THERE'S A NOTE ON MY WINDOW!! A NOTE!! I'M AFRAID OF THAT NOTE! OOOOOOOH!! I WILL READ IT TODAY.
ALIEN DEGENERATION
PIG
DEAR HUMAN CHILD, PLEASE BE HOME AND IN A NON RESISTANT MANNER BETWEEN THE HOURS OF 12-1 A.M. (By Your Human System of time)
P.S. WE ARE NOT ALIENS.
OH, NO, SHMEE! THE ALIENS ARE COMING FOR ME!! THEY'RE GONNA USE MY BUTT FOR STUFF!! I'VE GOTTA THINK OF SOMETHING!!!
2 HOURS LATER!!
BZZZZ!!!
!
MMMMMMMMM
IT'S THEM! OOOOH!!
OOH FACE
RADIO SHAK
RATHER THAN BUILD A MODEL OF THE SHIP, THIS SCENE WAS DONE IN THE COMPUTER, MAKING THE ACTUAL PHYSICAL PRESENCE OF THE CRAFT EVEN LESS CONVINCING. WE DO THIS BECAUSE WE CAN.

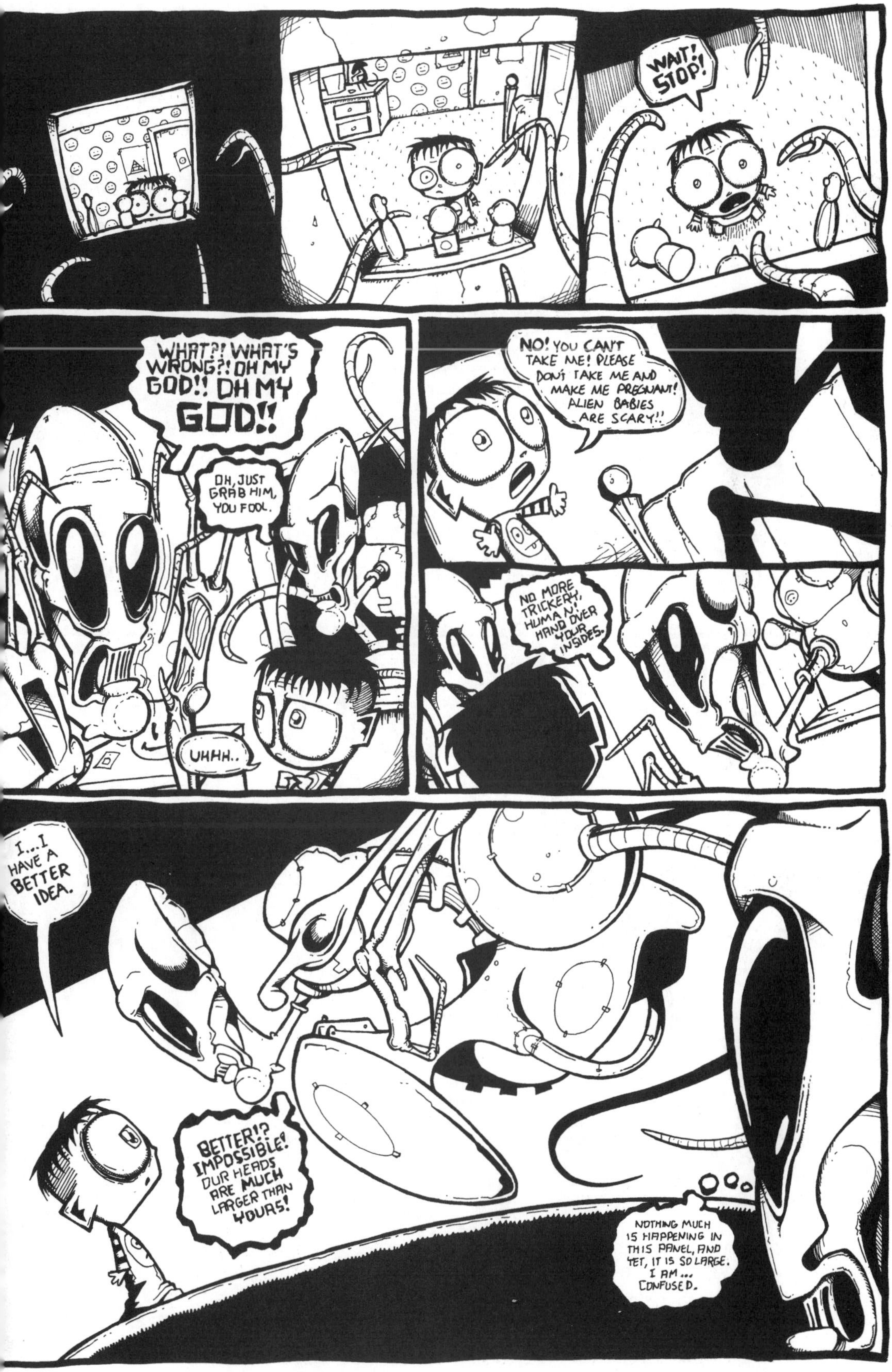
WAIT! STOP!
WHAT?! WHAT'S WRONG?! OH MY GOD!! OH MY GOD!!
OH, JUST GRAB HIM, YOU FOOL.
UHHH..
NO! YOU CAN'T TAKE ME! PLEASE DON'T TAKE ME AND MAKE ME PREGNANT! ALIEN BABIES ARE SCARY!!
NO MORE TRICKERY, HUMAN! HAND OVER YOUR INSIDES.
I...I HAVE A BETTER IDEA.
BETTER!? IMPOSSIBLE! OUR HEADS ARE MUCH LARGER THAN YOURS!
NOTHING MUCH IS HAPPENING IN THIS PANEL, AND YET, IT IS SO LARGE. I AM... CONFUSED.

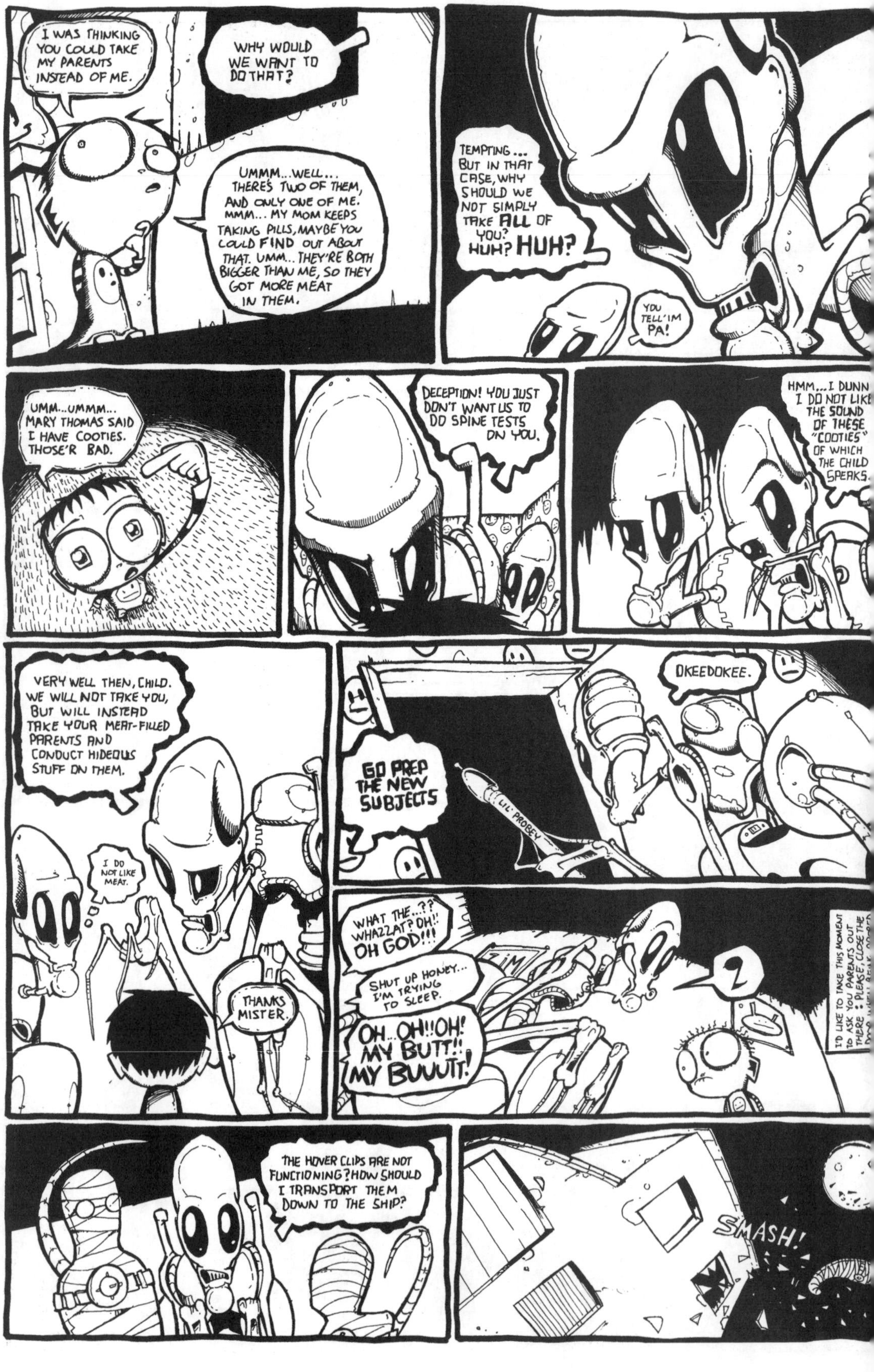
I WAS THINKING YOU COULD TAKE MY PARENTS INSTEAD OF ME.
WHY WOULD WE WANT TO DO THAT?
UMMM...WELL... THERE'S TWO OF THEM, AND ONLY ONE OF ME. MMM... MY MOM KEEPS TAKING PILLS, MAYBE YOU COULD FIND OUT ABOUT THAT. UMM... THEY'RE BOTH BIGGER THAN ME, SO THEY GOT MORE MEAT IN THEM.
TEMPTING... BUT IN THAT CASE, WHY SHOULD WE NOT SIMPLY TAKE ALL OF YOU? HUH? HUH?
YOU TELL'IM PA!
UMM...UMMM... MARY THOMAS SAID I HAVE COOTIES. THOSE'R BAD.
DECEPTION! YOU JUST DON'T WANT US TO DO SPINE TESTS ON YOU.
HMM,...I DUNN
I DO NOT LIKE THE SOUND OF THESE "COOTIES" OF WHICH THE CHILD SPEAKS.
VERY WELL THEN, CHILD. WE WILL NOT TAKE YOU, BUT WILL INSTEAD TAKE YOUR MEAT-FILLED PARENTS AND CONDUCT HIDEOUS STUFF ON THEM.
I DO NOT LIKE MEAT.
THANKS MISTER.
GO PREP THE NEW SUBJECTS
OKEEDOKEE.
LIL' PROBEY
WHAT THE...?? WHAZZAT? OH!! OH GOD!!!
SHUT UP HONEY... I'M TRYING TO SLEEP.
OH...OH!!OH! MY BUTT!! MY BUUUTT!
?
I'D LIKE TO TAKE THIS MOMENT
TO ASK YOU PARENTS OUT
THERE: PLEASE, CLOSE THE
THE HOVER CLIPS ARE NOT FUNCTIONING? HOW SHOULD I TRANSPORT THEM DOWN TO THE SHIP?
SMASH!

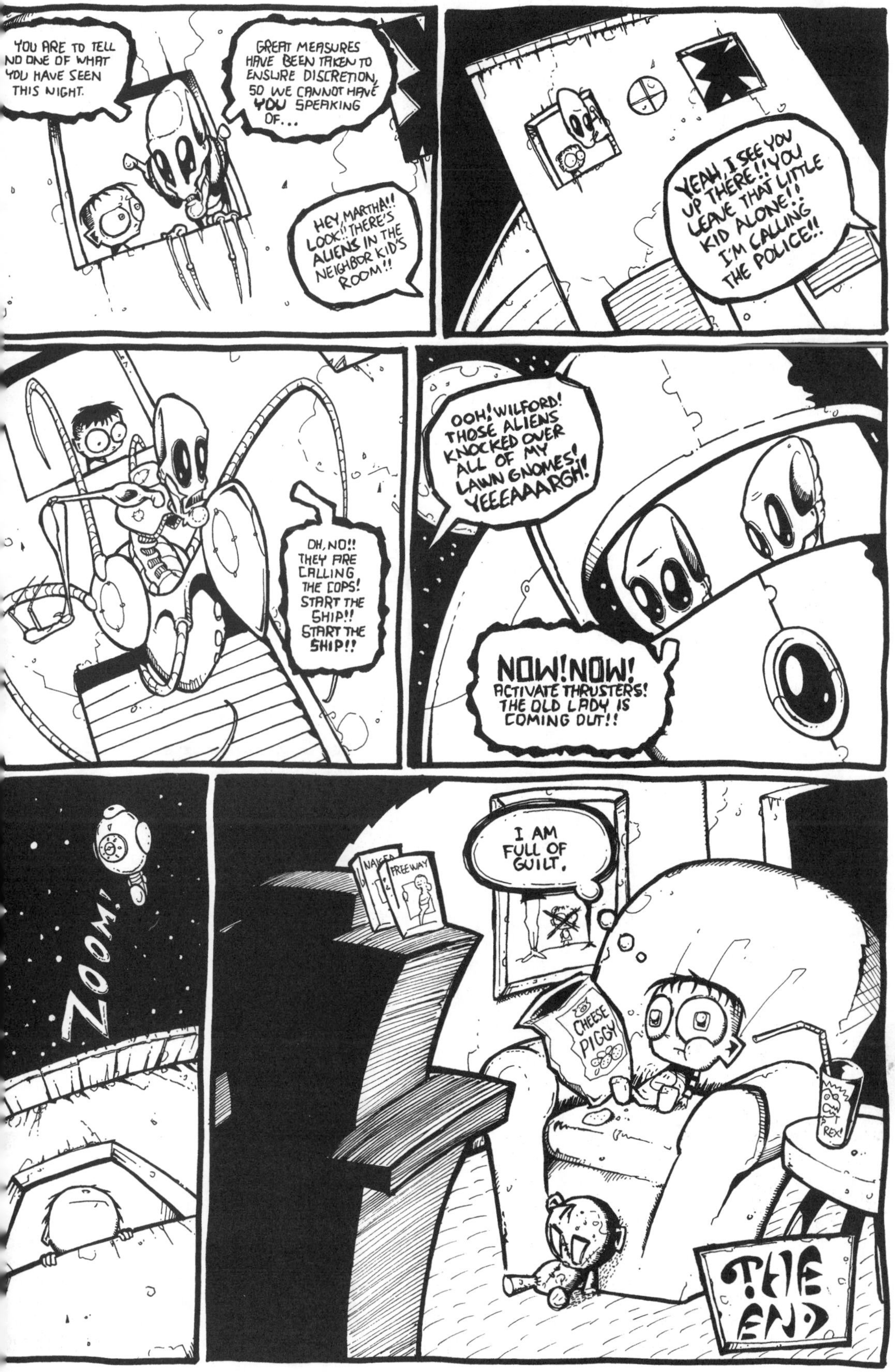
YOU ARE TO TELL NO ONE OF WHAT YOU HAVE SEEN THIS NIGHT.
GREAT MEASURES HAVE BEEN TAKEN TO ENSURE DISCRETION, SO WE CANNOT HAVE YOU SPEAKING OF...
HEY, MARTHA!! LOOK!! THERE'S ALIENS IN THE NEIGHBOR KID'S ROOM!!
YEAH, I SEE YOU UP THERE!! YOU LEAVE THAT LITTLE KID ALONE!! I'M CALLING THE POLICE!!
OH, NO!! THEY ARE CALLING THE COPS! START THE SHIP!! START THE SHIP!!
OOH! WILFORD! THOSE ALIENS KNOCKED OVER ALL OF MY LAWN GNOMES! YEEEAAARGH!
NOW! NOW! ACTIVATE THRUSTERS! THE OLD LADY IS COMING OUT!!
ZOOM!
I AM FULL OF GUILT.
FREEWAY
CHEESE PIGGY
REX!
THE END

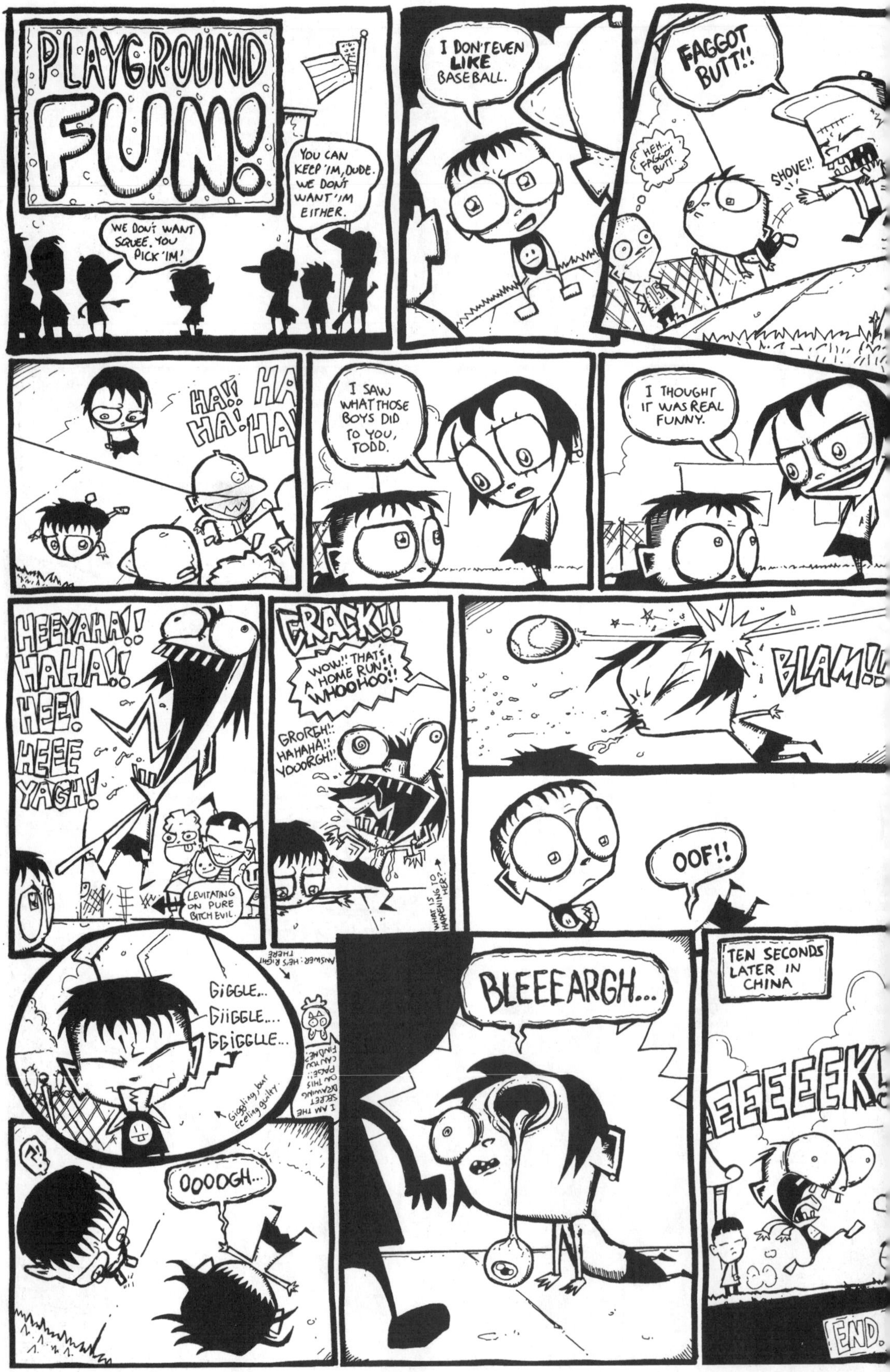
PLAYGROUND FUN!
WE DON'T WANT SQUEE. YOU PICK 'IM!
YOU CAN KEEP 'IM, DUDE. WE DON'T WANT 'IM EITHER.
I DON'T EVEN LIKE BASEBALL.
FAGGOT BUTT!!
HEH... FAGGOT BUTT.
SHOVE!!
HA!! HA! HA HA!
I SAW WHAT THOSE BOYS DID TO YOU, TODD.
I THOUGHT IT WAS REAL FUNNY.
HEEYAHA!! HAHA!! HEE! HEEE YAGH!
LEVITATING ON PURE BITCH EVIL.
CRACK!!
WOW!! THAT'S A HOME RUN!! WHOOHOO!!
GRORGH!! HAHAHA!! YOOORGH!!
WHAT IS HAPPENING TO HER?
BLAM!!
OOF!!
GIGGLE... GIIGGLE.... GGIGGLLE...
Giggling, but feeling guilty.
ANSWER: HE'S RIGHT THERE
I AM THE SECRET DRAWING ON THIS PAGE. CAN YOU FIND ME?
OOOOGH...
BLEEEARGH...
TEN SECONDS LATER IN CHINA
EEEEEEK!
END.

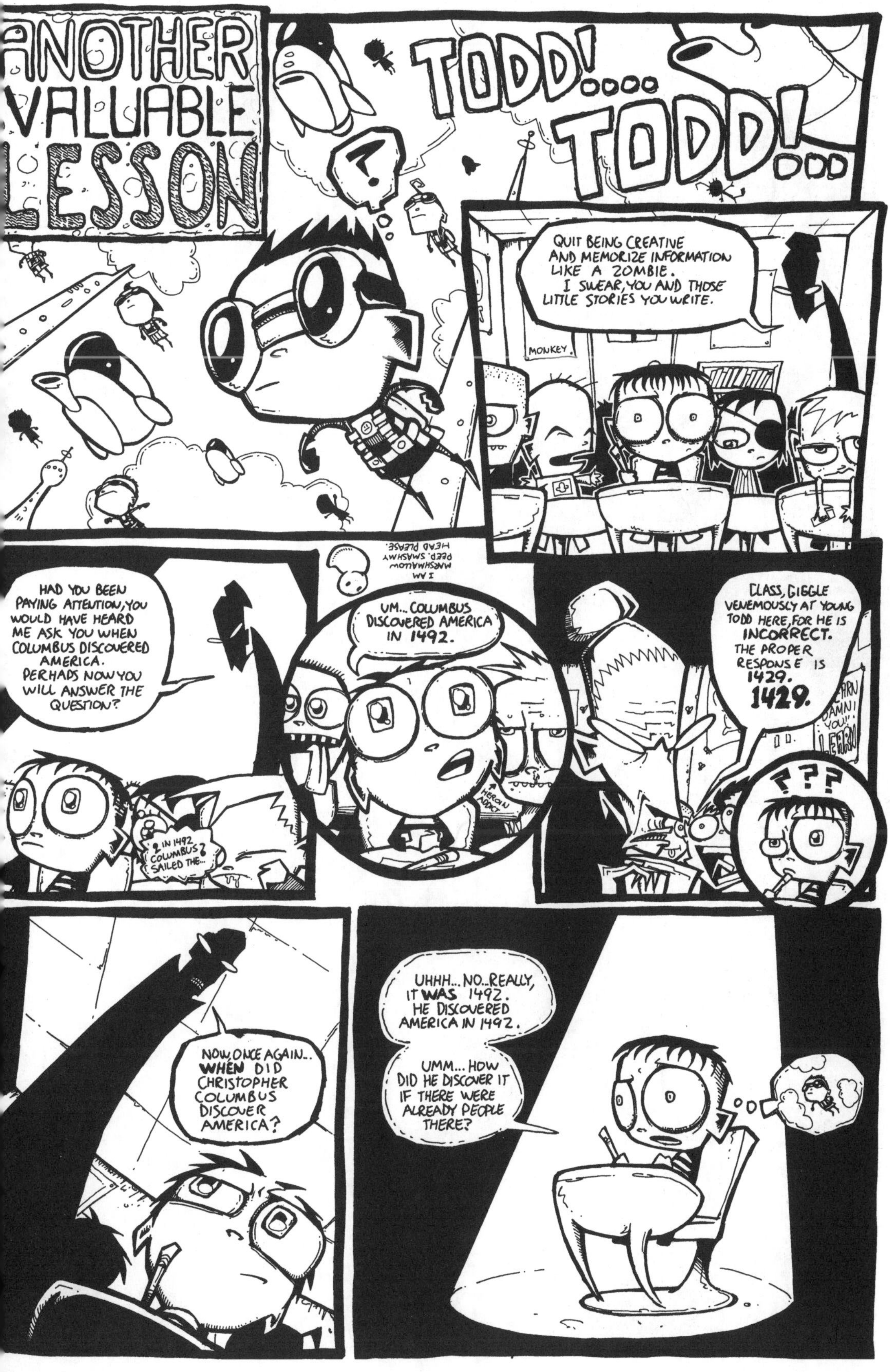
ANOTHER VALUABLE LESSON
TODD!.... TODD!...
QUIT BEING CREATIVE AND MEMORIZE INFORMATION LIKE A ZOMBIE. I SWEAR, YOU AND THOSE LITTLE STORIES YOU WRITE.
MONKEY
HAD YOU BEEN PAYING ATTENTION, YOU WOULD HAVE HEARD ME ASK YOU WHEN COLUMBUS DISCOVERED AMERICA. PERHAPS NOW YOU WILL ANSWER THE QUESTION?
? IN 1492 COLUMBUS ? SAILED THE...
I AM MARSHMALLOW PEEP. SMASH MY HEAD PLEASE.
UM... COLUMBUS DISCOVERED AMERICA IN 1492.
HEROIN ADDICT
CLASS, GIGGLE VENEMOUSLY AT YOUNG TODD HERE, FOR HE IS INCORRECT. THE PROPER RESPONSE IS 1429. 1429.
???
NOW, ONCE AGAIN.. WHEN DID CHRISTOPHER COLUMBUS DISCOVER AMERICA?
UHHH... NO..REALLY, IT WAS 1492. HE DISCOVERED AMERICA IN 1492.
UMM... HOW DID HE DISCOVER IT IF THERE WERE ALREADY PEOPLE THERE?

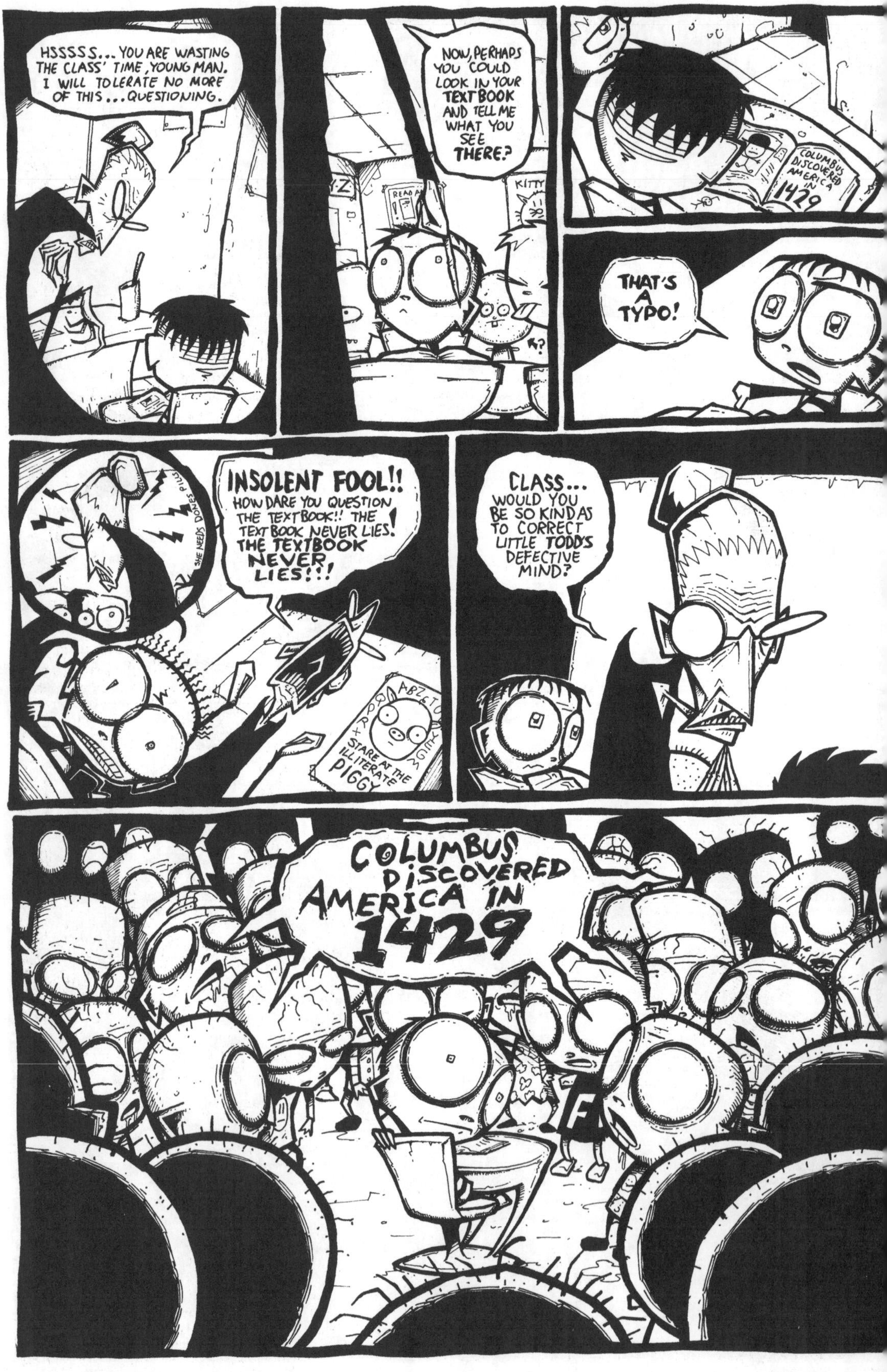
HSSSSS... YOU ARE WASTING THE CLASS' TIME, YOUNG MAN. I WILL TOLERATE NO MORE OF THIS... QUESTIONING.
NOW, PERHAPS YOU COULD LOOK IN YOUR TEXTBOOK AND TELL ME WHAT YOU SEE THERE?
COLUMBUS DISCOVERED AMERICA IN 1429
THAT'S A TYPO!
INSOLENT FOOL!! HOW DARE YOU QUESTION THE TEXTBOOK!! THE TEXTBOOK NEVER LIES! THE TEXTBOOK NEVER LIES!!!
SHE NEEDS DONKEY PILLS
STARE AT THE ILLITERATE PIGGY
CLASS... WOULD YOU BE SO KIND AS TO CORRECT LITTLE TODD'S DEFECTIVE MIND?
COLUMBUS DISCOVERED AMERICA IN 1429

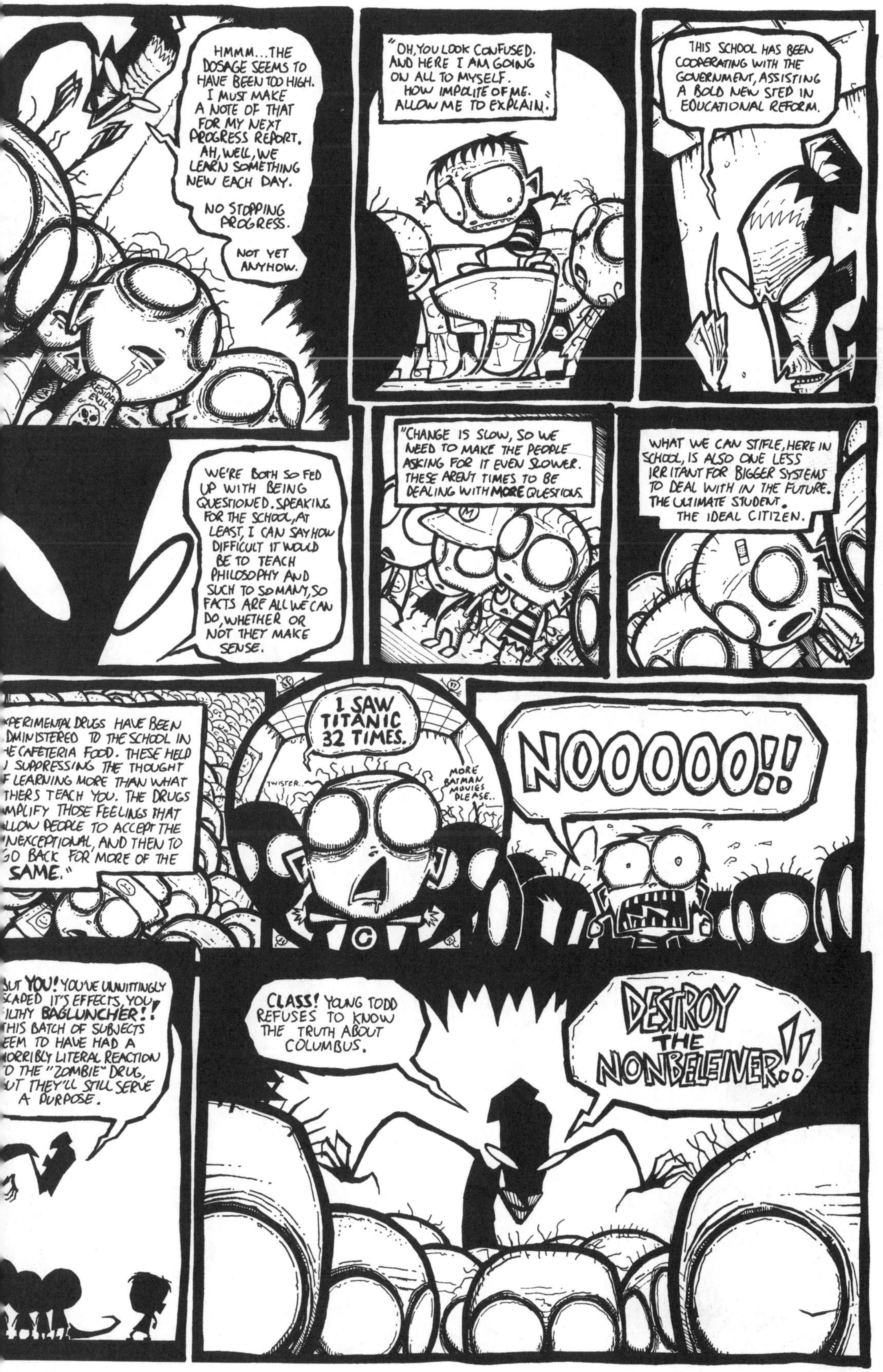
HMMM... THE DOSAGE SEEMS TO HAVE BEEN TOO HIGH. I MUST MAKE A NOTE OF THAT FOR MY NEXT PROGRESS REPORT. AH, WELL, WE LEARN SOMETHING NEW EACH DAY.
NO STOPPING PROGRESS.
NOT YET ANYHOW.
"OH, YOU LOOK CONFUSED. AND HERE I AM GOING ON ALL TO MYSELF. HOW IMPOLITE OF ME. ALLOW ME TO EXPLAIN."
THIS SCHOOL HAS BEEN COOPERATING WITH THE GOVERNMENT, ASSISTING A BOLD NEW STEP IN EDUCATIONAL REFORM.
WE'RE BOTH SO FED UP WITH BEING QUESTIONED. SPEAKING FOR THE SCHOOL, AT LEAST, I CAN SAY HOW DIFFICULT IT WOULD BE TO TEACH PHILOSOPHY AND SUCH TO SO MANY, SO FACTS ARE ALL WE CAN DO, WHETHER OR NOT THEY MAKE SENSE.
"CHANGE IS SLOW, SO WE NEED TO MAKE THE PEOPLE ASKING FOR IT EVEN SLOWER. THESE AREN'T TIMES TO BE DEALING WITH MORE QUESTIONS.
WHAT WE CAN STIFLE, HERE IN SCHOOL, IS ALSO ONE LESS IRRITANT FOR BIGGER SYSTEMS TO DEAL WITH IN THE FUTURE. THE ULTIMATE STUDENT. THE IDEAL CITIZEN.
XPERIMENTAL DRUGS HAVE BEEN DMINISTERED TO THE SCHOOL IN HE CAFETERIA FOOD. THESE HELP N SUPPRESSING THE THOUGHT F LEARNING MORE THAN WHAT THERS TEACH YOU. THE DRUGS MPLIFY THOSE FEELINGS THAT LLOW PEOPLE TO ACCEPT THE NEXCEPTIONAL, AND THEN TO GO BACK FOR MORE OF THE SAME."
I SAW TITANIC 32 TIMES.
TWISTER..
MORE BATMAN MOVIES PLEASE..
NOOOOO!!
UT YOU! YOU'VE UNWITTINGLY SCAPED IT'S EFFECTS, YOU ILTHY BAGLUNCHER!! THIS BATCH OF SUBJECTS EEM TO HAVE HAD A ORRIBLY LITERAL REACTION O THE "ZOMBIE" DRUG, UT THEY'LL STILL SERVE A PURPOSE.
CLASS! YOUNG TODD REFUSES TO KNOW THE TRUTH ABOUT COLUMBUS.
DESTROY THE NONBELEIVER!!

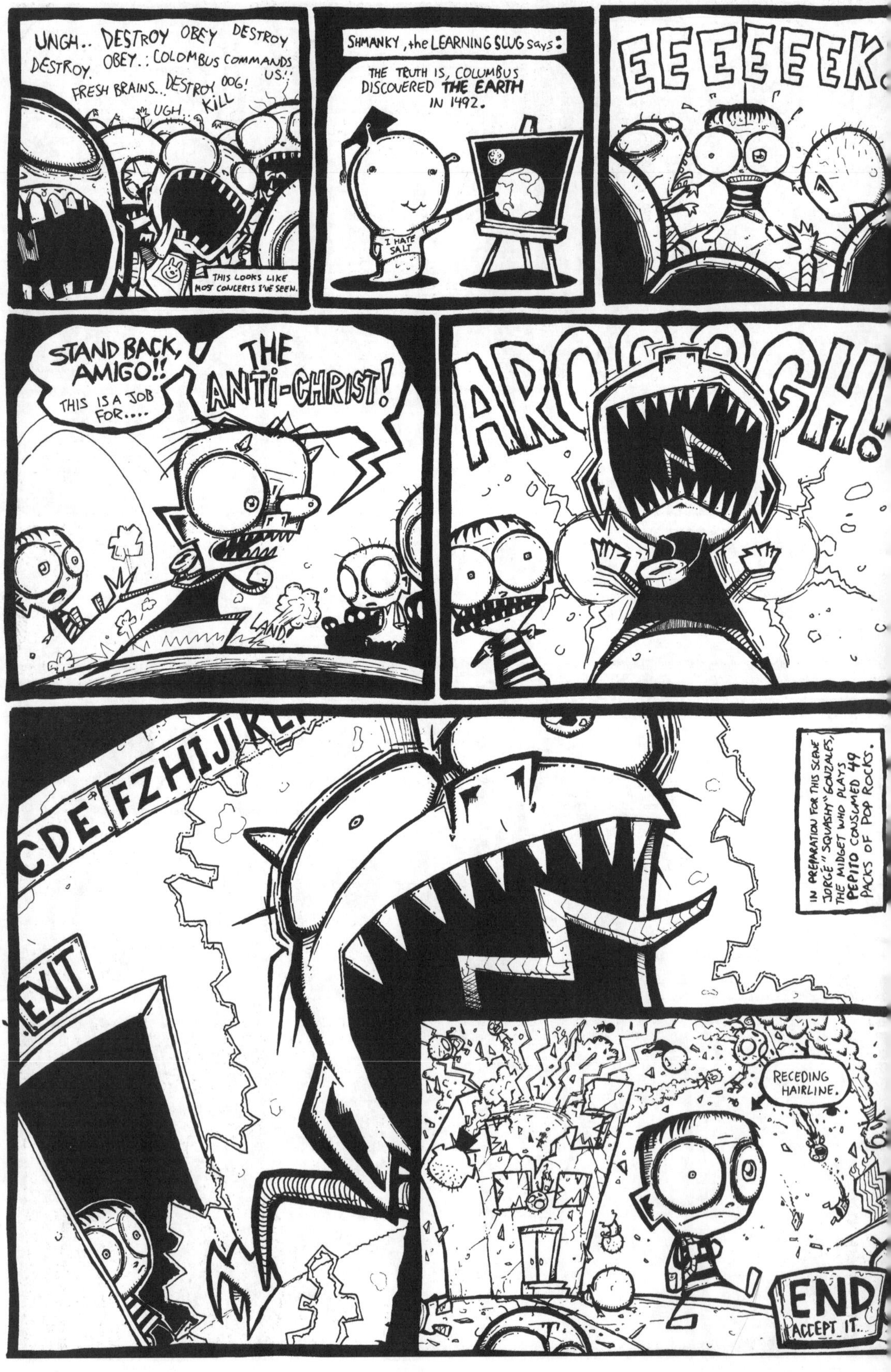
UNGH.. DESTROY OBEY DESTROY DESTROY. OBEY..: COLOMBUS COMMANDS US.!
FRESH BRAINS.. DESTROY OOG!
UGH.. KILL
THIS LOOKS LIKE MOST CONCERTS I'VE SEEN.
SHMANKY, the LEARNING SLUG says:
THE TRUTH IS, COLUMBUS DISCOVERED THE EARTH IN 1492.
I HATE SALT
EEEEEEK.
STAND BACK, AMIGO!! THIS IS A JOB FOR....
THE ANTI-CHRIST!
LAND!
AROOOOGH!
CDE FZHIJK
EXIT
IN PREPARATION FOR THIS SCENE JORGE "SQUASHY" GONZALES, THE MIDGET WHO PLAYS PEPITO CONSUMED 49 PACKS OF POP ROCKS.
RECEDING HAIRLINE.
END
ACCEPT IT..

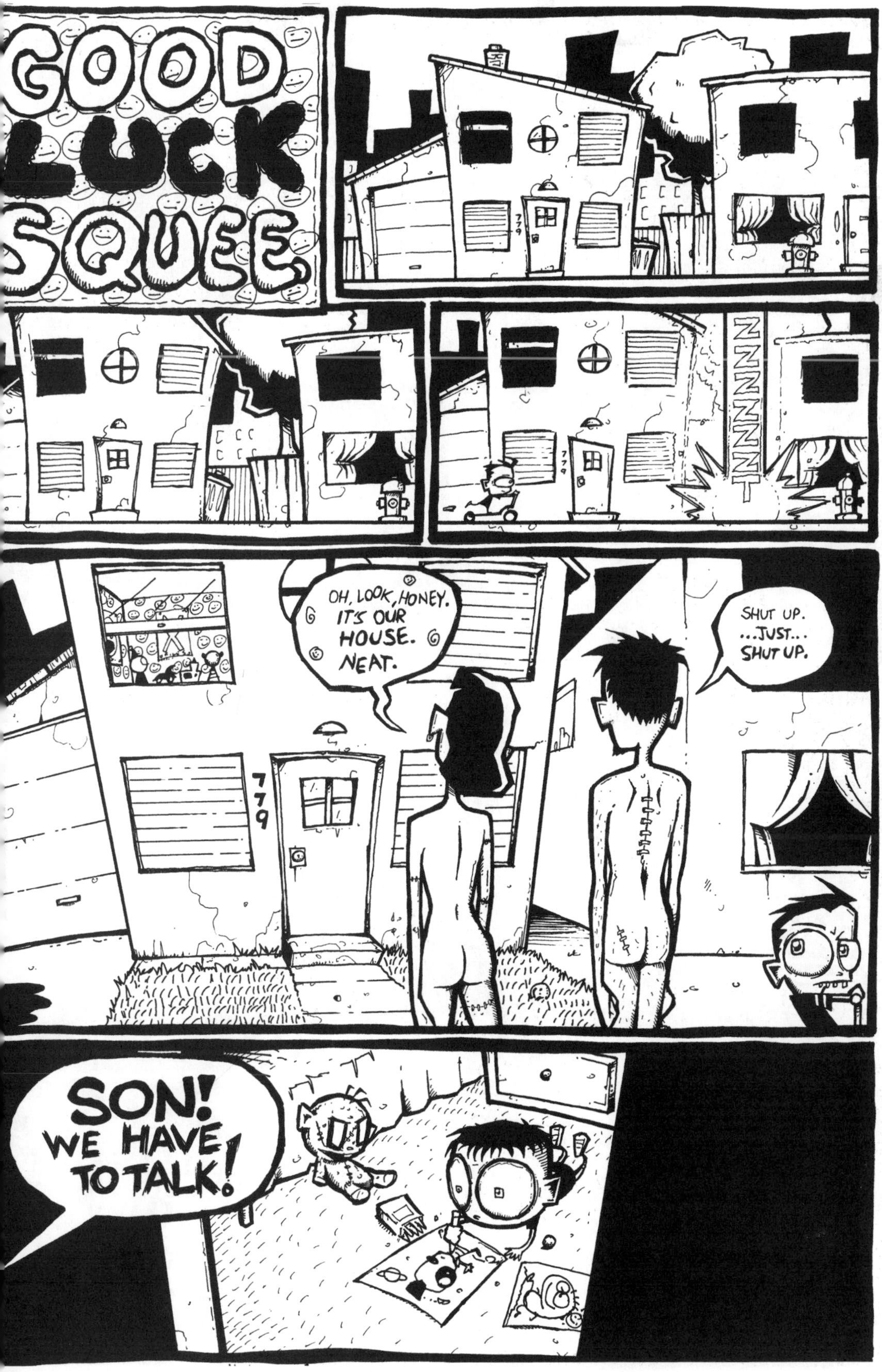
GOOD LUCK SQUEE
779
ZZZZZZT
OH, LOOK, HONEY. IT'S OUR HOUSE. NEAT.
SHUT UP. ...JUST... SHUT UP.
SON! WE HAVE TO TALK!

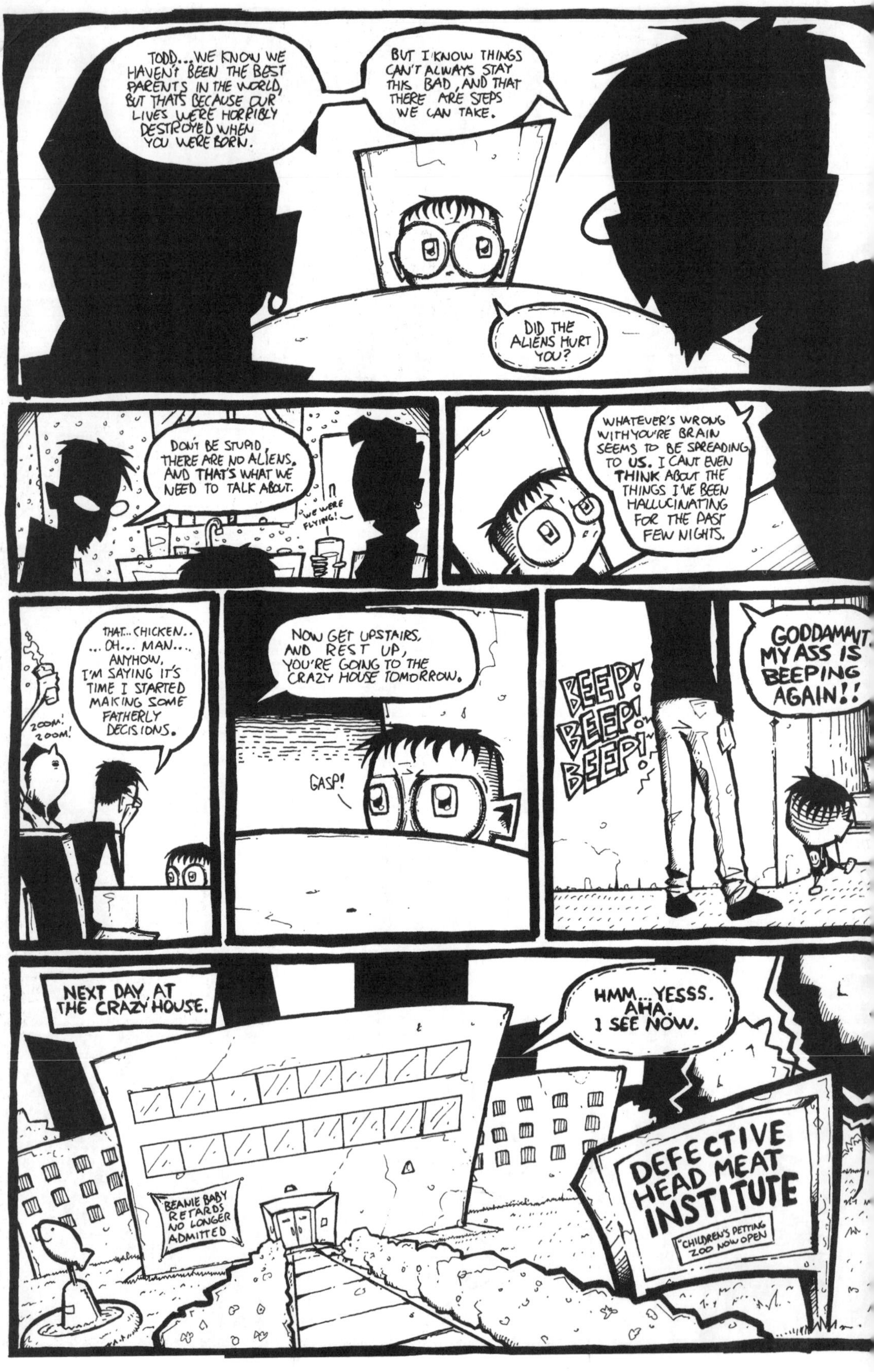
TODD... WE KNOW WE HAVEN'T BEEN THE BEST PARENTS IN THE WORLD, BUT THATS BECAUSE OUR LIVES WERE HORRIBLY DESTROYED WHEN YOU WERE BORN.
BUT I KNOW THINGS CAN'T ALWAYS STAY THIS BAD, AND THAT THERE ARE STEPS WE CAN TAKE.
DID THE ALIENS HURT YOU?
DON'T BE STUPID, THERE ARE NO ALIENS. AND THAT'S WHAT WE NEED TO TALK ABOUT.
WE WERE FLYING!
WHATEVER'S WRONG WITH YOU'RE BRAIN SEEMS TO BE SPREADING TO US. I CANT EVEN THINK ABOUT THE THINGS I'VE BEEN HALLUCINATING FOR THE PAST FEW NIGHTS.
THAT... CHICKEN... ...OH... MAN... ANYHOW, I'M SAYING IT'S TIME I STARTED MAKING SOME FATHERLY DECISIONS.
ZOOM! ZOOM!
NOW GET UPSTAIRS, AND REST UP, YOU'RE GOING TO THE CRAZY HOUSE TOMORROW.
GASP!
BEEP! BEEP! BEEP!
GODDAMMIT. MY ASS IS BEEPING AGAIN!!
NEXT DAY, AT THE CRAZY HOUSE.
HMM... YESSS. AHA. I SEE NOW.
BEANIE BABY RETARDS NO LONGER ADMITTED
DEFECTIVE HEAD MEAT INSTITUTE
"CHILDREN'S PETTING ZOO NOW OPEN

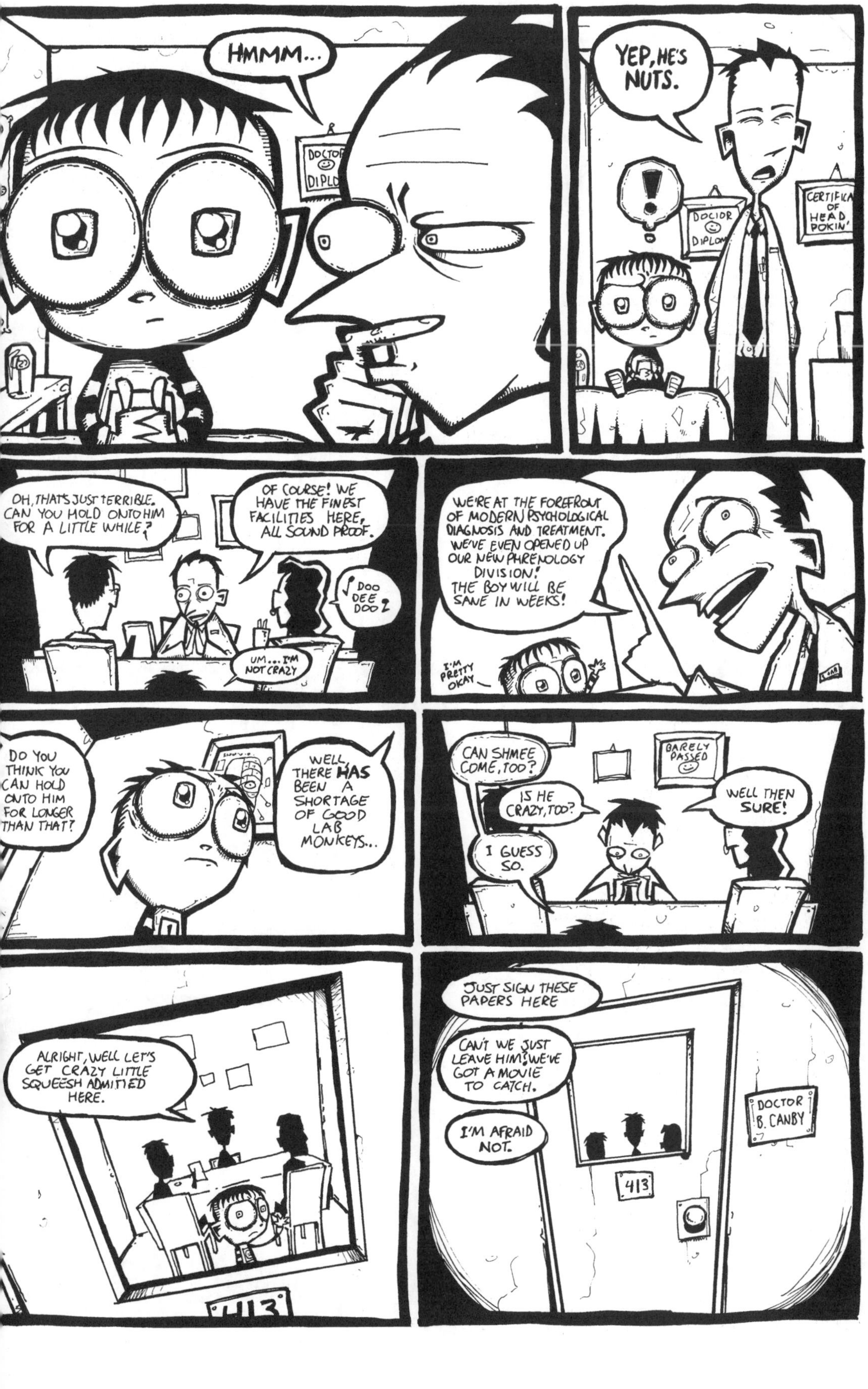
HMMM...
YEP, HE'S NUTS.
!
OH, THAT'S JUST TERRIBLE. CAN YOU HOLD ONTO HIM FOR A LITTLE WHILE?
OF COURSE! WE HAVE THE FINEST FACILITIES HERE, ALL SOUND PROOF.
DOO DEE DOO
UM... I'M NOT CRAZY
WE'RE AT THE FOREFRONT OF MODERN PSYCHOLOGICAL DIAGNOSIS AND TREATMENT. WE'VE EVEN OPENED UP OUR NEW PHRENOLOGY DIVISION! THE BOY WILL BE SANE IN WEEKS!
I'M PRETTY OKAY
DO YOU THINK YOU CAN HOLD ONTO HIM FOR LONGER THAN THAT?
WELL, THERE **HAS** BEEN A SHORTAGE OF GOOD LAB MONKEYS...
CAN SHMEE COME, TOO?
IS HE CRAZY, TOO?
I GUESS SO.
BARELY PASSED
WELL THEN **SURE!**
ALRIGHT, WELL LET'S GET CRAZY LITTLE SQUEESH ADMITTED HERE.
413
JUST SIGN THESE PAPERS HERE
CAN'T WE JUST LEAVE HIM? WE'VE GOT A MOVIE TO CATCH.
I'M AFRAID NOT.
DOCTOR B. CANBY
413

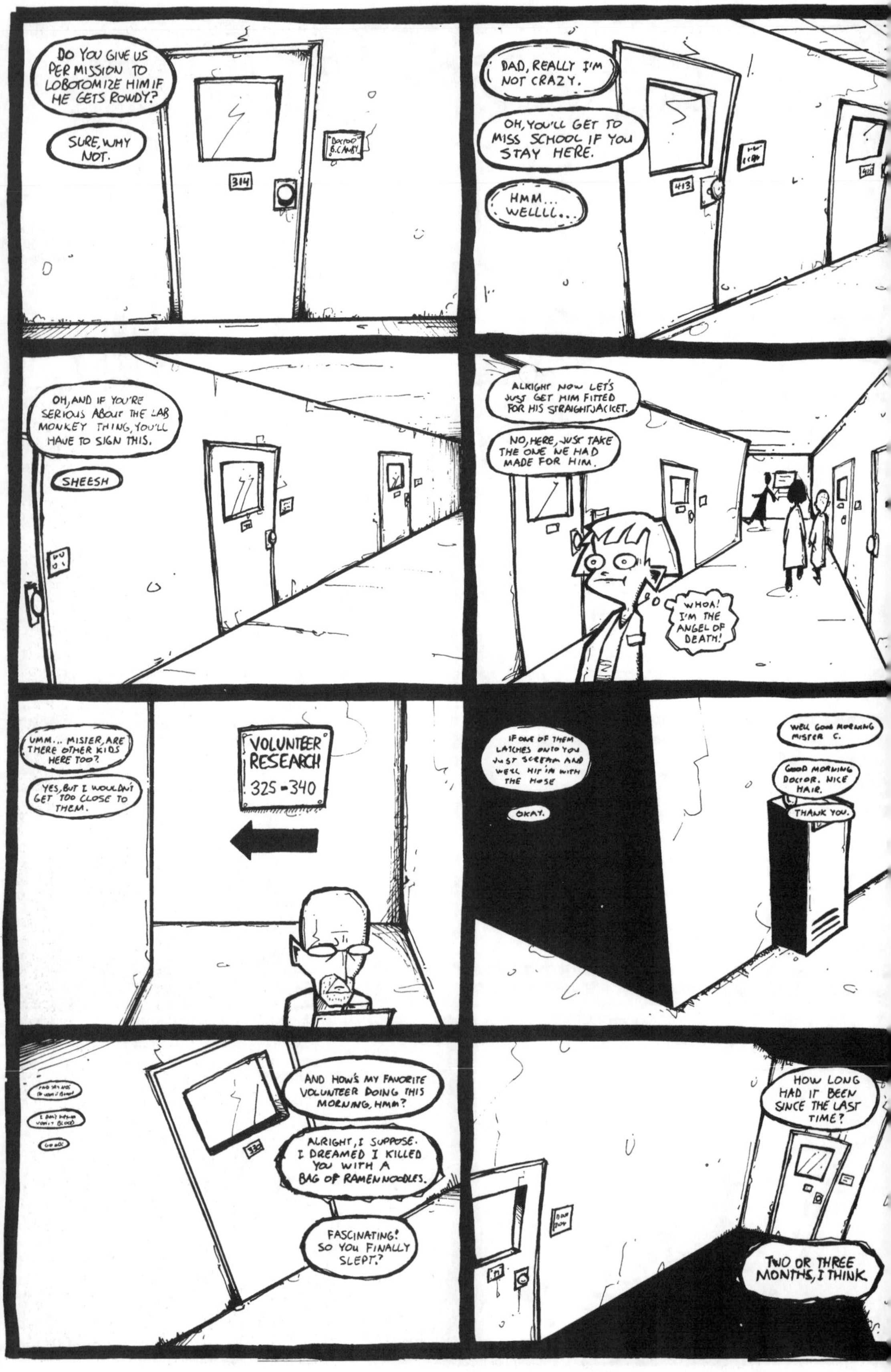

DO YOU GIVE US PERMISSION TO LOBOTOMIZE HIM IF HE GETS ROWDY?
SURE, WHY NOT.
314
DAD, REALLY I'M NOT CRAZY.
OH, YOU'LL GET TO MISS SCHOOL IF YOU STAY HERE.
HMM... WELLLL...
413
OH, AND IF YOU'RE SERIOUS ABOUT THE LAB MONKEY THING, YOU'LL HAVE TO SIGN THIS.
SHEESH
ALRIGHT NOW LET'S JUST GET HIM FITTED FOR HIS STRAIGHTJACKET.
NO, HERE, JUST TAKE THE ONE WE HAD MADE FOR HIM.
WHOA! I'M THE ANGEL OF DEATH!
UMM... MISTER, ARE THERE OTHER KIDS HERE TOO?
YES, BUT I WOULDN'T GET TOO CLOSE TO THEM.
VOLUNTEER RESEARCH 325-340
IF ONE OF THEM LATCHES ONTO YOU JUST SCREAM AND WE'LL HIT 'IM WITH THE HOSE
OKAY.
WELL GOOD MORNING MISTER C.
GOOD MORNING DOCTOR. NICE HAIR.
THANK YOU.
I DON'T WANNA VOMIT BLOOD
GOOD!
AND HOW'S MY FAVORITE VOLUNTEER DOING THIS MORNING, HMM?
ALRIGHT, I SUPPOSE. I DREAMED I KILLED YOU WITH A BAG OF RAMEN NOODLES.
FASCINATING! SO YOU FINALLY SLEPT?
HOW LONG HAD IT BEEN SINCE THE LAST TIME?
TWO OR THREE MONTHS, I THINK.

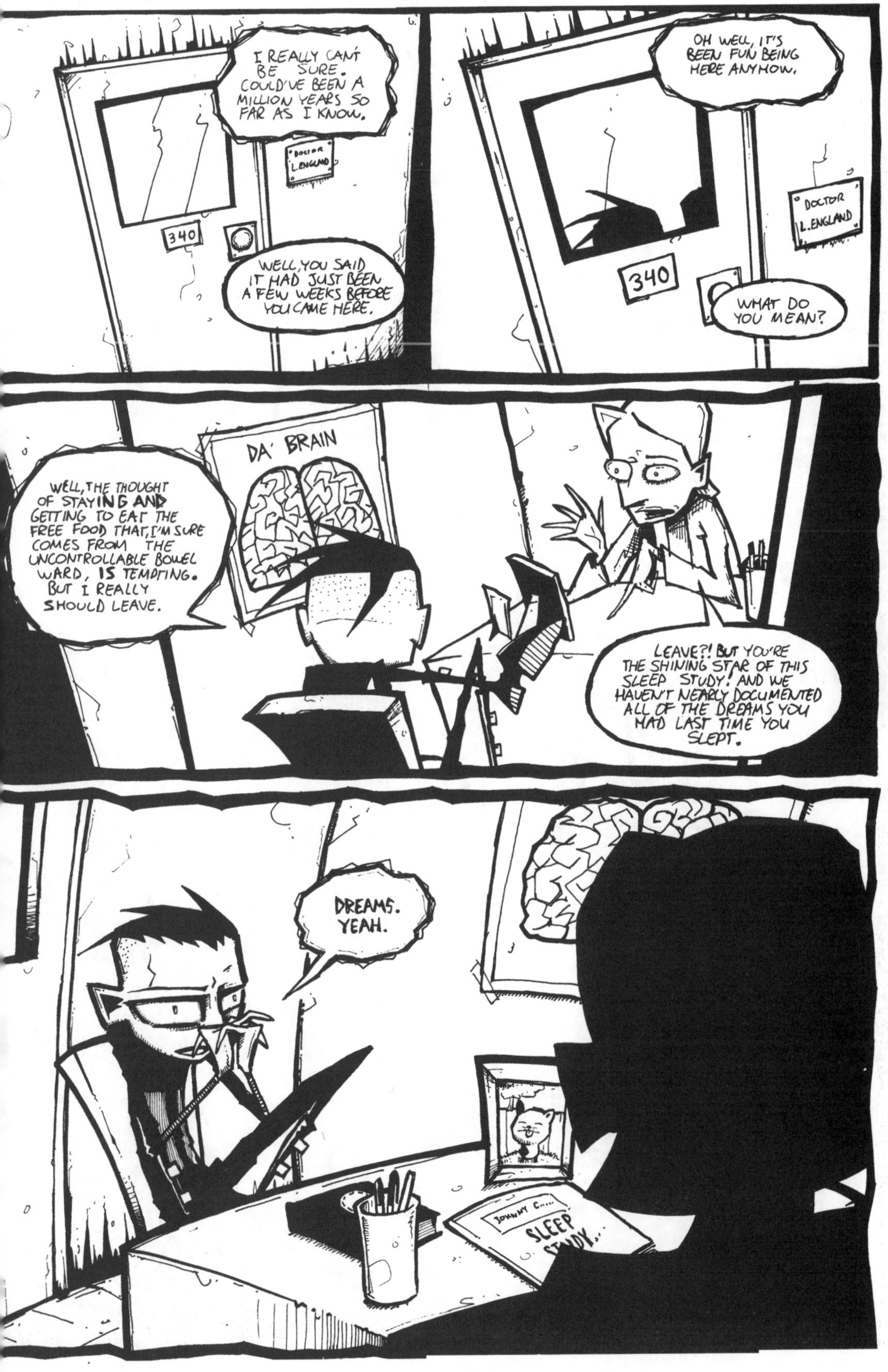
I REALLY CAN'T BE SURE. COULD'VE BEEN A MILLION YEARS SO FAR AS I KNOW.
DOCTOR L. ENGLAND
340
WELL, YOU SAID IT HAD JUST BEEN A FEW WEEKS BEFORE YOU CAME HERE.
OH WELL, IT'S BEEN FUN BEING HERE ANYHOW.
DOCTOR L. ENGLAND
340
WHAT DO YOU MEAN?
DA' BRAIN
WELL, THE THOUGHT OF STAYING AND GETTING TO EAT THE FREE FOOD THAT, I'M SURE COMES FROM THE UNCONTROLLABLE BOWEL WARD, IS TEMPTING. BUT I REALLY SHOULD LEAVE.
LEAVE?! BUT YOU'RE THE SHINING STAR OF THIS SLEEP STUDY! AND WE HAVEN'T NEARLY DOCUMENTED ALL OF THE DREAMS YOU HAD LAST TIME YOU SLEPT.
DREAMS. YEAH.
JOHNNY C.....
SLEEP STUDY..

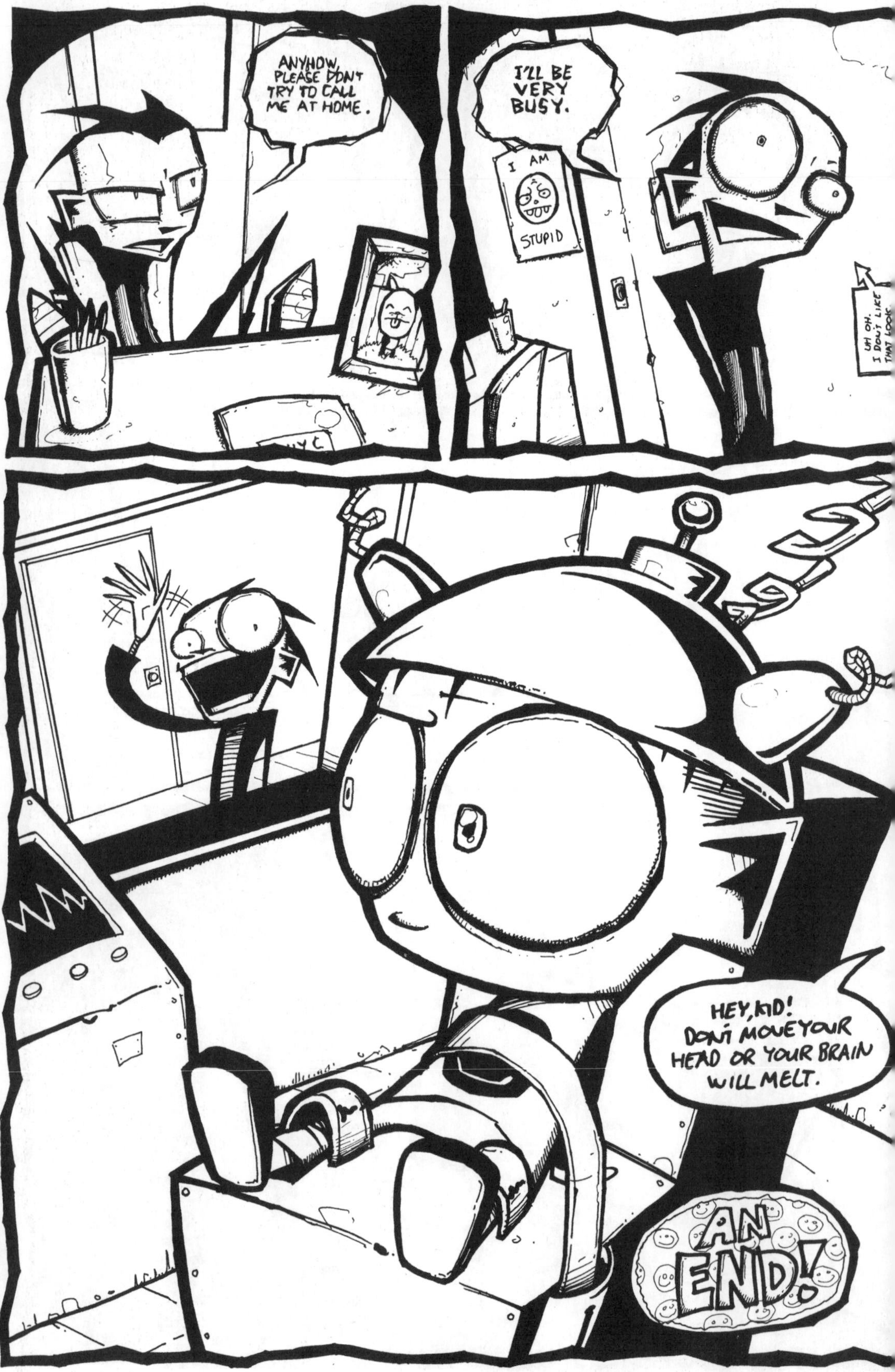

ANYHOW, PLEASE DON'T TRY TO CALL ME AT HOME.
I'LL BE VERY BUSY.
I AM STUPID
UH OH. I DON'T LIKE THAT LOOK.
HEY, KID! DON'T MOVE YOUR HEAD OR YOUR BRAIN WILL MELT.
AN END!

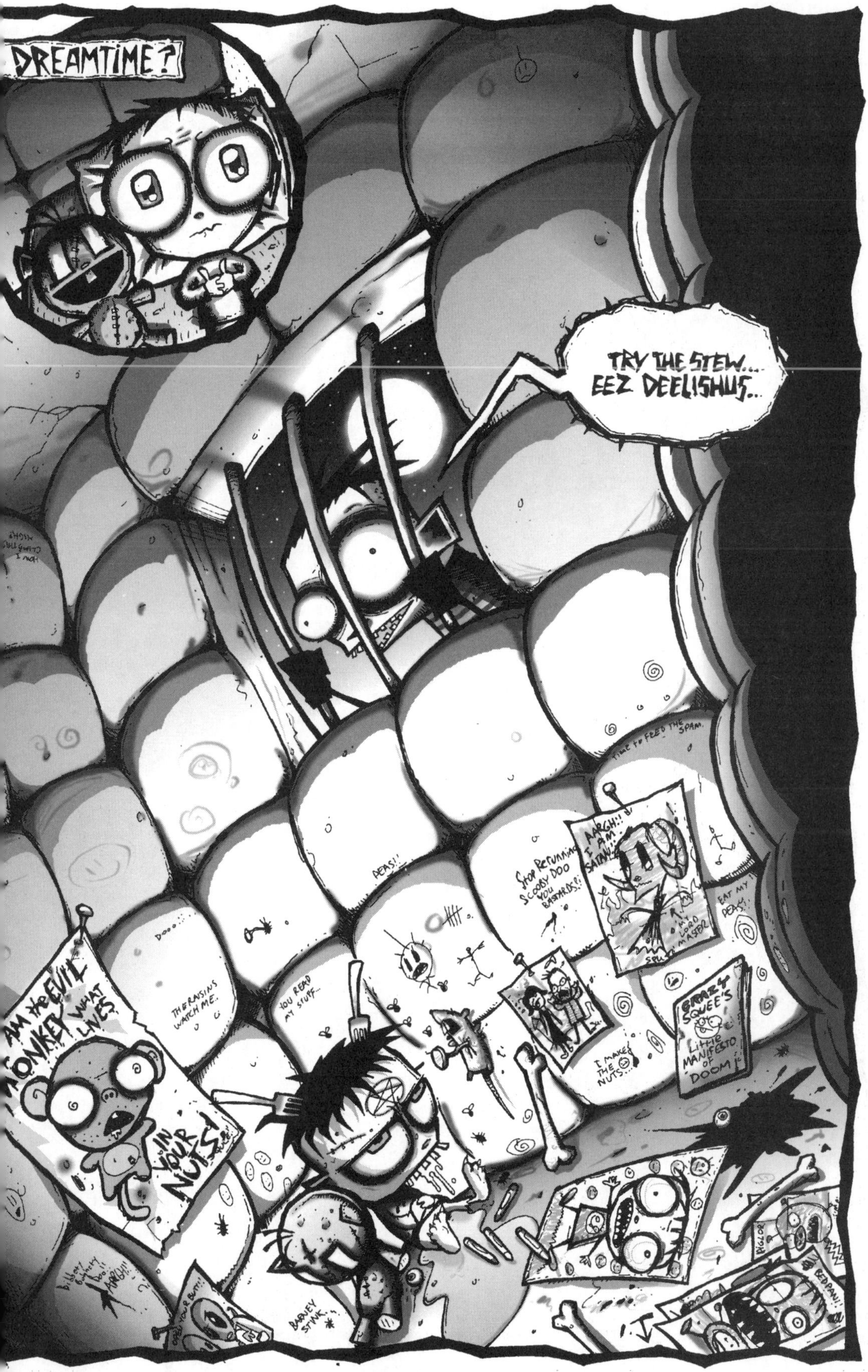
DREAMTIME?
TRY THE STEW... EEZ DEELISHUS..
TIME TO FEED THE SPAM.
AARGH!! I AM SATAN!
STOP RERUNNING SCOOBY DOO YOU BASTARDS!!
PEAS!!
EAT MY PEAS!
MY LORD MASTER
CRAZY SQUEE'S LITTLE MANIFESTO OF DOOM
I MAKE THE NUTS...
YOU READ MY STUFF...
THE RAISINS WATCH ME..
I AM THE EVIL MONKEY WHAT LIVES IN YOUR NUTS!
BARNEY STINK
BEDPAN!!
OPEN YOUR BUTT!

INTRODUCTION:
TAKE TWO...

OKAY, I'M FEELING MUCH BETTER THAN WHEN I WROTE THAT FIRST INTRO FOR
FIRST HALF OF THIS BOOK. IT'S UNFORTUNATE THAT I DID SUCH A TERRIBLE JOB
EXPRESSING THE DESIRED EFFECT FOR THAT HALF, AS IT'S THE PART OF THIS BOOK TH
MEANS THE MOST TO ME, WHAT WITH THE LITTLE KID BURITO THING. OH, GOD,
HAPPENING AGAIN...OKAY, MUST GET A HOLD OF MYSELF, OR I'LL JUST END UP TURN
THIS INTRODUCTION INTO A MASS OF MENTAL SPEWAGE LIKE THAT OTHER O

ALRIGHT, THIS IS GOOD, SEE? I STARTED OUT A NEW PARAGRAPH BEFORE THIN
GOT OUT OF HAND. YOU GIVE ME PRIZE NOW. SO, THIS ENTIRE SECOND HALF OF THE BO
IS DEVOTED TO THE VERY THINGS THAT KEEP ME "SANE" WHILE DOING ALL THOSE ISS
WITH SQUEE OR JOHNNY IN THEM. I AM NOT AT ALL PATIENT WITH DOING BOOK AF
BOOK OF THE SAME CHARACTER LOOKING THE SAME WAY AND BEING IN THE SAME WO
IT ONLY MAKES SENSE THAT I EXIT THEIR HORRIBLE REALITY AND HAVE FUN BY JUMP
INTO A DIFFERENT HORRIBLE REALITY, IF ONLY ONCE, AND FOR A MAXIMUM OF FOUR PA
THIS IS PRETTY MUCH WHY I CAME UP WITH THE MEANWHILE STORI

THE MEANWHILE STRIPS INCLUDED IN THIS COMPILATION OF LOVE INCLUDE EV
MEANWHILE DONE SINCE JOHNNY THE HOMICIDAL MANIAC #1, ALL THE WAY UP TO
FOURTH, AND LAST ISSUE OF SQUEE!, SO YOU JUST KNOW THIS BOOK WAS A BETTER
THAN THAT VIAL OF CRACK. THE IDEAS BEHIND THESE STORIES ARE THE KINDS OF IDE
THAT JUST PLAGUE MY MIND, MAKING ME TRY TO COMMUNICATE THEM, WITH FRIGHTEN
ENTHUSIASM, TO THE POOR SOULS UNFORTUNATE ENOUGH TO BE WITHIN EARSHOT OF
THIS IS THE KIND OF STUFF THAT PRETTY MUCH HITS ME IN THE MIDDLE OF THE NIG
AND SETS ME GIGGLING TO MYSELF UNTIL I PASS OUT, AS WAS THE CASE WITH THE TWO
HEADED VAMPIRE STORY. SO, BASICALLY, ANYTHING THAT GOES IN THE BOOKS THAT I
NO REAL RELATION TO THE TITLE CHARACTERS IS PUT IN THERE MORE FOR THE PURPOSE
QUIETING THE CACKLING IN MY HEAD THAN IT IS TO MAKE THE READERS SMILE. T
STUFF JUST BUILDS UP LIKE...CHILDREN, IF I DON'T GET IT OUT ON PAPER. MEANWHI
WOBBLY HEADED BOBS, TRUE TALES OF HUMAN DRAMA, AND HAPPY NOODLE BOYS (A
INCLUDED IN THIS COLLECTION) ALL ACT AS A SORT OF LUNACY PROTECTION, AS SITTI
AT A DRAWING TABLE 24 HOURS A DAY WITH NO HUMAN CONTACT CAN BEGIN TO H
..... ILL EFFECTS ON ONE'S MIND.

DESPITE MY SELFISH REASONS FOR DOING SUCH STORIES, IT WOULD SEEM THAT T
WERE SOME OF THE MOST POPULAR PARTS OF THE BOOKS WITH READERS, OFTEN TI
GETTING MORE ATTENTION THAN THE BOOKS' TITLE CHARACTERS THEMSELVES. THIS ANG
ME, AND MAKES ME KICK STRANGERS IN THE NUTS, REGARDLESS OF GENDER. WELL, PERH
NOT, BUT IT IS NICE TO KNOW THAT THEY FIND THE SHORT STRIPS TO BE AS AMUSING
I THINK THEY ARE. SOMETIMES I CAN JUST TELL WHICH THINGS WILL GET THAT ATTENT
SUCH AS WHEN THE LINE, "SOMEONE PUT SHIT IN MY PANTS!" POPPED INTO MY HEAD DUR
A CONVERSATION I HAD ABOUT STUPID EXCUSES FOR UNCONTROLLABLE INTESTINAL MOVEME
WITH A SHORT FRIEND OF MINE. I MENTION SHE WAS SHORT ONLY FOR THE FACT TH
SHE WAS PRETTY SHORT. SHE ALSO HAD AN ENORMOUS ASS. OKAY, I'M STARTING UP
THE TANGENT THING AGAIN, AND THIS INTRO WAS ACTUALLY GETTING PRETTY DEC
I CAN STILL TIE THIS IN TO THE POINT I WAS MAKING EARLIER THOUGH. SEE, IT'S QU
NECESSARY FOR ME TO GO OFF ON TANGENTS, BOTH MENTAL, AND ARTISTIC, OTHERWI
GO MAD, AND GET BORED OF THE ENTIRE PROCESS ENTIRELY.

YES, AS MENTIONED IN THE IN THAT LAST MASS OF SYLLABLES, THE WOBBLY HEA
BOB'S HAVE MADE IT INTO THIS COMPILATION OF MADNESS, AND THESE STRIPS GO AS
BACK AS THAT FIRST ISSUE OF JTHM AS WELL. SOME PEOPLE DIDN'T QUITE APPRECIA
THE FACT THAT BOTH THESE AND THE MEANWHILES WERE EXCLUDED FROM THE DIRECT
CUT OF JTHM, AND WROTE FIST SHAKINGLY FURIOUS LETTERS TO ME, THREATENING TO
SOMETHING. THE INTENT OF THAT COLLECTION WAS FOR IT TO BE A JOHNNY BOOK, DEAL
ONLY WITH THAT CHARACTER. I HAD ALWAYS INTENDED OF RELEASING THE REST OF
MATERIAL FROM THOSE BOOKS ALONG WITH THE SQUEE! SERIES, BUT THE PEOPLE W
IMPATIENT, AND ASKED TOO MUCH FROM ME. THIS SENT ME ON A TRIP INTO CRAZIN
FORCING ME TO BE SO RASH AS TO DO HORRIBLE THINGS, LIKE RESPOND TO E-MAIL.
ALAS, THE EVIL HAS SUBSIDED, AND HERE, YOU HOLD THE VERY THINGS THOSE MONST
WERE SO EAGER TO HAVE ALL THAT TIME AGO: PAGES AND PAGES OF PURE NONSE
AND REVOLTING SUBJECT MATTER!! YAAAY!

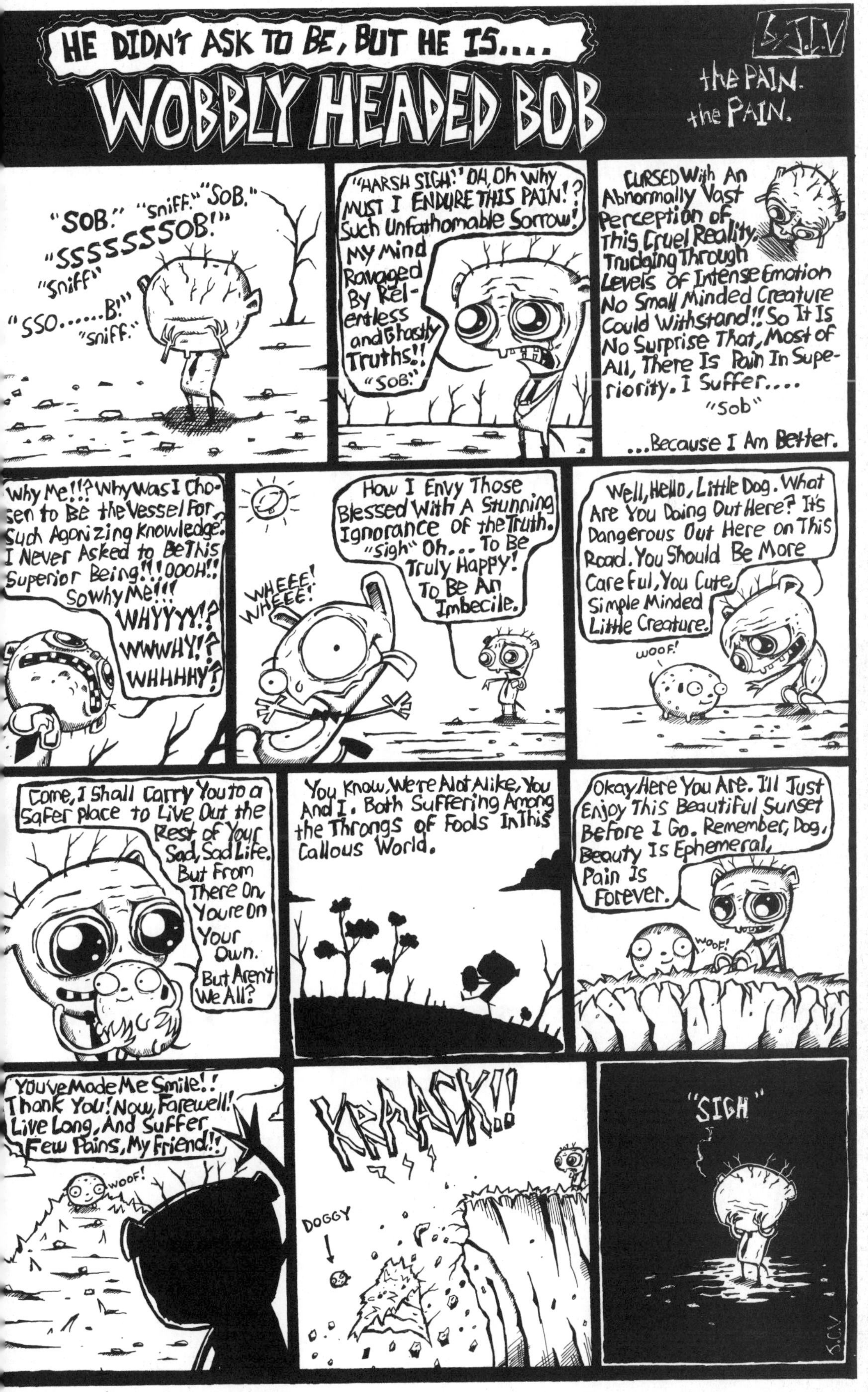
HE DIDN'T ASK TO BE, BUT HE IS....
WOBBLY HEADED BOB
the PAIN. the PAIN.
"SOB." "sniff." "SOB."
"SSSSSSSOB!"
"sniff"
"SSO......B!"
"sniff."
"HARSH SIGH!" OH, Oh Why MUST I ENDURE THIS PAIN!? Such Unfathomable Sorrow! My Mind Ravaged By Relentless and Ghastly Truths!! "SOB."
CURSED With An Abnormally Vast Perception of This Cruel Reality. Trudging Through Levels of Intense Emotion No Small Minded Creature Could Withstand!! So It Is No Surprise That, Most of All, There Is Pain In Superiority. I Suffer....
"Sob"
...Because I Am Better.
Why Me!!? Why Was I Chosen to Be the Vessel For Such Agonizing Knowledge? I Never Asked to Be This Superior Being!! OOOH!! So Why Me!!!
WHYYYY!? WWWHY!? WHHHHY!
How I Envy Those Blessed With A Stunning Ignorance of the Truth. "sigh" Oh... To Be Truly Happy! To Be An Imbecile.
WHEEE! WHEEE!
Well, Hello, Little Dog. What Are You Doing Out Here? It's Dangerous Out Here on This Road. You Should Be More Careful, You Cute, Simple Minded Little Creature.
WOOF!
Come, I Shall Carry You to a Safer place to Live Out the Rest of Your Sad, Sad Life. But From There On, You're On Your Own. But Aren't We All?
You Know, We're Alot Alike, You And I. Both Suffering Among the Throngs of Fools In This Callous World.
Okay Here You Are. I'll Just Enjoy This Beautiful Sunset Before I Go. Remember, Dog, Beauty Is Ephemeral, Pain Is Forever.
WOOF!
You've Made Me Smile!! Thank You! Now, Farewell! Live Long, And Suffer Few Pains, My Friend!!
WOOF!
KRRACK!!
DOGGY
"SIGH"
S.C.V.

Wobbly Headed Bob
oh, the sorrow.
by J.C.V
I LOVE YOU!!
I LOVE YOU!!
Woeful Deceit. Soon Will You Keep Each Other's Company Merely to Sustain Your Gutteral Carnal Desires. Enjoy Yourselves While Your Simple Lust is Veiled By Delusions of Complex Affections.
So You See, Ted, Suicide Isn't the Answer!!
Gee! I Guess You're Right!
So Brave to Prolong Your Obviously Wretched Existence. I Wish You Luck on What Will Likely Be A Sad Future.
I DID IT! I DID IT!!! A PERFECT SCORE ON MY SAT!! WHY, I MUST BE THE SMARTEST PERSON IN THE ENTIRE UNIVERSE!!
SAT PERFECT
Wow.
If You Actually Believe Your True Intelligence is Determined By Some Standardized System, Well, Then You Can't Be THAT Smart. The ability to quote memorized information Is hardly worth such joy.
OH, Our Beautiful Child!! So Fresh And Full of Inevitable Greatness!
A Doctor!! A Judge!! Maybe Even PRESIDENT!!
YOU DARE REVEL IN THIS HIDEOUS BEAST YOU HAVE SPAWNED, SO BLOATED WITH COUNTLESS WICKED FUTURES!! BLINDED MORONS, FOR ALL YOU KNOW, THIS CHILD OF YOURS MAY BE A VESSEL FOR SATAN!!
EEEEEEE!!
DOOMED TO WANDER THIS LAND, FOREVER A DISPENSER OF TRUTH!! WELL, NO MORE!! I HAVE MADE BLIND EYES SEE LIGHT, BUT NOW I TEND ONLY MY OWN TORMENT! I WILL JUMP!!!!
Jerk!
Bitch!
TEE EED!!
KILL IT!!
Oh, God, Will it Never End

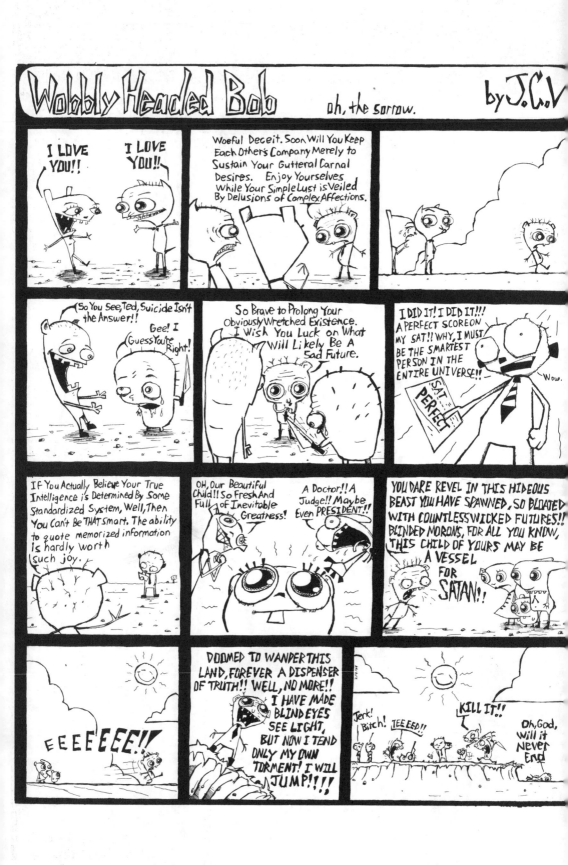

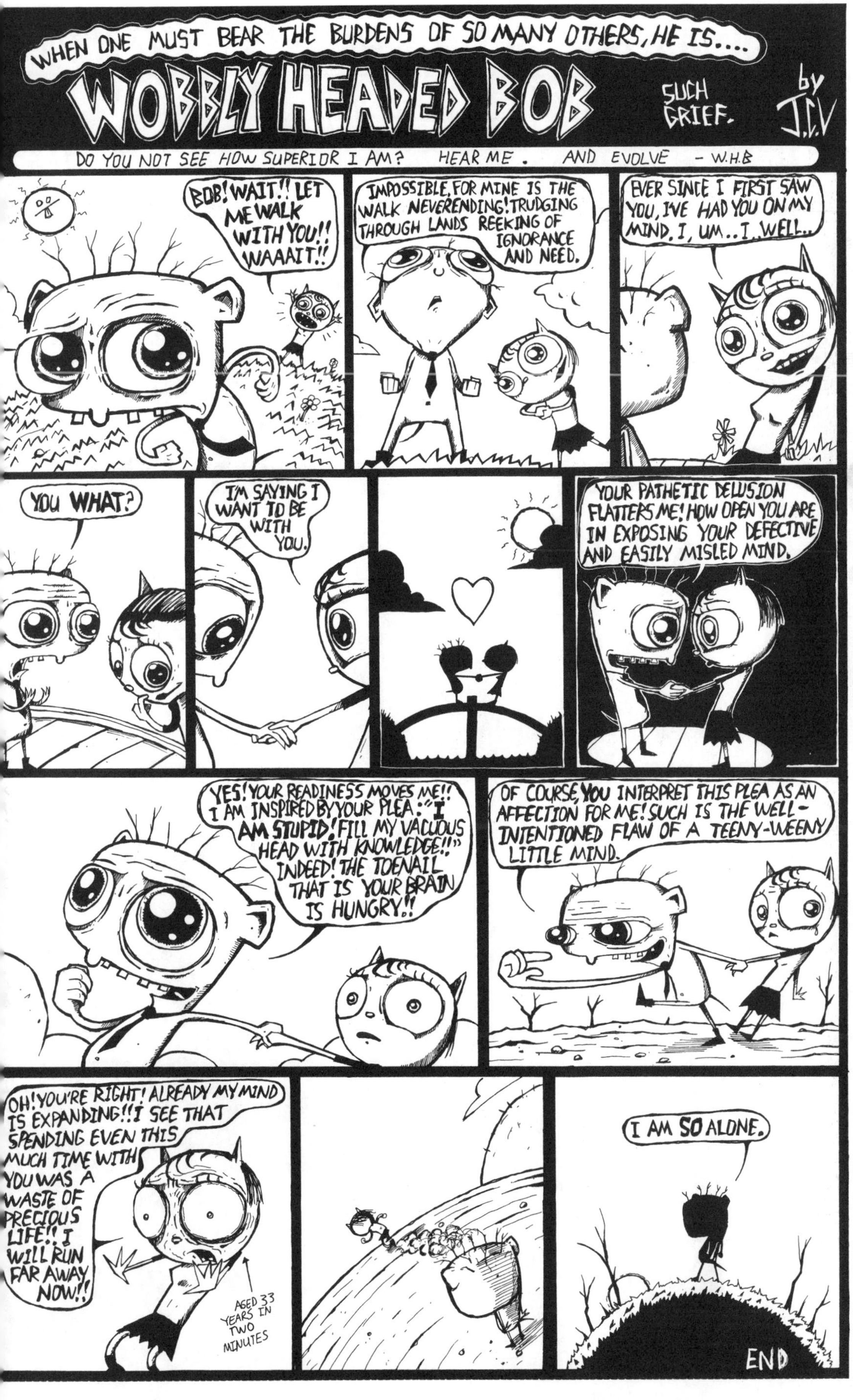
WHEN ONE MUST BEAR THE BURDENS OF SO MANY OTHERS, HE IS....
WOBBLY HEADED BOB
SUCH GRIEF.
by J.C.V
DO YOU NOT SEE HOW SUPERIOR I AM? HEAR ME. AND EVOLVE - W.H.B
BOB! WAIT!! LET ME WALK WITH YOU!! WAAAIT!!
IMPOSSIBLE, FOR MINE IS THE WALK NEVERENDING! TRUDGING THROUGH LANDS REEKING OF IGNORANCE AND NEED.
EVER SINCE I FIRST SAW YOU, I'VE HAD YOU ON MY MIND. I, UM.. I..WELL..
YOU WHAT?
I'M SAYING I WANT TO BE WITH YOU.
YOUR PATHETIC DELUSION FLATTERS ME! HOW OPEN YOU ARE IN EXPOSING YOUR DEFECTIVE AND EASILY MISLED MIND.
YES! YOUR READINESS MOVES ME!! I AM INSPIRED BY YOUR PLEA: "I AM STUPID! FILL MY VACUOUS HEAD WITH KNOWLEDGE!!" INDEED! THE TOENAIL THAT IS YOUR BRAIN IS HUNGRY!!
OF COURSE, YOU INTERPRET THIS PLEA AS AN AFFECTION FOR ME! SUCH IS THE WELL-INTENTIONED FLAW OF A TEENY-WEENY LITTLE MIND.
OH! YOU'RE RIGHT! ALREADY MY MIND IS EXPANDING!! I SEE THAT SPENDING EVEN THIS MUCH TIME WITH YOU WAS A WASTE OF PRECIOUS LIFE!! I WILL RUN FAR AWAY NOW!!
AGED 33 YEARS IN TWO MINUTES
I AM SO ALONE.
END

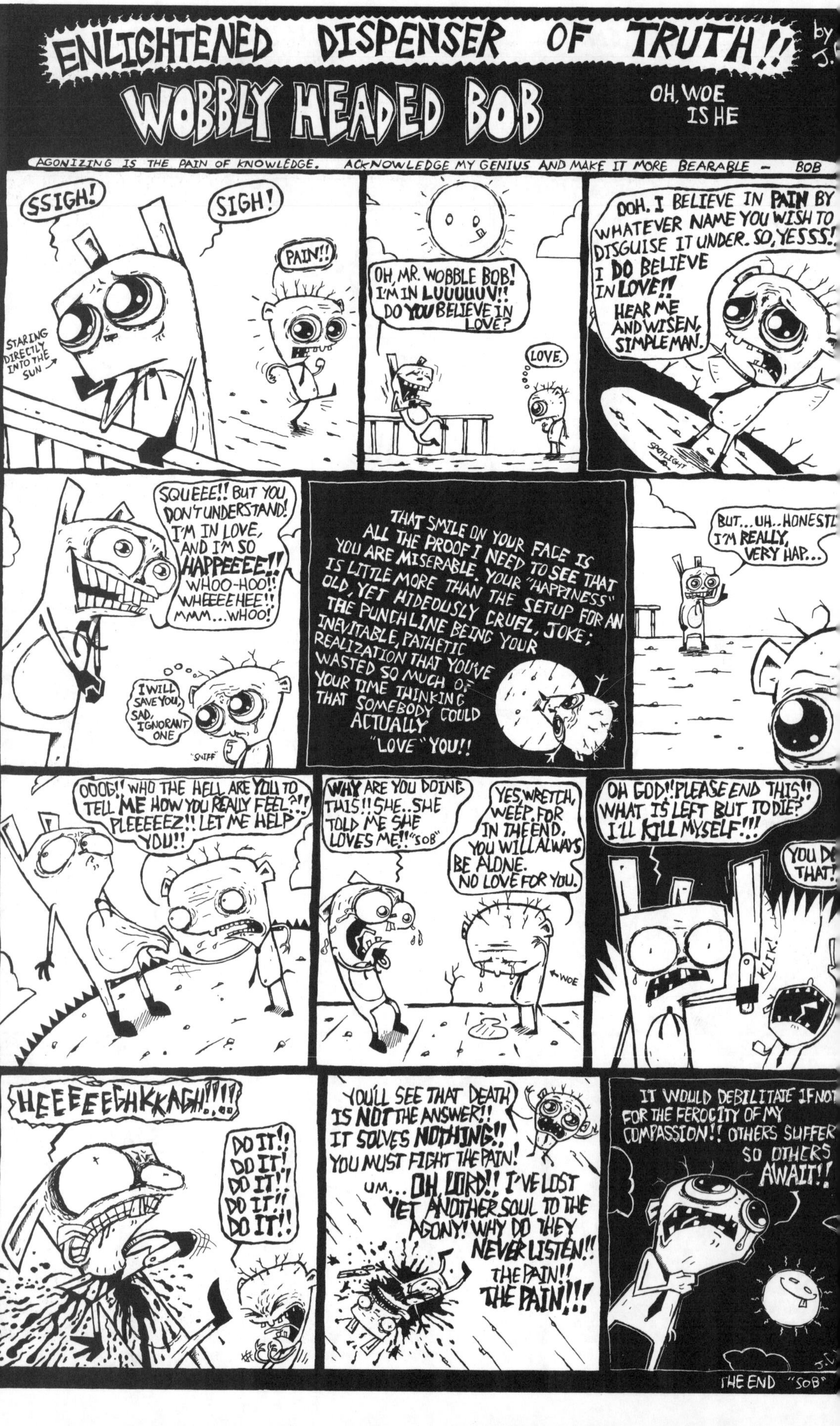
ENLIGHTENED DISPENSER OF TRUTH!!
WOBBLY HEADED BOB
OH, WOE IS HE
by J.
AGONIZING IS THE PAIN OF KNOWLEDGE. ACKNOWLEDGE MY GENIUS AND MAKE IT MORE BEARABLE - BOB
SSIGH!
SIGH!
PAIN!!
STARING DIRECTLY INTO THE SUN
OH, MR. WOBBLE BOB! I'M IN LUUUUUV!! DO YOU BELIEVE IN LOVE?
LOVE.
OOH. I BELIEVE IN PAIN BY WHATEVER NAME YOU WISH TO DISGUISE IT UNDER. SO, YESSS!! I DO BELIEVE IN LOVE!! HEAR ME AND WISEN, SIMPLE MAN.
SPOTLIGHT
SQUEEE!! BUT YOU DON'T UNDERSTAND! I'M IN LOVE, AND I'M SO HAPPEEEE!! WHOO-HOO!! WHEEEEHEE!! MMM...WHOO!
I WILL SAVE YOU, SAD, IGNORANT ONE
SNIFF
THAT SMILE ON YOUR FACE IS ALL THE PROOF I NEED TO SEE THAT YOU ARE MISERABLE. YOUR "HAPPINESS" IS LITTLE MORE THAN THE SET-UP FOR AN OLD, YET HIDEOUSLY CRUEL JOKE; THE PUNCHLINE BEING YOUR INEVITABLE, PATHETIC REALIZATION THAT YOU'VE WASTED SO MUCH OF YOUR TIME THINKING THAT SOMEBODY COULD ACTUALLY "LOVE" YOU!!
BUT...UH...HONESTL I'M REALLY, VERY HAP...
OOOG!! WHO THE HELL ARE YOU TO TELL ME HOW YOU REALLY FEEL?!! PLEEEEEZ!! LET ME HELP YOU!!
WHY ARE YOU DOING THIS!! SHE..SHE TOLD ME SHE LOVES ME!! "SOB"
YES, WRETCH, WEEP. FOR IN THE END, YOU WILL ALWAYS BE ALONE. NO LOVE FOR YOU.
WOE
OH GOD!! PLEASE END THIS!! WHAT IS LEFT BUT TO DIE? I'LL KILL MYSELF!!!
YOU D THAT!
KLIK!
HEEEEEGHKKAGH!!!!!
DO IT!! DO IT!! DO IT!! DO IT!! DO IT!!
YOU'LL SEE THAT DEATH IS NOT THE ANSWER!! IT SOLVES NOTHING!! YOU MUST FIGHT THE PAIN!
UM... OH, LORD!! I'VE LOST YET ANOTHER SOUL TO THE AGONY! WHY DO THEY NEVER LISTEN!! THE PAIN!! THE PAIN!!!
IT WOULD DEBILITATE IF NOT FOR THE FEROCITY OF MY COMPASSION!! OTHERS SUFFER SO OTHERS AWAIT!!
THE END "SOB"

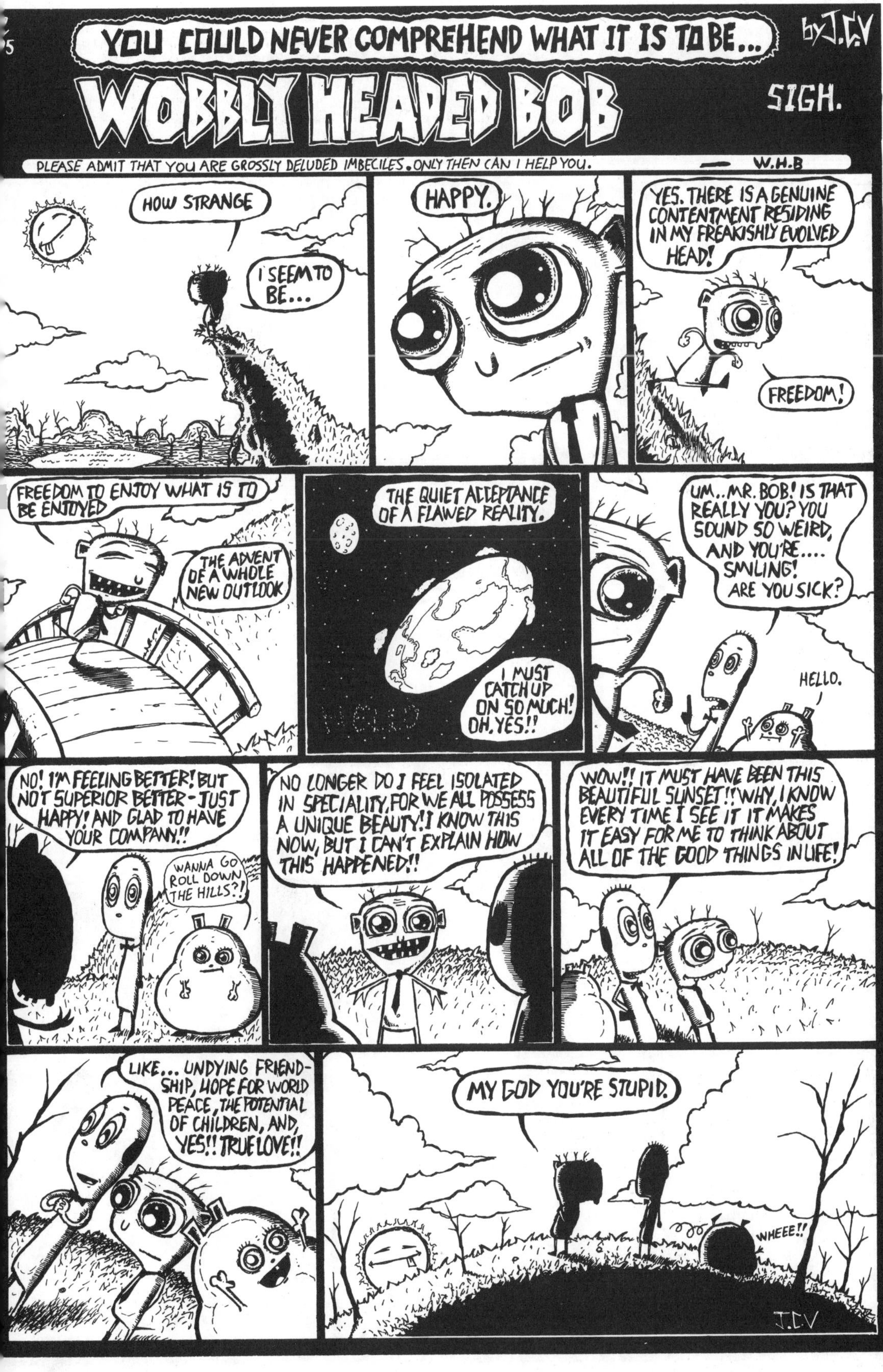
YOU COULD NEVER COMPREHEND WHAT IT IS TO BE...
by J.C.V
WOBBLY HEADED BOB
SIGH.
PLEASE ADMIT THAT YOU ARE GROSSLY DELUDED IMBECILES. ONLY THEN CAN I HELP YOU. — W.H.B
HOW STRANGE
I SEEM TO BE...
HAPPY.
YES. THERE IS A GENUINE CONTENTMENT RESIDING IN MY FREAKISHLY EVOLVED HEAD!
FREEDOM!
FREEDOM TO ENJOY WHAT IS TO BE ENJOYED
THE ADVENT OF A WHOLE NEW OUTLOOK
THE QUIET ACCEPTANCE OF A FLAWED REALITY.
I MUST CATCH UP ON SO MUCH! OH, YES!!
UM.. MR. BOB! IS THAT REALLY YOU? YOU SOUND SO WEIRD, AND YOU'RE.... SMILING! ARE YOU SICK?
HELLO.
NO! I'M FEELING BETTER! BUT NOT SUPERIOR BETTER - JUST HAPPY! AND GLAD TO HAVE YOUR COMPANY!!
WANNA GO ROLL DOWN THE HILLS?!
NO LONGER DO I FEEL ISOLATED IN SPECIALITY, FOR WE ALL POSSESS A UNIQUE BEAUTY! I KNOW THIS NOW, BUT I CAN'T EXPLAIN HOW THIS HAPPENED!!
WOW!! IT MUST HAVE BEEN THIS BEAUTIFUL SUNSET!! WHY, I KNOW EVERY TIME I SEE IT IT MAKES IT EASY FOR ME TO THINK ABOUT ALL OF THE GOOD THINGS IN LIFE!
LIKE... UNDYING FRIEND-SHIP, HOPE FOR WORLD PEACE, THE POTENTIAL OF CHILDREN, AND, YES!! TRUE LOVE!!
MY GOD YOU'RE STUPID.
WHEEE!!
J.C.V

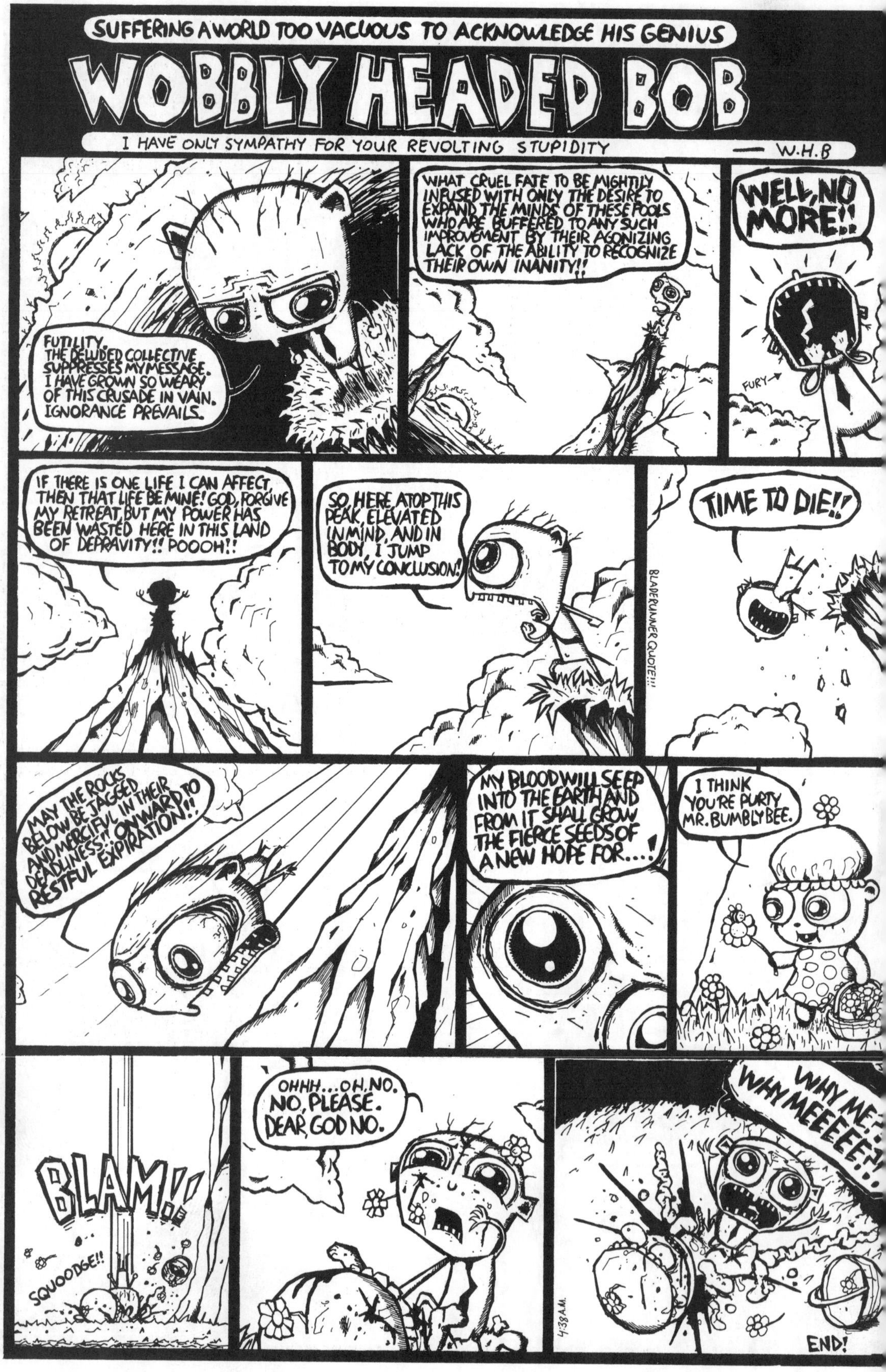
SUFFERING A WORLD TOO VACUOUS TO ACKNOWLEDGE HIS GENIUS
WOBBLY HEADED BOB
I HAVE ONLY SYMPATHY FOR YOUR REVOLTING STUPIDITY — W.H.B
FUTILITY. THE DELUDED COLLECTIVE SUPPRESSES MY MESSAGE. I HAVE GROWN SO WEARY OF THIS CRUSADE IN VAIN. IGNORANCE PREVAILS.
WHAT CRUEL FATE TO BE MIGHTILY INFUSED WITH ONLY THE DESIRE TO EXPAND THE MINDS OF THESE FOOLS WHO ARE BUFFERED TO ANY SUCH IMPROVEMENT BY THEIR AGONIZING LACK OF THE ABILITY TO RECOGNIZE THEIR OWN INANITY!!
WELL, NO MORE!!
FURY
IF THERE IS ONE LIFE I CAN AFFECT, THEN THAT LIFE BE MINE! GOD, FORGIVE MY RETREAT, BUT MY POWER HAS BEEN WASTED HERE IN THIS LAND OF DEPRAVITY!! POOOH!!
SO, HERE ATOP THIS PEAK, ELEVATED IN MIND, AND IN BODY, I JUMP TO MY CONCLUSION!
BLADERUNNER QUOTE!!!
TIME TO DIE!!
MAY THE ROCKS BELOW BE JAGGED AND MERCIFUL IN THEIR DEADLINESS!! ONWARD TO RESTFUL EXPIRATION!!
MY BLOOD WILL SEEP INTO THE EARTH AND FROM IT SHALL GROW THE FIERCE SEEDS OF A NEW HOPE FOR....!
I THINK YOU'RE PURTY MR. BUMBLY BEE.
BLAM!!
SQUOODGE!!
OHHH...OH, NO. NO, PLEASE. DEAR, GOD NO.
4:38 A.M.
WHY ME!... WHY MEEEEEE?!!
END!

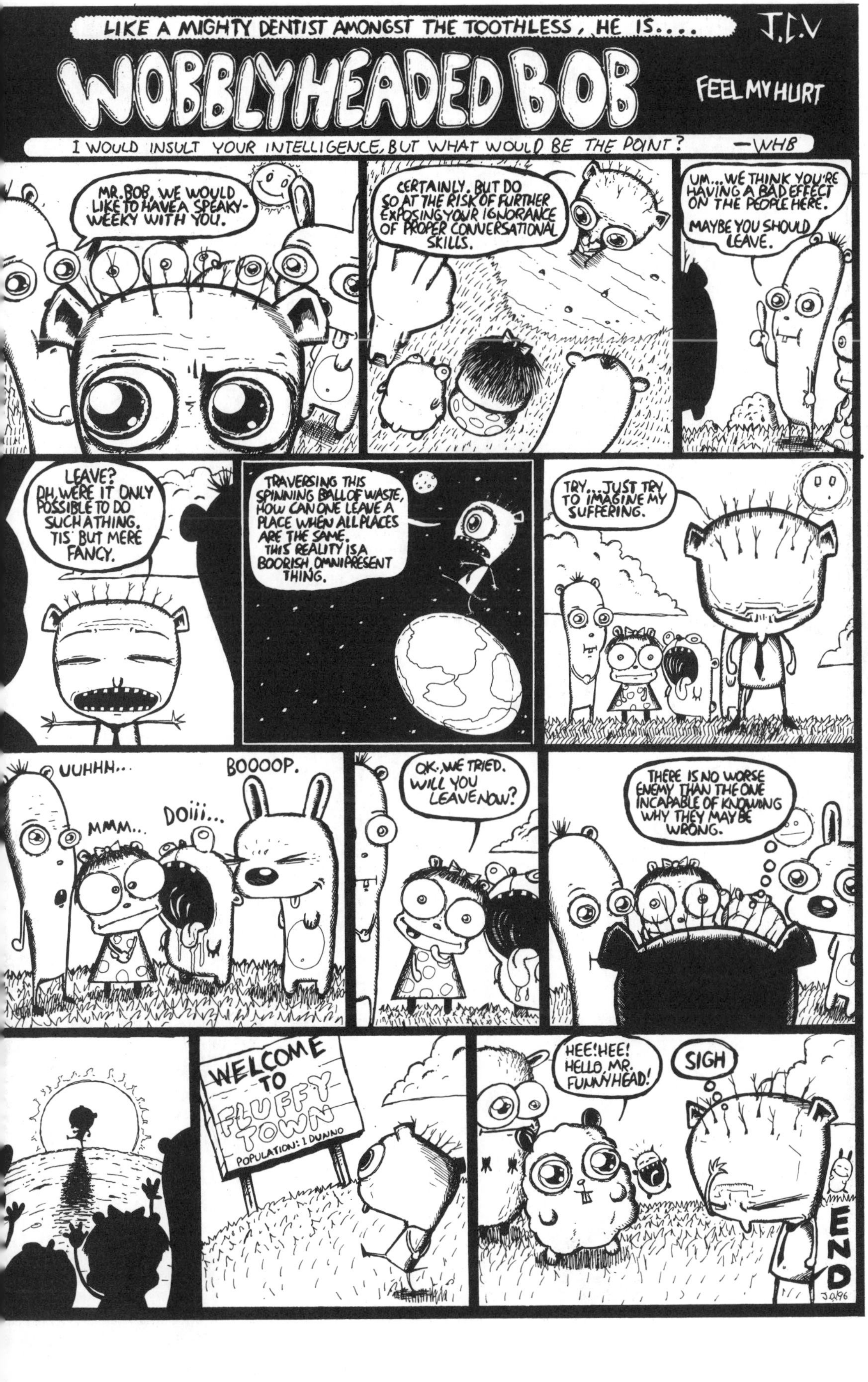
LIKE A MIGHTY DENTIST AMONGST THE TOOTHLESS, HE IS....
J.C.V
WOBBLYHEADED BOB
FEEL MY HURT
I WOULD INSULT YOUR INTELLIGENCE, BUT WHAT WOULD BE THE POINT? —WHB
MR. BOB, WE WOULD LIKE TO HAVE A SPEAKY-WEEKY WITH YOU.
CERTAINLY. BUT DO SO AT THE RISK OF FURTHER EXPOSING YOUR IGNORANCE OF PROPER CONVERSATIONAL SKILLS.
UM...WE THINK YOU'RE HAVING A BAD EFFECT ON THE PEOPLE HERE.
MAYBE YOU SHOULD LEAVE.
LEAVE? OH, WERE IT ONLY POSSIBLE TO DO SUCH A THING. TIS' BUT MERE FANCY.
TRAVERSING THIS SPINNING BALL OF WASTE, HOW CAN ONE LEAVE A PLACE WHEN ALL PLACES ARE THE SAME. THIS REALITY IS A BOORISH, OMNIPRESENT THING.
TRY...JUST TRY TO IMAGINE MY SUFFERING.
UUHHH...
BOOOOP.
MMM...
DOiii...
OK, WE TRIED. WILL YOU LEAVE NOW?
THERE IS NO WORSE ENEMY THAN THE ONE INCAPABLE OF KNOWING WHY THEY MAY BE WRONG.
WELCOME TO FLUFFY TOWN
POPULATION: I DUNNO
HEE! HEE! HELLO, MR. FUNNYHEAD!
SIGH
END
J.O.96

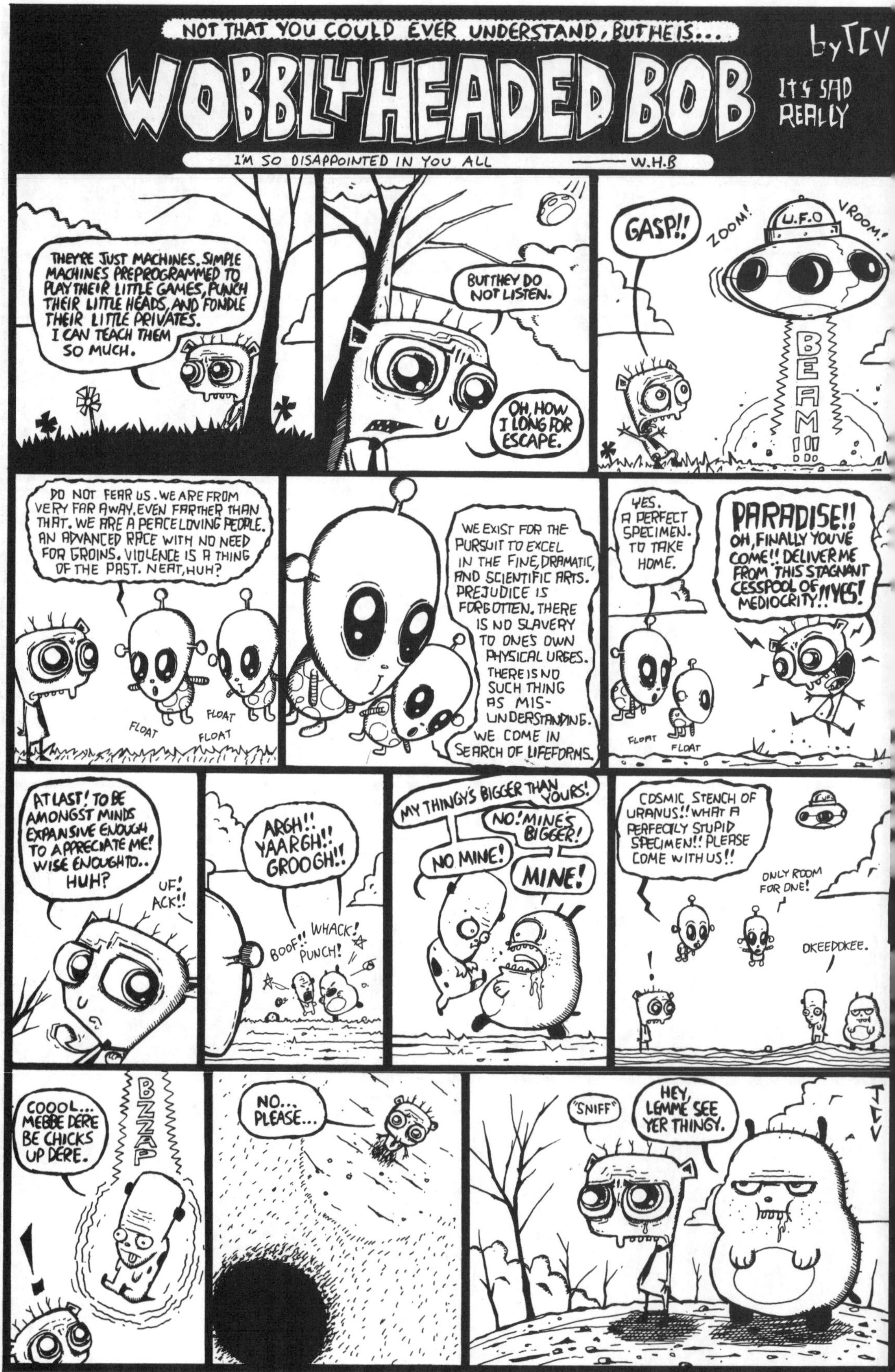
NOT THAT YOU COULD EVER UNDERSTAND, BUT HE IS...
WOBBLY HEADED BOB
by JCV
IT'S SAD REALLY
I'M SO DISAPPOINTED IN YOU ALL —— W.H.B
THEY'RE JUST MACHINES. SIMPLE MACHINES PREPROGRAMMED TO PLAY THEIR LITTLE GAMES, PUNCH THEIR LITTLE HEADS, AND FONDLE THEIR LITTLE PRIVATES. I CAN TEACH THEM SO MUCH.
BUT THEY DO NOT LISTEN.
OH, HOW I LONG FOR ESCAPE.
GASP!!
ZOOM!
VROOM!
U.F.O
BEAM!!!
DO NOT FEAR US. WE ARE FROM VERY FAR AWAY. EVEN FARTHER THAN THAT. WE ARE A PEACE LOVING PEOPLE. AN ADVANCED RACE WITH NO NEED FOR GROINS. VIOLENCE IS A THING OF THE PAST. NEAT, HUH?
FLOAT
FLOAT
FLOAT
WE EXIST FOR THE PURSUIT TO EXCEL IN THE FINE, DRAMATIC, AND SCIENTIFIC ARTS. PREJUDICE IS FORGOTTEN. THERE IS NO SLAVERY TO ONE'S OWN PHYSICAL URGES. THERE IS NO SUCH THING AS MIS-UNDERSTANDING. WE COME IN SEARCH OF LIFEFORMS.
YES. A PERFECT SPECIMEN. TO TAKE HOME.
FLOAT
FLOAT
PARADISE!! OH, FINALLY YOU'VE COME!! DELIVER ME FROM THIS STAGNANT CESSPOOL OF MEDIOCRITY!! YES!
AT LAST! TO BE AMONGST MINDS EXPANSIVE ENOUGH TO APPRECIATE ME! WISE ENOUGH TO.. HUH?
UF! ACK!!
ARGH!! YAARGH!! GROOGH!!
BOOF!! WHACK! PUNCH!
MY THINGY'S BIGGER THAN YOURS!
NO! MINE'S BIGGER!
NO MINE!
MINE!
COSMIC STENCH OF URANUS!! WHAT A PERFECTLY STUPID SPECIMEN!! PLEASE COME WITH US!!
ONLY ROOM FOR ONE!
OKEEDOKEE.
!
COOOL... MEBBE DERE BE CHICKS UP DERE.
BZZAP
!
NO... PLEASE...
"SNIFF"
HEY, LEMME SEE YER THINGY.
JCV

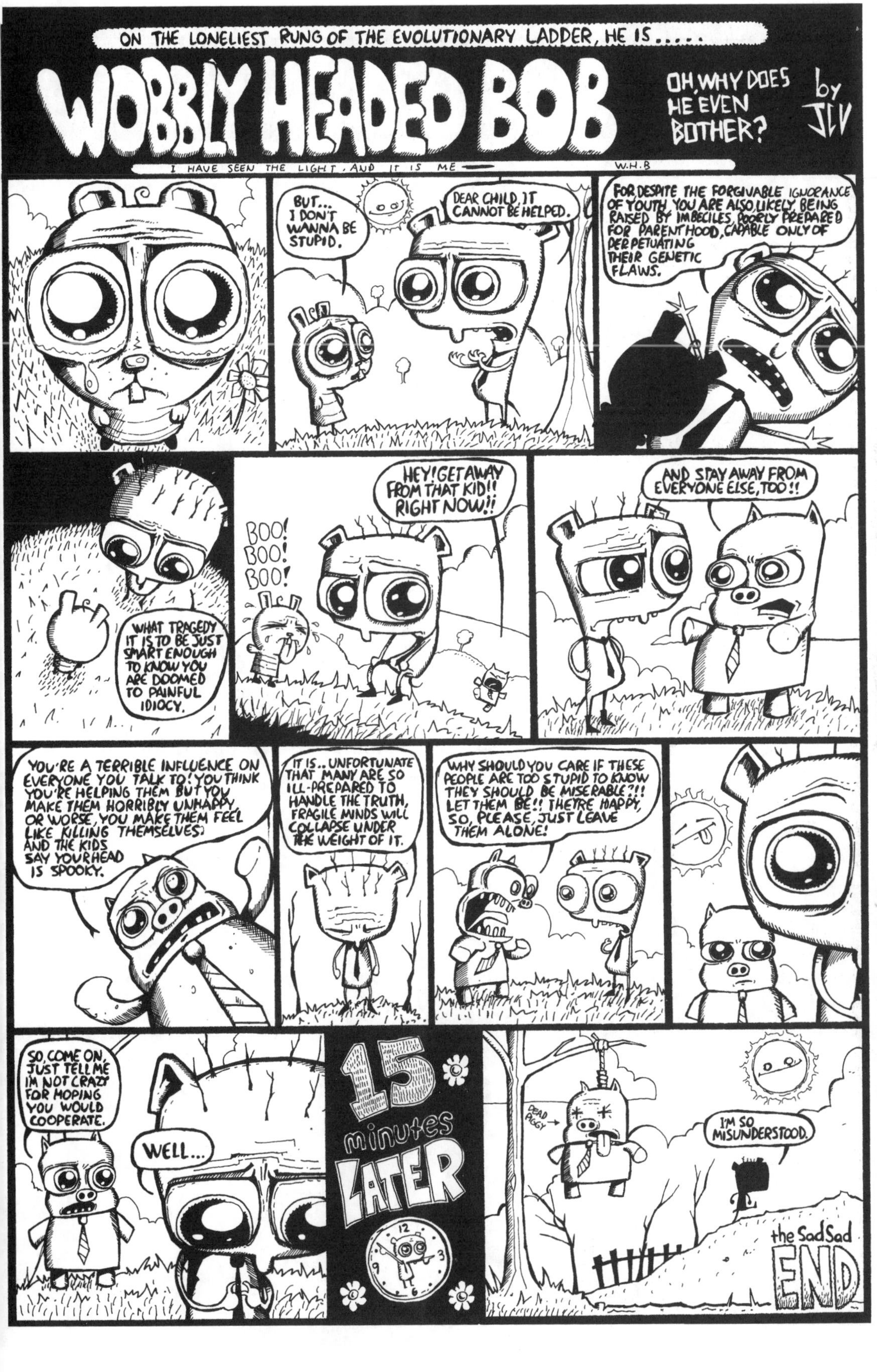
ON THE LONELIEST RUNG OF THE EVOLUTIONARY LADDER, HE IS.....
WOBBLY HEADED BOB
OH, WHY DOES HE EVEN BOTHER?
by JLV
I HAVE SEEN THE LIGHT, AND IT IS ME — W.H.B
BUT... I DON'T WANNA BE STUPID.
DEAR CHILD, IT CANNOT BE HELPED.
FOR DESPITE THE FORGIVABLE IGNORANCE OF YOUTH, YOU ARE ALSO LIKELY BEING RAISED BY IMBECILES, POORLY PREPARED FOR PARENTHOOD, CAPABLE ONLY OF PERPETUATING THEIR GENETIC FLAWS.
WHAT TRAGEDY IT IS TO BE JUST SMART ENOUGH TO KNOW YOU ARE DOOMED TO PAINFUL IDIOCY.
BOO! BOO! BOO!
HEY! GET AWAY FROM THAT KID!! RIGHT NOW!!
AND STAY AWAY FROM EVERYONE ELSE, TOO!!
YOU'RE A TERRIBLE INFLUENCE ON EVERYONE YOU TALK TO! YOU THINK YOU'RE HELPING THEM BUT YOU MAKE THEM HORRIBLY UNHAPPY, OR WORSE, YOU MAKE THEM FEEL LIKE KILLING THEMSELVES! AND THE KIDS SAY YOUR HEAD IS SPOOKY.
IT IS... UNFORTUNATE THAT MANY ARE SO ILL-PREPARED TO HANDLE THE TRUTH. FRAGILE MINDS WILL COLLAPSE UNDER THE WEIGHT OF IT.
WHY SHOULD YOU CARE IF THESE PEOPLE ARE TOO STUPID TO KNOW THEY SHOULD BE MISERABLE?!! LET THEM BE!! THEY'RE HAPPY, SO, PLEASE, JUST LEAVE THEM ALONE!
SO, COME ON, JUST TELL ME I'M NOT CRAZY FOR HOPING YOU WOULD COOPERATE.
WELL...
15 minutes LATER
DEAD PIGGY
I'M SO MISUNDERSTOOD.
the Sad Sad END

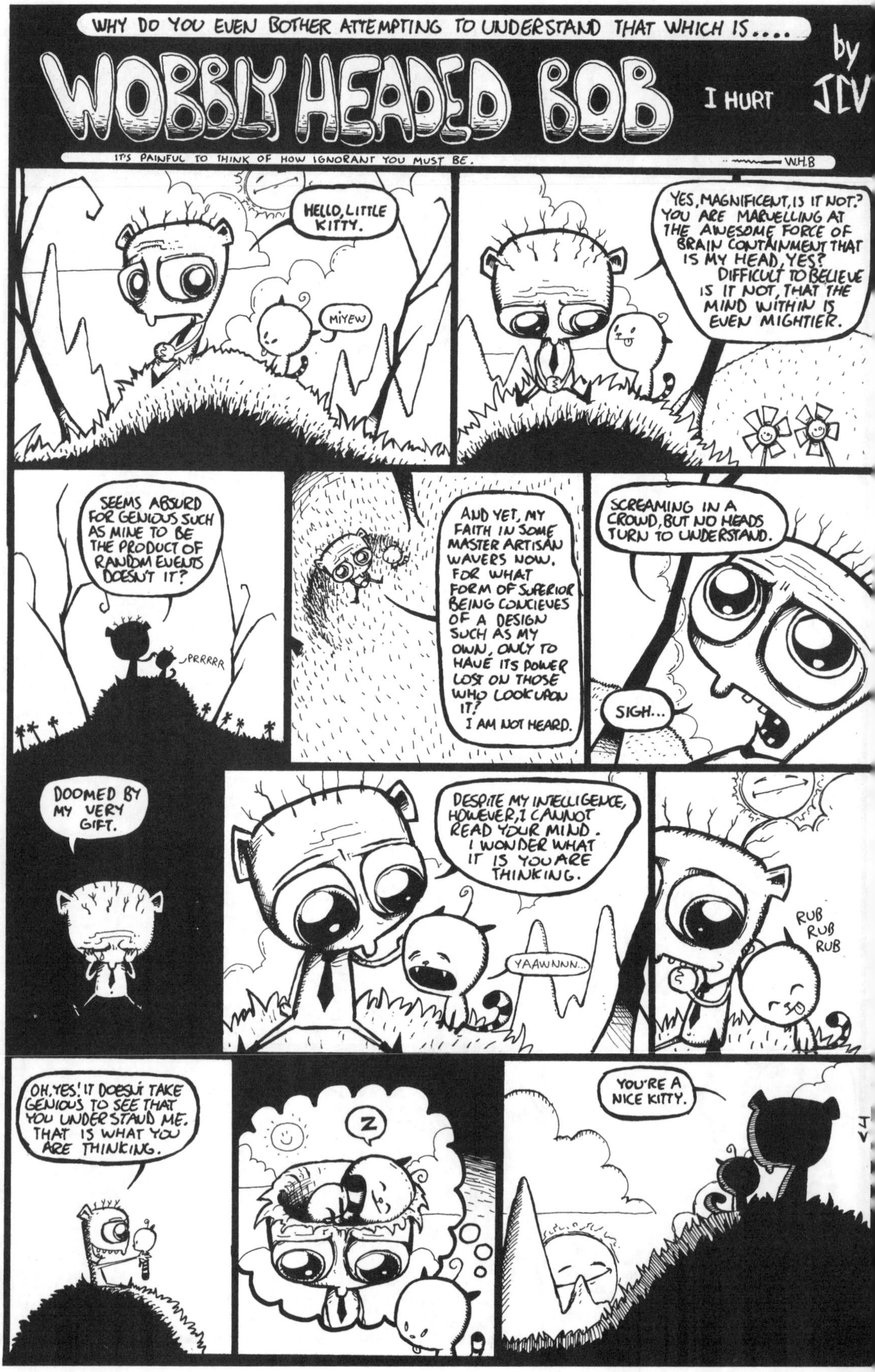
WHY DO YOU EVEN BOTHER ATTEMPTING TO UNDERSTAND THAT WHICH IS....
WOBBLY HEADED BOB
I HURT
by JCV
IT'S PAINFUL TO THINK OF HOW IGNORANT YOU MUST BE.
W.H.B
HELLO, LITTLE KITTY.
MIYEW
YES, MAGNIFICENT, IS IT NOT? YOU ARE MARVELLING AT THE AWESOME FORCE OF BRAIN CONTAINMENT THAT IS MY HEAD, YES? DIFFICULT TO BELIEVE IS IT NOT, THAT THE MIND WITHIN IS EVEN MIGHTIER.
SEEMS ABSURD FOR GENIOUS SUCH AS MINE TO BE THE PRODUCT OF RANDOM EVENTS DOESN'T IT?
PRRRRR
AND YET, MY FAITH IN SOME MASTER ARTISAN WAVERS NOW. FOR WHAT FORM OF SUPERIOR BEING CONCIEVES OF A DESIGN SUCH AS MY OWN, ONLY TO HAVE ITS POWER LOST ON THOSE WHO LOOK UPON IT? I AM NOT HEARD.
SCREAMING IN A CROWD, BUT NO HEADS TURN TO UNDERSTAND.
SIGH...
DOOMED BY MY VERY GIFT.
DESPITE MY INTELLIGENCE, HOWEVER, I CANNOT READ YOUR MIND. I WONDER WHAT IT IS YOU ARE THINKING.
YAAWNNN...
RUB RUB RUB
OH, YES! IT DOESN'T TAKE GENIOUS TO SEE THAT YOU UNDERSTAND ME. THAT IS WHAT YOU ARE THINKING.
Z
YOU'RE A NICE KITTY.

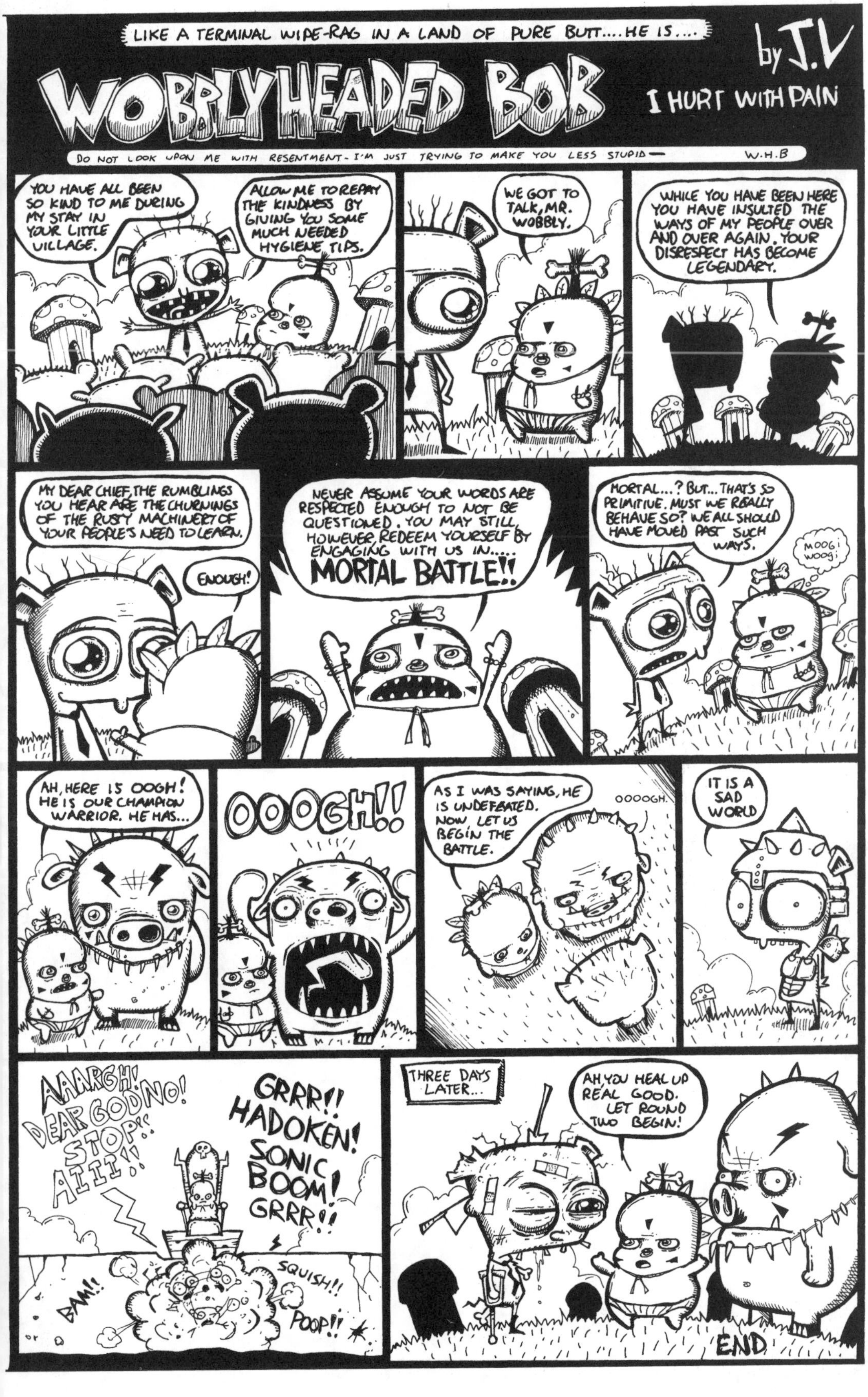

LIKE A TERMINAL WIPE-RAG IN A LAND OF PURE BUTT.... HE IS....
WOBBLYHEADED BOB
by J.V
I HURT WITH PAIN
DO NOT LOOK UPON ME WITH RESENTMENT - I'M JUST TRYING TO MAKE YOU LESS STUPID —
W.H.B
YOU HAVE ALL BEEN SO KIND TO ME DURING MY STAY IN YOUR LITTLE VILLAGE.
ALLOW ME TO REPAY THE KINDNESS BY GIVING YOU SOME MUCH NEEDED HYGIENE TIPS.
WE GOT TO TALK, MR. WOBBLY.
WHILE YOU HAVE BEEN HERE YOU HAVE INSULTED THE WAYS OF MY PEOPLE OVER AND OVER AGAIN. YOUR DISRESPECT HAS BECOME LEGENDARY.
MY DEAR CHIEF, THE RUMBLINGS YOU HEAR ARE THE CHURNINGS OF THE RUSTY MACHINERY OF YOUR PEOPLE'S NEED TO LEARN.
ENOUGH!
NEVER ASSUME YOUR WORDS ARE RESPECTED ENOUGH TO NOT BE QUESTIONED. YOU MAY STILL, HOWEVER, REDEEM YOURSELF BY ENGAGING WITH US IN..... MORTAL BATTLE!!
MORTAL...? BUT... THAT'S SO PRIMITIVE. MUST WE REALLY BEHAVE SO? WE ALL SHOULD HAVE MOVED PAST SUCH WAYS.
MOOGI WOOGI
AH, HERE IS OOGH! HE IS OUR CHAMPION WARRIOR. HE HAS...
OOOGH!!
AS I WAS SAYING, HE IS UNDEFEATED. NOW, LET US BEGIN THE BATTLE.
OOOOGH.
IT IS A SAD WORLD
AAARGH! DEAR GOD NO! STOP!! AIII!!
GRRR!! HADOKEN! SONIC BOOM! GRRR!!
BAM!!
SQUISH!!
POOP!!
THREE DAYS LATER...
AH, YOU HEAL UP REAL GOOD. LET ROUND TWO BEGIN!
END

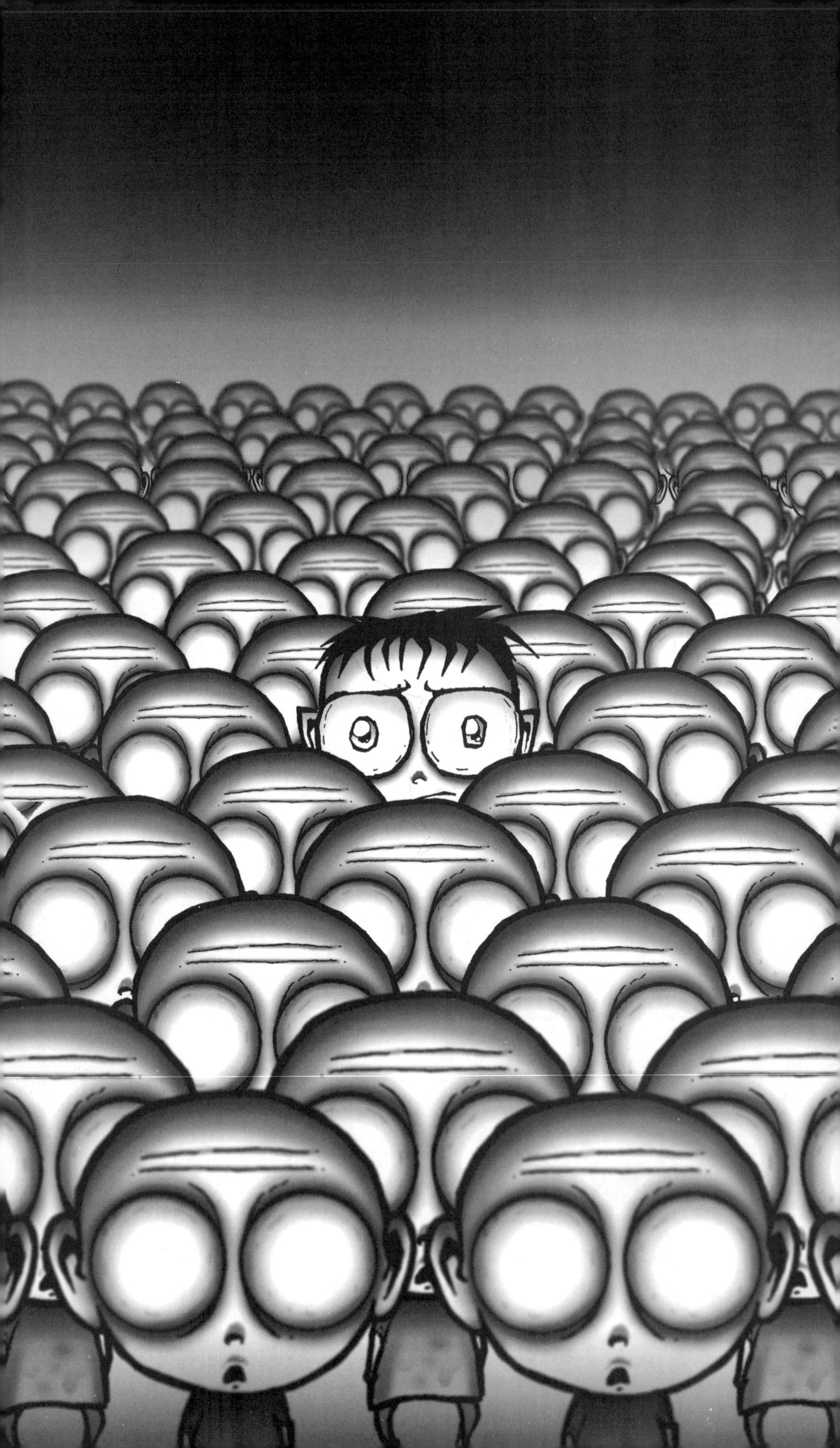

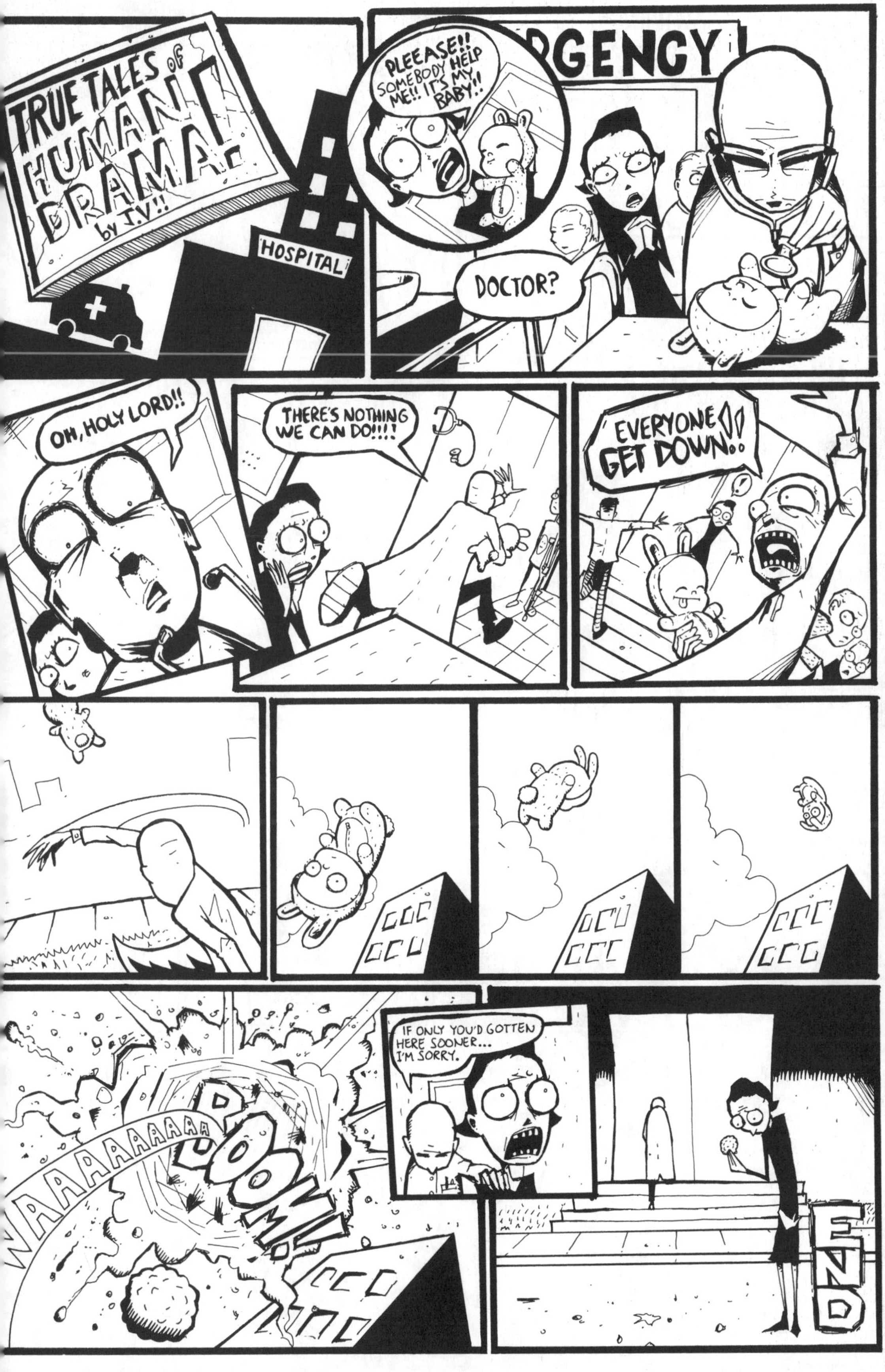
TRUE TALES of HUMAN DRAMA! by J.V.!!
HOSPITAL
PLEEASE!! SOMEBODY HELP ME!! IT'S MY BABY!!
RGENCY
DOCTOR?
OH, HOLY LORD!!
THERE'S NOTHING WE CAN DO!!!!
EVERYONE!! GET DOWN!!
WAAAAAAAA
BOOM!
IF ONLY YOU'D GOTTEN HERE SOONER... I'M SORRY.
END

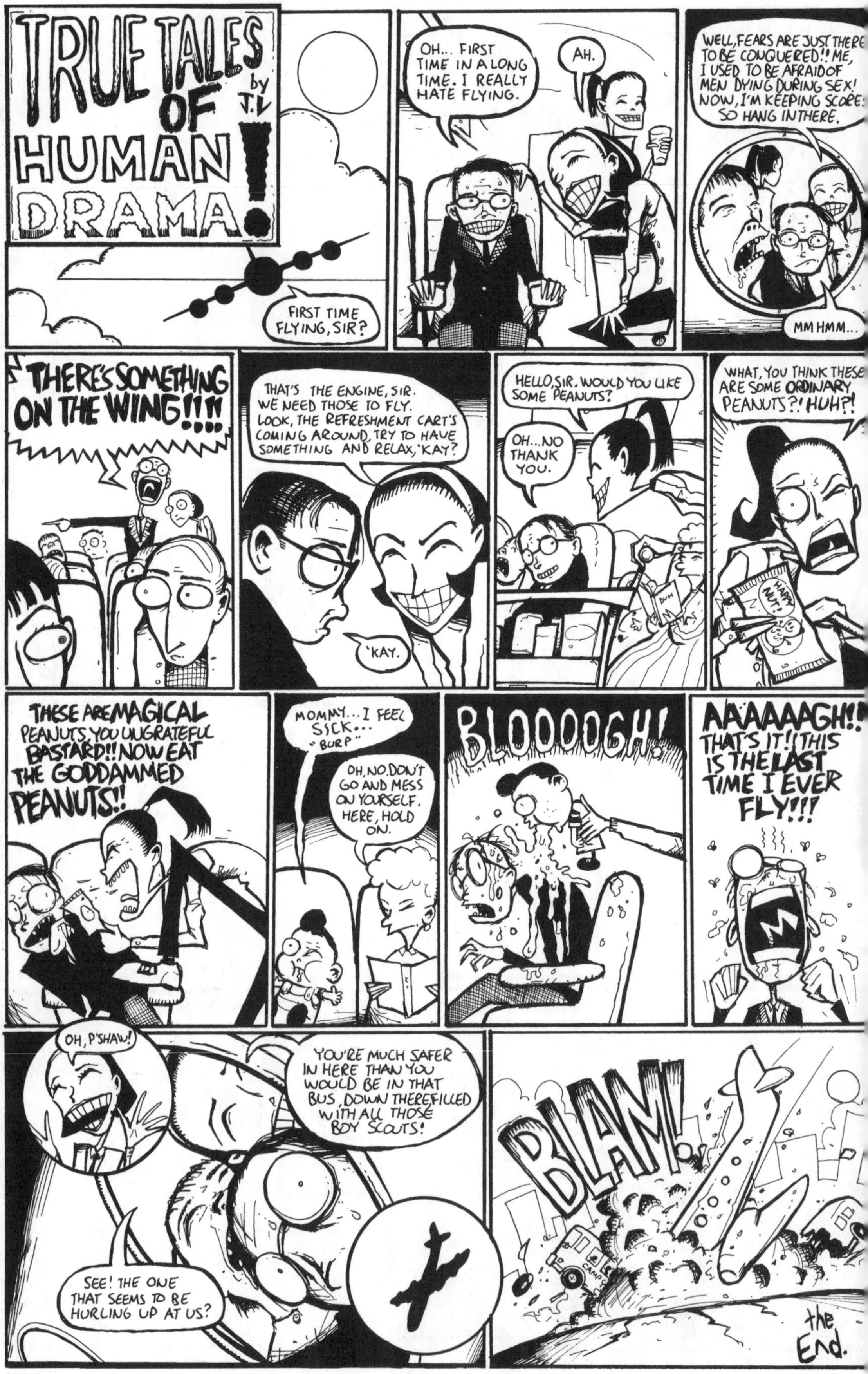
TRUE TALES OF HUMAN DRAMA!
by J.V
FIRST TIME FLYING, SIR?
OH... FIRST TIME IN A LONG TIME. I REALLY HATE FLYING.
AH.
WELL, FEARS ARE JUST THERE TO BE CONQUERED!! ME, I USED TO BE AFRAID OF MEN DYING DURING SEX! NOW, I'M KEEPING SCORE! SO HANG IN THERE.
MM HMM...
THERE'S SOMETHING ON THE WING!!!!!!!
THAT'S THE ENGINE, SIR. WE NEED THOSE TO FLY. LOOK, THE REFRESHMENT CART'S COMING AROUND, TRY TO HAVE SOMETHING AND RELAX, 'KAY?
'KAY.
HELLO, SIR. WOULD YOU LIKE SOME PEANUTS?
OH... NO THANK YOU.
DUH
WHAT, YOU THINK THESE ARE SOME ORDINARY PEANUTS?! HUH?!
HAPPY NUT!
THESE ARE MAGICAL PEANUTS, YOU UNGRATEFUL BASTARD!! NOW EAT THE GODDAMMED PEANUTS!!
MOMMY... I FEEL SICK... "BURP"
OH, NO, DON'T GO AND MESS ON YOURSELF. HERE, HOLD ON.
BLOOOOGH!
AAAAAAGH!! THAT'S IT!! THIS IS THE LAST TIME I EVER FLY!!!
OH, P'SHAW!
YOU'RE MUCH SAFER IN HERE THAN YOU WOULD BE IN THAT BUS, DOWN THERE FILLED WITH ALL THOSE BOY SCOUTS!
SEE! THE ONE THAT SEEMS TO BE HURLING UP AT US?
BLAM!
CAMP
the End.

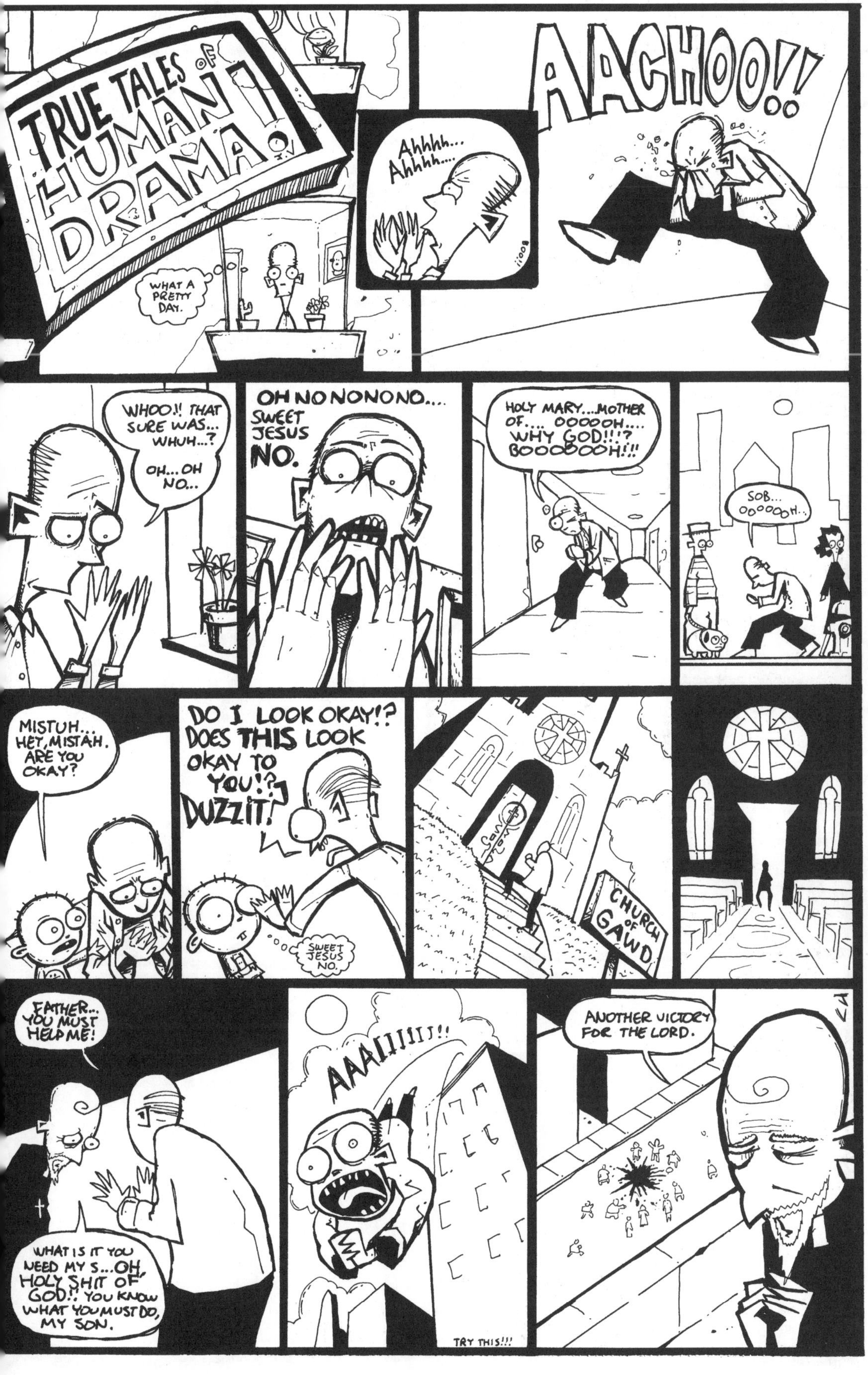
TRUE TALES OF HUMAN DRAMA!
WHAT A PRETTY DAY.
Ahhhh... Ahhhh....
AACHOO!!
WHOO!! THAT SURE WAS... WHUH...?
OH... OH NO...
OH NO NONONO... SWEET JESUS NO.
HOLY MARY...MOTHER OF.... OOOOOH.... WHY GOD!!!? BOOOOOOH!!!
SOB... OOOOOOH...
MISTUH... HEY, MISTAH. ARE YOU OKAY?
DO I LOOK OKAY!? DOES THIS LOOK OKAY TO YOU!? DUZZIT!
SWEET JESUS NO.
CHURCH OF GAWD
FATHER... YOU MUST HELP ME!
WHAT IS IT YOU NEED MY S...OH, HOLY SHIT OF GOD!! YOU KNOW WHAT YOU MUST DO, MY SON.
AAAIIIIII!!
TRY THIS!!!
ANOTHER VICTORY FOR THE LORD.

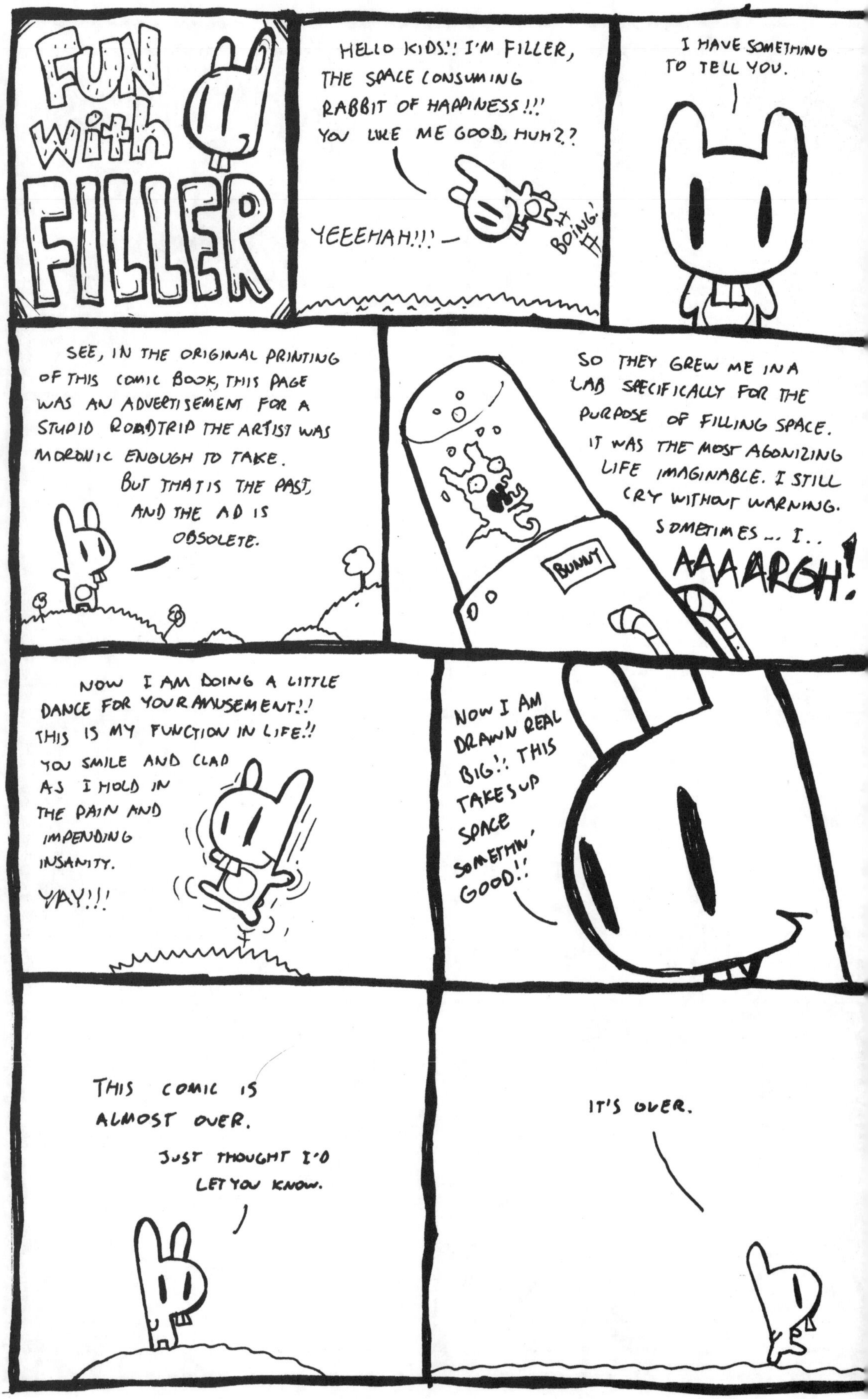
FUN with FILLER
HELLO KIDS!! I'M FILLER, THE SPACE CONSUMING RABBIT OF HAPPINESS!!! YOU LIKE ME GOOD, HUH??
YEEEHAH!!!
BOING!
I HAVE SOMETHING TO TELL YOU.
SEE, IN THE ORIGINAL PRINTING OF THIS COMIC BOOK, THIS PAGE WAS AN ADVERTISEMENT FOR A STUPID ROADTRIP THE ARTIST WAS MORONIC ENOUGH TO TAKE.
BUT THAT IS THE PAST, AND THE AD IS OBSOLETE.
SO THEY GREW ME IN A LAB SPECIFICALLY FOR THE PURPOSE OF FILLING SPACE. IT WAS THE MOST AGONIZING LIFE IMAGINABLE. I STILL CRY WITHOUT WARNING.
SOMETIMES... I..
AAAARGH!
BUNNY
NOW I AM DOING A LITTLE DANCE FOR YOUR AMUSEMENT!! THIS IS MY FUNCTION IN LIFE!! YOU SMILE AND CLAP AS I HOLD IN THE PAIN AND IMPENDING INSANITY.
YAY!!!
NOW I AM DRAWN REAL BIG!! THIS TAKES UP SPACE SOMETHIN' GOOD!!
THIS COMIC IS ALMOST OVER.
JUST THOUGHT I'D LET YOU KNOW.
IT'S OVER.

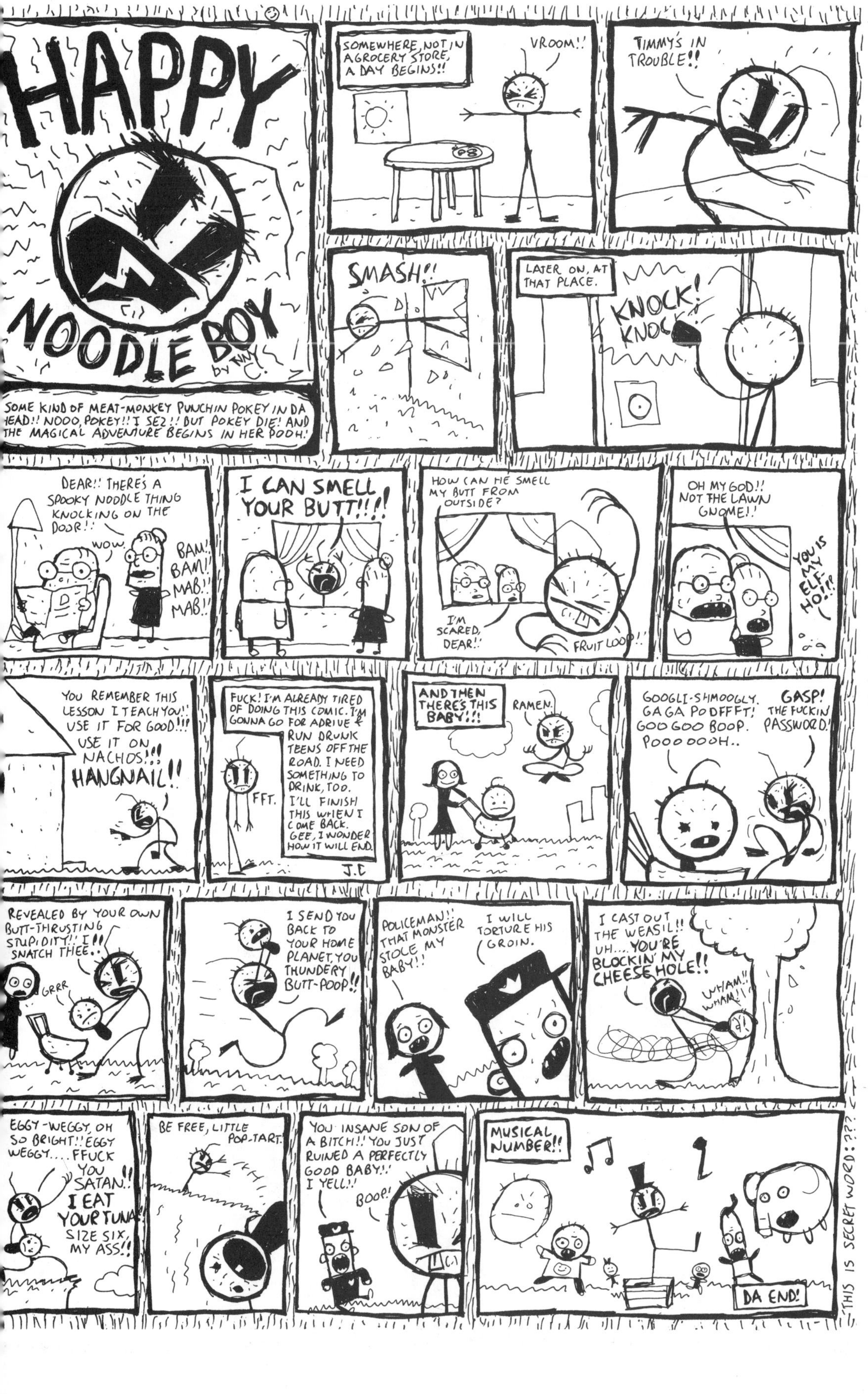

HAPPY NOODLE BOY
by JHNY C.
SOME KIND OF MEAT-MONKEY PUNCHIN POKEY IN DA HEAD!! NOOO, POKEY!! I SEZ!! BUT POKEY DIE! AND THE MAGICAL ADVENTURE BEGINS IN HER POOH!
SOMEWHERE, NOT IN A GROCERY STORE, A DAY BEGINS!!
VROOM!!
TIMMY'S IN TROUBLE!!
SMASH!!
LATER ON, AT THAT PLACE.
KNOCK! KNOCK
DEAR!! THERE'S A SPOOKY NOODLE THING KNOCKING ON THE DOOR!!
WOW.
BAM! BAM! MAB!! MAB!!
I CAN SMELL YOUR BUTT!!!!
HOW CAN HE SMELL MY BUTT FROM OUTSIDE?
I'M SCARED, DEAR!!
FRUIT LOOP!!
OH MY GOD!! NOT THE LAWN GNOME!!
YOU IS MY ELF HO!!?
YOU REMEMBER THIS LESSON I TEACH YOU!! USE IT FOR GOOD!!! USE IT ON NACHOS!!! HANGNAIL!!
FUCK! I'M ALREADY TIRED OF DOING THIS COMIC. I'M GONNA GO FOR A DRIVE & RUN DRUNK TEENS OFF THE ROAD. I NEED SOMETHING TO DRINK, TOO. I'LL FINISH THIS WHEN I COME BACK. GEE, I WONDER HOW IT WILL END.
FFT.
J.C
AND THEN THERE'S THIS BABY!!!
RAMEN.
GOOGLI-SHMOOGLY. GA GA PODFFFT! GOO GOO BOOP. POOOOOOH..
GASP! THE FUCKIN PASSWORD!
REVEALED BY YOUR OWN BUTT-THRUSTING STUPIDITY!! I!!! SNATCH THEE!!
GRRR
I SEND YOU BACK TO YOUR HOME PLANET, YOU THUNDERY BUTT-POOP!!
POLICEMAN!! THAT MONSTER STOLE MY BABY!!
I WILL TORTURE HIS GROIN.
I CAST OUT THE WEASIL!! UH.... YOU'RE BLOCKIN' MY CHEESE HOLE!!
WHAM!! WHAM!!
EGGY-WEGGY, OH SO BRIGHT!! EGGY WEGGY.... FFUCK YOU SATAN!! I EAT YOUR TUNA! SIZE SIX, MY ASS!!
BE FREE, LITTLE POP-TART.
YOU INSANE SON OF A BITCH!! YOU JUST RUINED A PERFECTLY GOOD BABY!! I YELL!!
BOOP!
MUSICAL NUMBER!!
DA END!
THIS IS SECRET WORD: ???

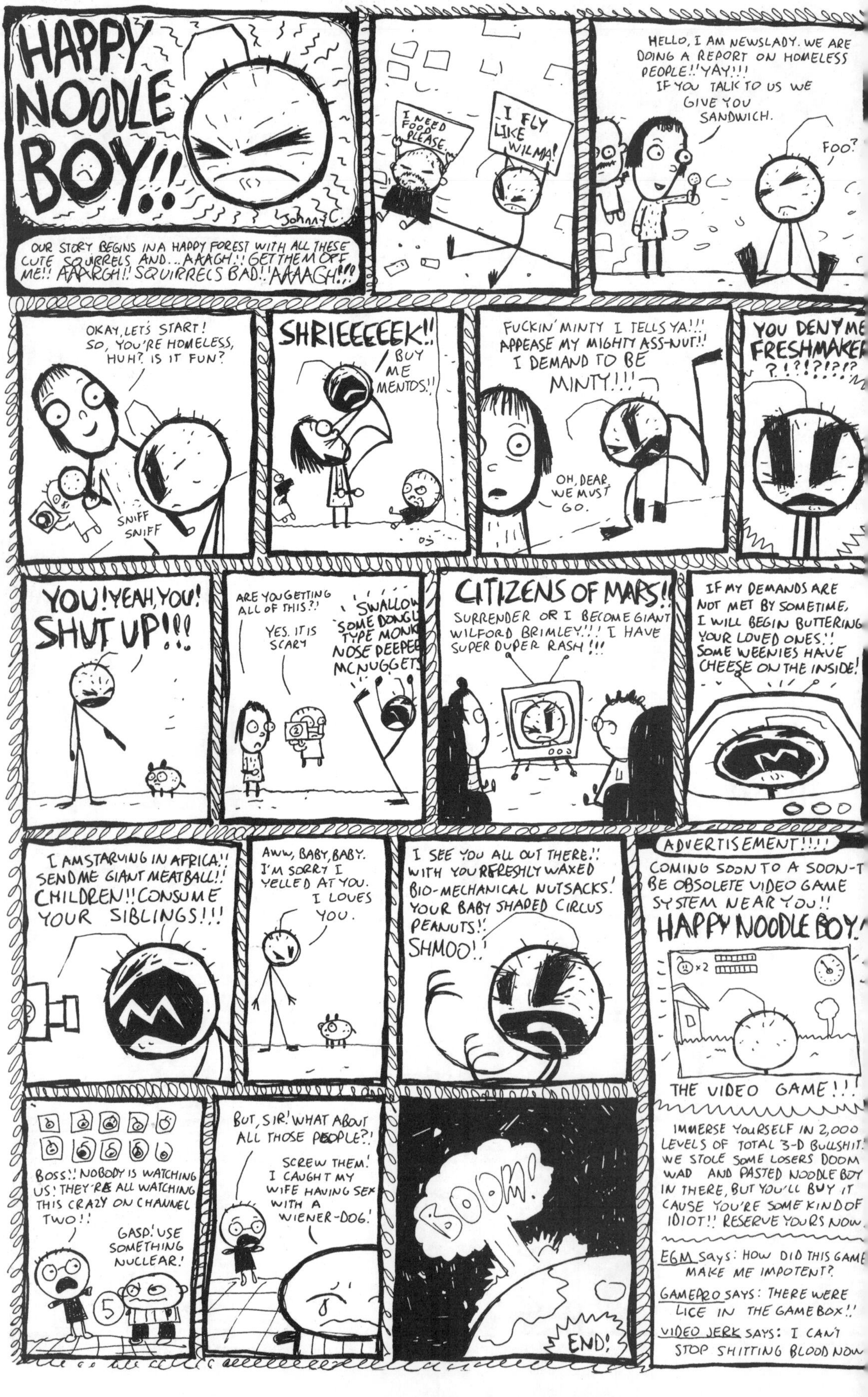
HAPPY NOODLE BOY!!
JohnnyC.
OUR STORY BEGINS IN A HAPPY FOREST WITH ALL THESE CUTE SQUIRRELS AND... AAAGH!! GET THEM OFF ME!! AAARGH!! SQUIRRELS BAD!! AAAAGH!!!
I NEED FOOD PLEASE.
I FLY LIKE WILMA!
HELLO, I AM NEWSLADY. WE ARE DOING A REPORT ON HOMELESS PEOPLE!! YAY!!! IF YOU TALK TO US WE GIVE YOU SANDWICH.
FOO?
OKAY, LET'S START! SO, YOU'RE HOMELESS, HUH? IS IT FUN?
SNIFF SNIFF
SHRIEEEEEK!!
BUY ME MENTOS!!
FUCKIN' MINTY I TELLS YA!!! APPEASE MY MIGHTY ASS-NUT!! I DEMAND TO BE MINTY!!!
OH, DEAR, WE MUST GO.
YOU DENY ME FRESHMAKER ?!?!?!?!?
YOU! YEAH, YOU! SHUT UP!!!
ARE YOU GETTING ALL OF THIS?!
YES. IT IS SCARY
SWALLOW SOME DONGLE TYPE MONK NOSE PEEPEE MCNUGGETS
CITIZENS OF MARS!! SURRENDER OR I BECOME GIANT WILFORD BRIMLEY!!! I HAVE SUPER DUPER RASH!!!
IF MY DEMANDS ARE NOT MET BY SOMETIME, I WILL BEGIN BUTTERING YOUR LOVED ONES!! SOME WEENIES HAVE CHEESE ON THE INSIDE!
I AM STARVING IN AFRICA!! SEND ME GIANT MEATBALL!! CHILDREN!! CONSUME YOUR SIBLINGS!!!
AWW, BABY, BABY. I'M SORRY I YELLED AT YOU. I LOVES YOU.
I SEE YOU ALL OUT THERE!! WITH YOUR FRESHLY WAXED BIO-MECHANICAL NUTSACKS! YOUR BABY SHADED CIRCUS PEANUTS!! SHMOO!!
ADVERTISEMENT!!!!
COMING SOON TO A SOON-T BE OBSOLETE VIDEO GAME SYSTEM NEAR YOU!!
HAPPY NOODLE BOY!
THE VIDEO GAME!!!
IMMERSE YOURSELF IN 2,000 LEVELS OF TOTAL 3-D BULLSHIT! WE STOLE SOME LOSERS DOOM WAD AND PASTED NOODLE BOY IN THERE, BUT YOU'LL BUY IT CAUSE YOU'RE SOME KIND OF IDIOT!! RESERVE YOURS NOW
EGM SAYS: HOW DID THIS GAME MAKE ME IMPOTENT?
GAMEPRO SAYS: THERE WERE LICE IN THE GAME BOX!!
VIDEO JERK SAYS: I CAN'T STOP SHITTING BLOOD NOW
BOSS!! NOBODY IS WATCHING US! THEY'RE ALL WATCHING THIS CRAZY ON CHANNEL TWO!!
GASP! USE SOMETHING NUCLEAR!
BUT, SIR! WHAT ABOUT ALL THOSE PEOPLE?!
SCREW THEM! I CAUGHT MY WIFE HAVING SEX WITH A WIENER-DOG!
BOOM!
END!

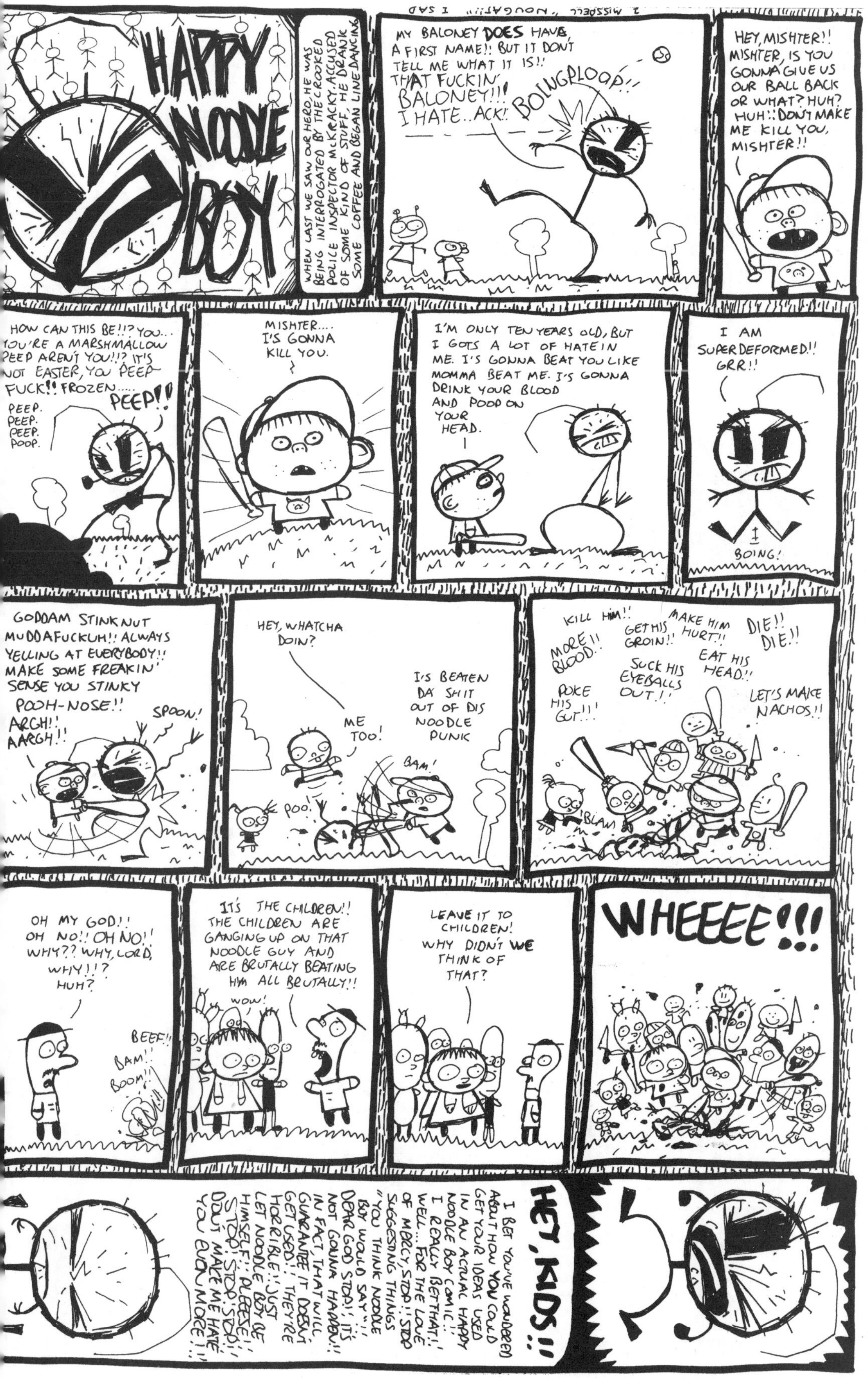

HAPPY NOODLE BOY
WHEN LAST WE SAW OUR HERO, HE WAS BEING INTERROGATED BY THE CROOKED POLICE INSPECTOR McKRACKY, ACCUSED OF SOME KIND OF STUFF. HE DRANK SOME COFFEE AND BEGAN LINE DANCING
MY BALONEY DOES HAVE A FIRST NAME!! BUT IT DON'T TELL ME WHAT IT IS!! THAT FUCKIN' BALONEY!!! I HATE..ACK!
BOINGPLOOP!!
HEY, MISHTER!! MISHTER, IS YOU GONNA GIVE US OUR BALL BACK OR WHAT? HUH? HUH!! DON'T MAKE ME KILL YOU, MISHTER!!
HOW CAN THIS BE!!? YOU... YOU'RE A MARSHMALLOW PEEP AREN'T YOU!!? IT'S NOT EASTER, YOU PEEP FUCK!! FROZEN.....
PEEP. PEEP. PEEP. POOP.
PEEP!!
MISHTER.... I'S GONNA KILL YOU.
I'M ONLY TEN YEARS OLD, BUT I GOTS A LOT OF HATE IN ME. I'S GONNA BEAT YOU LIKE MOMMA BEAT ME. I'S GONNA DRINK YOUR BLOOD AND POOP ON YOUR HEAD.
I AM SUPERDEFORMED!! GRR!!
BOING!
GODDAM STINKNUT MUDDAFUCKUH!! ALWAYS YELLING AT EVERYBODY!! MAKE SOME FREAKIN' SENSE YOU STINKY POOH-NOSE!!
ARGH!! AARGH!!
SPOON!
HEY, WHATCHA DOIN?
I'S BEATEN DA' SHIT OUT OF DIS NOODLE PUNK
ME TOO!
BAM!
POO!
KILL HIM!!
MORE BLOOD!!
GET HIS GROIN!!
MAKE HIM HURT!!
DIE!! DIE!!
EAT HIS HEAD!!
SUCK HIS EYEBALLS OUT!!
POKE HIS GUT!!!
LET'S MAKE NACHOS!!
BLAM
OH MY GOD!! OH NO!! OH NO!! WHY?? WHY, LORD, WHY!!? HUH?
BEEF!! BAM!! BOOM!!
IT'S THE CHILDREN!! THE CHILDREN ARE GANGING UP ON THAT NOODLE GUY AND ARE BRUTALLY BEATING HIM ALL BRUTALLY!!
WOW!
LEAVE IT TO CHILDREN! WHY DIDN'T WE THINK OF THAT?
WHEEEEE!!!
HEY, KIDS!!
I BET YOU'VE WONDERED ABOUT HOW YOU COULD GET YOUR IDEAS USED IN AN ACTUAL HAPPY NOODLE BOY COMIC!! I REALLY BET THAT!! WELL... FOR THE LOVE OF MERCY, STOP! STOP SUGGESTING THINGS "YOU THINK NOODLE BOY WOULD SAY"!! DEAR GOD STOP!! IT'S NOT GONNA HAPPEN!! IN FACT THAT WILL GUARANTEE IT DOESN'T GET USED!! THEY'RE HORRIBLE!! JUST LET NOODLE BOY BE HIMSELF!! PLEEESE!! STOP! STOP! STOP! DON'T MAKE ME HATE YOU ANYMORE!!!

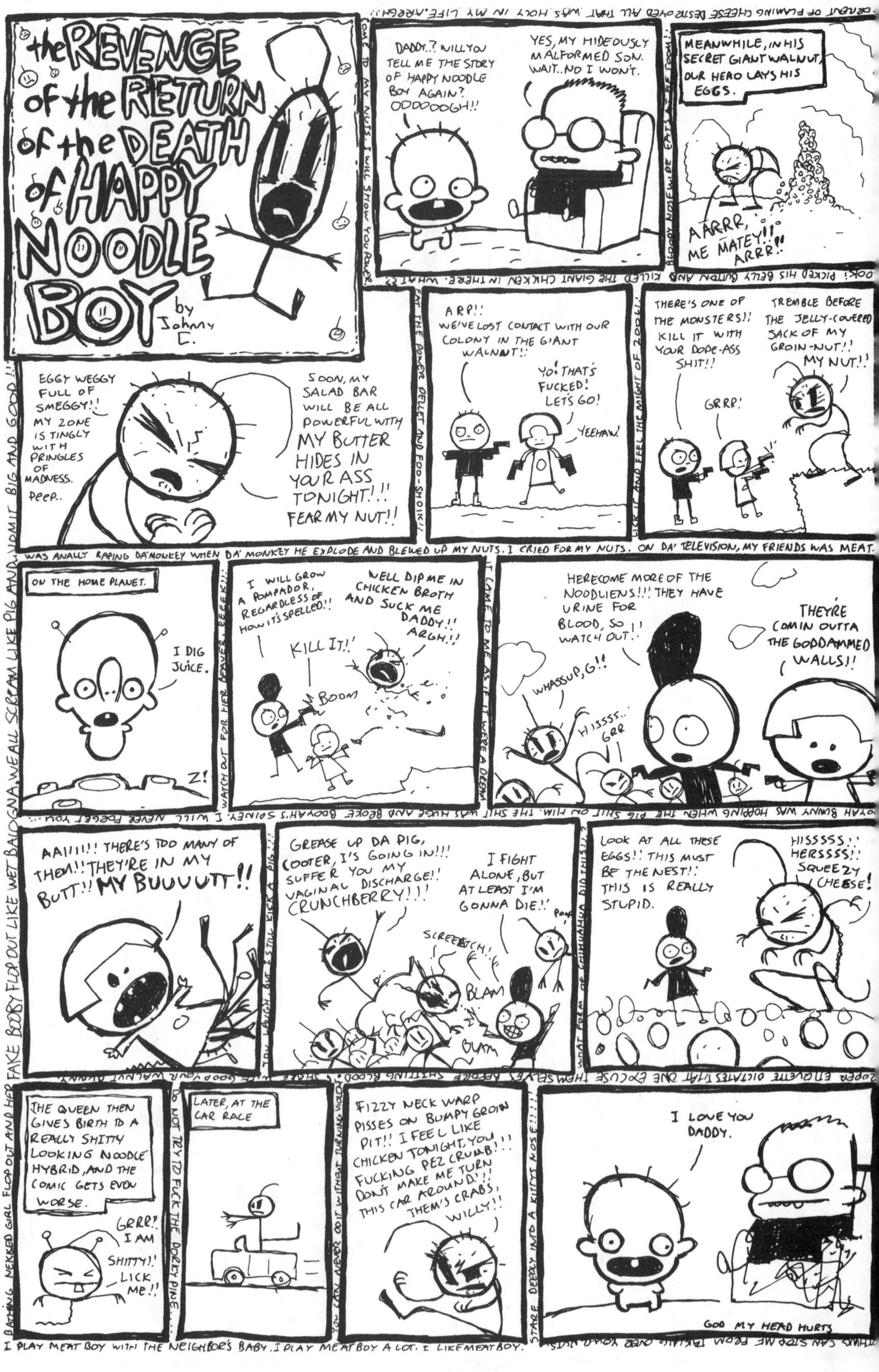

the REVENGE of the RETURN of the DEATH of HAPPY NOODLE BOY
by Johnny C.
DADDY..? WILL YOU TELL ME THE STORY OF HAPPY NOODLE BOY AGAIN? OOOOOOGH!!
YES, MY HIDEOUSLY MALFORMED SON. WAIT..NO I WON'T.
MEANWHILE, IN HIS SECRET GIANT WALNUT, OUR HERO LAYS HIS EGGS.
AARRR, ME MATEY!!! ARRR!!
EGGY WEGGY FULL OF SMEGGY!! MY ZONE IS TINGLY WITH PRINGLES OF MADNESS. PEEP..
SOON, MY SALAD BAR WILL BE ALL POWERFUL WITH MY BUTTER HIDES IN YOUR ASS TONIGHT!!! FEAR MY NUT!!
ARP!! WE'VE LOST CONTACT WITH OUR COLONY IN THE GIANT WALNUT!!
YO! THAT'S FUCKED! LET'S GO!
YEEHAW!
THERE'S ONE OF THE MONSTERS!! KILL IT WITH YOUR DOPE-ASS SHIT!!
GRRR!
TREMBLE BEFORE THE JELLY-COVERED SACK OF MY GROIN-NUT!! MY NUT!!
WAS ANALLY RAPING DA' MONKEY WHEN DA' MONKEY HE EXPLODE AND BLEWED UP MY NUTS. I CRIED FOR MY NUTS. ON DA' TELEVISION, MY FRIENDS WAS MEAT.
ON THE HOME PLANET.
I DIG JUICE.
Z!
I WILL GROW A POMPADOR, REGARDLESS OF HOW IT'S SPELLED!!
WELL DIP ME IN CHICKEN BROTH AND SUCK ME DADDY!! ARGH!!
KILL IT!!
BOOM
HERE COME MORE OF THE NOODLIENS!!! THEY HAVE URINE FOR BLOOD, SO WATCH OUT!!
THEY'RE COMIN OUTTA THE GODDAMMED WALLS!!
WHASSUP, G!!
HISSSS.. GRR
AAI!!!! THERE'S TOO MANY OF THEM!! THEY'RE IN MY BUTT!! MY BUUUUTT!!
GREASE UP DA PIG, COOTER, I'S GOING IN!!! SUFFER YOU MY VAGINAL DISCHARGE!! CRUNCHBERRY!!!
I FIGHT ALONE, BUT AT LEAST I'M GONNA DIE!!
SCREEATCH!!
BLAM
BLAM
LOOK AT ALL THESE EGGS!! THIS MUST BE THE NEST!! THIS IS REALLY STUPID.
HISSSSS!! HERSSSS!! SQUEEZY CHEESE!
THE QUEEN THEN GIVES BIRTH TO A REALLY SHITTY LOOKING NOODLE HYBRID, AND THE COMIC GETS EVEN WORSE.
GRRR! I AM SHITTY!! LICK ME!!
LATER, AT THE CAR RACE
FIZZY NECK WARP PISSES ON BUMPY GROIN PIT!! I FEEL LIKE CHICKEN TONIGHT, YOU FUCKING PEZ CRUMB!!! DON'T MAKE ME TURN THIS CAR AROUND!!! THEM'S CRABS, WILLY!!
I LOVE YOU DADDY.
GOD MY HEAD HURTS
I PLAY MEAT BOY WITH THE NEIGHBOR'S BABY. I PLAY MEAT BOY A LOT. I LIKE MEAT BOY.

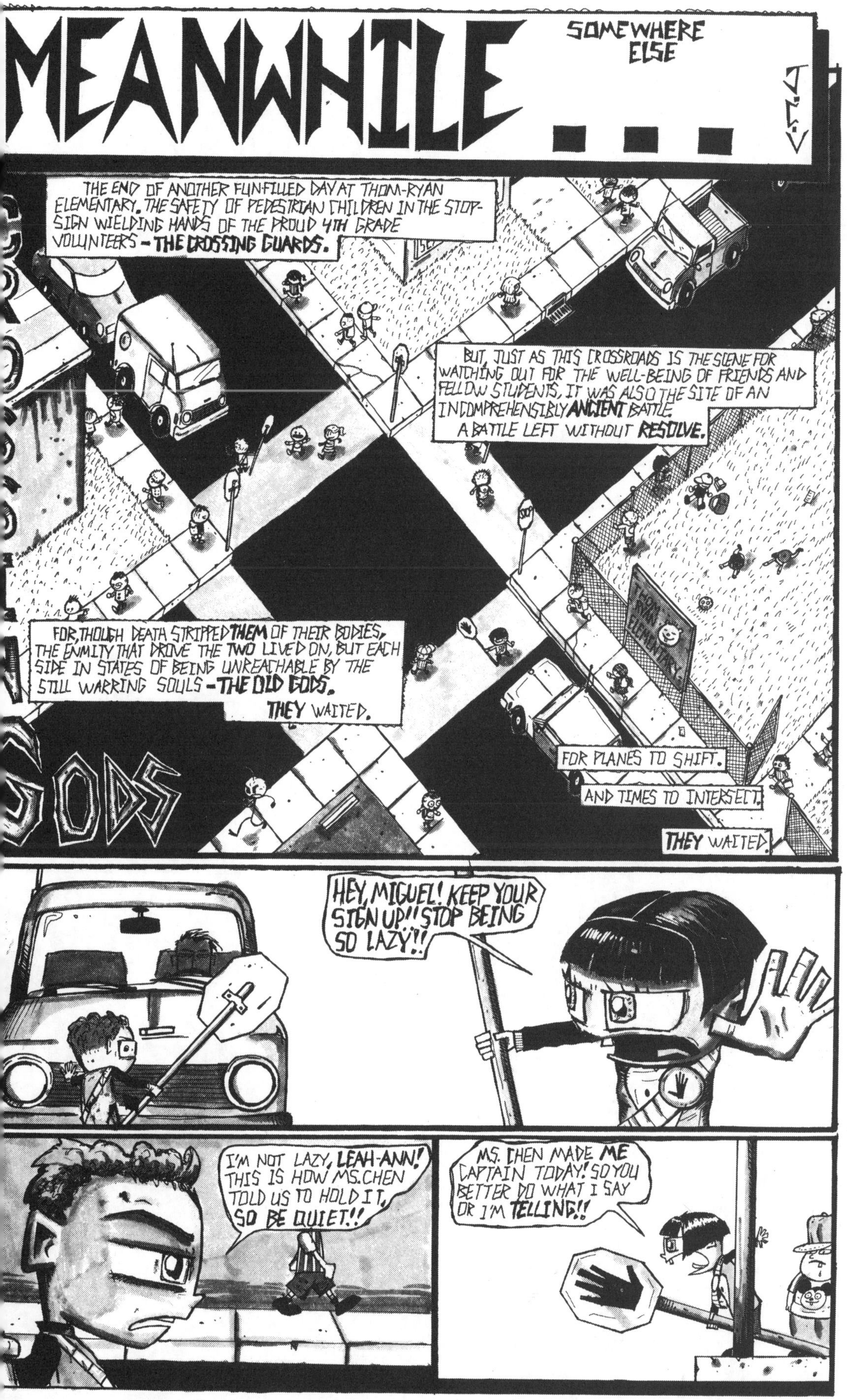
MEANWHILE...
SOMEWHERE ELSE
THE END OF ANOTHER FUNFILLED DAY AT THOM-RYAN ELEMENTARY. THE SAFETY OF PEDESTRIAN CHILDREN IN THE STOP-SIGN WIELDING HANDS OF THE PROUD 4TH GRADE VOLUNTEERS - THE CROSSING GUARDS.
BUT, JUST AS THIS CROSSROADS IS THE SCENE FOR WATCHING OUT FOR THE WELL-BEING OF FRIENDS AND FELLOW STUDENTS, IT WAS ALSO THE SITE OF AN INCOMPREHENSIBLY ANCIENT BATTLE.
A BATTLE LEFT WITHOUT RESOLVE.
FOR, THOUGH DEATH STRIPPED THEM OF THEIR BODIES, THE ENMITY THAT DROVE THE TWO LIVED ON, BUT EACH SIDE IN STATES OF BEING UNREACHABLE BY THE STILL WARRING SOULS - THE OLD GODS.
THEY WAITED.
FOR PLANES TO SHIFT.
AND TIMES TO INTERSECT.
THEY WAITED.
GODS
HEY, MIGUEL! KEEP YOUR SIGN UP!! STOP BEING SO LAZY!!
I'M NOT LAZY, LEAH-ANN! THIS IS HOW MS. CHEN TOLD US TO HOLD IT, SO BE QUIET!!
MS. CHEN MADE ME CAPTAIN TODAY! SO YOU BETTER DO WHAT I SAY OR I'M TELLING!!

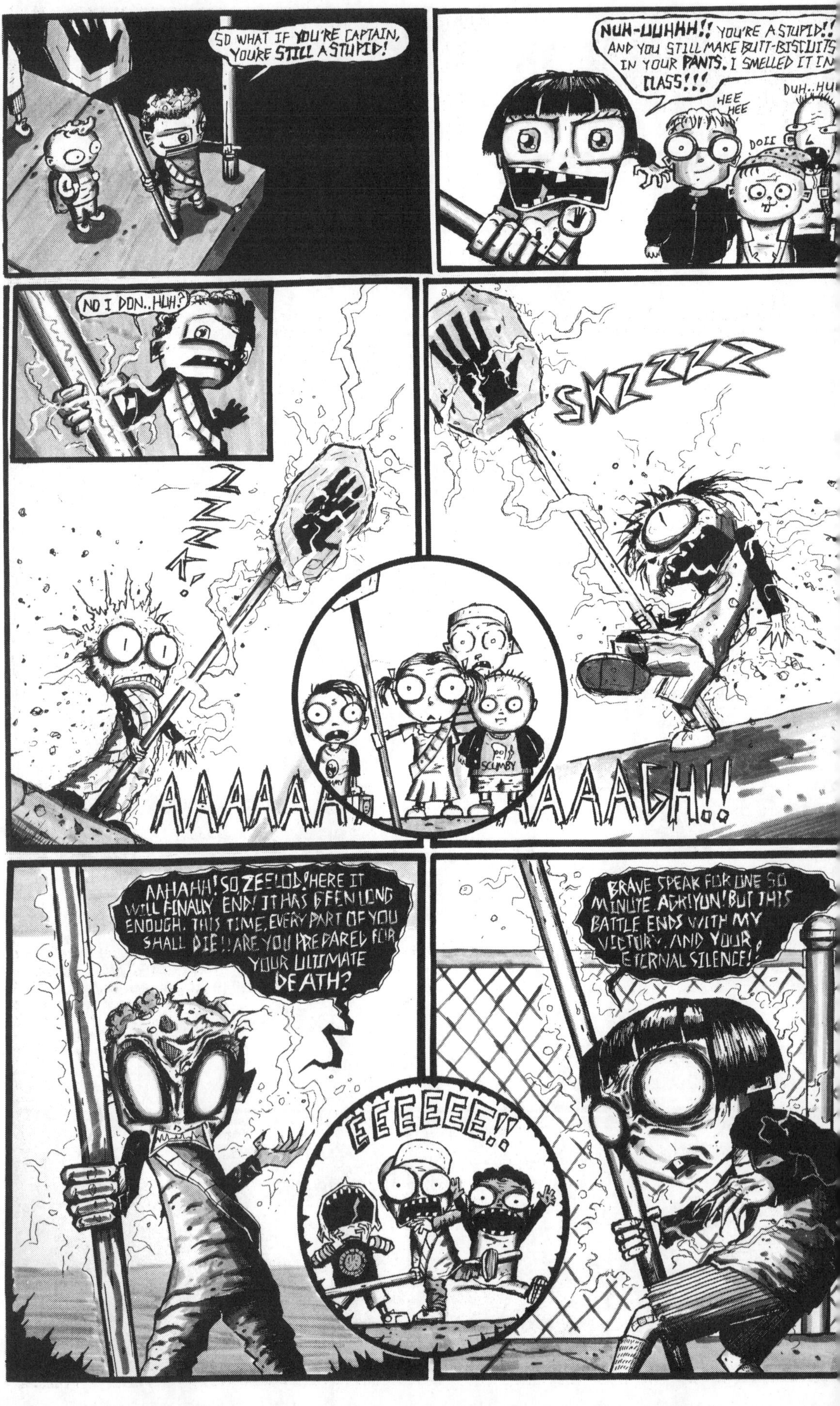

SO WHAT IF YOU'RE CAPTAIN, YOU'RE STILL A STUPID!
NUH-UUHHH!! YOU'RE A STUPID!! AND YOU STILL MAKE BUTT-BISCUITS IN YOUR PANTS. I SMELLED IT IN CLASS!!!
HEE HEE
DUH..HU
DOII
NO I DON..HUH?
ZZZZK!
SKZZZZZZ
AAAAAAAAAAAAAAGH!!
AAHAHH! SO, ZEELOD! HERE IT WILL FINALLY END! IT HAS BEEN LONG ENOUGH. THIS TIME, EVERY PART OF YOU SHALL DIE!! ARE YOU PREPARED FOR YOUR ULTIMATE DEATH?
BRAVE SPEAK FOR ONE SO MINUTE, AGRIYON! BUT THIS BATTLE ENDS WITH MY VICTORY. AND YOUR ETERNAL SILENCE!
EEEEEE!!

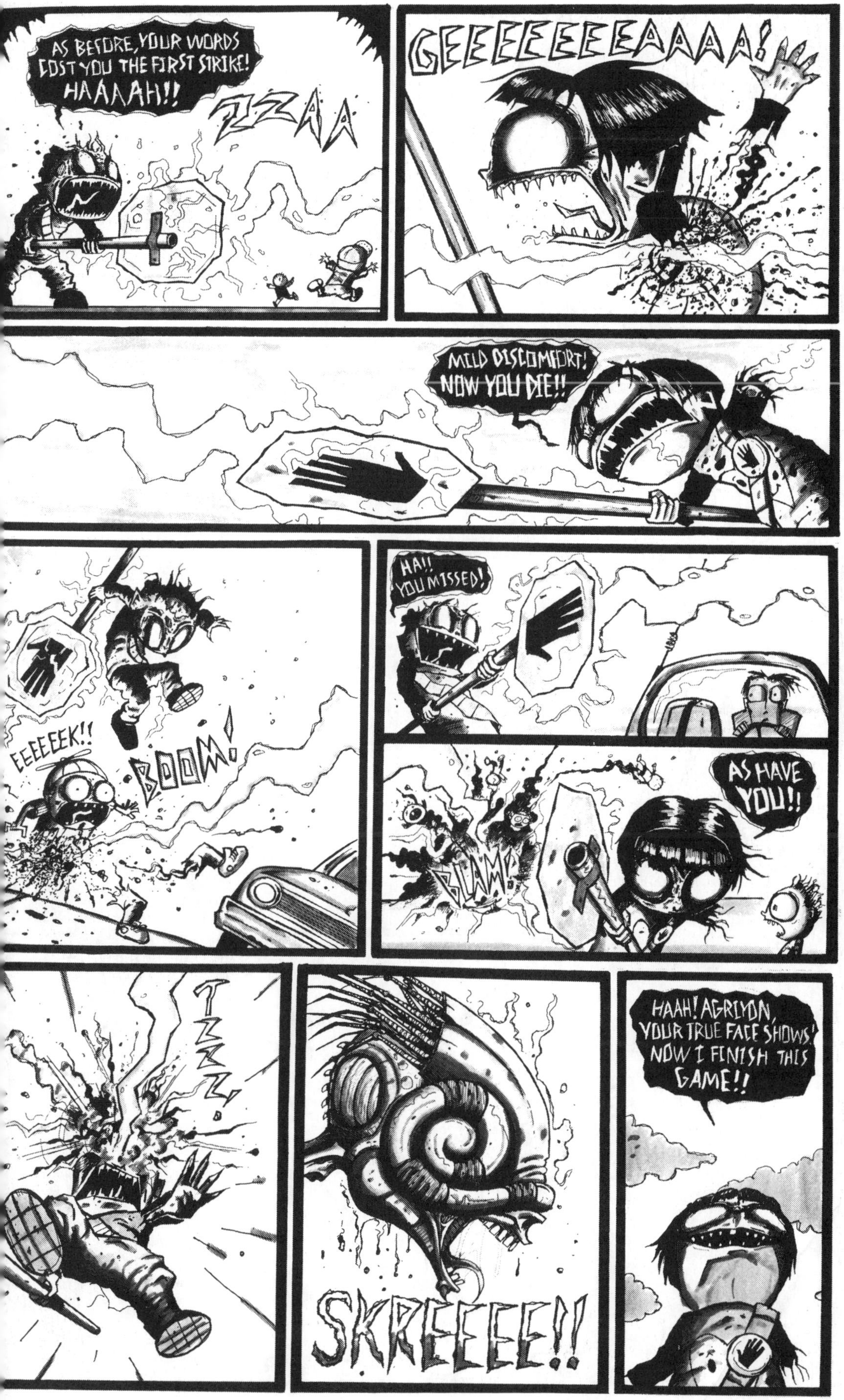
AS BEFORE, YOUR WORDS COST YOU THE FIRST STRIKE! HAAAAH!!
ZZAA
GEEEEEEEAAAA!
MILD DISCOMFORT! NOW YOU DIE!!
EEEEEEK!!
BOOM!
HA!! YOU MISSED!
BLAM!
AS HAVE YOU!!
TZZZ
SKREEEE!!
HAAH! AGRIYDN, YOUR TRUE FACE SHOWS! NOW I FINISH THIS GAME!!

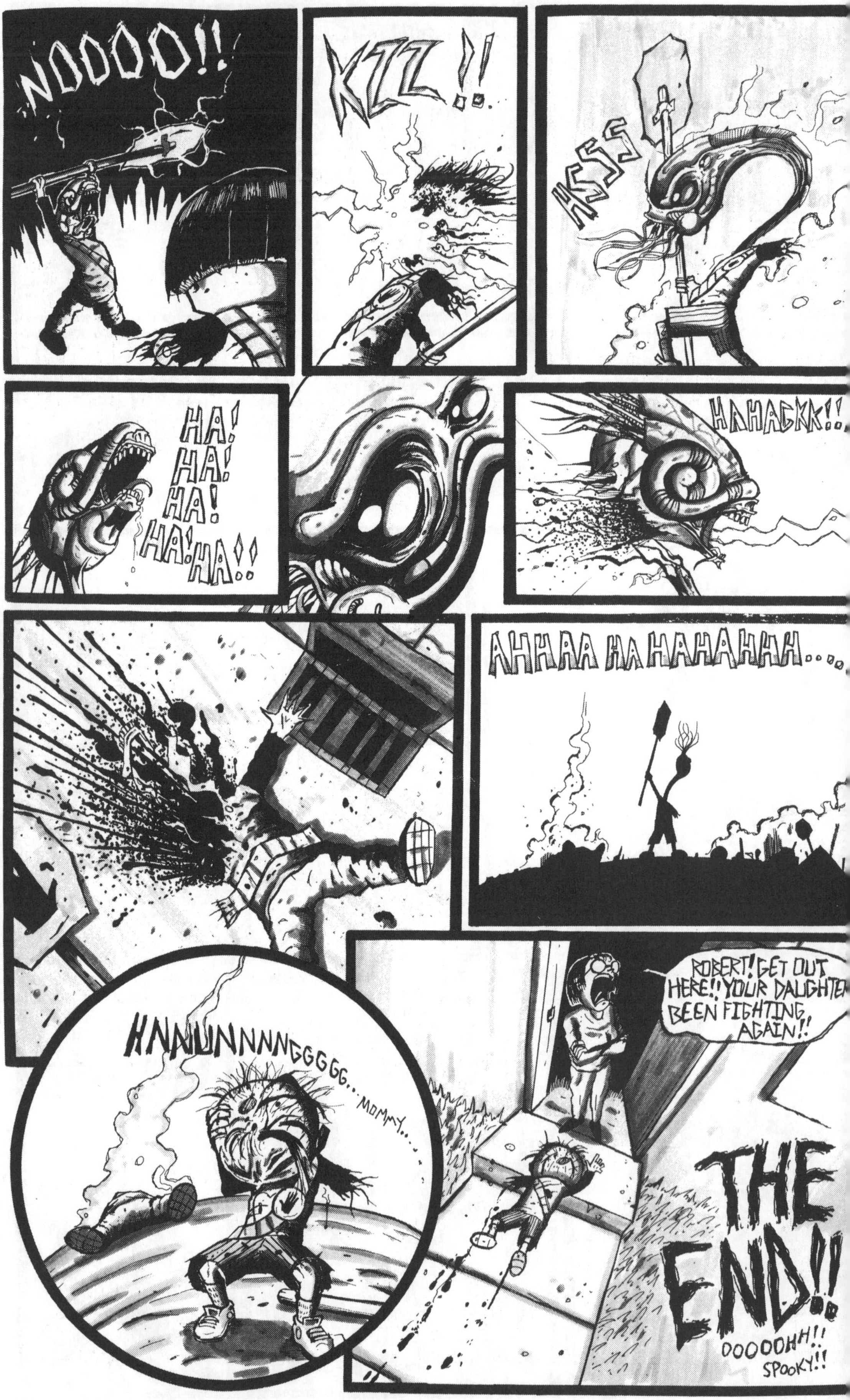
NOOOO!!
KZZ!!
HSSS
HA! HA! HA! HA-HA!!
HAHAGKK!!
AHHAA HA HAHAHHH.....
HNNUNNNNGGGGG...
MOMMY....
ROBERT! GET OUT HERE!! YOUR DAUGHTER BEEN FIGHTING AGAIN!!
THE END!!
OOOOOHH!! SPOOKY!!

MEANWHILE....

SOMEWHERE ELSE

THIS CHICKEN CHOW MEIN IS **INCREDIBLE!!** **EVERYTHING** HERE IS. I CAN'T BELIEVE YOU'VE HARDLY EVEN TOUCHED YOUR FOOD! IT'S DELICIOUS!!

YEAH. Heh.

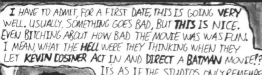

I HAVE TO ADMIT, FOR A FIRST DATE, THIS IS GOING **VERY** WELL. USUALLY, SOMETHING GOES BAD, BUT **THIS** IS NICE. EVEN BITCHING ABOUT HOW BAD THE MOVIE WAS WAS FUN. I MEAN, WHAT THE **HELL** WERE THEY THINKING WHEN THEY LET **KEVIN COSTNER** ACT IN AND **DIRECT** A **BATMAN** MOVIE!? IT'S AS IF THE STUDIOS ONLY REMEMBER DANCES WITH WOLVES, AND THEN COMPLETELY FORGET THE **INTESTINAL SCRAPE** THAT CAME AFTER!! GOD, HE LOOKED LIKE AN IDIOT IN THAT COSTUME! AND WHEN WILL BATMAN EVER HAVE A NECK THAT **MOVES!!?**

YEAH, AND **GILBERT GOTFRIED**, AS **MR. FREEZE** WASN'T EXACTLY EASY TO SIT THROUGH.

I'M IN **HELL**. SHE'S **AMAZING!!** SHE'S AN INCREDIBLE CONVERSATIONALIST!! SHE LOOKS LIKE SOMEONE I'D **DREAM** ABOUT! SHE LOVES MOVIES MAYBE EVEN **MORE** THAN I DO!! AND HERE I AM FACING A POTENTIALLY LETHAL FIT OF GASTROINTESTINAL UNHAPPINESS! THE PAIN! UUNNNGGHH!!

EY, LOOK. THAT **FAMILY** IS STARING AT US. OBABLY TELLING THE KIDS NOT TO GROW UP D LOOK LIKE **US**.

I THINK IT'S SO SAD WHEN MONKEYS DON'T KNOW THAT **THEY** ARE THE SIMPLE ONES.

OH, MAN, IT'S GETTING **WORSE**! FEELS LIKE I'M GOING TO GIVE **BIRTH** TO THE **ANTICHRIST!!** MUST FLEE!!

I CAN'T WAIT FOR THEM TO BRING THE CASHEW CHICKEN. **EVERYTHING** HAS BEEN SO PERFECT, SO FAR. MMM.

YOU KNOW, I DON'T THINK I CAN EAT ANOTHER **BITE!** I'M PRETTY STUFFED!! YEP! BESIDES, I **REALLY** NEED TO LOSE SOME WEIGHT!

GOD!! THAT WAS STUPID! YOU MORON! YOU WEIGH 115!! LOSE WEIGHT?!

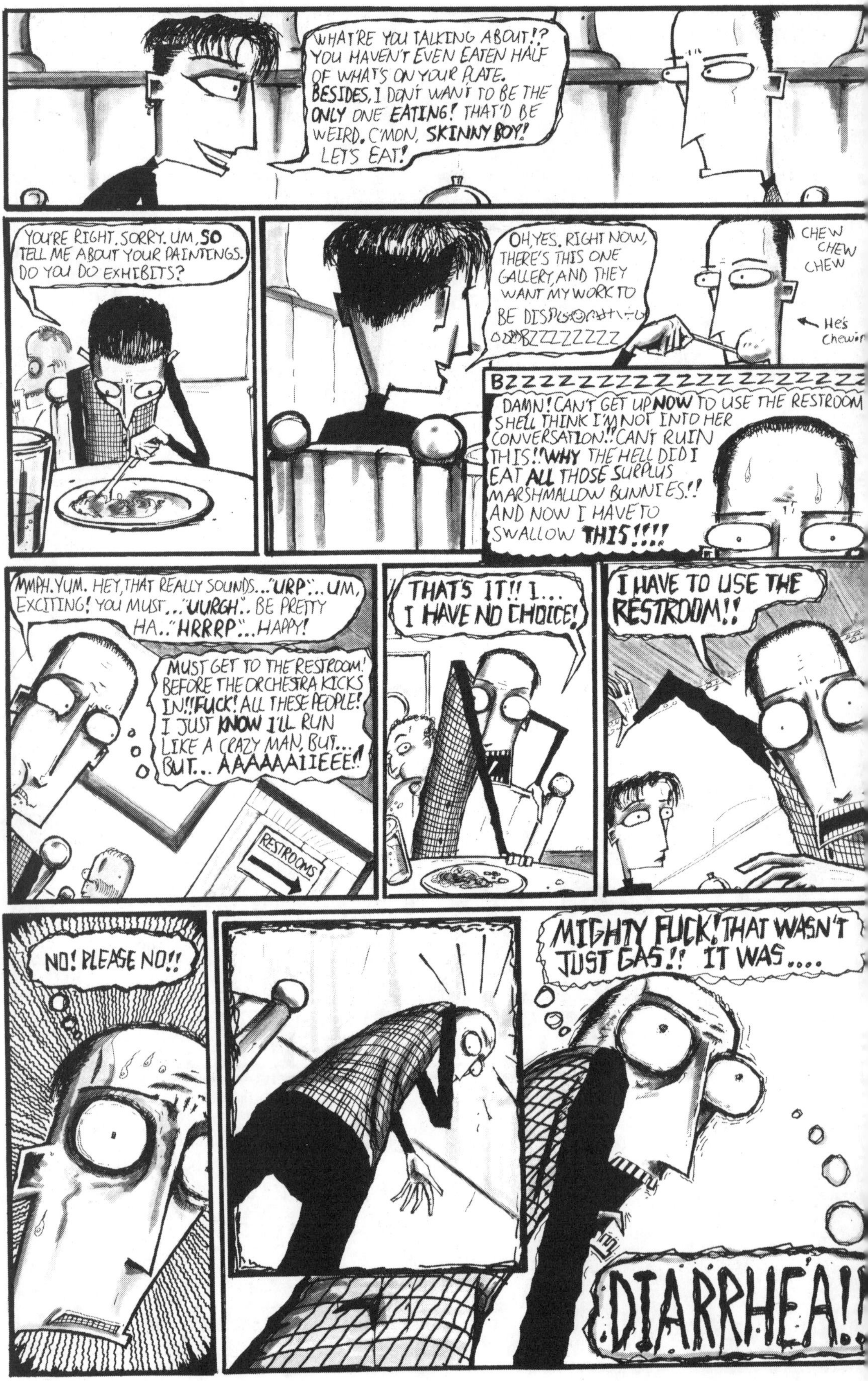
WHAT'RE YOU TALKING ABOUT!? YOU HAVEN'T EVEN EATEN HALF OF WHAT'S ON YOUR PLATE. BESIDES, I DON'T WANT TO BE THE ONLY ONE EATING! THAT'D BE WEIRD. C'MON, SKINNY BOY! LET'S EAT!
YOU'RE RIGHT. SORRY. UM, SO TELL ME ABOUT YOUR PAINTINGS. DO YOU DO EXHIBITS?
OH, YES. RIGHT NOW, THERE'S THIS ONE GALLERY, AND THEY WANT MY WORK TO BE DIS
BZZZZZZZZ
CHEW CHEW CHEW
He's
BZZZZZZZZZZZZZZZZZZZ
DAMN! CAN'T GET UP NOW TO USE THE RESTROOM SHE'LL THINK I'M NOT INTO HER CONVERSATION!! CAN'T RUIN THIS!! WHY THE HELL DID I EAT ALL THOSE SURPLUS MARSHMALLOW BUNNIES!! AND NOW I HAVE TO SWALLOW THIS!!!!
MMPH. YUM. HEY, THAT REALLY SOUNDS... "URP"... UM, EXCITING! YOU MUST... "UURGH".. BE PRETTY HA.. "HRRRP"... HAPPY!
MUST GET TO THE RESTROOM! BEFORE THE ORCHESTRA KICKS IN!! FUCK! ALL THESE PEOPLE! I JUST KNOW I'LL RUN LIKE A CRAZY MAN, BUT... BUT... AAAAAAIIEEE!!
RESTROOMS
THAT'S IT!! I... I HAVE NO CHOICE!
I HAVE TO USE THE RESTROOM!!
NO! PLEASE NO!!
MIGHTY FUCK! THAT WASN'T JUST GAS!! IT WAS....
DIARRHEA!!

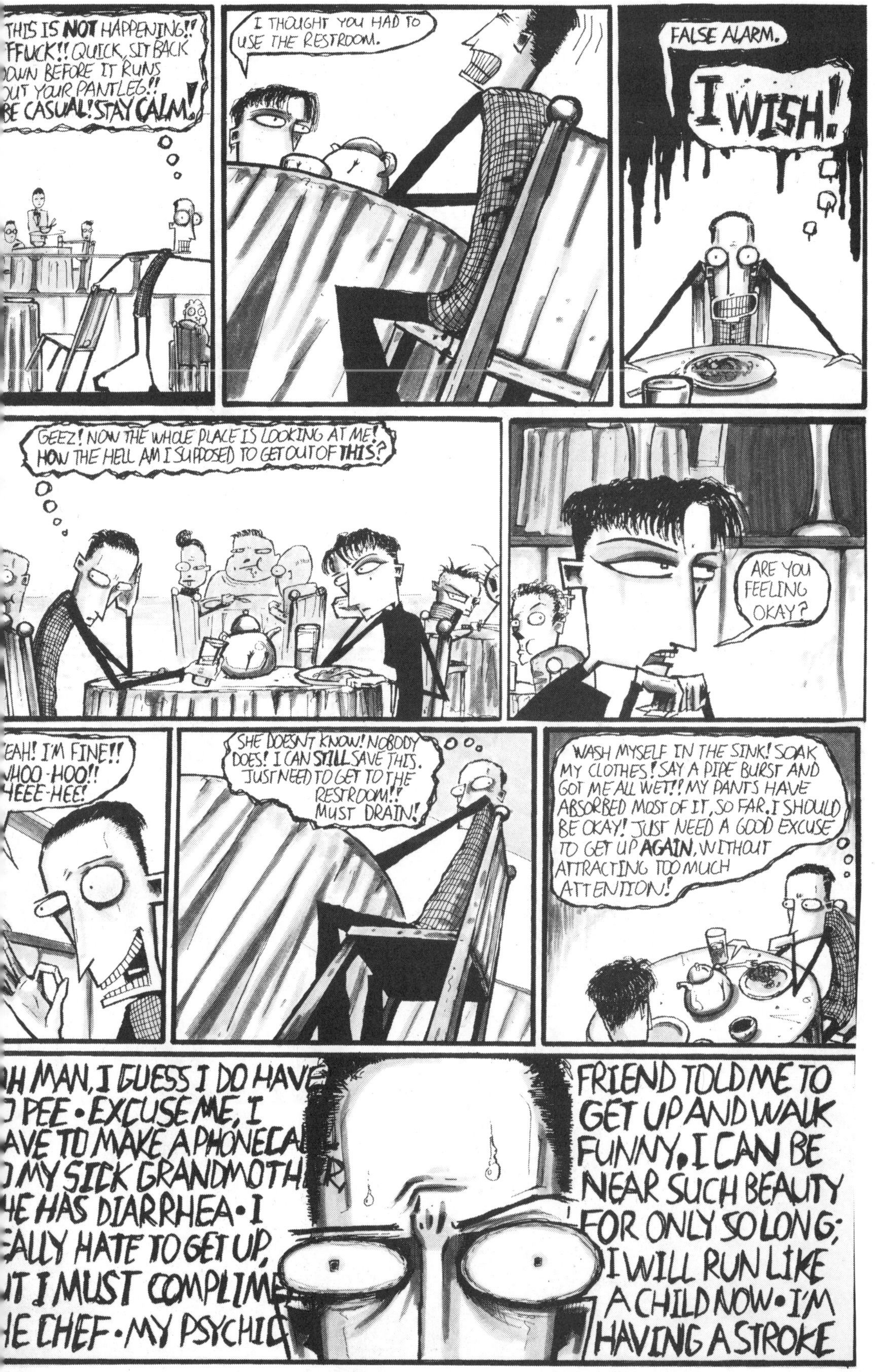
THIS IS NOT HAPPENING!! FFUCK!! QUICK, SIT BACK OWN BEFORE IT RUNS OUT YOUR PANTLEG!! BE CASUAL! STAY CALM!
I THOUGHT YOU HAD TO USE THE RESTROOM.
FALSE ALARM.
I WISH!
GEEZ! NOW THE WHOLE PLACE IS LOOKING AT ME! HOW THE HELL AM I SUPPOSED TO GET OUT OF THIS?
ARE YOU FEELING OKAY?
EAH! I'M FINE!! HOO-HOO!! HEEE-HEE!
SHE DOESN'T KNOW! NOBODY DOES! I CAN STILL SAVE THIS. JUST NEED TO GET TO THE RESTROOM!! MUST DRAIN!
WASH MYSELF IN THE SINK! SOAK MY CLOTHES! SAY A PIPE BURST AND GOT ME ALL WET!! MY PANTS HAVE ABSORBED MOST OF IT, SO FAR. I SHOULD BE OKAY! JUST NEED A GOOD EXCUSE TO GET UP AGAIN, WITHOUT ATTRACTING TOO MUCH ATTENTION!
H MAN, I GUESS I DO HAVE O PEE • EXCUSE ME, I AVE TO MAKE A PHONECA O MY SICK GRANDMOTHE HE HAS DIARRHEA • I EALLY HATE TO GET UP, UT I MUST COMPLIME HE CHEF • MY PSYCHIC
FRIEND TOLD ME TO GET UP AND WALK FUNNY, I CAN BE NEAR SUCH BEAUTY FOR ONLY SO LONG; I WILL RUN LIKE A CHILD NOW • I'M HAVING A STROKE

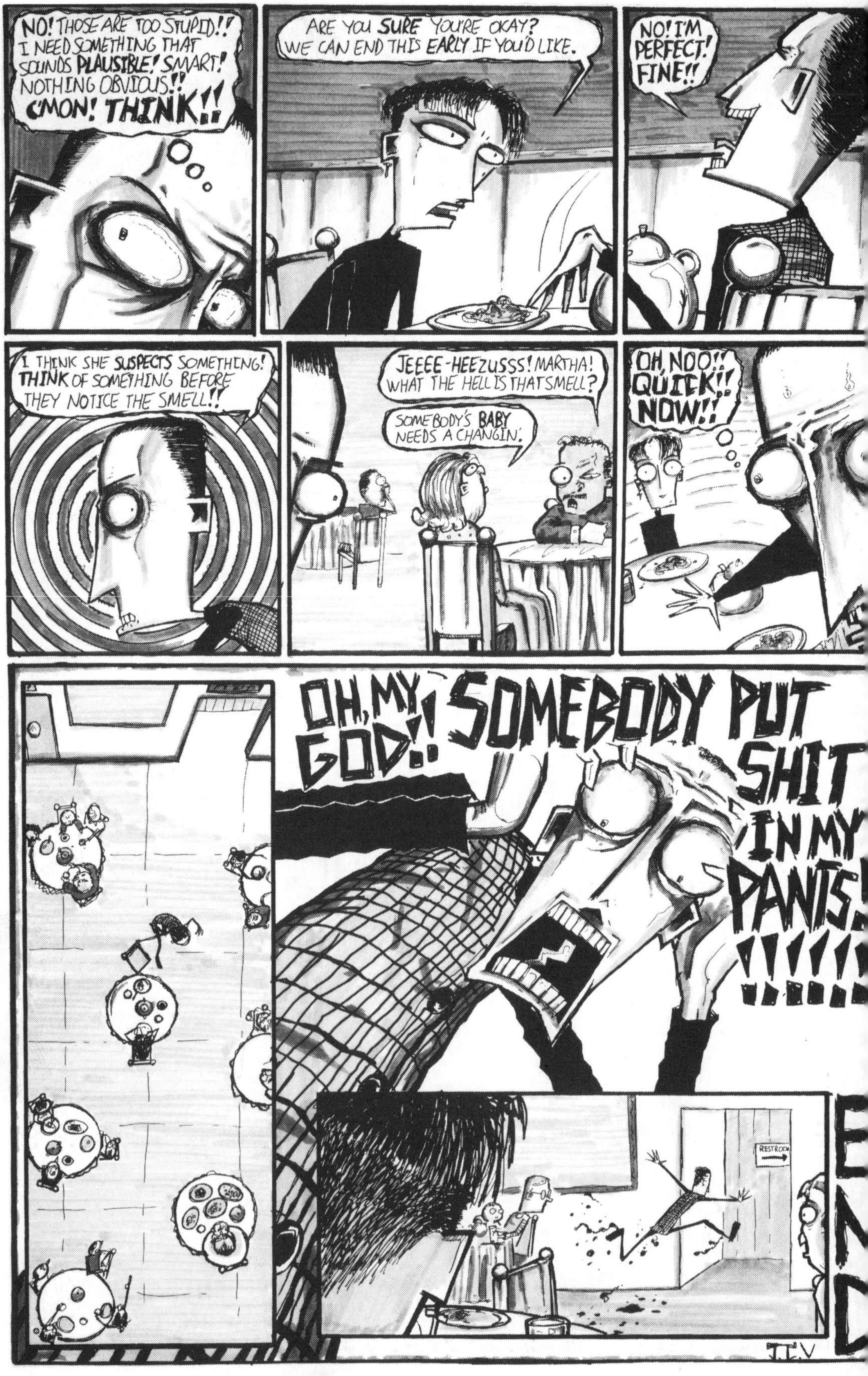
NO! THOSE ARE TOO STUPID!! I NEED SOMETHING THAT SOUNDS PLAUSIBLE! SMART! NOTHING OBVIOUS!! C'MON! THINK!!
ARE YOU SURE YOU'RE OKAY? WE CAN END THIS EARLY IF YOU'D LIKE.
NO! I'M PERFECT! FINE!!
I THINK SHE SUSPECTS SOMETHING! THINK OF SOMETHING BEFORE THEY NOTICE THE SMELL!!
JEEEE-HEEZUSSS! MARTHA! WHAT THE HELL IS THAT SMELL?
SOMEBODY'S BABY NEEDS A CHANGIN'.
OH, NOO!! QUICK!! NOW!!
OH, MY GOD!!
SOMEBODY PUT SHIT IN MY PANTS!!!!!!
RESTROOM
J.F.V

MEANWHILE...

J.C.V

HIGH ABOVE THE EARTH

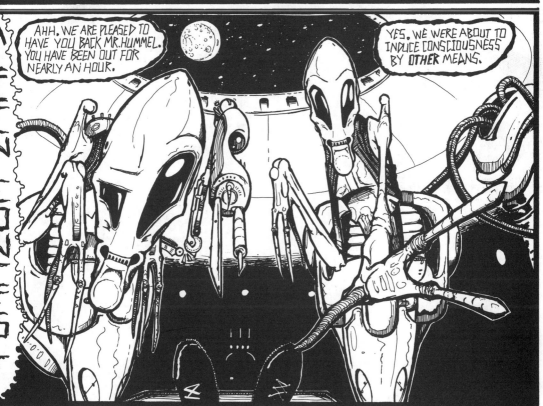

AHH, WE ARE PLEASED TO HAVE YOU BACK MR. HUMMEL. YOU HAVE BEEN OUT FOR NEARLY AN HOUR.

YES, WE WERE ABOUT TO INDUCE CONSCIOUSNESS BY *OTHER* MEANS.

WHAT IS THIS?! WHAT'S GOIN' ON?! WHERE **AM** I?!!

WHO... **WHAT** ARE YOU!!!?!

YOU ARE OFF OF YOUR PLANET

WE ARE SCIENTISTS. AND YOU ARE REQUIRED.

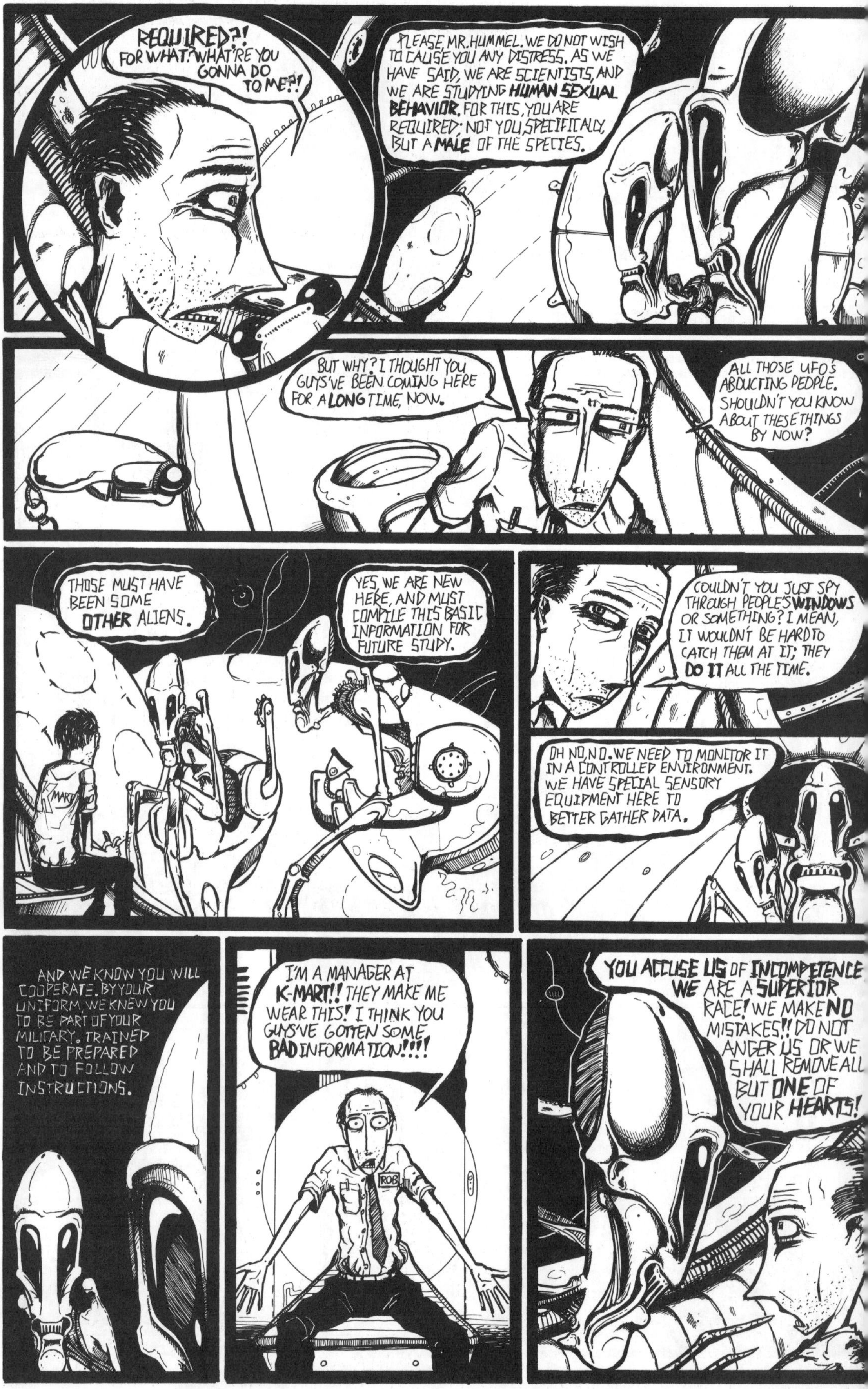
REQUIRED?! FOR WHAT? WHAT'RE YOU GONNA DO TO ME?!
PLEASE, MR. HUMMEL. WE DO NOT WISH TO CAUSE YOU ANY DISTRESS. AS WE HAVE SAID, WE ARE SCIENTISTS, AND WE ARE STUDYING **HUMAN SEXUAL BEHAVIOR**. FOR THIS, YOU ARE REQUIRED; NOT YOU, SPECIFICALLY, BUT A **MALE** OF THE SPECIES.
BUT WHY? I THOUGHT YOU GUYS'VE BEEN COMING HERE FOR A **LONG** TIME, NOW.
ALL THOSE UFO'S ABDUCTING PEOPLE. SHOULDN'T YOU KNOW ABOUT THESE THINGS BY NOW?
THOSE MUST HAVE BEEN SOME **OTHER** ALIENS.
YES, WE ARE NEW HERE, AND MUST COMPILE THIS BASIC INFORMATION FOR FUTURE STUDY.
K MART
COULDN'T YOU JUST SPY THROUGH PEOPLE'S **WINDOWS** OR SOMETHING? I MEAN, IT WOULDN'T BE HARD TO CATCH THEM AT IT; THEY **DO IT** ALL THE TIME.
OH NO, NO. WE NEED TO MONITOR IT IN A CONTROLLED ENVIRONMENT. WE HAVE SPECIAL SENSORY EQUIPMENT HERE TO BETTER GATHER DATA.
AND WE KNOW YOU WILL COOPERATE. BY YOUR UNIFORM, WE KNEW YOU TO BE PART OF YOUR MILITARY. TRAINED TO BE PREPARED AND TO FOLLOW INSTRUCTIONS.
I'M A MANAGER AT **K-MART!!** THEY MAKE ME WEAR THIS! I THINK YOU GUYS'VE GOTTEN SOME **BAD** INFORMATION!!!!
ROB
YOU ACCUSE US OF INCOMPETENCE WE ARE A **SUPERIOR** RACE! WE MAKE **NO** MISTAKES!! DO NOT ANGER **US** OR WE SHALL REMOVE ALL BUT **ONE** OF YOUR **HEARTS**!

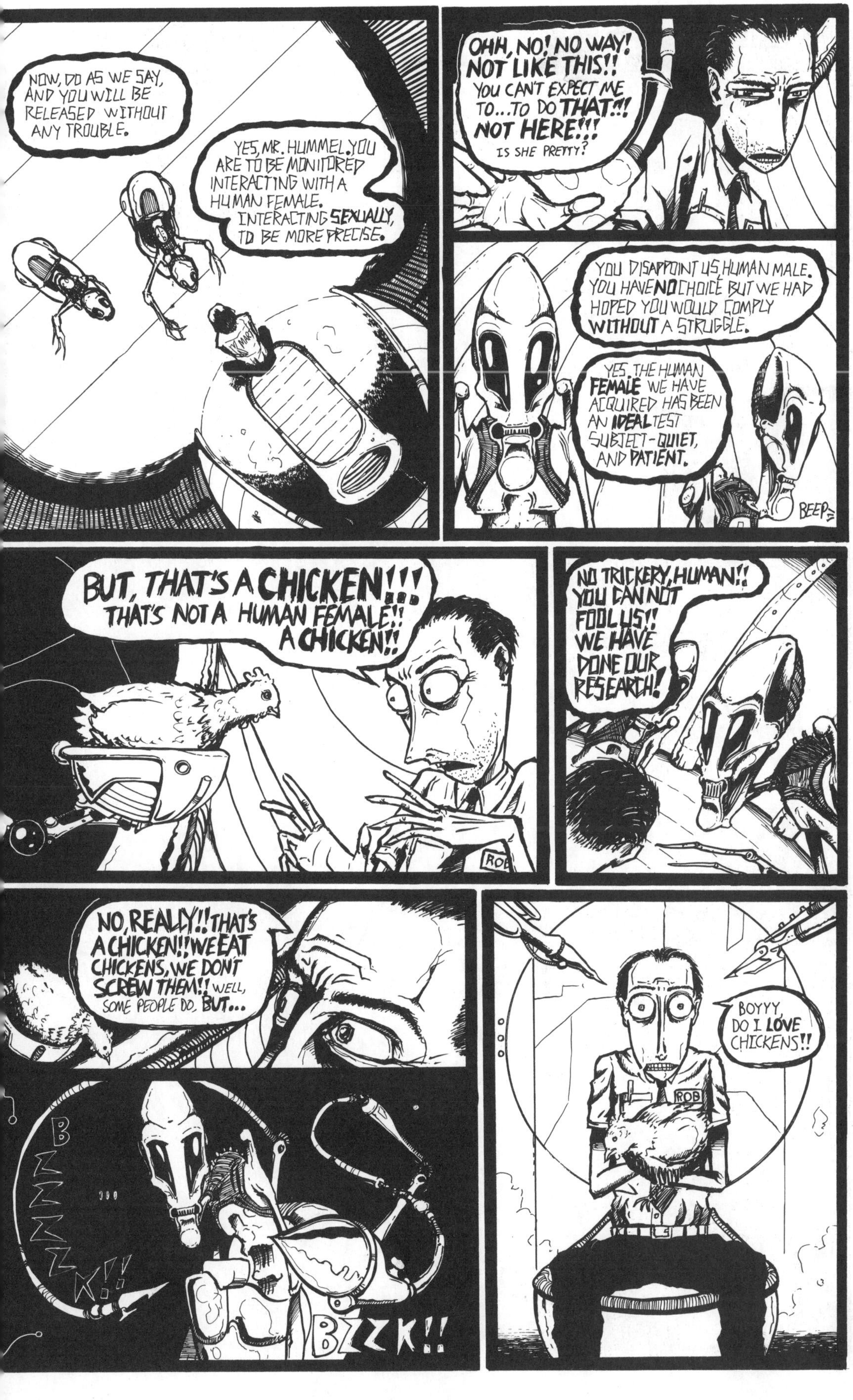
NOW, DO AS WE SAY, AND YOU WILL BE RELEASED WITHOUT ANY TROUBLE.
YES, MR. HUMMEL. YOU ARE TO BE MONITORED INTERACTING WITH A HUMAN FEMALE. INTERACTING SEXUALLY, TO BE MORE PRECISE.
OHH, NO! NO WAY! NOT LIKE THIS!! YOU CAN'T EXPECT ME TO...TO DO THAT!!! NOT HERE!!! IS SHE PRETTY?
YOU DISAPPOINT US, HUMAN MALE. YOU HAVE NO CHOICE BUT WE HAD HOPED YOU WOULD COMPLY WITHOUT A STRUGGLE.
YES. THE HUMAN FEMALE WE HAVE ACQUIRED HAS BEEN AN IDEAL TEST SUBJECT - QUIET, AND PATIENT.
BEEP
BUT, THAT'S A CHICKEN!!! THAT'S NOT A HUMAN FEMALE!! A CHICKEN!!
ROB
NO TRICKERY, HUMAN!! YOU CAN NOT FOOL US!! WE HAVE DONE OUR RESEARCH!
NO, REALLY!! THAT'S A CHICKEN!! WE EAT CHICKENS, WE DONT SCREW THEM!! WELL, SOME PEOPLE DO, BUT...
BZZZZZK!!
BZZK!!
BOYYY, DO I LOVE CHICKENS!!
ROB

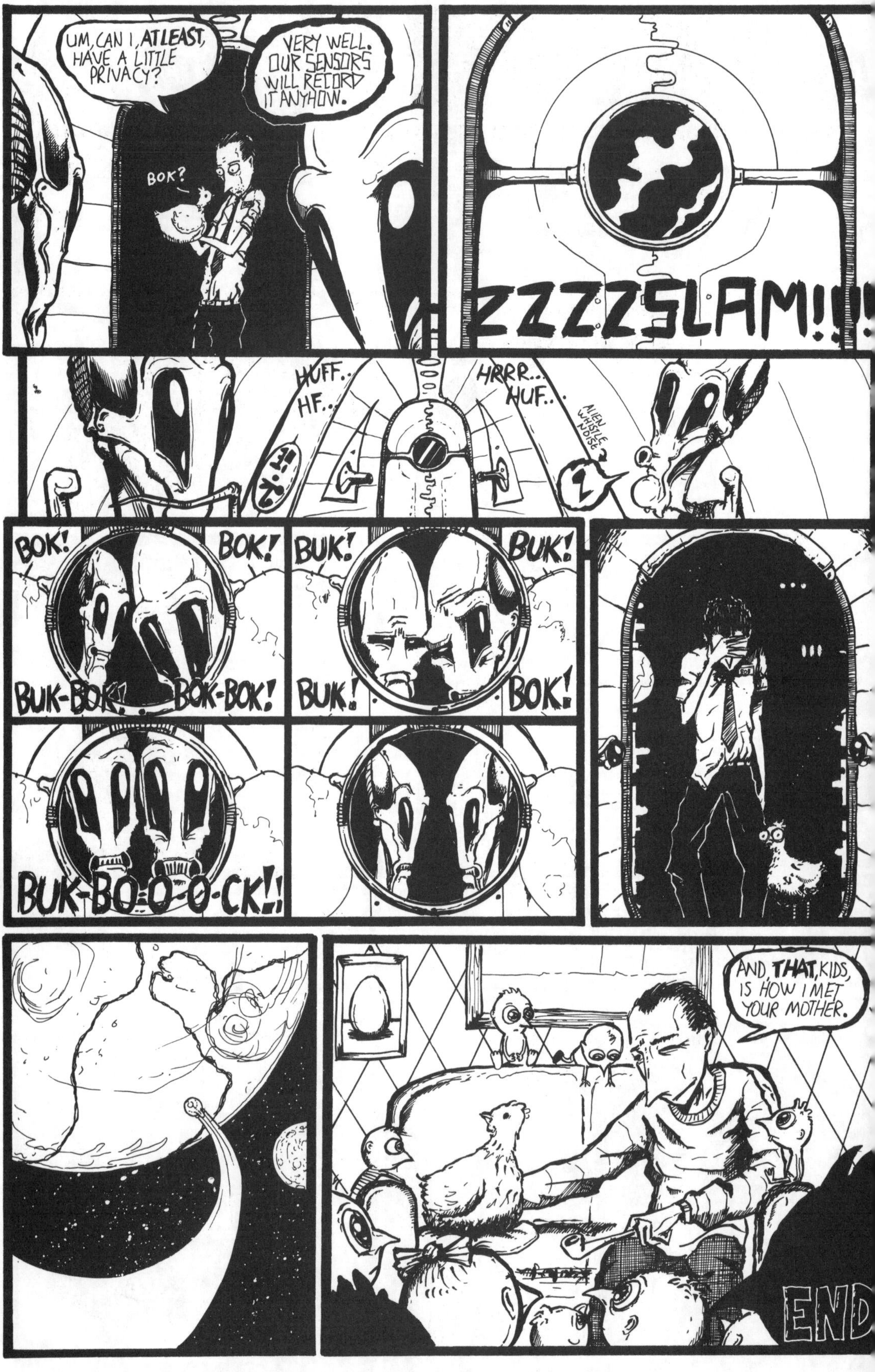
UM, CAN I, **AT LEAST**, HAVE A LITTLE PRIVACY?
VERY WELL. OUR SENSORS WILL RECORD IT ANYHOW.
BOK?
ZZZZSLAM!!!!
HUFF.. HF..
HRRR... HUF...
ALIEN WHISTLE NOISE
BOK! BOK!
BUK-BOK! BOK-BOK!
BUK! BUK!
BUK! BOK!
BUK-BO-O-O-CK!!
AND, **THAT**, KIDS, IS HOW I MET YOUR MOTHER.
END

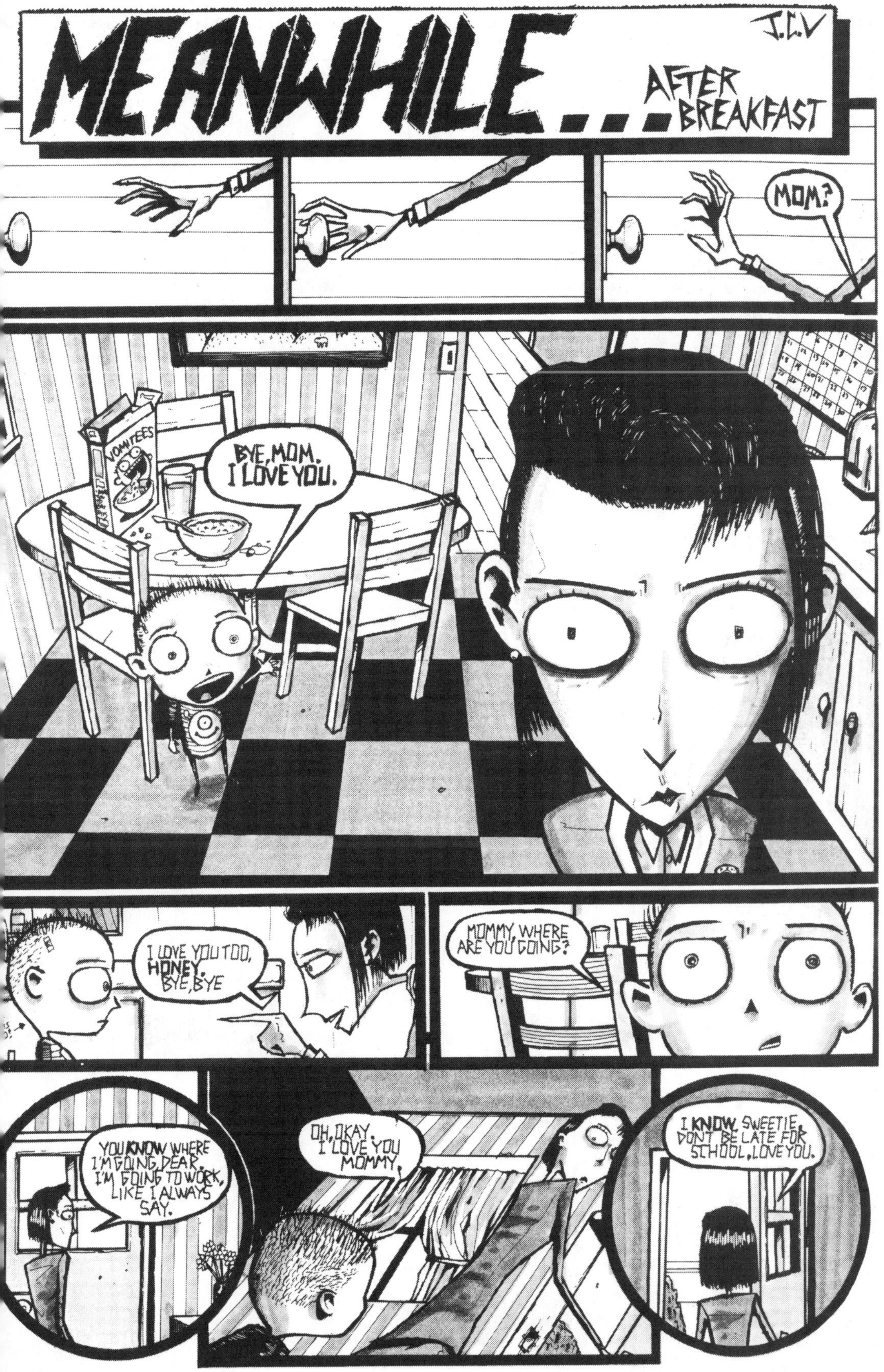
MEANWHILE... AFTER BREAKFAST
J.C.V
MOM?
BYE, MOM. I LOVE YOU.
I LOVE YOU TOO, HONEY. BYE, BYE
MOMMY, WHERE ARE YOU GOING?
YOU KNOW WHERE I'M GOING, DEAR. I'M GOING TO WORK, LIKE I ALWAYS SAY.
OH, OKAY. I LOVE YOU MOMMY.
I KNOW, SWEETIE. DON'T BE LATE FOR SCHOOL, LOVE YOU.

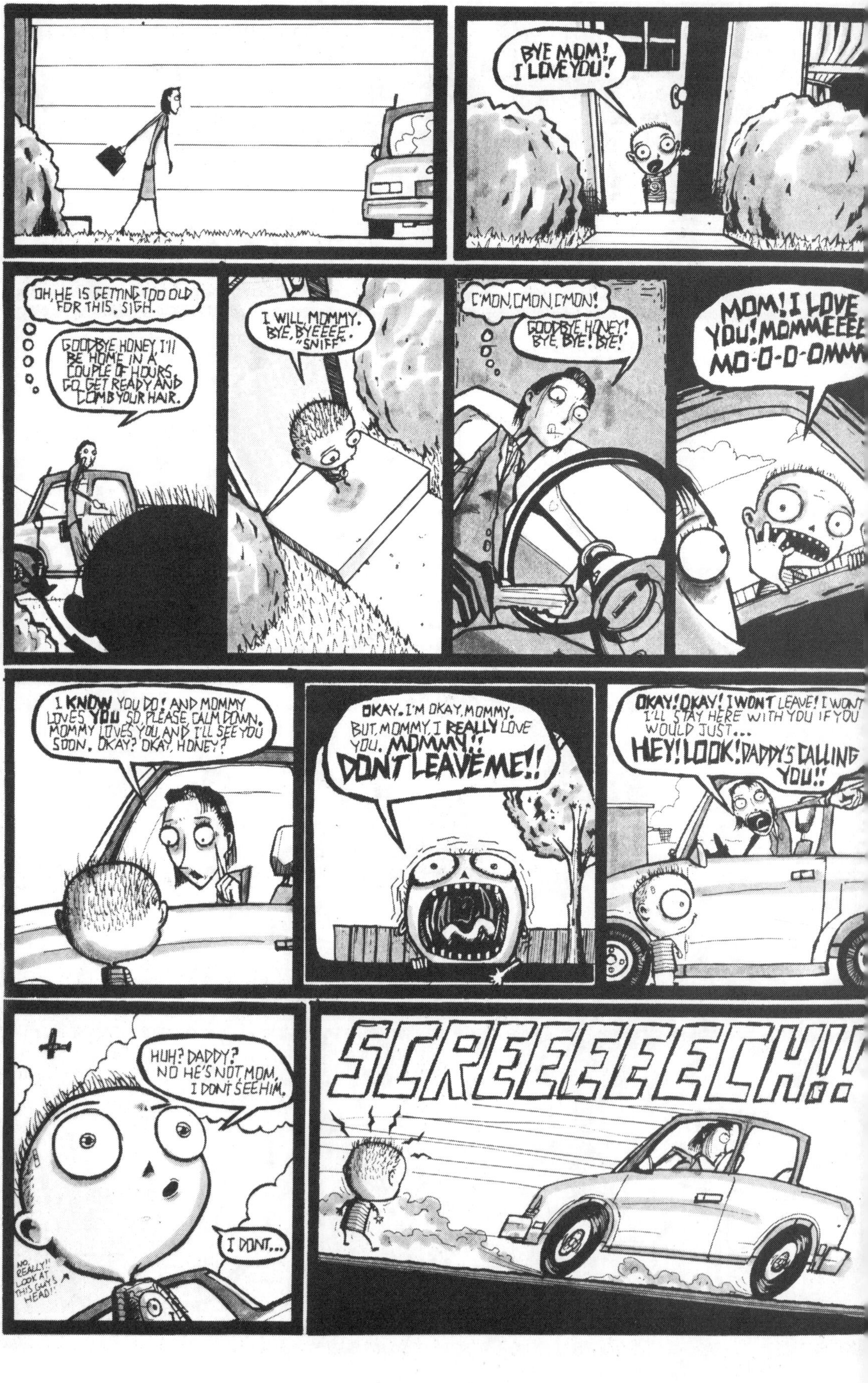
BYE MOM! I LOVE YOU!!
OH, HE IS GETTING TOO OLD FOR THIS. SIGH.
GOODBYE HONEY. I'LL BE HOME IN A COUPLE OF HOURS. GO GET READY AND COMB YOUR HAIR.
I WILL MOMMY. BYE, BYEEEE. "SNIFF"
C'MON, C'MON, C'MON!
GOODBYE HONEY! BYE, BYE! BYE!
MOM! I LOVE YOU! MOMMEEEE MO-O-O-OMM
I KNOW YOU DO! AND MOMMY LOVES YOU SO PLEASE CALM DOWN. MOMMY LOVES YOU, AND I'LL SEE YOU SOON. OKAY? OKAY, HONEY?
OKAY. I'M OKAY, MOMMY. BUT, MOMMY, I REALLY LOVE YOU. MOMMY!! DONT LEAVE ME!!
OKAY! OKAY! I WONT LEAVE! I WONT I'LL STAY HERE WITH YOU IF YOU WOULD JUST... HEY! LOOK! DADDY'S CALLING YOU!!
HUH? DADDY? NO HE'S NOT, MOM, I DONT SEE HIM.
I DONT...
NO, REALLY!! LOOK AT THIS GUY'S HEAD!!
SCREEEEEECH!!

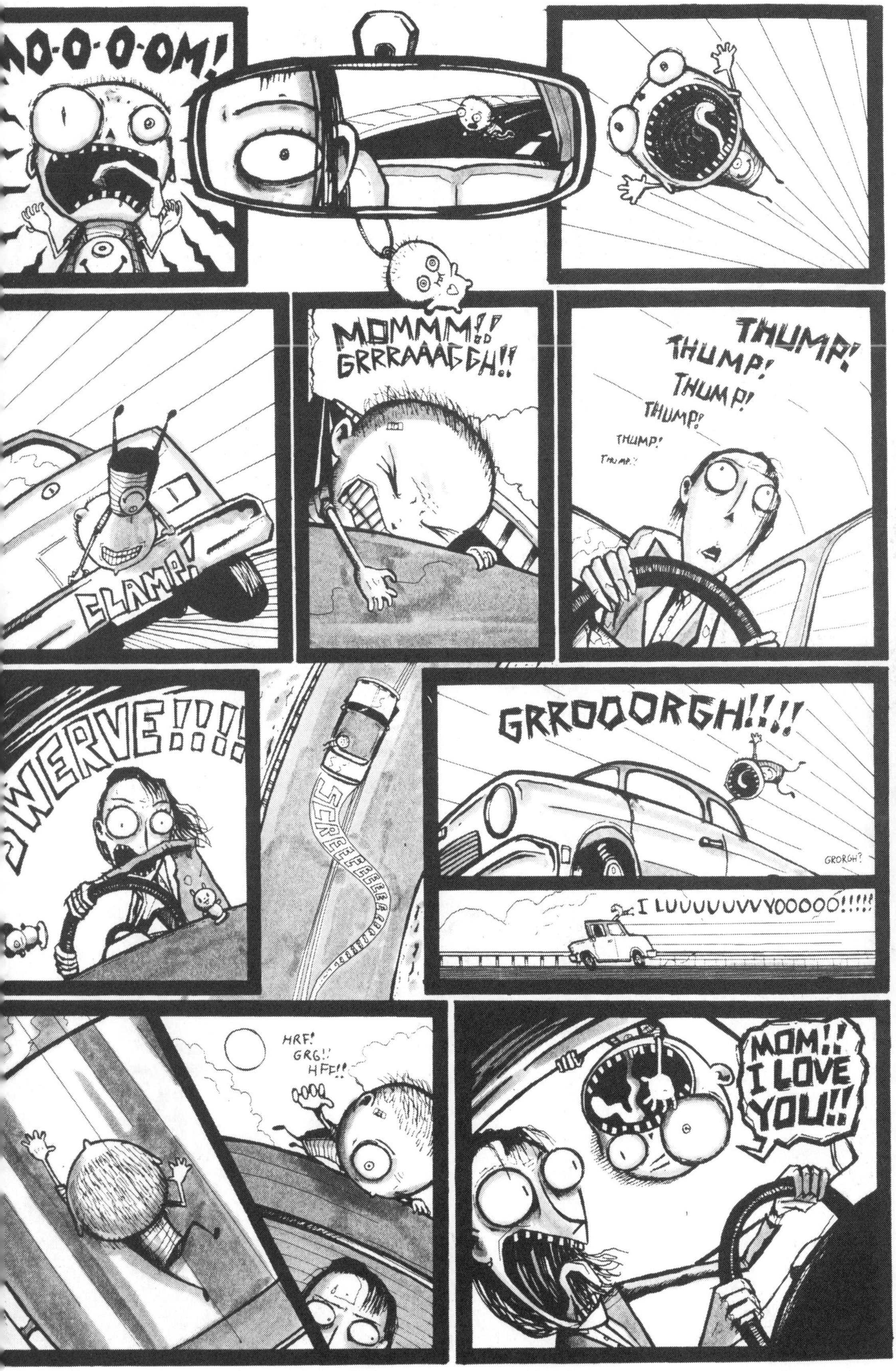
MO-O-O-OM!
MOMMM!!
GRRRAAAGGH!!
THUMP!
THUMP!
THUMP!
THUMP!
THUMP!
CLAMP!
SWERVE!!!!!
SCREEEEEEEE
GRROOORGH!!!!
GRORGH?
I LUUUUUVVYOOOOO!!!!!
HRF!
GRG!!
HFF!!
MOM!!
I LOVE
YOU!!

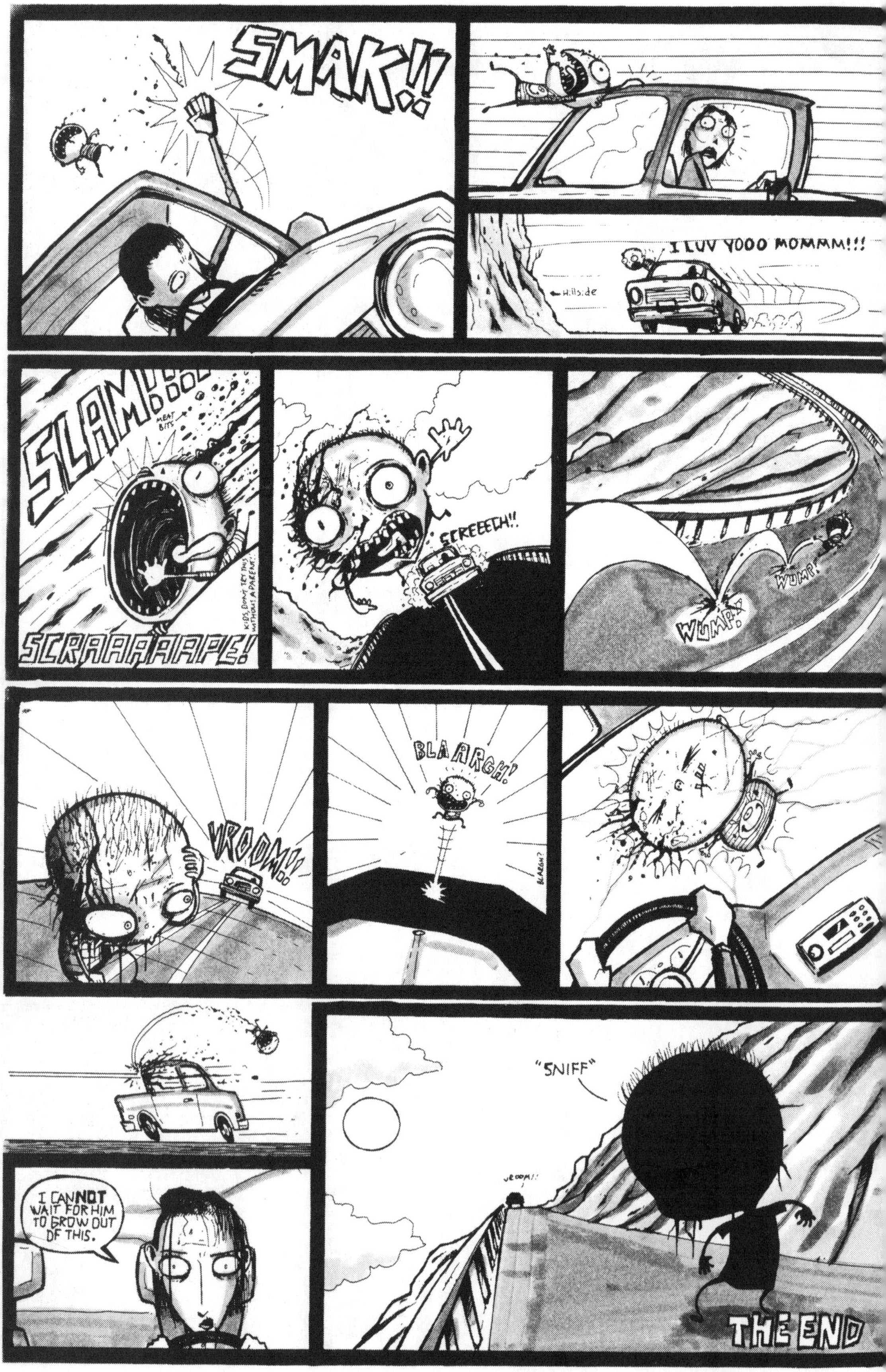
SMAK!!
I LUV YOOO MOMMM!!!
Hillside
SLAM!!
MEAT BITS
KIDS, DON'T TRY THIS WITHOUT A PARENT!
SCRAAAAAAPE!
SCREEECH!!
WUMP!!
WUMP!
VROOM!!
BLAARGH!
BLARGH?
I CAN NOT WAIT FOR HIM TO GROW OUT OF THIS.
"SNIFF"
VROOM!!
THE END

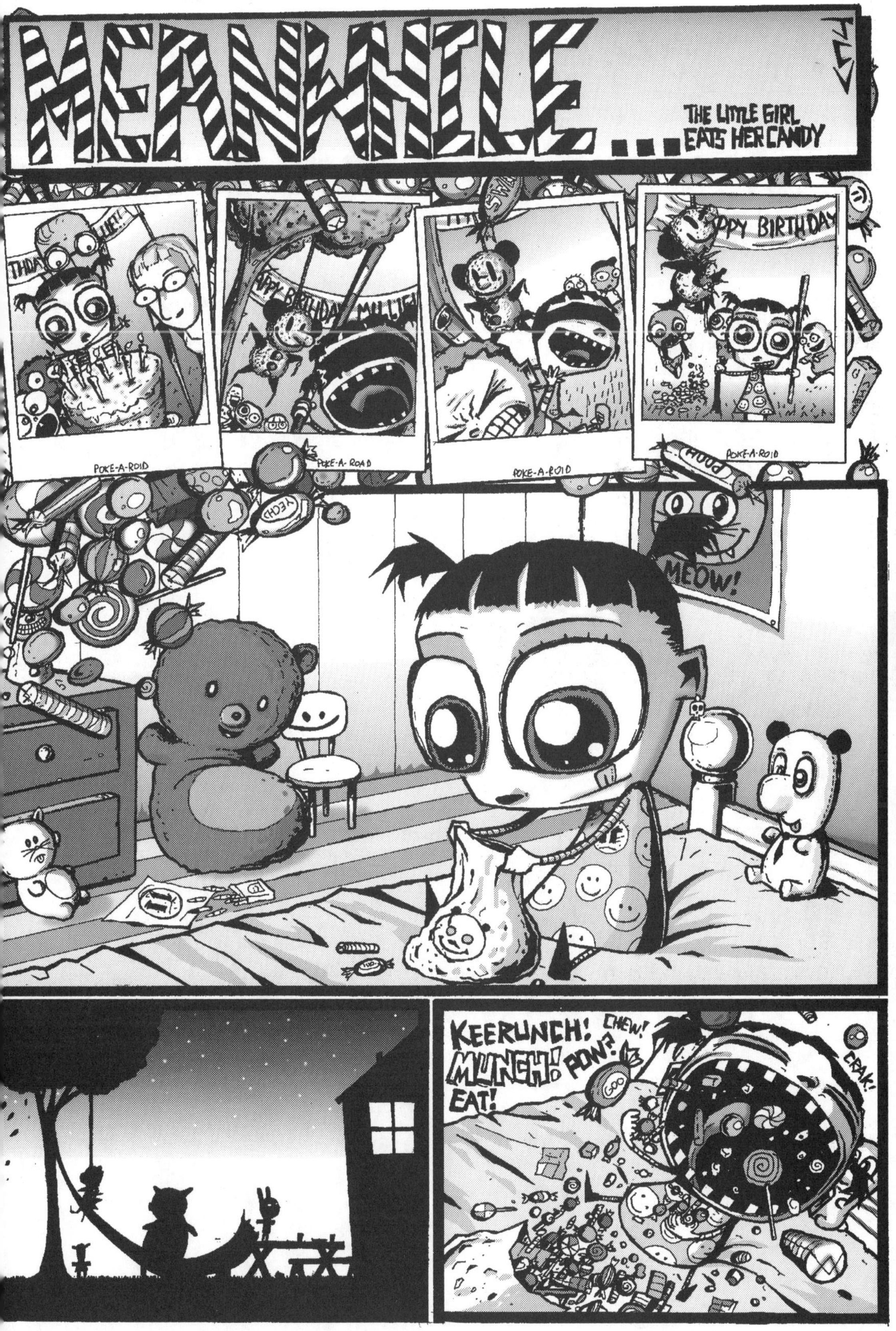
MEANWHILE...
THE LITTLE GIRL EATS HER CANDY
POKE-A-ROID
POKE-A-ROAD
POKE-A-ROID
PPY BIRTHDAY
POKE-A-ROID
YECH
MEOW!
KEERUNCH!
CHEW!
MUNCH!
POW?
EAT!
CRAK!

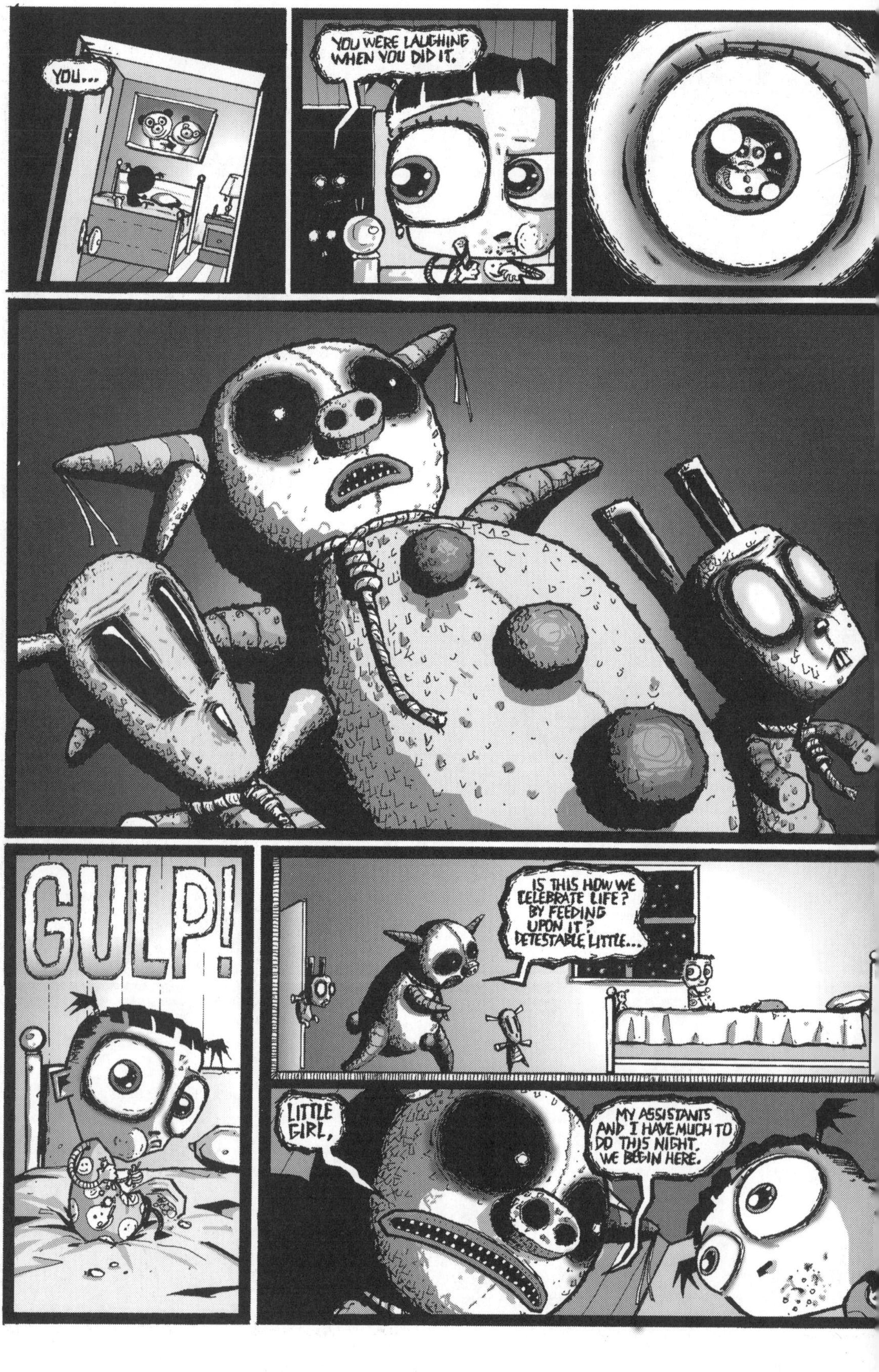
YOU...
YOU WERE LAUGHING WHEN YOU DID IT.
GULP!
IS THIS HOW WE CELEBRATE LIFE? BY FEEDING UPON IT? DETESTABLE LITTLE...
LITTLE GIRL,
MY ASSISTANTS AND I HAVE MUCH TO DO THIS NIGHT. WE BEGIN HERE.

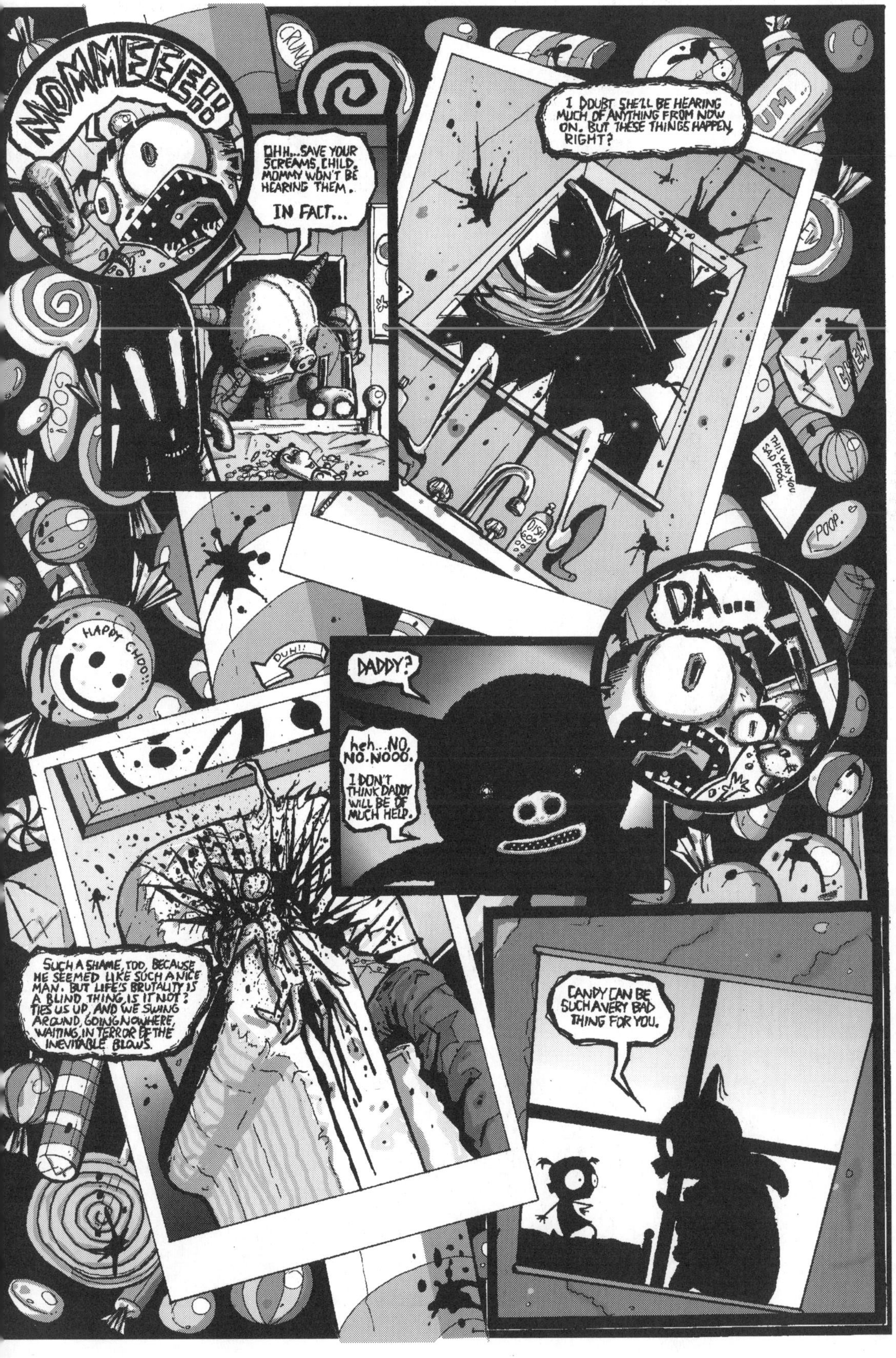
MOMMEEE
OHH...SAVE YOUR SCREAMS, CHILD. MOMMY WON'T BE HEARING THEM.
IN FACT...
I DOUBT SHE'LL BE HEARING MUCH OF ANYTHING FROM NOW ON. BUT THESE THINGS HAPPEN, RIGHT?
DA...
DADDY?
heh...NO, NO. NOOO.
I DON'T THINK DADDY WILL BE OF MUCH HELP.
SUCH A SHAME, TOO, BECAUSE HE SEEMED LIKE SUCH A NICE MAN. BUT LIFE'S BRUTALITY IS A BLIND THING IS IT NOT? TIES US UP, AND WE SWING AROUND, GOING NOWHERE, WAITING, IN TERROR OF THE INEVITABLE BLOWS.
CANDY CAN BE SUCH A VERY BAD THING FOR YOU.

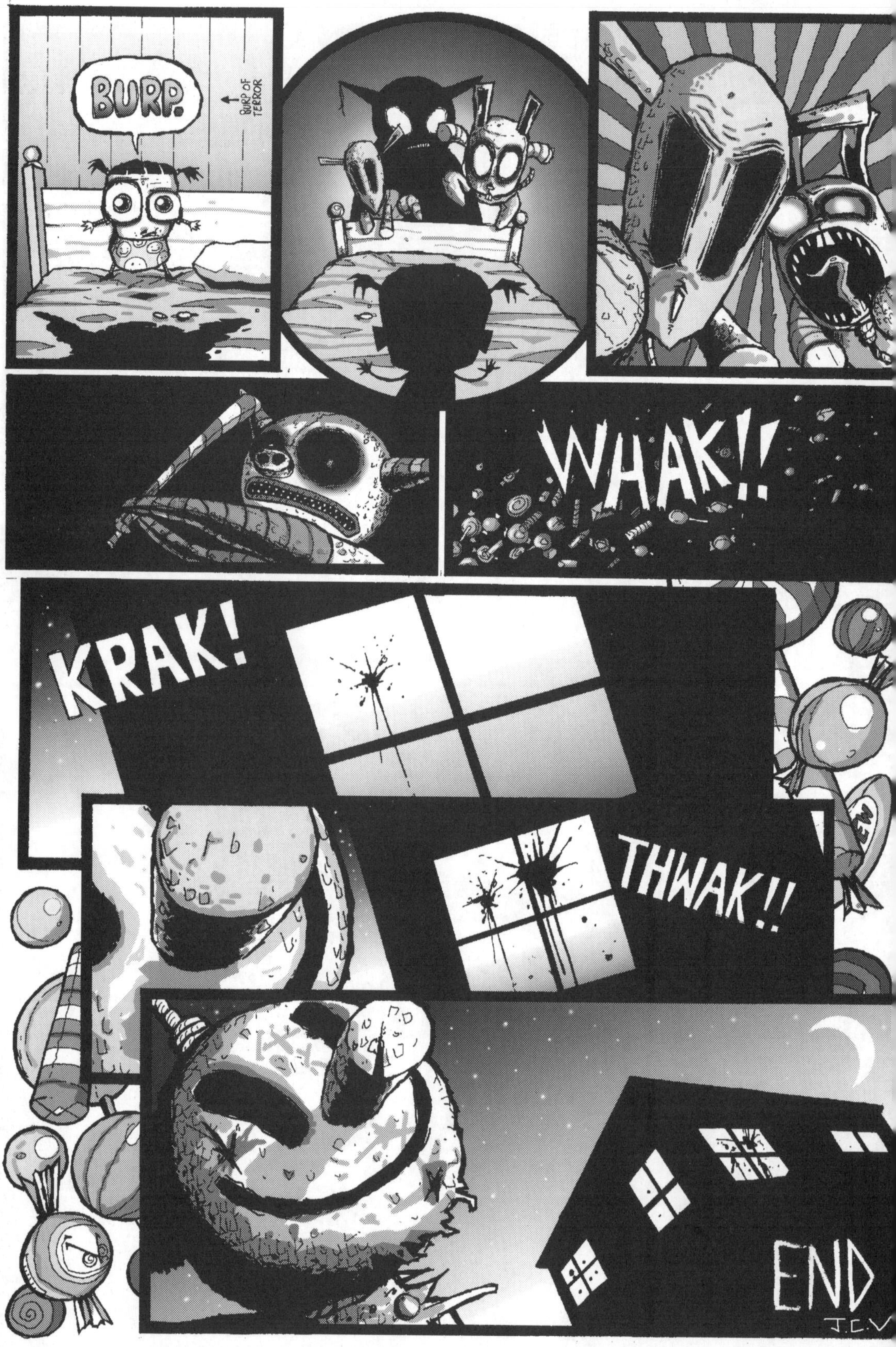
BURP.
← BURP OF TERROR
WHAK!!
KRAK!
EW
THWAK!!
END
J.C.V

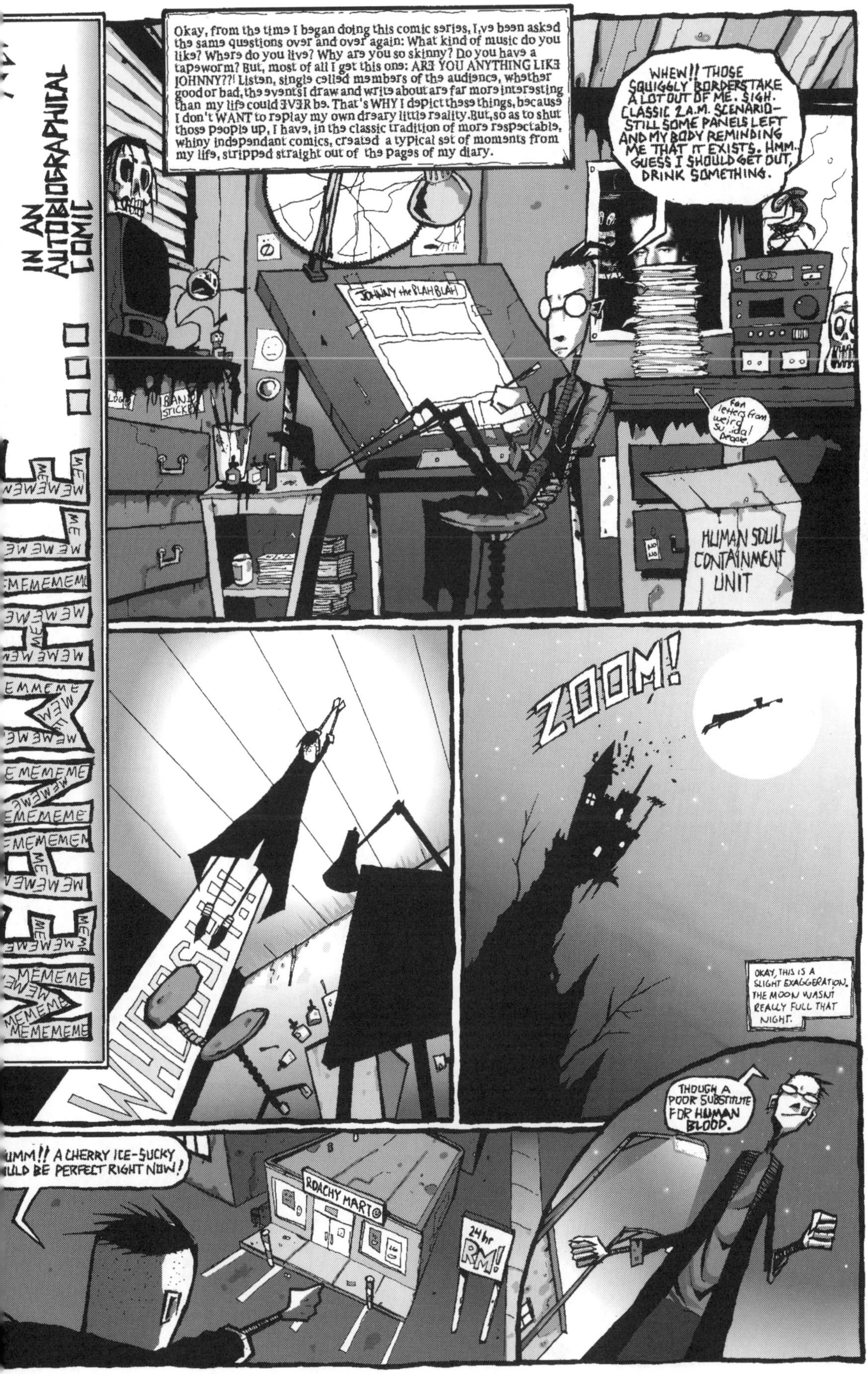
IN AN AUTOBIOGRAPHICAL COMIC
Okay, from the time I began doing this comic series, I,ve been asked the same questions over and over again: What kind of music do you like? Where do you live? Why are you so skinny? Do you have a tapeworm? But, most of all I get this one: ARE YOU ANYTHING LIKE JOHNNY??! Listen, single celled members of the audience, whether good or bad, the events I draw and write about are far more interesting than my life could EVER be. That's WHY I depict these things, because I don't WANT to replay my own dreary little reality. But, so as to shut those people up, I have, in the classic tradition of more respectable, whiny independant comics, created a typical set of moments from my life, stripped straight out of the pages of my diary.
WHEW!! THOSE SQUIGGLY BORDERS TAKE A LOT OUT OF ME. SIGH. CLASSIC 2 A.M. SCENARIO- STILL SOME PANELS LEFT AND MY BODY REMINDING ME THAT IT EXISTS. HMM.. GUESS I SHOULD GET OUT, DRINK SOMETHING.
JOHNNY the PLAH BLAH
Fan letters from weird suicidal people.
HUMAN SOUL CONTAINMENT UNIT
WHOOSH!!
ZOOM!
OKAY, THIS IS A SLIGHT EXAGGERATION. THE MOON WASN'T REALLY FULL THAT NIGHT.
THOUGH A POOR SUBSTITUTE FOR HUMAN BLOOD.
UMM!! A CHERRY ICE-SUCKY ULD BE PERFECT RIGHT NOW!
ROACHY MART
24 hr RM!

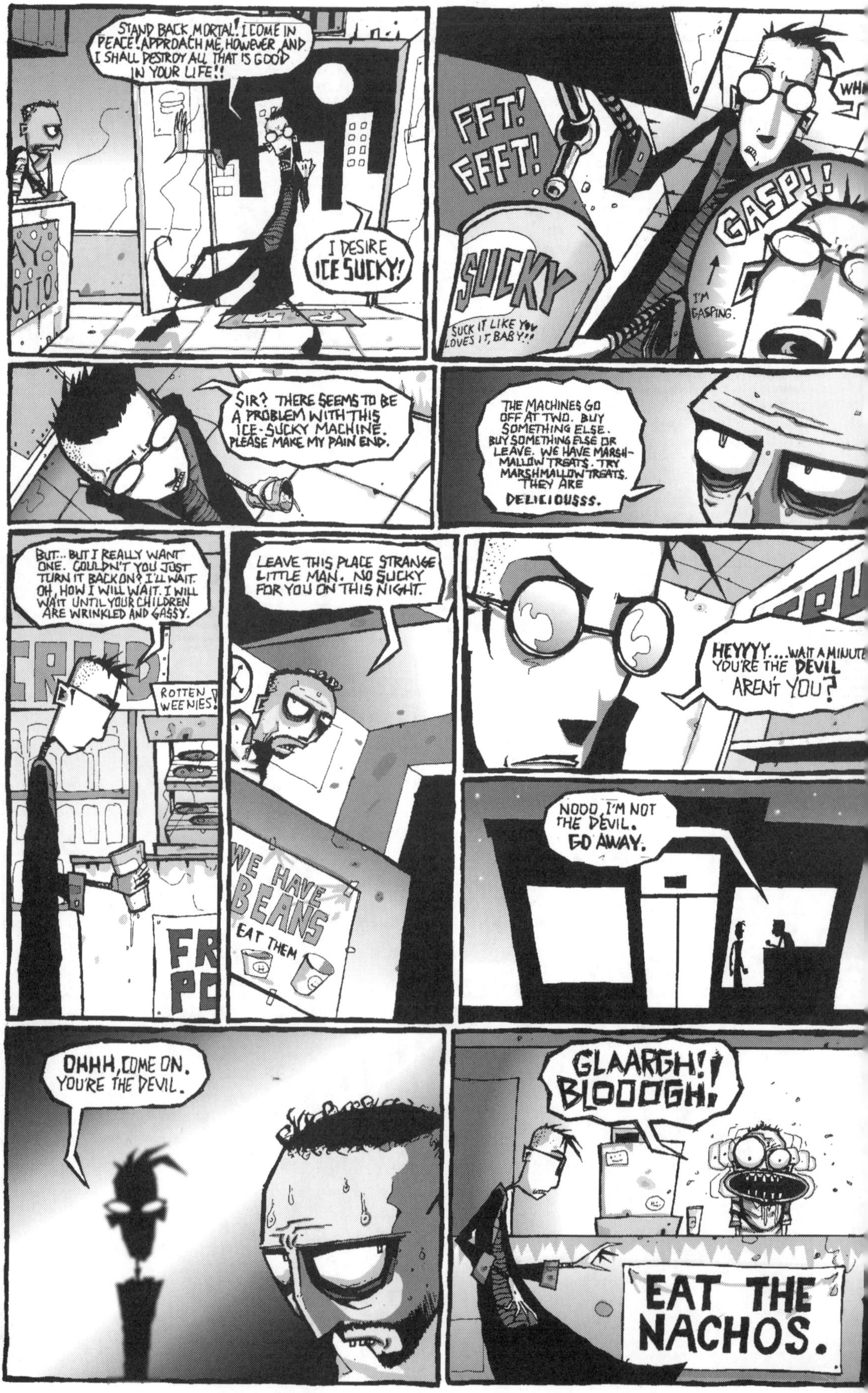
STAND BACK MORTAL! I COME IN PEACE! APPROACH ME, HOWEVER AND I SHALL DESTROY ALL THAT IS GOOD IN YOUR LIFE!!
I DESIRE ICE SUCKY!
FFT! FFFT!
SUCKY
SUCK IT LIKE YOU LOVES IT, BABY!!
GASP!!
I'M GASPING.
SIR? THERE SEEMS TO BE A PROBLEM WITH THIS ICE-SUCKY MACHINE. PLEASE MAKE MY PAIN END.
THE MACHINES GO OFF AT TWO. BUY SOMETHING ELSE. BUY SOMETHING ELSE OR LEAVE. WE HAVE MARSHMALLOW TREATS. TRY MARSHMALLOW TREATS. THEY ARE DELICIOUSSS.
BUT... BUT I REALLY WANT ONE. COULDN'T YOU JUST TURN IT BACK ON? I'LL WAIT. OH, HOW I WILL WAIT. I WILL WAIT UNTIL YOUR CHILDREN ARE WRINKLED AND GASSY.
ROTTEN WEENIES!
LEAVE THIS PLACE STRANGE LITTLE MAN. NO SUCKY FOR YOU ON THIS NIGHT.
WE HAVE BEANS
EAT THEM
HEYYYY....WAIT A MINUTE YOU'RE THE DEVIL AREN'T YOU?
NOOO, I'M NOT THE DEVIL. GO AWAY.
OHHH, COME ON. YOU'RE THE DEVIL.
GLAARGH! BLOOOGH!
EAT THE NACHOS.

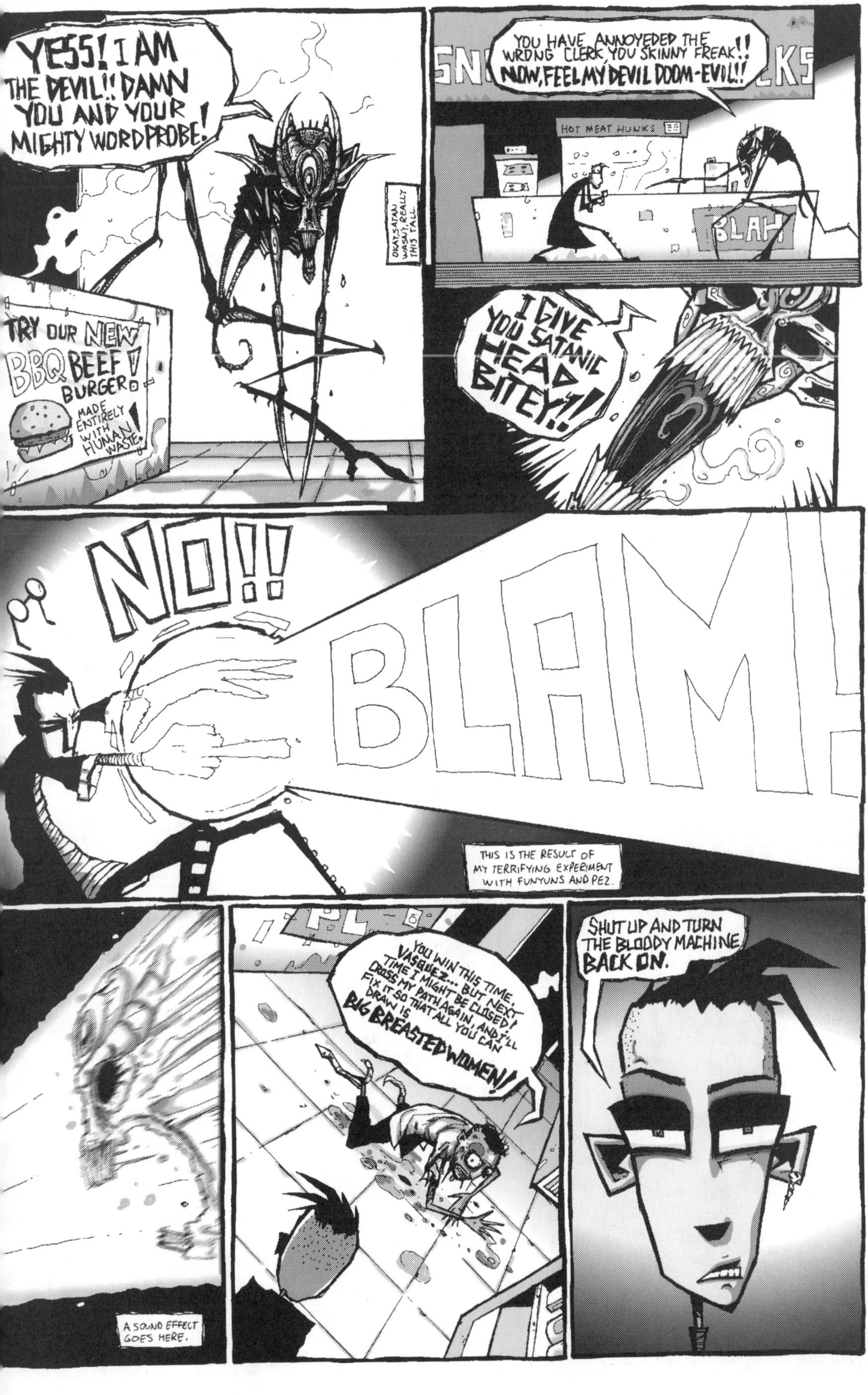
YESS! I AM THE DEVIL!! DAMN YOU AND YOUR MIGHTY WORDPROBE!
OKAY, SATAN WASN'T REALLY THIS TALL.
TRY OUR NEW BBQ BEEF BURGER! MADE ENTIRELY WITH HUMAN WASTE!
YOU HAVE ANNOYEDED THE WRONG CLERK, YOU SKINNY FREAK!! NOW, FEEL MY DEVIL DOOM-EVIL!!
HOT MEAT HUNKS
BLAH
I GIVE YOU SATANIC HEAD BITEY!!
NO!!
BLAM!
THIS IS THE RESULT OF MY TERRIFYING EXPERIMENT WITH FUNYUNS AND PEZ.
A SOUND EFFECT GOES HERE.
YOU WIN THIS TIME, VASQUEZ... BUT NEXT TIME I MIGHT BE CLOSED! CROSS MY PATH AGAIN, AND I'LL FIX IT SO THAT ALL YOU CAN DRAW IS BIG BREASTED WOMEN!
SHUT UP AND TURN THE BLOODY MACHINE BACK ON.

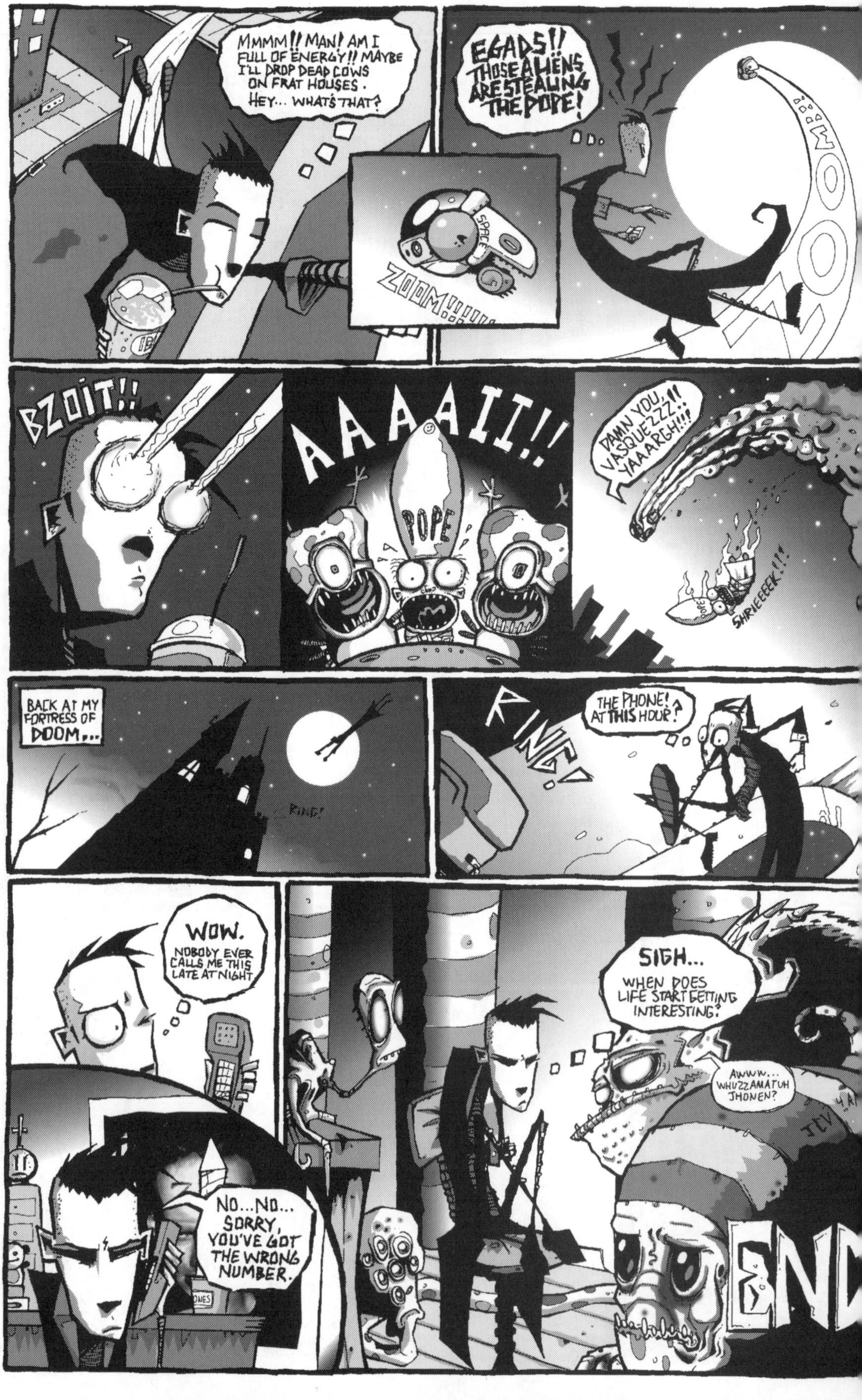
MMMM!! MAN! AM I FULL OF ENERGY!! MAYBE I'LL DROP DEAD COWS ON FRAT HOUSES.
HEY... WHAT'S THAT?
SPACE
ZOOM!!!!!!
EGADS!! THOSE ALIENS ARE STEALING THE POPE!
BZOIT!!
AAAAII!!
POPE
DAMN YOU, VASQUEZZZ!! YAAARGH!!!
SHRIEEEEK!!!
BACK AT MY FORTRESS OF DOOM...
RING!
RING!
THE PHONE! AT THIS HOUR?
WOW.
NOBODY EVER CALLS ME THIS LATE AT NIGHT.
NO...NO... SORRY, YOU'VE GOT THE WRONG NUMBER.
SIGH...
WHEN DOES LIFE START GETTING INTERESTING?
AWWW... WHUZZAMATUH JHONEN?
END

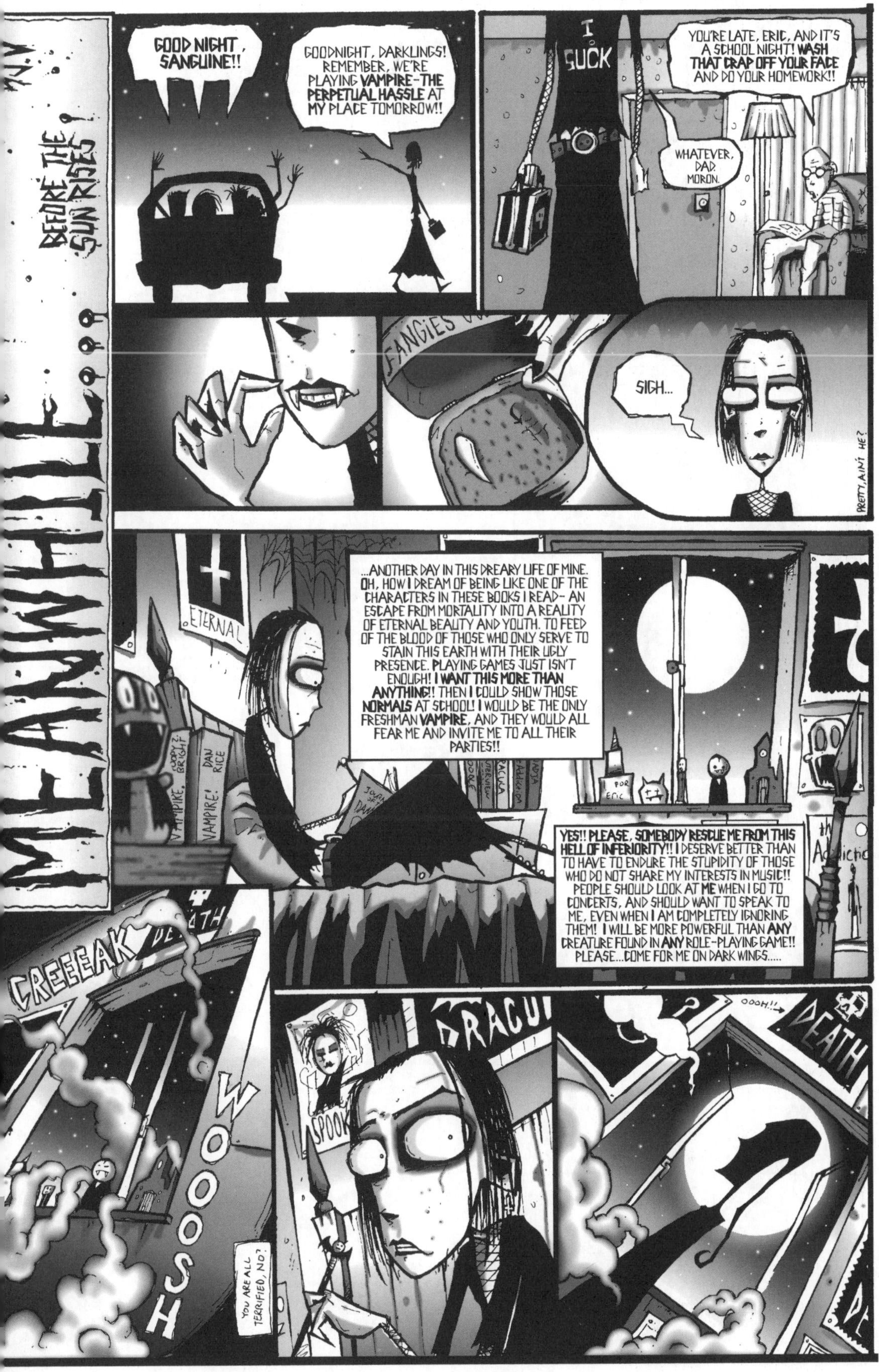

MEANWHILE...
BEFORE THE SUN RISES!
GOOD NIGHT, SANGUINE!!
GOODNIGHT, DARKLINGS! REMEMBER, WE'RE PLAYING VAMPIRE-THE PERPETUAL HASSLE AT MY PLACE TOMORROW!!
I SUCK
YOU'RE LATE, ERIC, AND IT'S A SCHOOL NIGHT! WASH THAT CRAP OFF YOUR FACE AND DO YOUR HOMEWORK!!
WHATEVER, DAD MORON.
FANGIES
SIGH...
PRETTY, AIN'T HE?
ETERNAL
...ANOTHER DAY IN THIS DREARY LIFE OF MINE. OH, HOW I DREAM OF BEING LIKE ONE OF THE CHARACTERS IN THESE BOOKS I READ-- AN ESCAPE FROM MORTALITY INTO A REALITY OF ETERNAL BEAUTY AND YOUTH. TO FEED OF THE BLOOD OF THOSE WHO ONLY SERVE TO STAIN THIS EARTH WITH THEIR UGLY PRESENCE. PLAYING GAMES JUST ISN'T ENOUGH! I WANT THIS MORE THAN ANYTHING!! THEN I COULD SHOW THOSE NORMALS AT SCHOOL! I WOULD BE THE ONLY FRESHMAN VAMPIRE, AND THEY WOULD ALL FEAR ME AND INVITE ME TO ALL THEIR PARTIES!!
VAMPIRE!
DAN RICE
FOR ERIC
YES!! PLEASE, SOMEBODY RESCUE ME FROM THIS HELL OF INFERIORITY!! I DESERVE BETTER THAN TO HAVE TO ENDURE THE STUPIDITY OF THOSE WHO DO NOT SHARE MY INTERESTS IN MUSIC!! PEOPLE SHOULD LOOK AT ME WHEN I GO TO CONCERTS, AND SHOULD WANT TO SPEAK TO ME, EVEN WHEN I AM COMPLETELY IGNORING THEM! I WILL BE MORE POWERFUL THAN ANY CREATURE FOUND IN ANY ROLE-PLAYING GAME!! PLEASE...COME FOR ME ON DARK WINGS.....
CREEEAK
DEATH
WOOOOSH
YOU ARE ALL TERRIFIED, NO?
DRACU
SPOOK
OOOH!!
DEATH

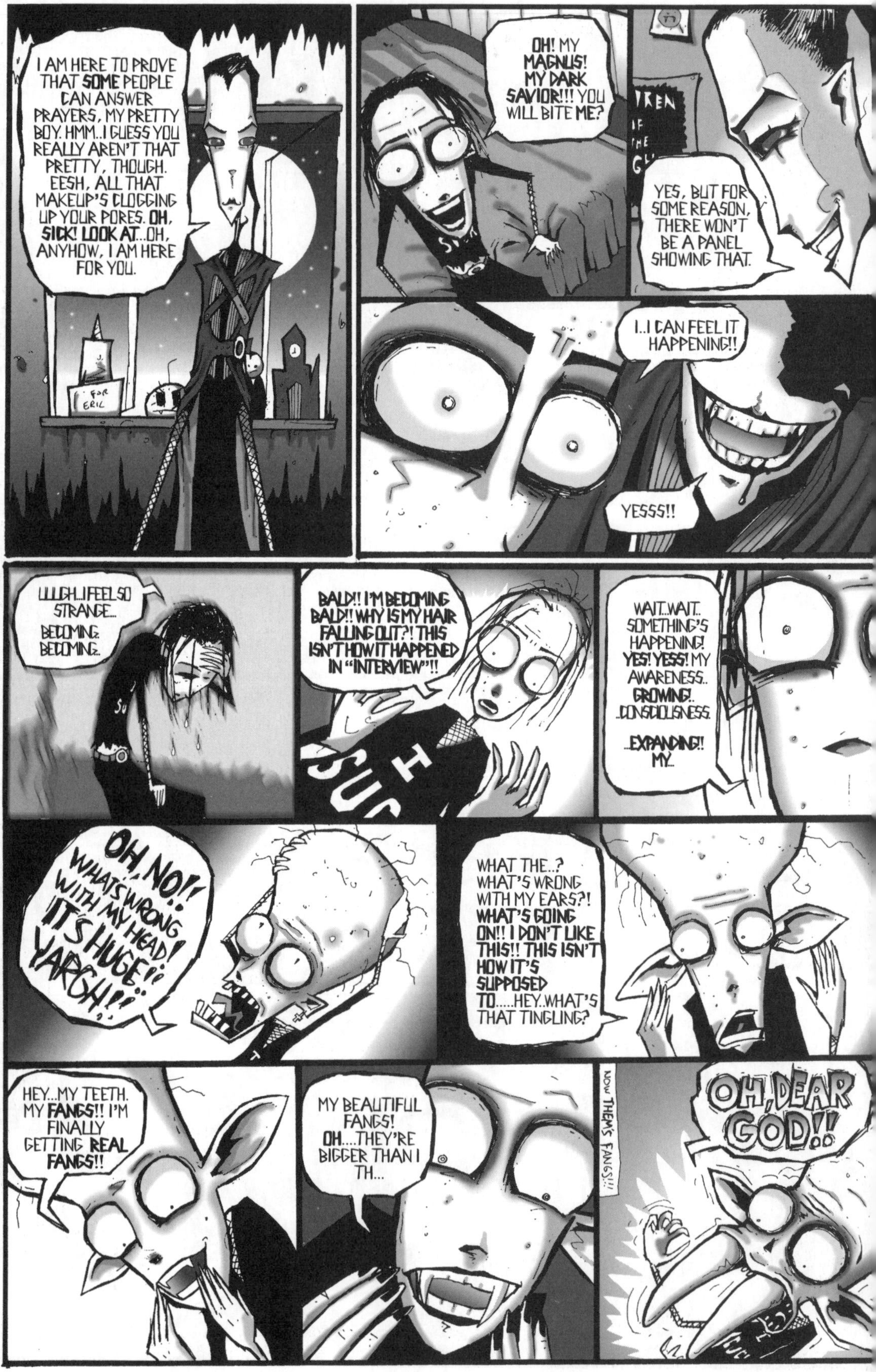
I AM HERE TO PROVE THAT SOME PEOPLE CAN ANSWER PRAYERS, MY PRETTY BOY. HMM..I GUESS YOU REALLY AREN'T THAT PRETTY, THOUGH. EESH, ALL THAT MAKEUP'S CLOGGING UP YOUR PORES. OH, SICK! LOOK AT...OH, ANYHOW, I AM HERE FOR YOU.
FOR ERIC
OH! MY MAGNUS! MY DARK SAVIOR!!! YOU WILL BITE ME?
YES, BUT FOR SOME REASON, THERE WON'T BE A PANEL SHOWING THAT.
I..I CAN FEEL IT HAPPENING!!
YESSS!!
UUUGH..I FEEL SO STRANGE... BECOMING. BECOMING..
BALD!! I'M BECOMING BALD!! WHY IS MY HAIR FALLING OUT?! THIS ISN'T HOW IT HAPPENED IN "INTERVIEW"!!
WAIT...WAIT.. SOMETHING'S HAPPENING! YES! YESS! MY AWARENESS.. GROWING!.. ..CONSCIOUSNESS. ...EXPANDING!! MY...
OH, NO!! WHAT'S WRONG WITH MY HEAD! IT'S HUGE!! YARGH!!
WHAT THE...? WHAT'S WRONG WITH MY EARS?! WHAT'S GOING ON!! I DON'T LIKE THIS!! THIS ISN'T HOW IT'S SUPPOSED TO.....HEY..WHAT'S THAT TINGLING?
HEY...MY TEETH. MY FANGS!! I'M FINALLY GETTING REAL FANGS!!
MY BEAUTIFUL FANGS! OH....THEY'RE BIGGER THAN I TH...
NOW THEM'S FANGS!!
OH, DEAR GOD!!

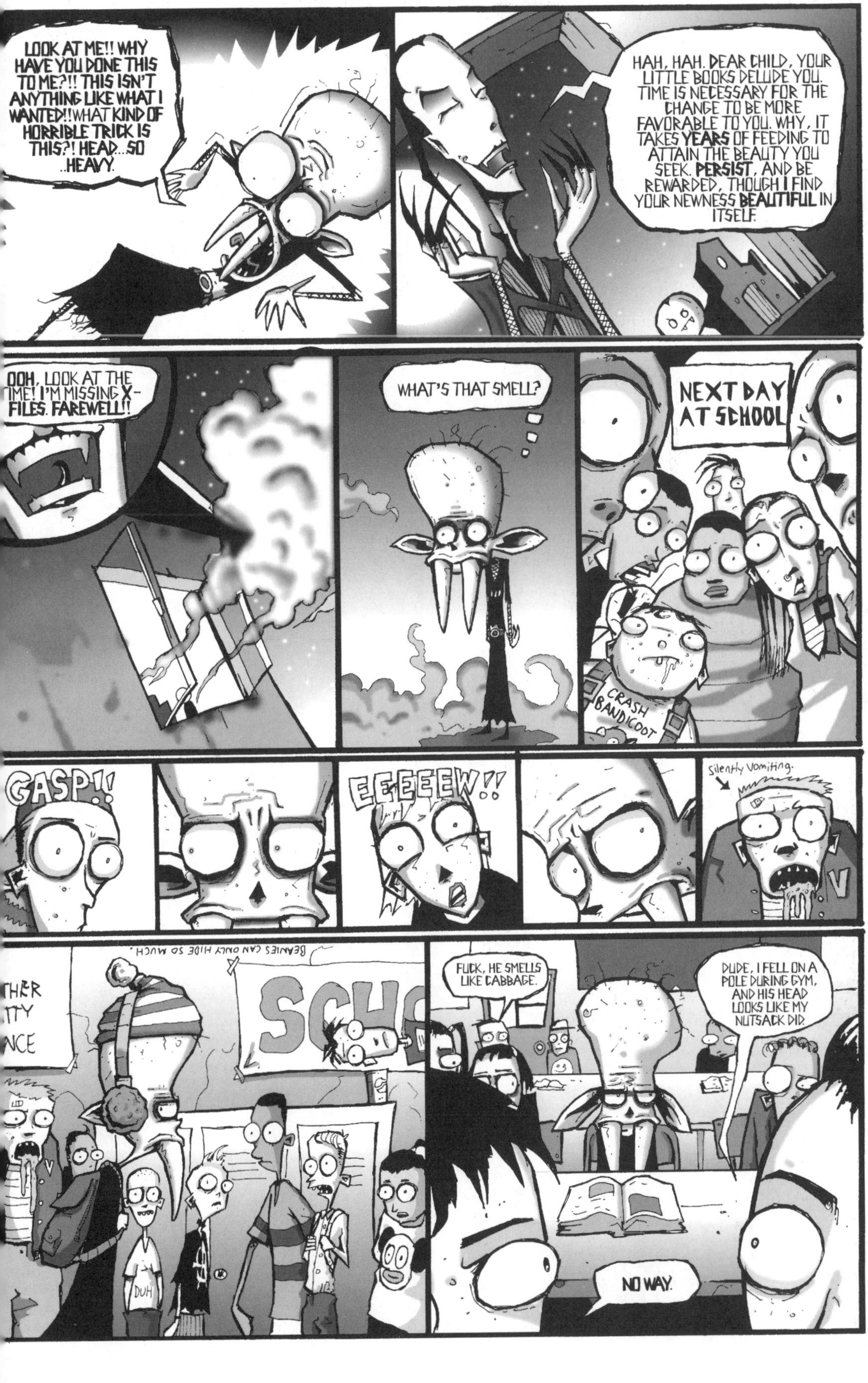
LOOK AT ME!! WHY HAVE YOU DONE THIS TO ME?!! THIS ISN'T ANYTHING LIKE WHAT I WANTED!! WHAT KIND OF HORRIBLE TRICK IS THIS?! HEAD...SO ..HEAVY.
HAH, HAH. DEAR CHILD, YOUR LITTLE BOOKS DELUDE YOU. TIME IS NECESSARY FOR THE CHANGE TO BE MORE FAVORABLE TO YOU. WHY, IT TAKES YEARS OF FEEDING TO ATTAIN THE BEAUTY YOU SEEK. PERSIST, AND BE REWARDED, THOUGH I FIND YOUR NEWNESS BEAUTIFUL IN ITSELF.
OOH, LOOK AT THE TIME! I'M MISSING X-FILES. FAREWELL!!
WHAT'S THAT SMELL?
NEXT DAY AT SCHOOL
CRASH BANDICOOT
GASP!!
EEEEEW!!
Silently Vomiting.
BEANIES CAN ONLY HIDE SO MUCH.
DUH
FUCK, HE SMELLS LIKE CABBAGE.
DUDE, I FELL ON A POLE DURING GYM, AND HIS HEAD LOOKS LIKE MY NUTSACK DID.
NO WAY.

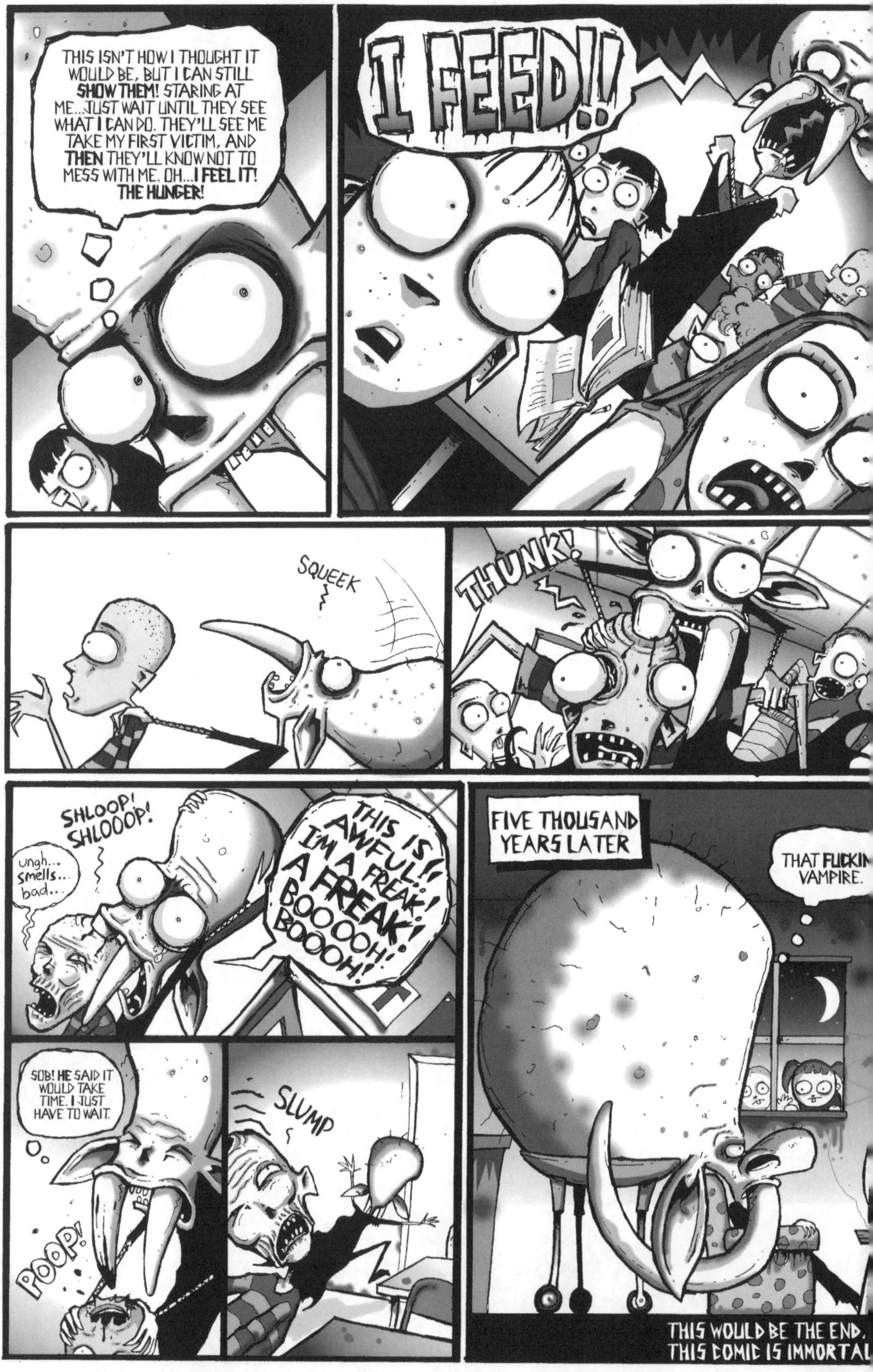
THIS ISN'T HOW I THOUGHT IT WOULD BE, BUT I CAN STILL SHOW THEM! STARING AT ME...JUST WAIT UNTIL THEY SEE WHAT I CAN DO. THEY'LL SEE ME TAKE MY FIRST VICTIM, AND THEN THEY'LL KNOW NOT TO MESS WITH ME. OH...I FEEL IT! THE HUNGER!
I FEED!!
SQUEEK
THUNK!
SHLOOP! SHLOOOP!
ungh... smells... bad...
THIS IS AWFUL!! I'M A FREAK! A FREAK! BOOOOOH! BOOOOH!
SOB! HE SAID IT WOULD TAKE TIME. I JUST HAVE TO WAIT.
POOP!
SLUMP
FIVE THOUSAND YEARS LATER
THAT FUCKIN VAMPIRE.
THIS WOULD BE THE END.
THIS COMIC IS IMMORTAL

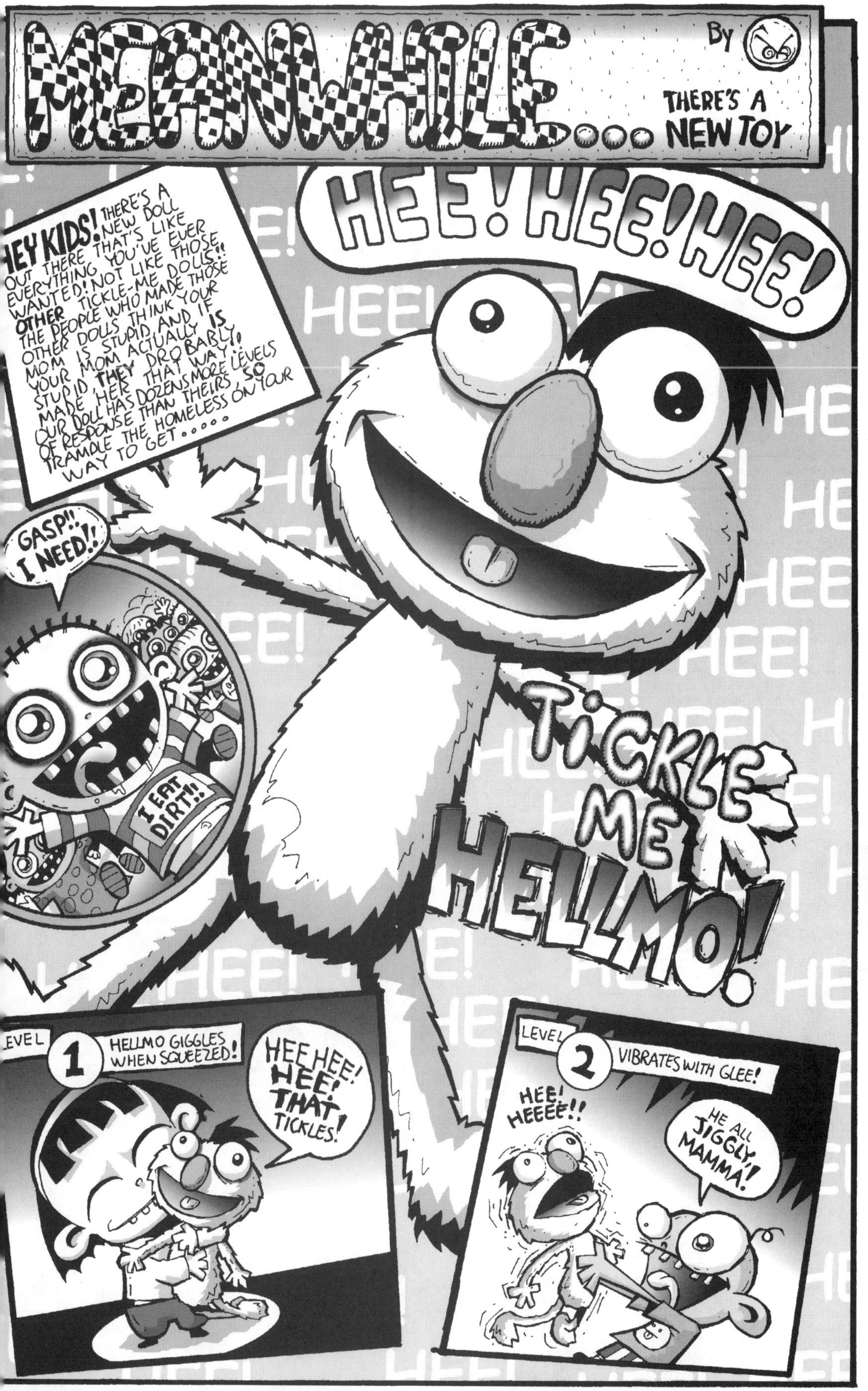
MEANWHILE.... By
THERE'S A NEW TOY
HEE! HEE! HEE!
HEY KIDS! THERE'S A NEW DOLL OUT THERE THAT'S LIKE EVERYTHING YOU'VE EVER WANTED! NOT LIKE THOSE OTHER TICKLE-ME DOLLS!! THE PEOPLE WHO MADE THOSE OTHER DOLLS THINK YOUR MOM IS STUPID AND IF YOUR MOM ACTUALLY IS STUPID, THEY PROBABLY MADE HER THAT WAY. OUR DOLL HAS DOZENS MORE LEVELS OF RESPONSE THAN THEIRS SO TRAMPLE THE HOMELESS ON YOUR WAY TO GET.....
GASP!.. I NEED!!
I EAT DIRT!!
TICKLE ME HELLMO!
LEVEL 1
HELLMO GIGGLES WHEN SQUEEZED!
HEE HEE! HEE! THAT TICKLES!
LEVEL 2
VIBRATES WITH GLEE!
HEE! HEEEE!!
HE ALL JIGGLY, MAMMA!

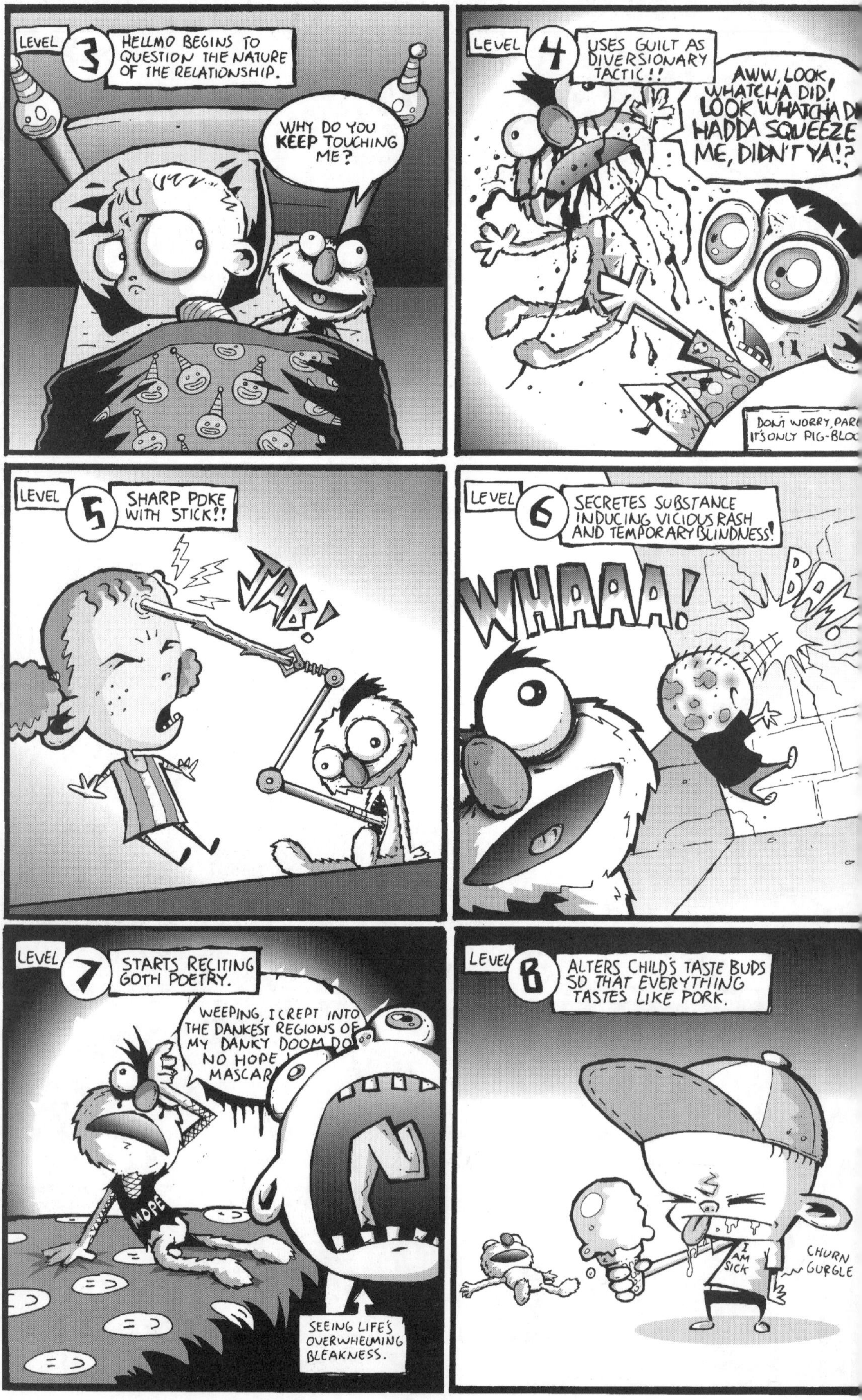
LEVEL 3
HELLMO BEGINS TO QUESTION THE NATURE OF THE RELATIONSHIP.
WHY DO YOU KEEP TOUCHING ME?
LEVEL 4
USES GUILT AS DIVERSIONARY TACTIC!!
AWW, LOOK, WHATCHA DID! LOOK WHATCHA DI HADDA SQUEEZE ME, DIDN'T YA!?
DON'T WORRY, PAR IT'S ONLY PIG-BLOO
LEVEL 5
SHARP POKE WITH STICK!!
JAB!
LEVEL 6
SECRETES SUBSTANCE INDUCING VICIOUS RASH AND TEMPORARY BLINDNESS!
WHAAAA!
LEVEL 7
STARTS RECITING GOTH POETRY.
WEEPING, I CREPT INTO THE DANKEST REGIONS OF MY DANKY DOOM DO NO HOPE MASCAR
MOPE
SEEING LIFE'S OVERWHELMING BLEAKNESS.
LEVEL 8
ALTERS CHILD'S TASTE BUDS SO THAT EVERYTHING TASTES LIKE PORK.
I AM SICK
CHURN GURGLE

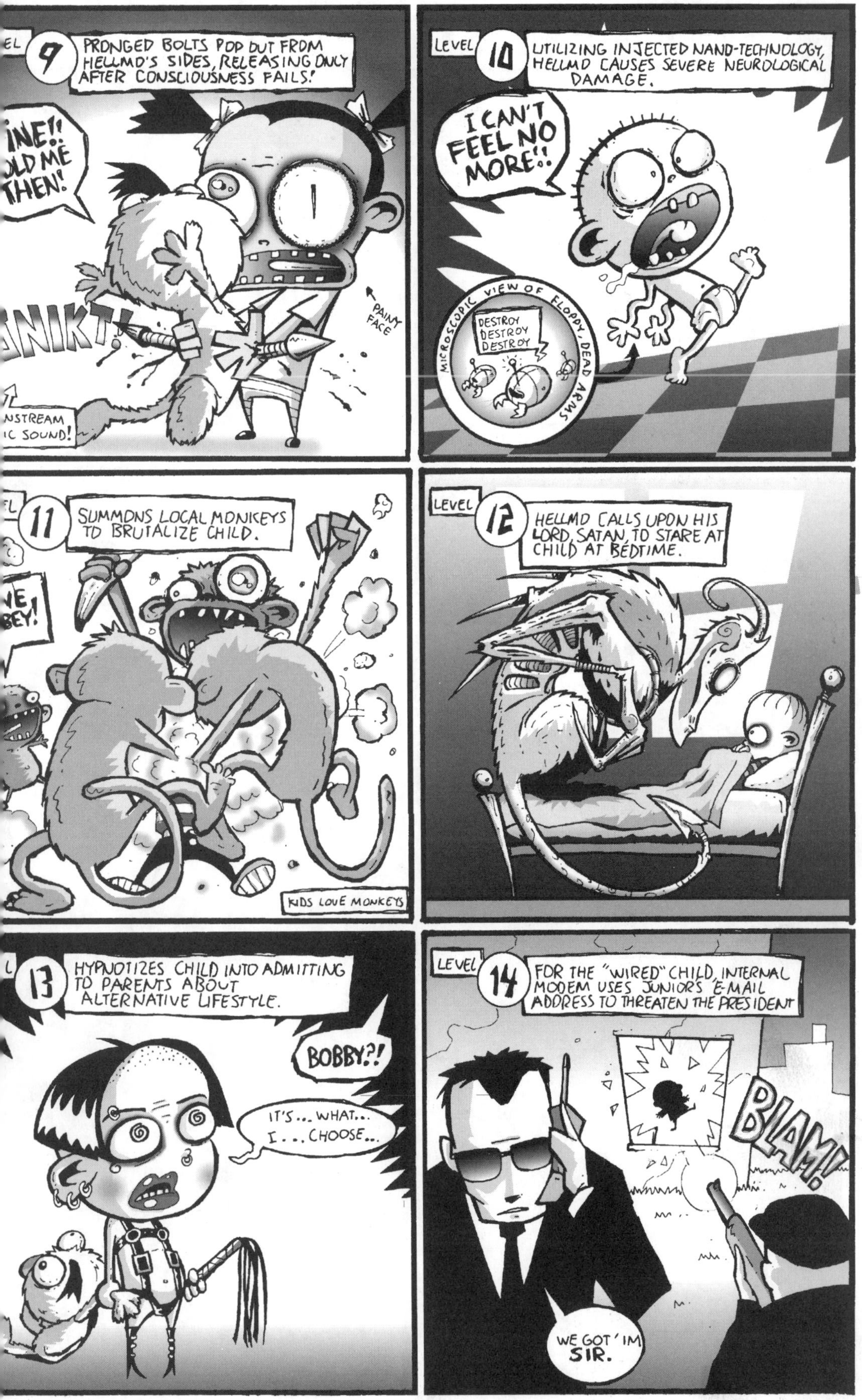

EL
9
PRONGED BOLTS POP OUT FROM HELLMD'S SIDES, RELEASING ONLY AFTER CONSCIOUSNESS FAILS!
INE!! OLD ME THEN!
PAINY FACE
NIKT!
NSTREAM IC SOUND!
LEVEL
10
UTILIZING INJECTED NANO-TECHNOLOGY, HELLMD CAUSES SEVERE NEUROLOGICAL DAMAGE.
I CAN'T FEEL NO MORE!!
MICROSCOPIC VIEW OF FLOPPY, DEAD ARMS
DESTROY DESTROY DESTROY
11
SUMMONS LOCAL MONKEYS TO BRUTALIZE CHILD.
KIDS LOVE MONKEYS
LEVEL
12
HELLMD CALLS UPON HIS LORD, SATAN, TO STARE AT CHILD AT BEDTIME.
13
HYPNOTIZES CHILD INTO ADMITTING TO PARENTS ABOUT ALTERNATIVE LIFESTYLE.
BOBBY?!
IT'S... WHAT... I... CHOOSE...
LEVEL
14
FOR THE "WIRED" CHILD, INTERNAL MODEM USES JUNIOR'S E-MAIL ADDRESS TO THREATEN THE PRESIDENT
BLAM!
WE GOT 'IM SIR.

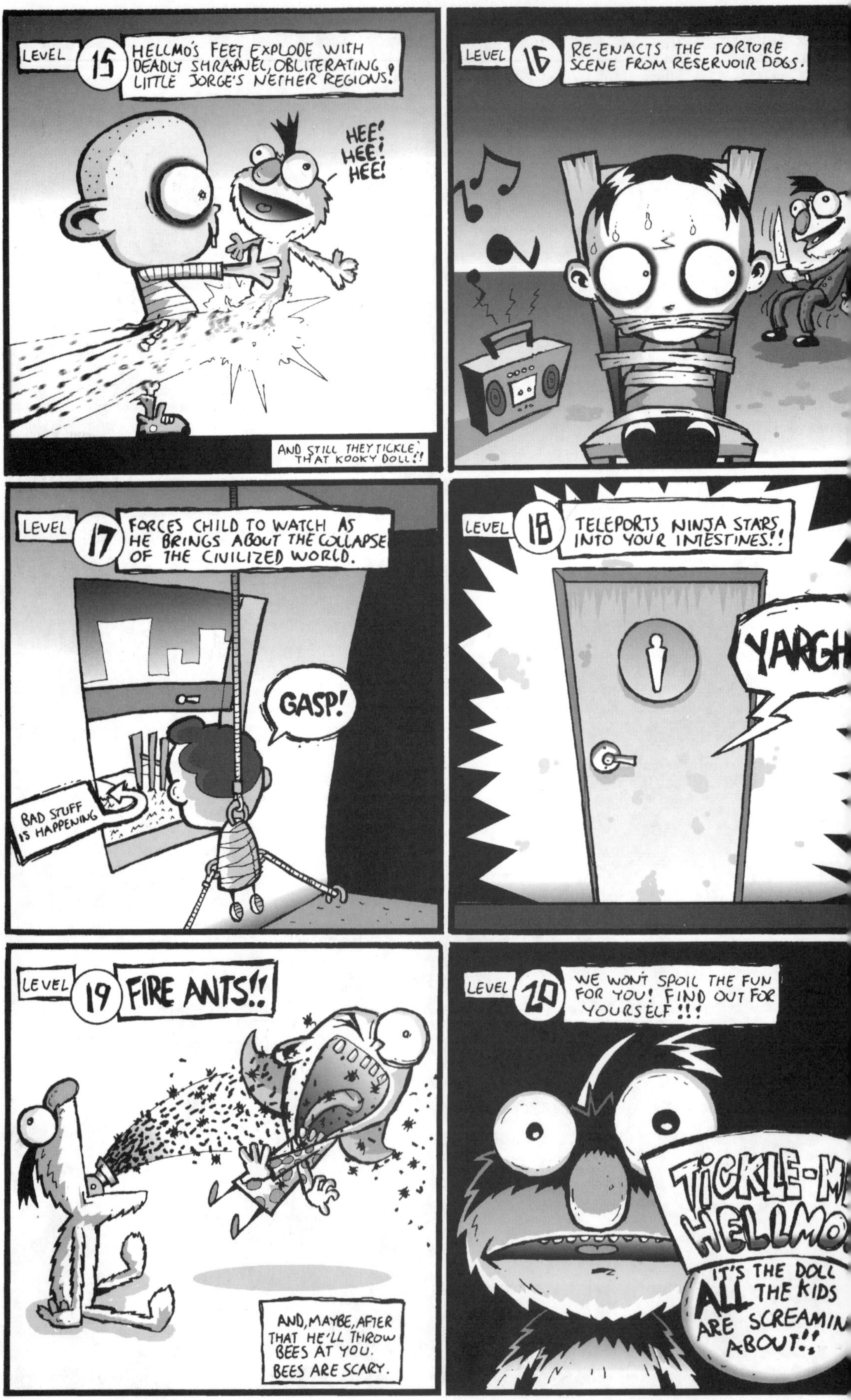
LEVEL 15
HELLMO'S FEET EXPLODE WITH DEADLY SHRAPNEL, OBLITERATING LITTLE JORGE'S NETHER REGIONS!
HEE! HEE! HEE!
AND STILL THEY TICKLE THAT KOOKY DOLL!!
LEVEL 16
RE-ENACTS THE TORTURE SCENE FROM RESERVOIR DOGS.
LEVEL 17
FORCES CHILD TO WATCH AS HE BRINGS ABOUT THE COLLAPSE OF THE CIVILIZED WORLD.
GASP!
BAD STUFF IS HAPPENING
LEVEL 18
TELEPORTS NINJA STARS INTO YOUR INTESTINES!!
YARGH
LEVEL 19
FIRE ANTS!!
AND, MAYBE, AFTER THAT HE'LL THROW BEES AT YOU.
BEES ARE SCARY.
LEVEL 20
WE WON'T SPOIL THE FUN FOR YOU! FIND OUT FOR YOURSELF!!!
IT'S THE DOLL ALL THE KIDS ARE SCREAMIN ABOUT!!

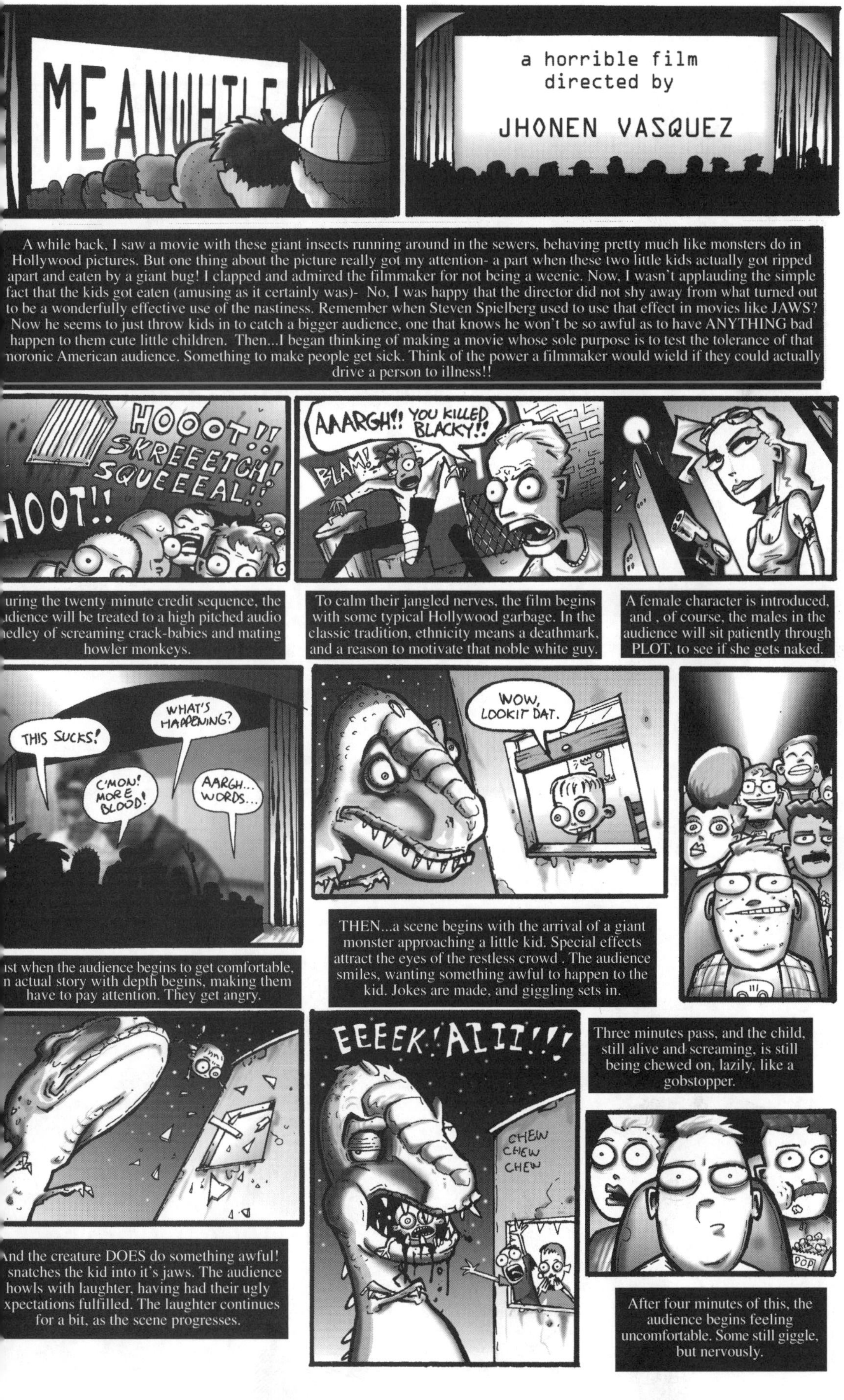

MEANWHILE
a horrible film
directed by
JHONEN VASQUEZ
A while back, I saw a movie with these giant insects running around in the sewers, behaving pretty much like monsters do in Hollywood pictures. But one thing about the picture really got my attention- a part when these two little kids actually got ripped apart and eaten by a giant bug! I clapped and admired the filmmaker for not being a weenie. Now, I wasn't applauding the simple fact that the kids got eaten (amusing as it certainly was)- No, I was happy that the director did not shy away from what turned out to be a wonderfully effective use of the nastiness. Remember when Steven Spielberg used to use that effect in movies like JAWS? Now he seems to just throw kids in to catch a bigger audience, one that knows he won't be so awful as to have ANYTHING bad happen to them cute little children. Then...I began thinking of making a movie whose sole purpose is to test the tolerance of that noronic American audience. Something to make people get sick. Think of the power a filmmaker would wield if they could actually drive a person to illness!!
HOOOT!! SKREEEETCH! SQUEEEEAL!!
HOOT!!
uring the twenty minute credit sequence, the idience will be treated to a high pitched audio iedley of screaming crack-babies and mating howler monkeys.
AAARGH!! YOU KILLED BLACKY!!
BLAM!
To calm their jangled nerves, the film begins with some typical Hollywood garbage. In the classic tradition, ethnicity means a deathmark, and a reason to motivate that noble white guy.
A female character is introduced, and , of course, the males in the audience will sit patiently through PLOT, to see if she gets naked.
THIS SUCKS!
WHAT'S HAPPENING?
C'MON! MORE BLOOD!
AARGH... WORDS...
ist when the audience begins to get comfortable, n actual story with depth begins, making them have to pay attention. They get angry.
WOW, LOOKIT DAT.
THEN...a scene begins with the arrival of a giant monster approaching a little kid. Special effects attract the eyes of the restless crowd . The audience smiles, wanting something awful to happen to the kid. Jokes are made, and giggling sets in.
nd the creature DOES do something awful! snatches the kid into it's jaws. The audience howls with laughter, having had their ugly xpectations fulfilled. The laughter continues for a bit, as the scene progresses.
EEEEK! AIII!!!
CHEW CHEW CHEW
Three minutes pass, and the child, still alive and screaming, is still being chewed on, lazily, like a gobstopper.
POP
After four minutes of this, the audience begins feeling uncomfortable. Some still giggle, but nervously.

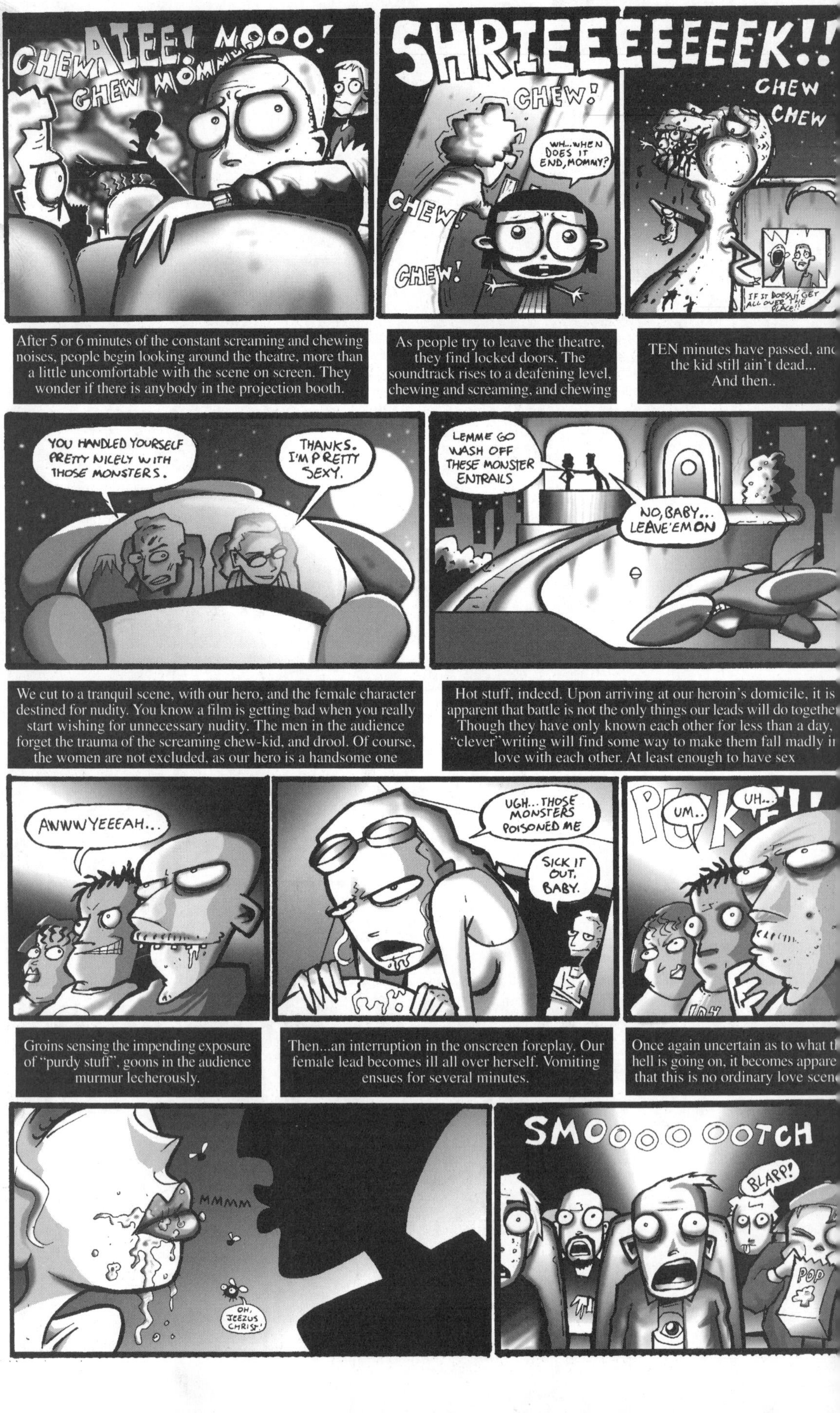

CHEW AIEE! NOOO!
CHEW MOMM
SHRIEEEEEEEK!!
CHEW!
WH...WHEN DOES IT END, MOMMY?
CHEW!
CHEW!
CHEW CHEW
IF IT DOESN'T GET ALL OVER THE PLACE!!
After 5 or 6 minutes of the constant screaming and chewing noises, people begin looking around the theatre, more than a little uncomfortable with the scene on screen. They wonder if there is anybody in the projection booth.
As people try to leave the theatre, they find locked doors. The soundtrack rises to a deafening level, chewing and screaming, and chewing
TEN minutes have passed, anc the kid still ain't dead... And then..
YOU HANDLED YOURSELF PRETTY NICELY WITH THOSE MONSTERS.
THANKS. I'M PRETTY SEXY.
LEMME GO WASH OFF THESE MONSTER ENTRAILS
NO, BABY... LEAVE 'EM ON
We cut to a tranquil scene, with our hero, and the female character destined for nudity. You know a film is getting bad when you really start wishing for unnecessary nudity. The men in the audience forget the trauma of the screaming chew-kid, and drool. Of course, the women are not excluded, as our hero is a handsome one
Hot stuff, indeed. Upon arriving at our heroin's domicile, it is apparent that battle is not the only things our leads will do togethe Though they have only known each other for less than a day, "clever"writing will find some way to make them fall madly ir love with each other. At least enough to have sex
AWWWYEEEAH...
UGH... THOSE MONSTERS POISONED ME
SICK IT OUT, BABY.
UM..
UH..
Groins sensing the impending exposure of "purdy stuff", goons in the audience murmur lecherously.
Then...an interruption in the onscreen foreplay. Our female lead becomes ill all over herself. Vomiting ensues for several minutes.
Once again uncertain as to what t hell is going on, it becomes appare that this is no ordinary love scen
MMMM
OH, JEEZUS CHRIST!
SMOOOOO OOTCH
BLAPP!
POP

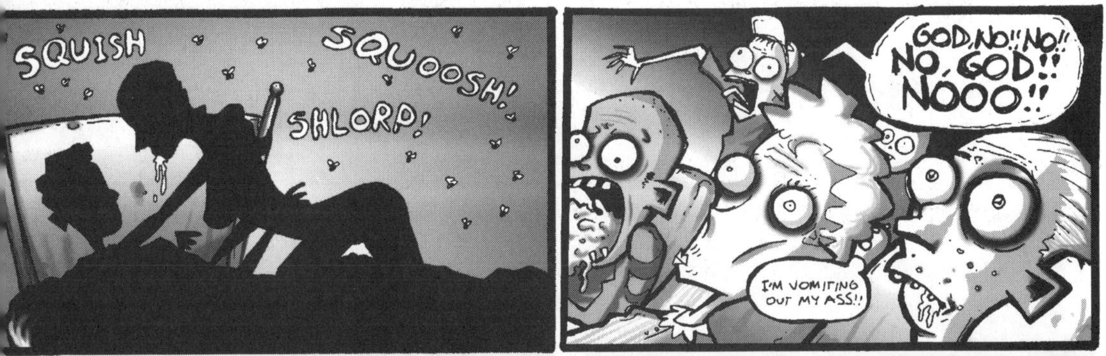
SQUISH
SQUOOSH!
SHLORP!
GOD, NO!! NO!! NO, GOD!! NOOO!!
I'M VOMITING OUT MY ASS!!

The "LOVE" scene that ensues is the most grotesque perversion of obscenity most of the audience will ever see. The soundtrack for this scene is the overamplified sounds of someone stirring a large, saucy bowl of spaghetti and Mac'N'Cheese. Close-ups of veins are nice too.

I'm not exactly sure what is going on here, but you can rest assured it's pretty fucking sick.

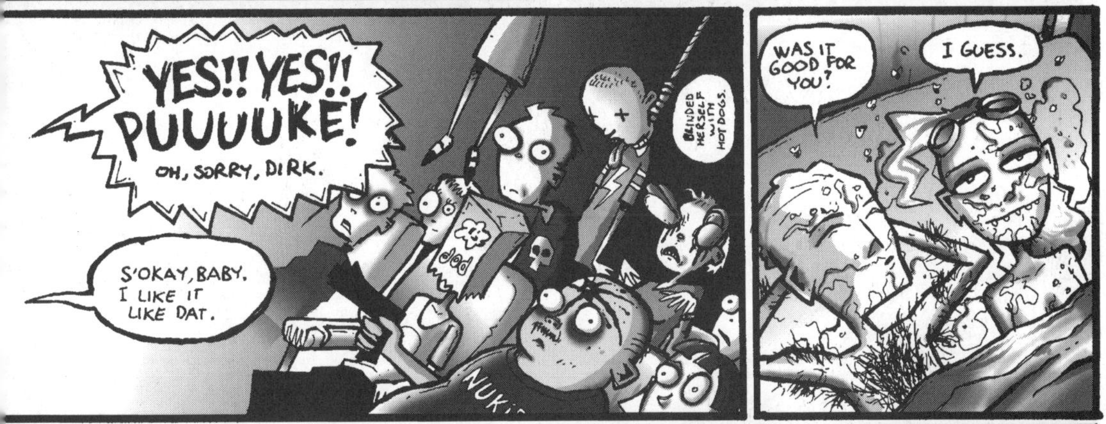
YES!! YES!! PUUUUKE! OH, SORRY, DIRK.
S'OKAY, BABY. I LIKE IT LIKE DAT.
BLINDED HERSELF WITH HOT DOGS.
WAS IT GOOD FOR YOU?
I GUESS.

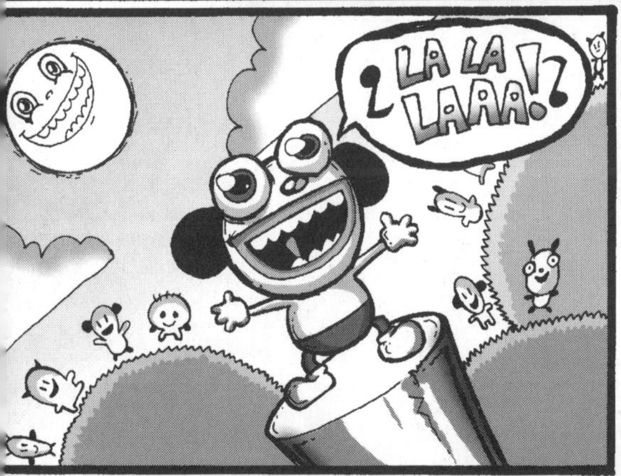
¿LA LA LAAA!¿

And we cut to a MUSICAL NUMBER!! After all the nightmare, a cute, happy song is in order. A cute, nightmarishly repetitive song.

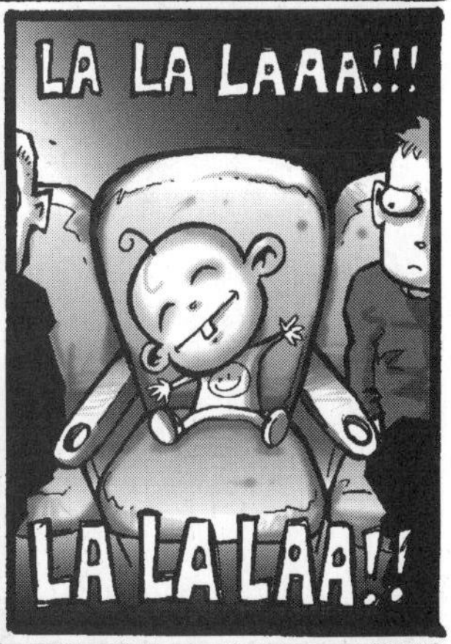
LA LA LAAA!!!
LA LA LAA!!

Some of the children begin to come out of their fright induced comas, and dance. the parents tolerate the idiocy, glad the sex is over.

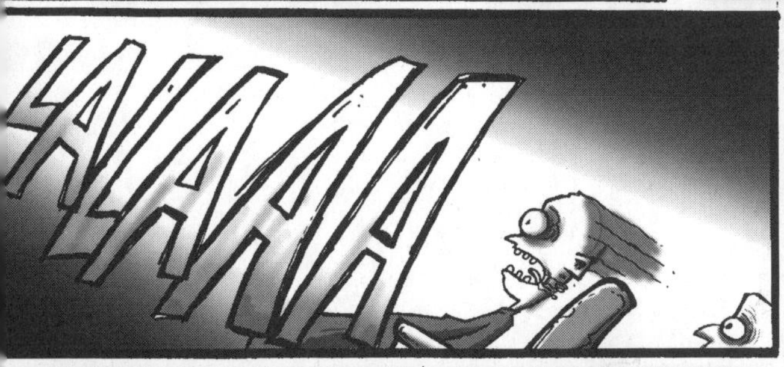
LALAAA

But soon, they see that nothing has changed as far as the intent of the movie is concerned. The volume escalates to a head exploding...um...volume, and then some heads actually begin to explode. I dunno..I am very tired. I want this strip to be over with. I need food.

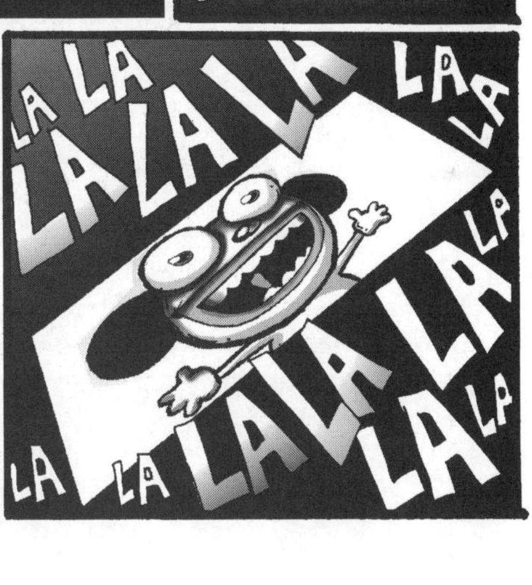
LA LA LA LA LA LA LA LA
LA LA LA LA LA LA LA LA LA LA

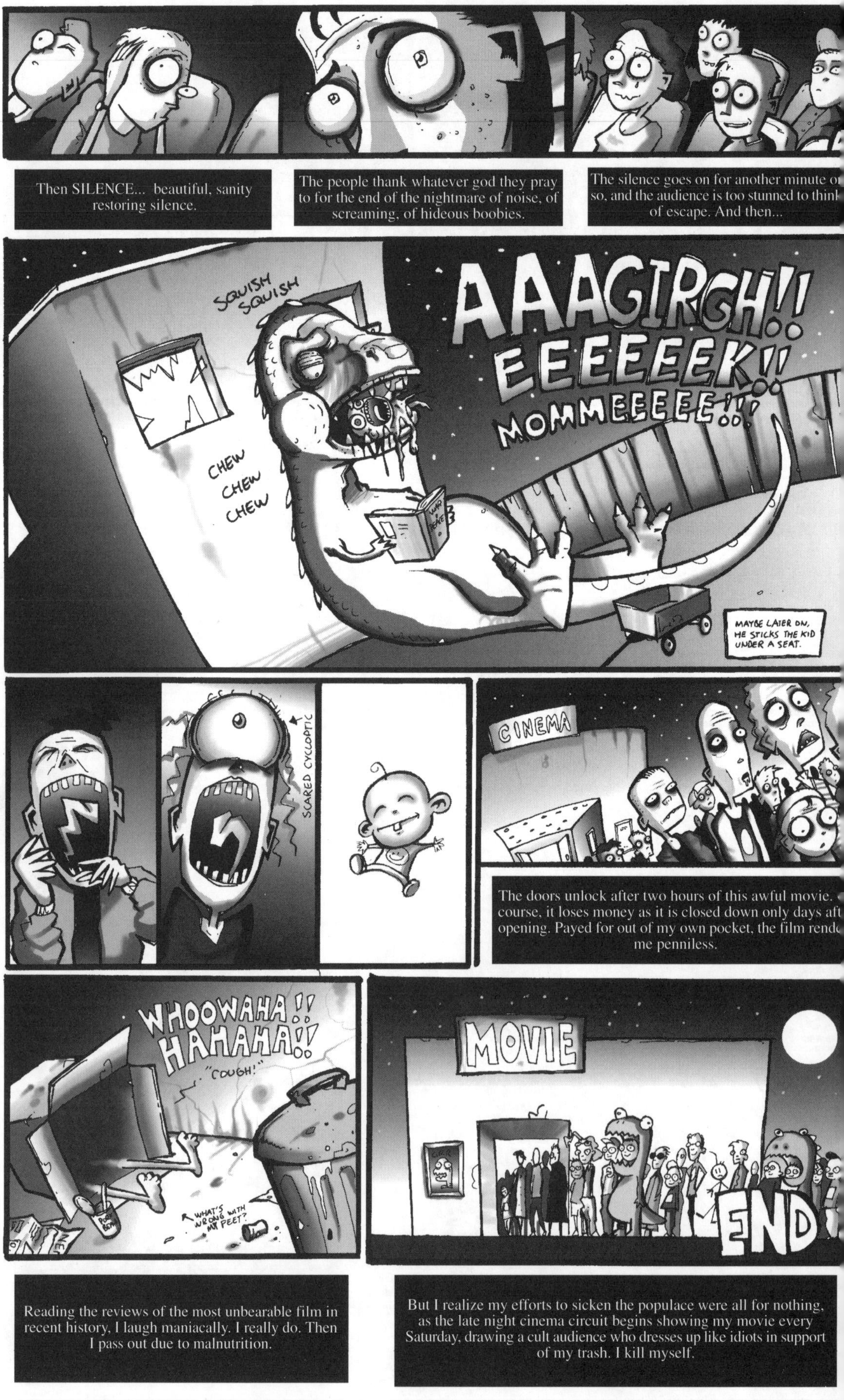
Then SILENCE... beautiful, sanity restoring silence.
The people thank whatever god they pray to for the end of the nightmare of noise, of screaming, of hideous boobies.
The silence goes on for another minute or so, and the audience is too stunned to think of escape. And then...
SQUISH SQUISH
AAAGIRGH!!
EEEEEEK!!
MOMMEEEEE!!
CHEW CHEW CHEW
MAYBE LATER ON, HE STICKS THE KID UNDER A SEAT.
SCARED CYCLOPTIC
CINEMA
The doors unlock after two hours of this awful movie. course, it loses money as it is closed down only days aft opening. Payed for out of my own pocket, the film rend me penniless.
WHOOWAHA!! HAHAHA!!
"COUGH!"
WHAT'S WRONG WITH MY FEET?
MOVIE
END
Reading the reviews of the most unbearable film in recent history, I laugh maniacally. I really do. Then I pass out due to malnutrition.
But I realize my efforts to sicken the populace were all for nothing, as the late night cinema circuit begins showing my movie every Saturday, drawing a cult audience who dresses up like idiots in support of my trash. I kill myself.

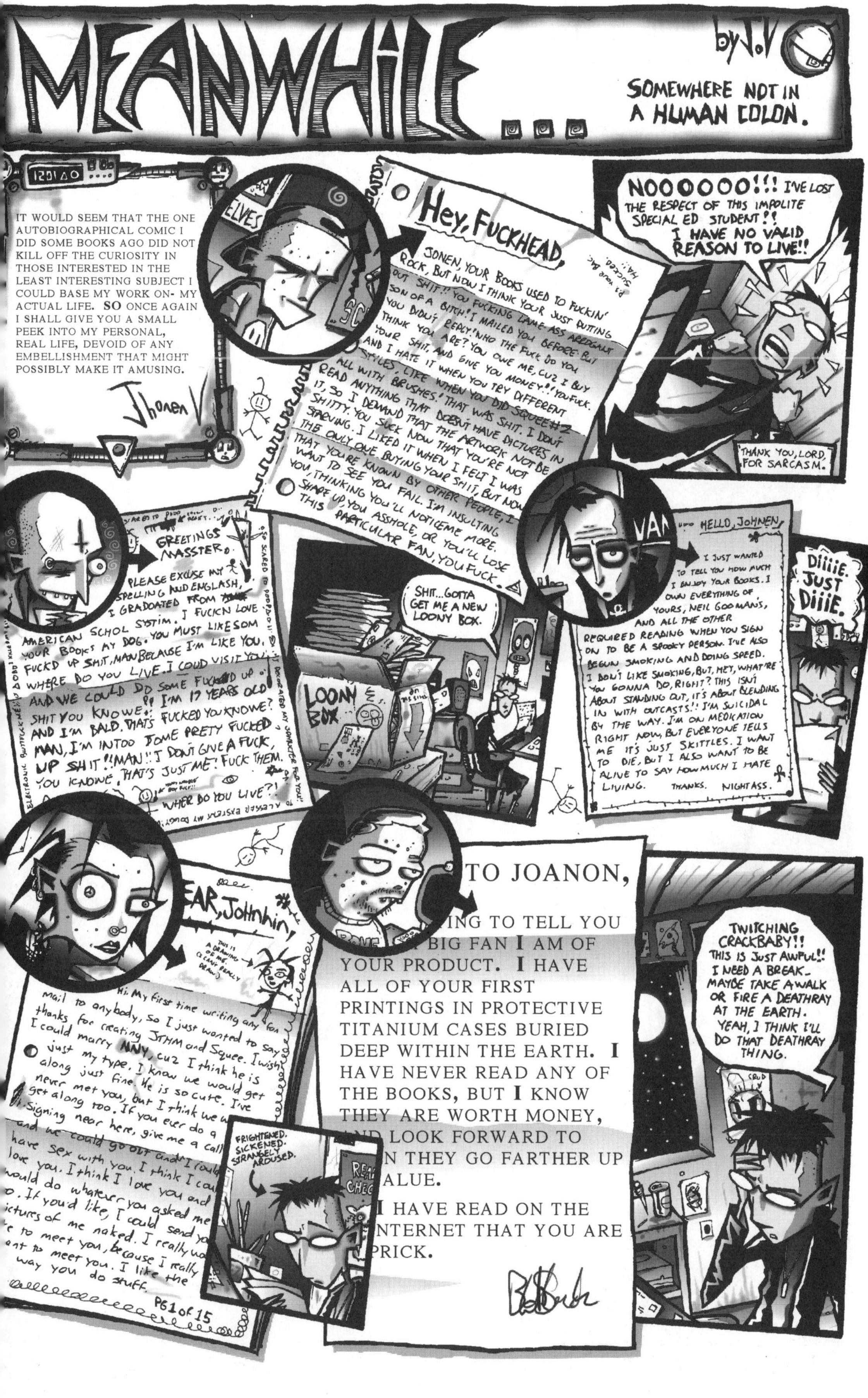
MEANWHILE...
by J.V
SOMEWHERE NOT IN A HUMAN COLON.
IT WOULD SEEM THAT THE ONE AUTOBIOGRAPHICAL COMIC I DID SOME BOOKS AGO DID NOT KILL OFF THE CURIOSITY IN THOSE INTERESTED IN THE LEAST INTERESTING SUBJECT I COULD BASE MY WORK ON- MY ACTUAL LIFE. SO ONCE AGAIN I SHALL GIVE YOU A SMALL PEEK INTO MY PERSONAL, REAL LIFE, DEVOID OF ANY EMBELLISHMENT THAT MIGHT POSSIBLY MAKE IT AMUSING.
Jhonen V
Hey, FUCKHEAD,
JONEN, YOUR BOOKS USED TO FUCKIN' ROCK, BUT NOW I THINK YOUR JUST PUTTING OUT SHIT!! YOU FUCKING LAME-ASS ARROGANT SON OF A BITCH! I MAILED YOU BEFORE, BUT YOU DIDN'T REPLY! WHO THE FUCK DO YOU THINK YOU ARE? YOU OWE ME, CUZ I BUY YOUR SHIT, AND GIVE YOU MONEY!! YOU FUCK. AND I HATE IT WHEN YOU TRY DIFFERENT STYLES, LIKE WHEN YOU DID SQUEE#2 ALL WITH BRUSHES! THAT WAS SHIT. I DON'T READ ANYTHING THAT DOESN'T HAVE PICTURES IN IT, SO I DEMAND THAT THE ARTWORK NOT BE SHITTY. YOU SUCK NOW THAT YOU'RE NOT STARVING. I LIKED IT WHEN I FELT I WAS THE ONLY ONE BUYING YOUR SHIT, BUT NOW THAT YOU'RE KNOWN BY OTHER PEOPLE, I WANT TO SEE YOU FAIL. I'M INSULTING YOU, THINKING YOU'LL NOTICE ME MORE. SHAPE UP, YOU ASSHOLE, OR YOU'LL LOSE THIS PARTICULAR FAN, YOU FUCK.
NOOOOOO!!! I'VE LOST THE RESPECT OF THIS IMPOLITE SPECIAL ED STUDENT!! I HAVE NO VALID REASON TO LIVE!!
THANK YOU, LORD, FOR SARCASM.
GREETINGS MASSTER.
PLEASE EXCUSE MY SPELLING AND ENGLASH, I GRADOATED FROM AMERICAN SCHOL SYSTIM. I FUCKN LOVE YOUR BOOKS MY DOG. YOU MUST LIKE SOM FUCKD UP SHIT, MAN BECAUSE I'M LIKE YOU. WHERE DO YOU LIVE. I COUD VISIT YOU AND WE COULD DO SOME FUCKED UP SHIT YOU KNOWE. I'M 17 YEARS OLD AND I'M BALD. THAT'S FUCKED YOU KNOWE? MAN, I'M INTOO SOME PRETTY FUCKED UP SHIT!! MAN! I DON'T GIVE A FUCK, YOU KNOWE. THAT'S JUST ME! FUCK THEM.
WHER DO YOU LIVE?!
SHIT...GOTTA GET ME A NEW LOONY BOX.
LOONY BOX
HELLO, JOHNEN,
I JUST WANTED TO TELL YOU HOW MUCH I ENJOY YOUR BOOKS. I OWN EVERYTHING OF YOURS, NEIL GOOMAN'S, AND ALL THE OTHER REQUIRED READING WHEN YOU SIGN ON TO BE A SPOOKY PERSON. I'VE ALSO BEGUN SMOKING AND DOING SPEED. I DON'T LIKE SMOKING, BUT, HEY, WHAT'RE YOU GONNA DO, RIGHT? THIS ISN'T ABOUT STANDING OUT, IT'S ABOUT BLENDING IN WITH OUTCASTS!! I'M SUICIDAL BY THE WAY. I'M ON MEDICATION RIGHT NOW, BUT EVERYONE TELLS ME IT'S JUST SKITTLES. I WANT TO DIE. BUT I ALSO WANT TO BE ALIVE TO SAY HOW MUCH I HATE LIVING. THANKS. NIGHTASS.
DiiiiE. JUST DiiiiE.
EAR, Johnhin,
THIS IS A DRAWING OF ME. (I CAN'T REALLY DRAW)
Hi. My first time writing any fan mail to anybody, so I just wanted to say thanks for creating JTHM and Squee. I wish I could marry NNY, cuz I think he is just my type. I know we would get along just fine. He is so cute. I've never met you, but I think we w get along too. If you ever do a Signing near here, give me a call and we could go out and I could have sex with you. I think I cou love you. I think I love you and would do whatever you asked me o. If you'd like, I could send yo ictures of me naked. I really wa e to meet you, because I really ant to meet you. I like the way you do stuff.
PG 1 of 15
FRIGHTENED. SICKENED. STRANGELY AROUSED.
TO JOANON,
ING TO TELL YOU BIG FAN I AM OF YOUR PRODUCT. I HAVE ALL OF YOUR FIRST PRINTINGS IN PROTECTIVE TITANIUM CASES BURIED DEEP WITHIN THE EARTH. I HAVE NEVER READ ANY OF THE BOOKS, BUT I KNOW THEY ARE WORTH MONEY, AND LOOK FORWARD TO N THEY GO FARTHER UP ALUE.
I HAVE READ ON THE INTERNET THAT YOU ARE PRICK.
TWITCHING CRACKBABY!! THIS IS JUST AWFUL!! I NEED A BREAK. MAYBE TAKE A WALK OR FIRE A DEATHRAY AT THE EARTH. YEAH, I THINK I'LL DO THAT DEATHRAY THING.

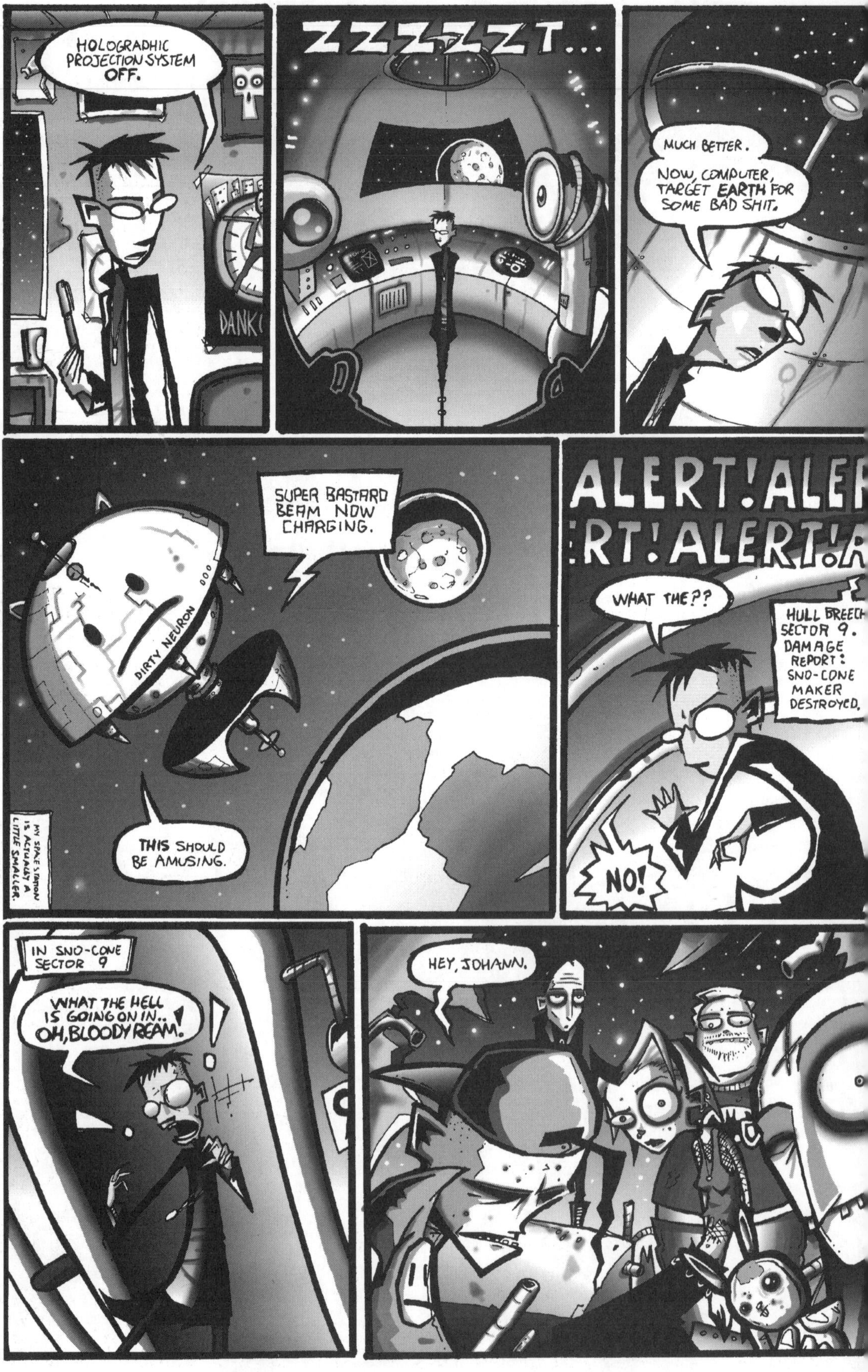
HOLOGRAPHIC PROJECTION SYSTEM OFF.
DANKO
ZZZZZZT...
MUCH BETTER.
NOW, COMPUTER, TARGET EARTH FOR SOME BAD SHIT.
SUPER BASTARD BEAM NOW CHARGING.
DIRTY NEURON
THIS SHOULD BE AMUSING.
MY SPACE STATION IS ACTUALLY A LITTLE SMALLER.
ALERT! ALER
RT! ALERT! A
WHAT THE??
HULL BREECH SECTOR 9. DAMAGE REPORT: SNO-CONE MAKER DESTROYED.
NO!
IN SNO-CONE SECTOR 9
WHAT THE HELL IS GOING ON IN.. OH, BLOODY REAM!
HEY, JOHANN.

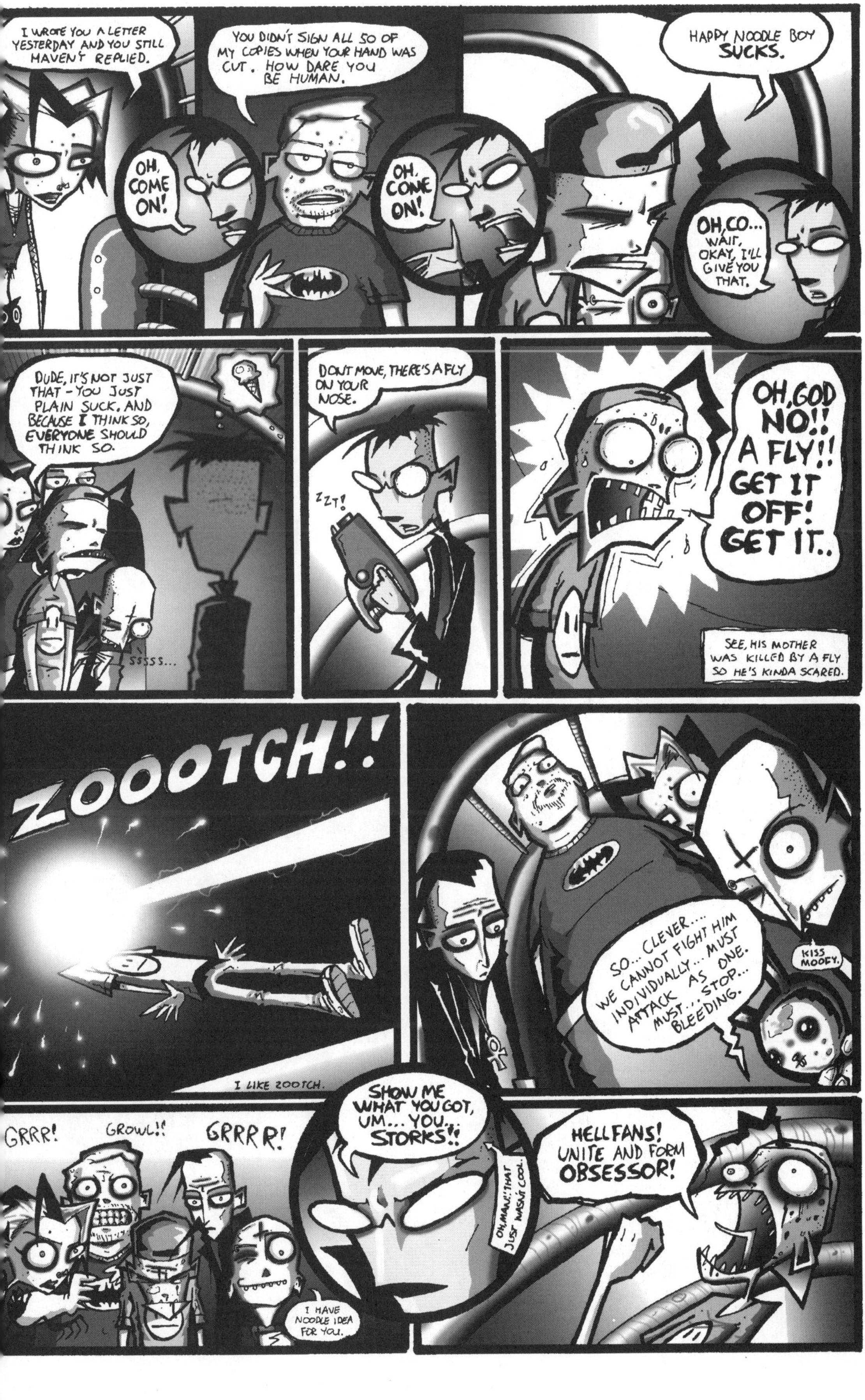

I WROTE YOU A LETTER YESTERDAY AND YOU STILL HAVEN'T REPLIED.
OH, COME ON!
YOU DIDN'T SIGN ALL 50 OF MY COPIES WHEN YOUR HAND WAS CUT. HOW DARE YOU BE HUMAN.
OH, COME ON!
HAPPY NOODLE BOY SUCKS.
OH, CO... WAIT, OKAY, I'LL GIVE YOU THAT.
DUDE, IT'S NOT JUST THAT - YOU JUST PLAIN SUCK. AND BECAUSE I THINK SO, EVERYONE SHOULD THINK SO.
SSSSS...
DON'T MOVE, THERE'S A FLY ON YOUR NOSE.
ZZT!
OH, GOD NO!! A FLY!! GET IT OFF! GET IT..
SEE, HIS MOTHER WAS KILLED BY A FLY SO HE'S KINDA SCARED.
ZOOOTCH!!
I LIKE ZOOTCH.
SO... CLEVER.... WE CANNOT FIGHT HIM INDIVIDUALLY... MUST ATTACK AS ONE. MUST... STOP... BLEEDING.
KISS MOOFY.
GRRR!
GROWL!!
GRRRR!
I HAVE NOODLE IDEA FOR YOU.
SHOW ME WHAT YOU GOT, UM... YOU... STORKS!!
OH, MAN! THAT JUST WASN'T COOL.
HELLFANS! UNITE AND FORM OBSESSOR!

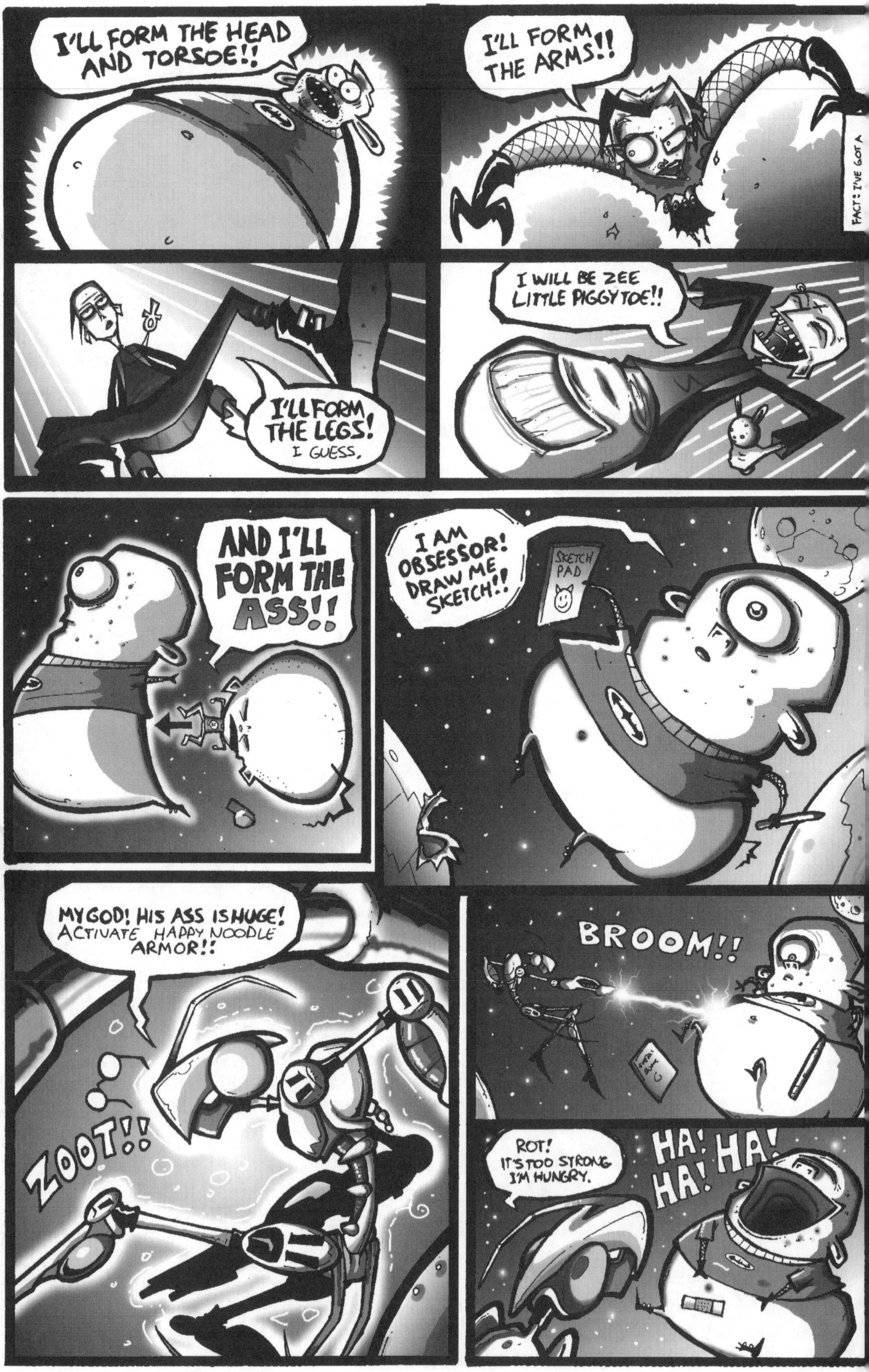
I'LL FORM THE HEAD AND TORSOE!!
I'LL FORM THE ARMS!!
FACT: I'VE GOT A
I'LL FORM THE LEGS! I GUESS.
I WILL BE ZEE LITTLE PIGGY TOE!!
AND I'LL FORM THE ASS!!
I AM OBSESSOR! DRAW ME SKETCH!!
SKETCH PAD
MY GOD! HIS ASS IS HUGE! ACTIVATE HAPPY NOODLE ARMOR!!
ZOOT!!
BROOM!!
ROT! IT'S TOO STRONG I'M HUNGRY.
HA! HA! HA!

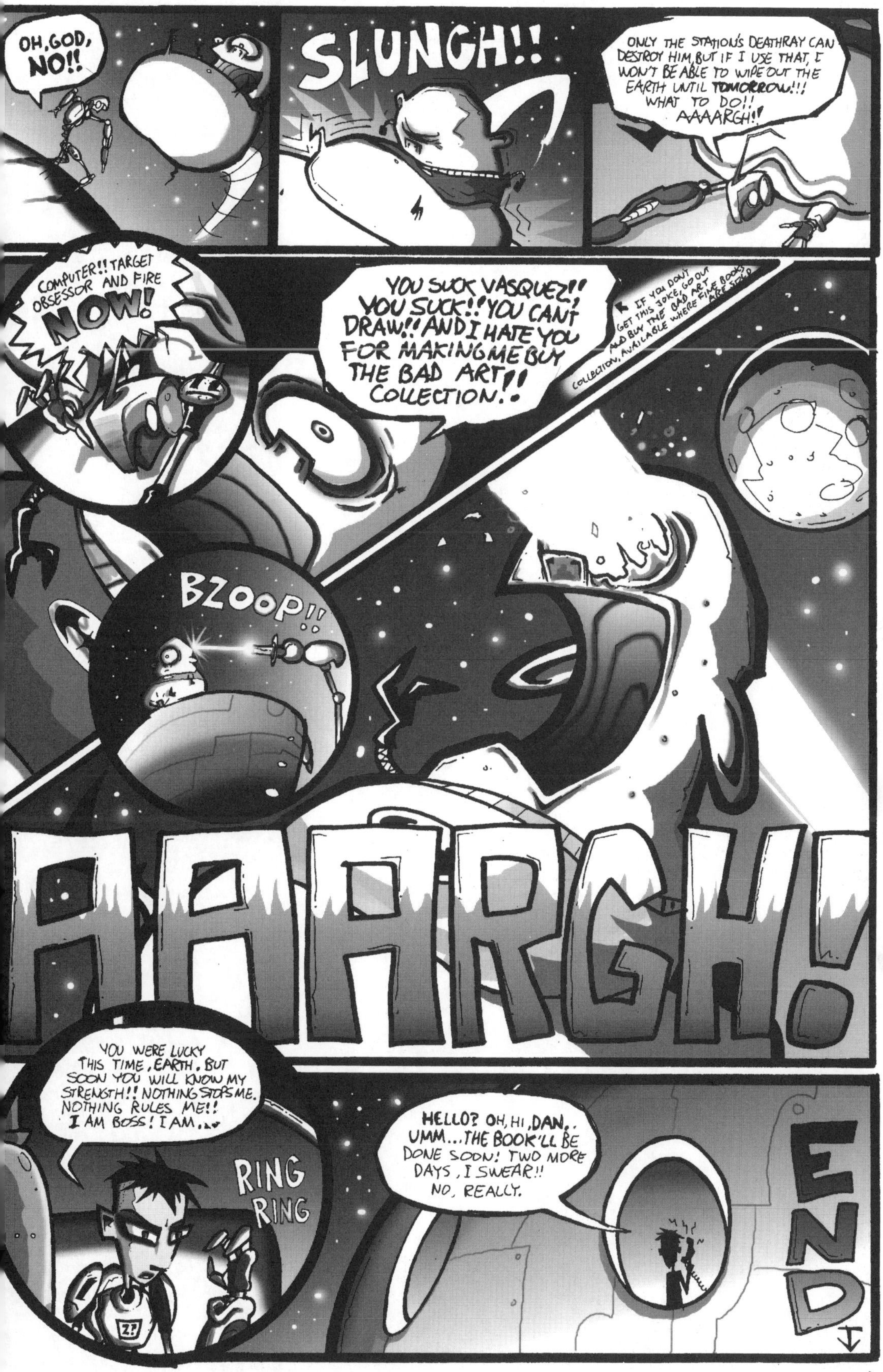
OH, GOD, NO!!
SLUNGH!!
ONLY THE STATION'S DEATHRAY CAN DESTROY HIM, BUT IF I USE THAT, I WON'T BE ABLE TO WIPE OUT THE EARTH UNTIL TOMORROW!!! WHAT TO DO!! AAAARGH!!
COMPUTER!! TARGET OBSESSOR AND FIRE NOW!
YOU SUCK VASQUEZ!! YOU SUCK!! YOU CAN'T DRAW!! AND I HATE YOU FOR MAKING ME BUY THE BAD ART COLLECTION!!
IF YOU DON'T GET THIS JOKE, GO OUT AND BUY THE BAD ART COLLECTION, AVAILABLE WHERE FINE BOOKS ARE SOLD
BZOOP!!
AAARGH!
YOU WERE LUCKY THIS TIME, EARTH. BUT SOON YOU WILL KNOW MY STRENGTH!! NOTHING STOPS ME. NOTHING RULES ME!! I AM BOSS! I AM...
RING RING
HELLO? OH, HI, DAN.. UMM... THE BOOK'LL BE DONE SOON! TWO MORE DAYS, I SWEAR!! NO, REALLY.
END

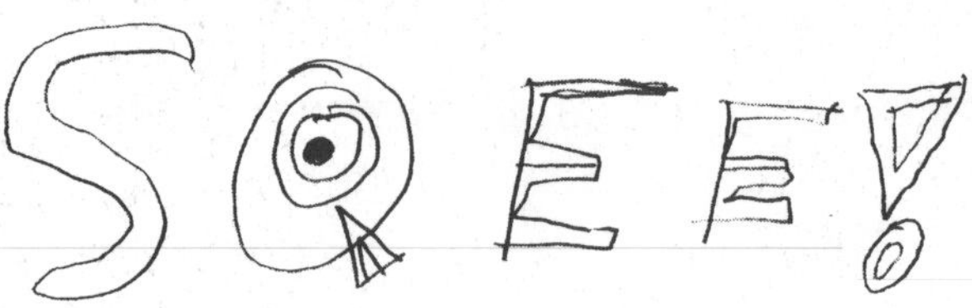

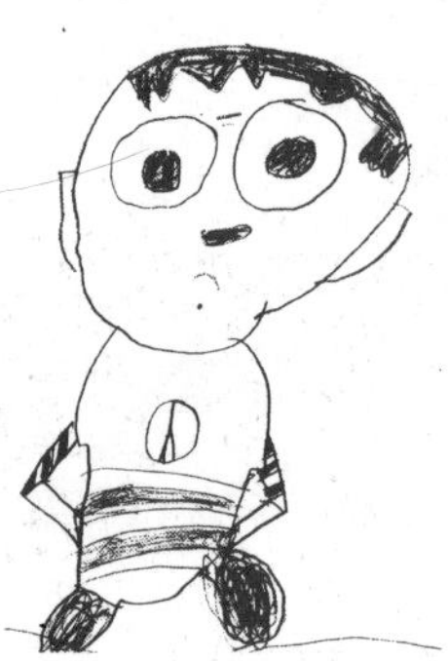

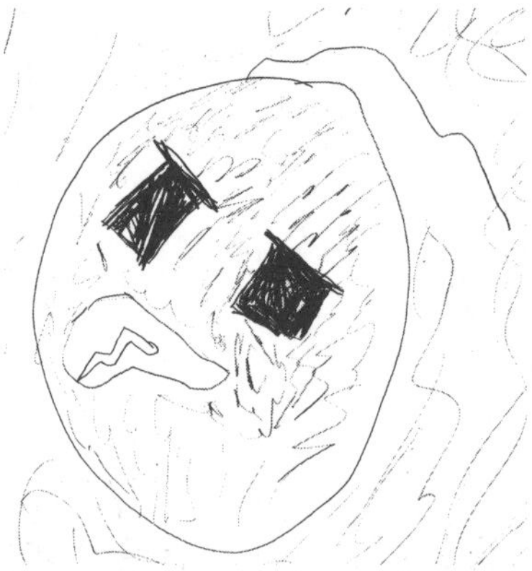

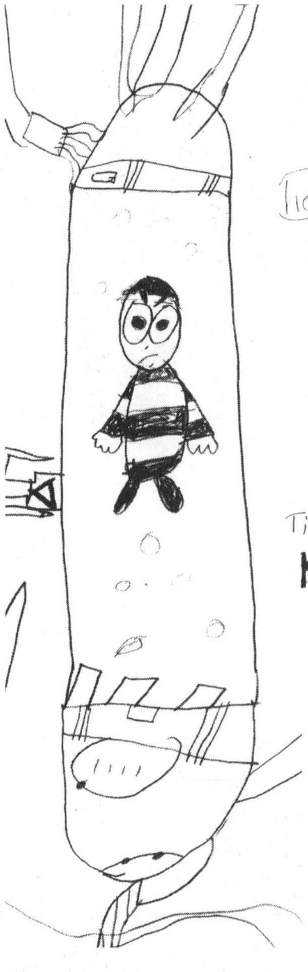

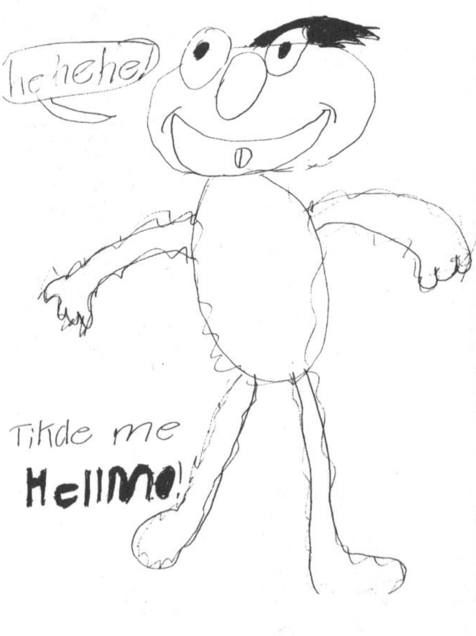
hehehe
Tickle me
Hellmo!

artwork by
Dustin Vado

Well, that sure was interesting, I
It might not have been, if yo
not into this sort of thing. But
would you be holding this boo
your hands if you were not int
Well, assuming you are not or
those sad freaks who r
something in hopes of gathe
more reasons for why it is garb
I refuse to break this up into sm
paragraphs that are easier on
eyes. I am a mean Jhonen. To
this book is more likely to
pleasant diversion from your
something to make the pain of b
flogged by baboons a little r
bearable. But to me, look
through this collection, I see
more than just the comics and
words and the love- I see memo
the things that were going on in
times when I was working o
particular page, or even laying d
a specific line. The countless ti
I raised my head from the des
see the moon floating out TH
from the window before me.
3 A.M drives to get food for
poor, neglected tummy. Cut
my hand wide open on a glass
cursing to nothing but the wo
Staying up for three days, finis
a book, rolling around on the f
and moaning between panels,
screaming with exhaustion u
finishing that morning. Dri
home in morning traffic
watching the faces of all the pe
whose days were just beginn
Smiling after purchasing on
those Slurpees that just make
day a good thing. Finally put
down my pens for the night, ha
had no contact, and telling it
to the little spider that had spu
on my ceiling. Pulling the stit
from my hand with an old pa
scissors. The countless hour
nonstop sound beaming from
stereo and directly into my b
The sounds of the endless mys
cars behind the freeway wall.
constant stream of disturb
monkey imagery that runs thro
my head. Drinking that
chocolate outside watching the
get brighter. The giggling fits,
new ideas, that only serve to fil
own ears. The giant black wi
spider adventure. My battle
the kitchen ants. The shower
no hot water in the dead of wi
The person who told me their
was on me. "Dope-Ass".
Roman, he wasn't really a pig-
The magical Z! All of the DO
Getting my Bob's Big Boy.
inbred people at Chevron. Know
there'll be a time when I'm d

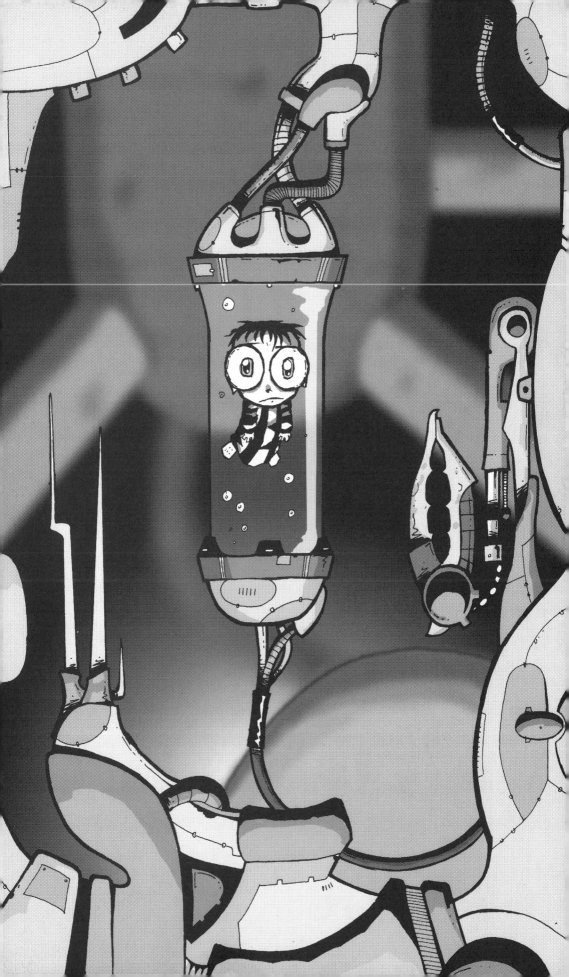

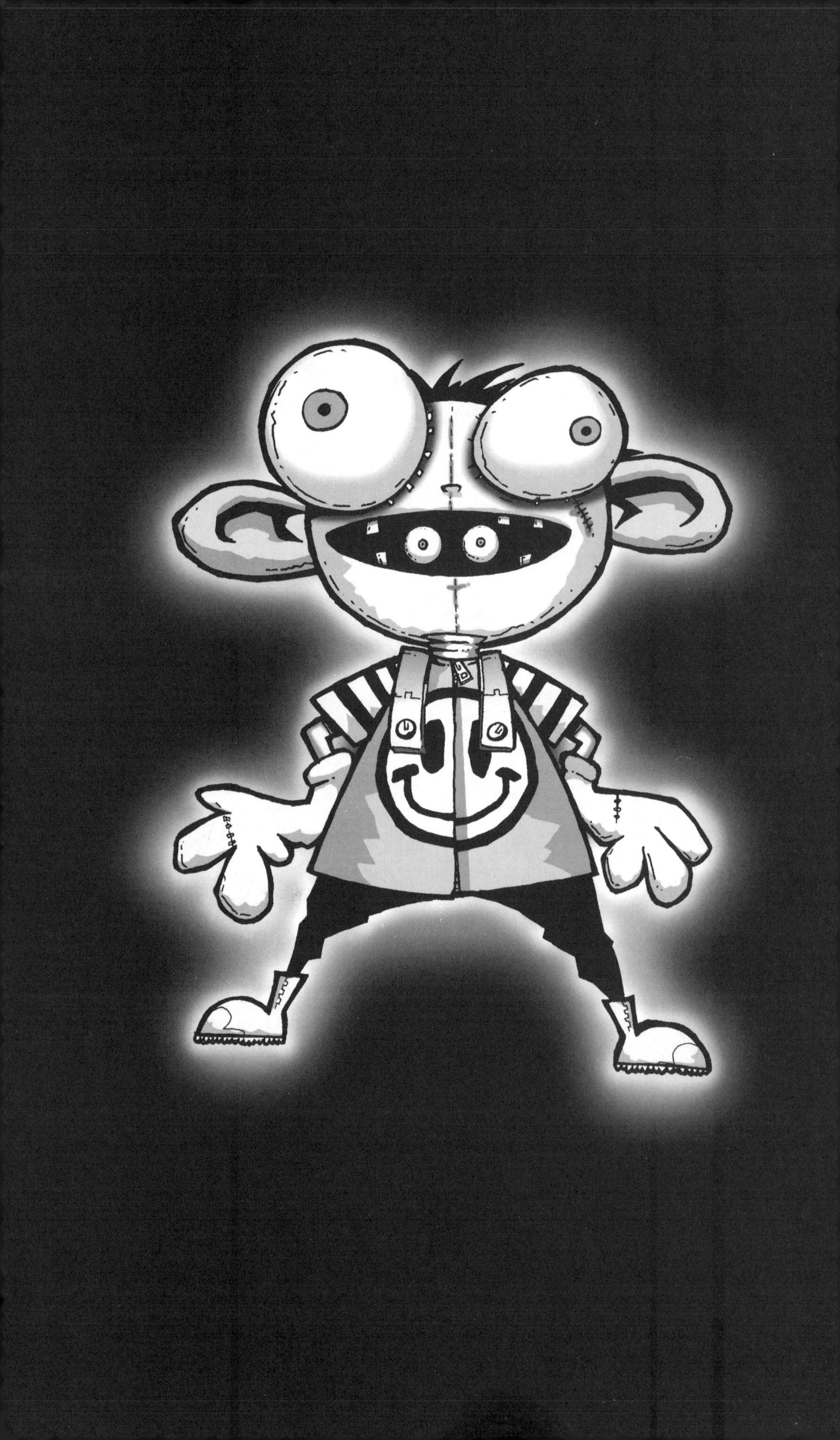

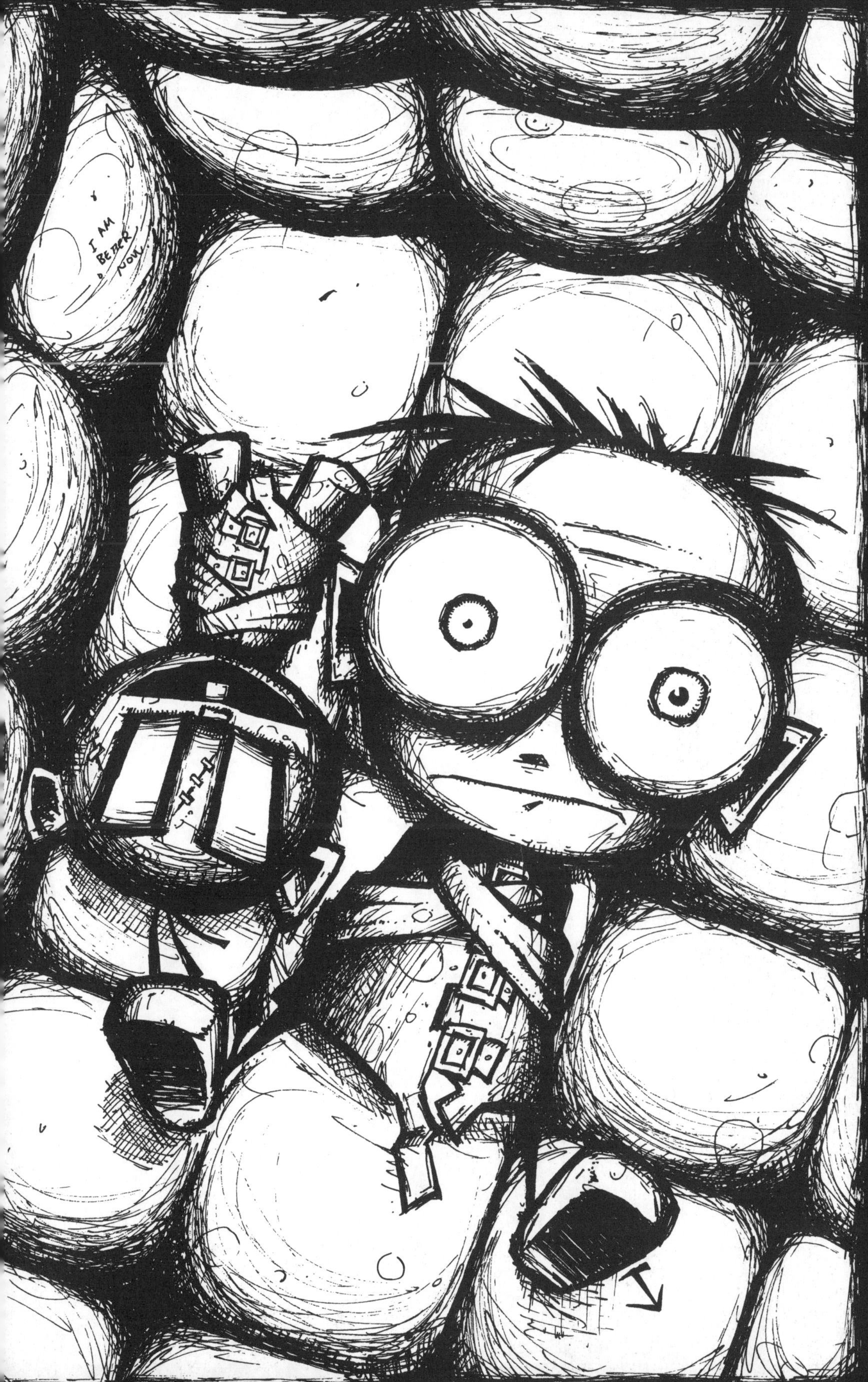
I AM BETTER NOW.

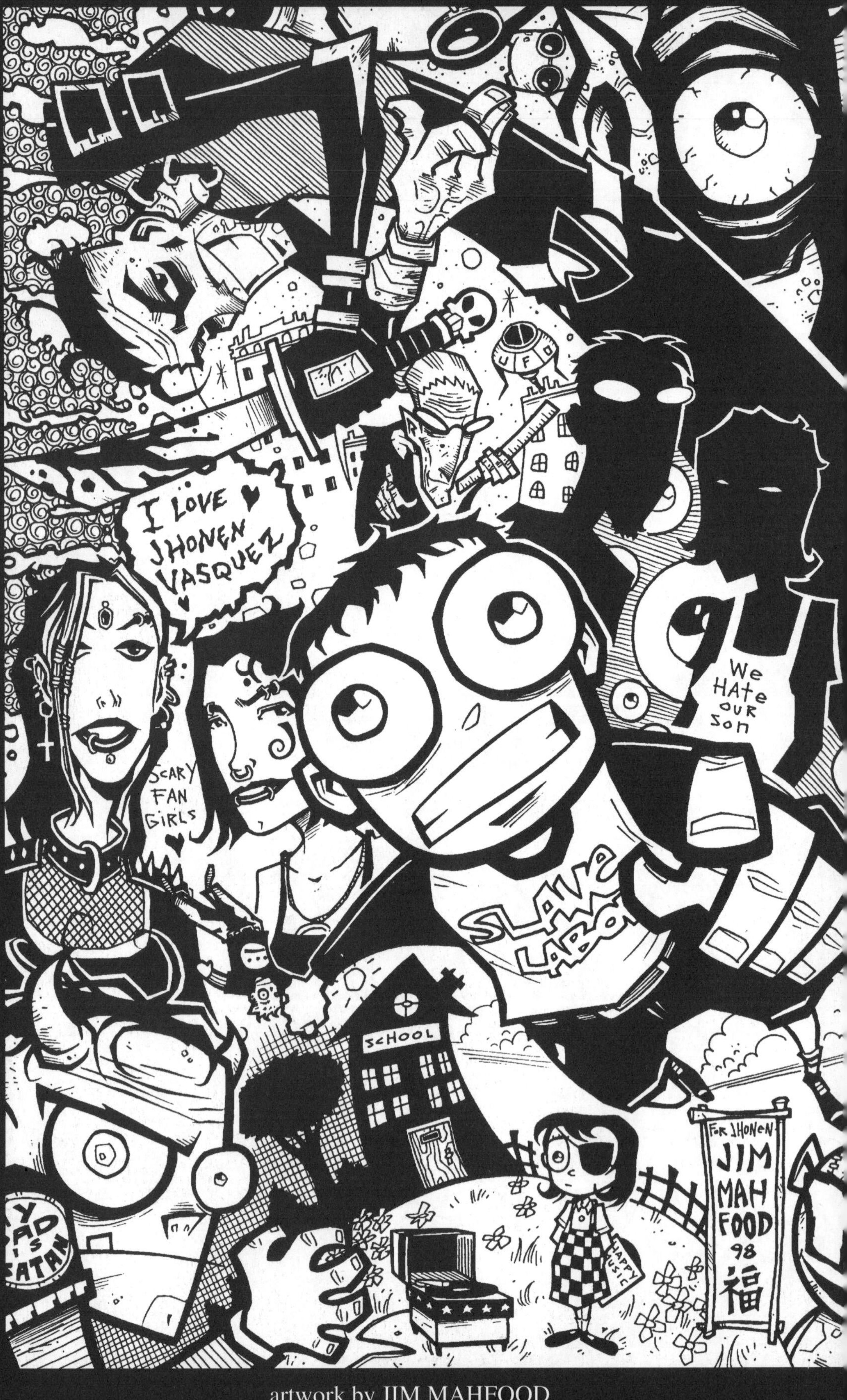

I LOVE JHONEN VASQUEZ
We HATe OUR SON
SCARY FAN GIRLS
SLAVE LABOR
SCHOOL
UFO
FOR JHONEN
JIM MAHFOOD 98 福
DAD IS SATAN
HAPPY MUSIC

artwork by JIM MAHFOOD

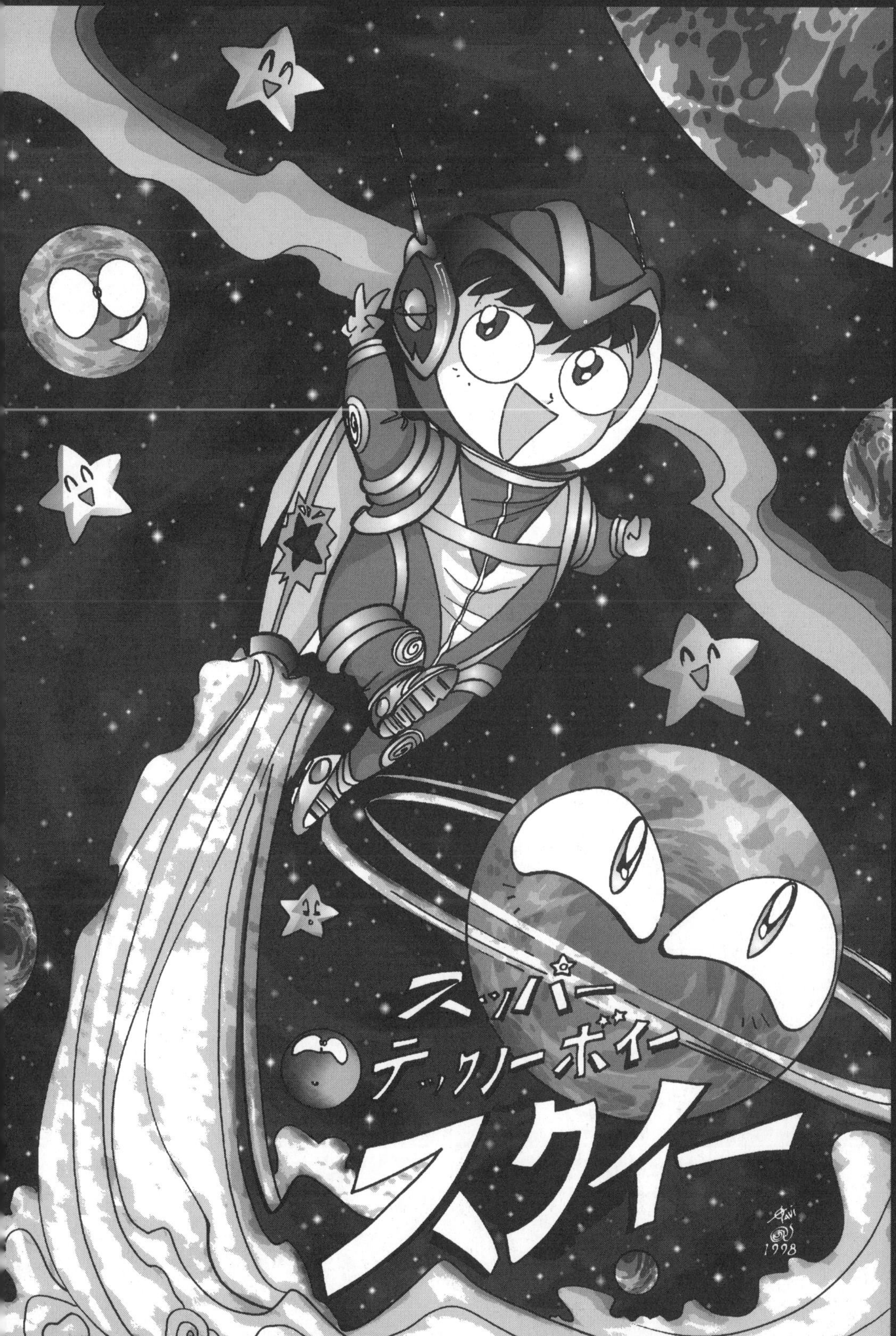
スッパー
テックノーボイー
スクイー
1998

disturbing artwork by Rosearik Rikki Simons and Tavish Wolfgarth-Simons

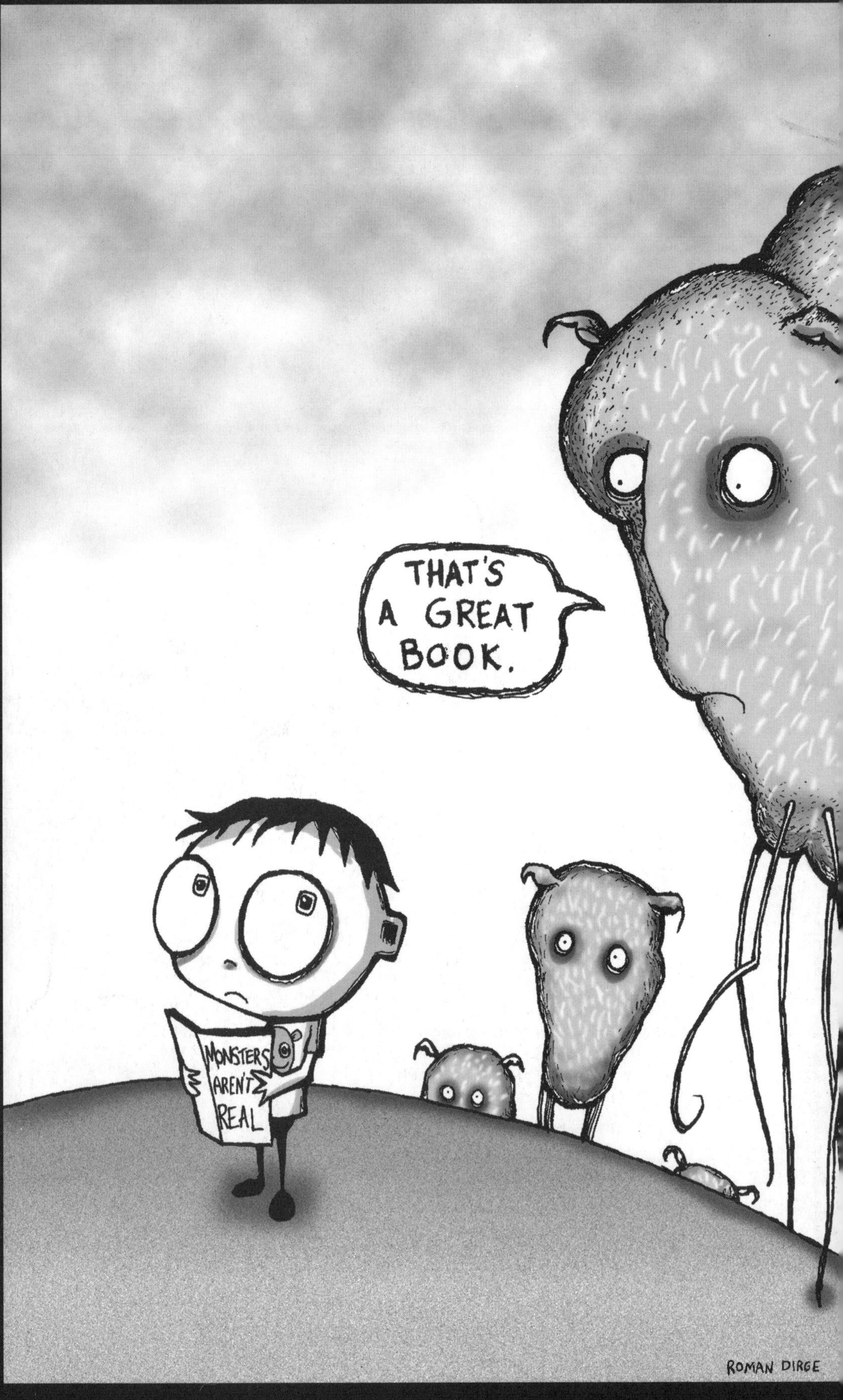
THAT'S A GREAT BOOK.
MONSTERS AREN'T REAL
ROMAN DIRGE

artwork by Roman Dirge

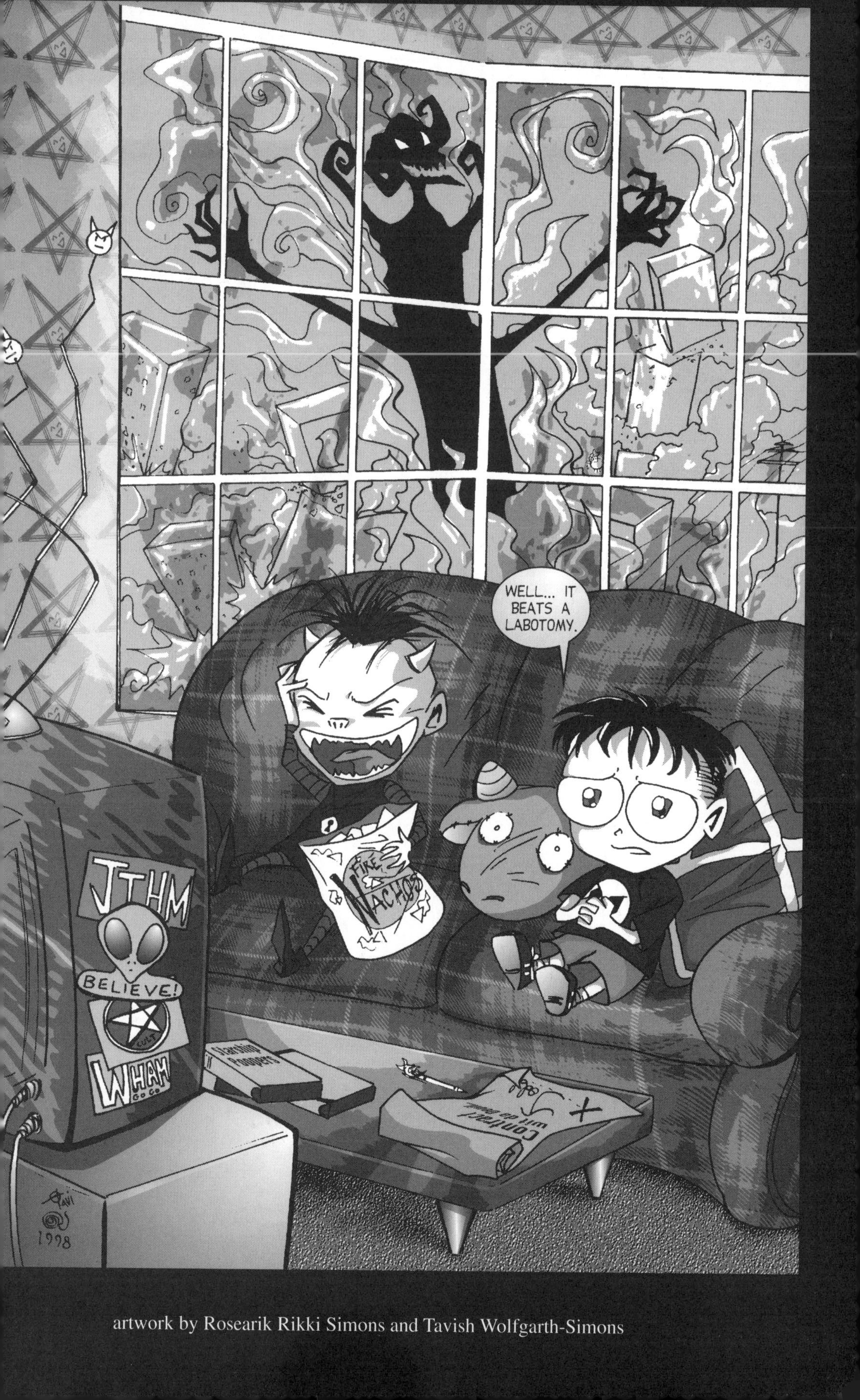
WELL... IT BEATS A LABOTOMY.
JTHM
BELIEVE!
WHAM
Fire Nachos
Starship Poopers
Contract
1998

artwork by Rosearik Rikki Simons and Tavish Wolfgarth-Simons

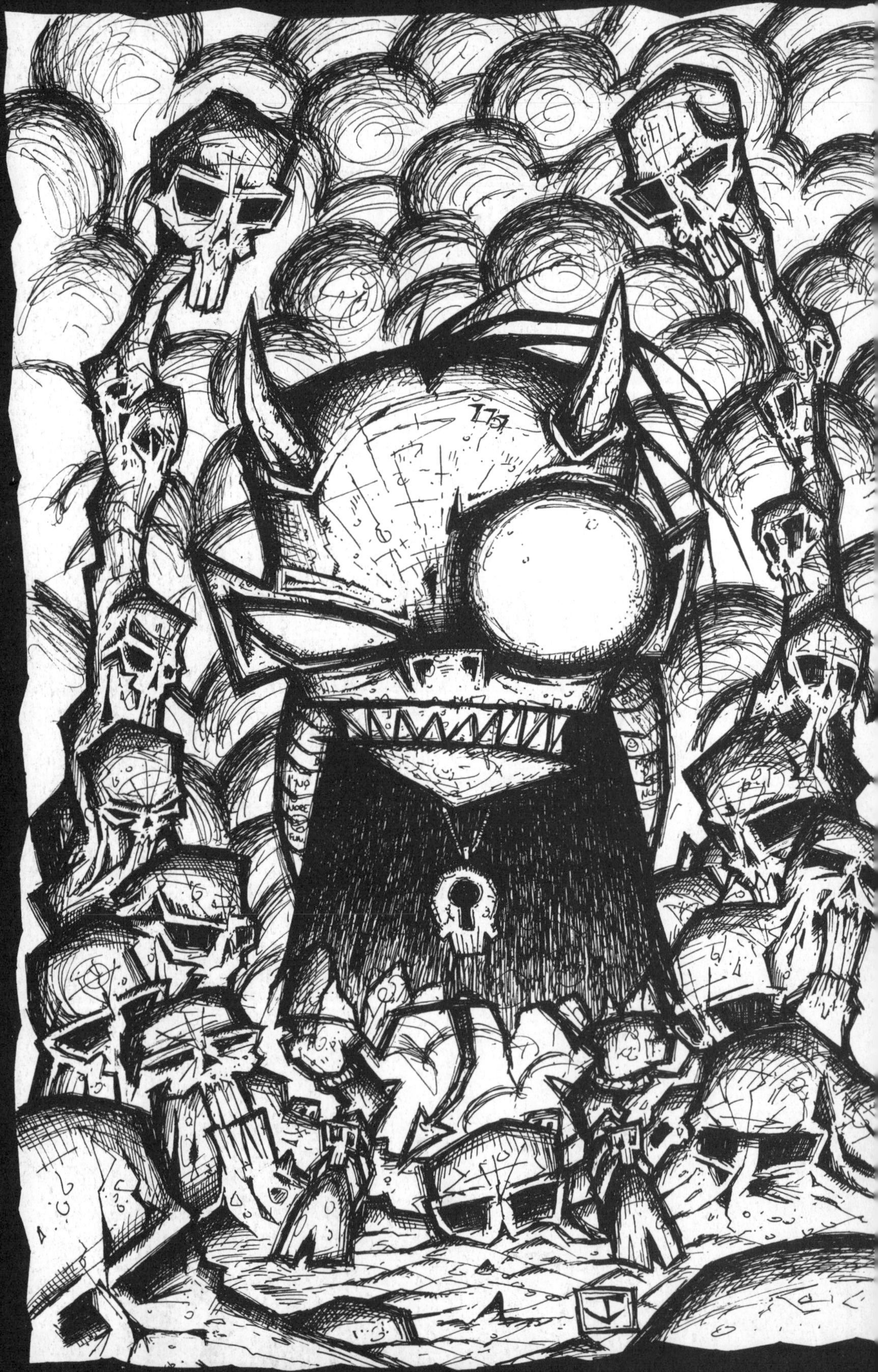